Slavoj Žižek was born in Ljublj
a professor at the European C
Director of the Birkbeck Institute
of London, and a senior research..... ... .,
University of Ljubljana. He has been a visiting professor at
Columbia University and the University of Paris VIII, as well as
at a number of other prestigious institutions on both sides of the
Atlantic.

In his native Slovenia, he was a prominent political figure in the
1980s. He wrote a regular column for the newspaper *Mladina* and,
in 1990, finished fifth in the election for the nation's four-person
presidency. His international reputation as a writer and philosopher was secured in 1989 with the publication of *The Sublime
Object of Ideology*, a book that applied the author's original distil-
lation of Lacan and Marx to an analysis of agency and modern
ideology. A string of much lauded works has followed, including
Repeating Lenin (1997), *The Ticklish Subject* (1999), *Iraq: The
Borrowed Kettle* (2004) and *Living in the End Times* (2010).

As well as providing original insights into psychoanalysis, philosophy and radical political theory, he has, through employing his
extraordinary scholarship to the examination of popular enter-
tainment, established himself as a witty and deeply moral cultural
critic. He has been the subject of two feature-length documenta-
ries, *Slavoj Žižek: The Reality of the Virtual* (2004) and *Žižek!*
(2005). He also presented and wrote the three-part British TV
documentary *A Pervert's Guide to Cinema* (2006).

His compelling, charismatic presence and puckish sense of
the absurd have prompted the press to dub him "the Elvis of
cultural theory" and an "intellectual rock star." However, these
jocular monikers belie a seriousness of purpose that has been
nothing short of startling in an era marked by despondency and
disengagement on the Left. More than an academic or theorist,
Žižek has the gravitas and drive of a breed once thought extinct:
the revolutionary. He has made philosophy relevant again for a
whole generation of politically committed readers.

THE ESSENTIAL ŽIŽEK
A series of classic philosophical texts from Verso

Did Somebody Say Totalitarianism? Five Interventions in the
(Mis)Use of a Notion
The Fragile Absolute
The Plague of Fantasies
Revolution at the Gates, Žižek on Lenin: The 1917 Writings
The Sublime Object of Ideology
The Ticklish Subject

Also available from Verso by the same author:

In Defense of Lost Causes
First as Tragedy, Then as Farce
Iraq: The Borrowed Kettle
Lacan: The Silent Partners
Living in the End Times
Welcome to the Desert of the Real

REVOLUTION AT THE GATES

A Selection of Writings from February to October 1917

V. I. Lenin

◆

Edited and with an Introduction and Afterword by

Slavoj Žižek

VERSO

London • New York

First published by Verso 2002
Introduction and afterword © Slavoj Žižek 2002
Original Lenin texts: see p. vii
Paperback edition first published by Verso 2004
Reprinted by Verso 2011 as part of the Essential Žižek series

3 5 7 9 10 8 6 4 2

Verso
UK: 6 Meard Street, London W1F 0EG
US: 20 Jay Street, Suite 1010, Brooklyn, NY 11201
www.versobooks.com

Verso is the imprint of New Left Books

ISBN-13: 978-1-84467-714-6

British Library Cataloguing in Publication Data
A catalogue record for this book is available from the British Library

Library of Congress Cataloging-in-Publication Data
A catalog record for this book is available from the Library of Congress

Typeset in Sabon by Hewer Text UK Ltd, Edinburgh
Printed in the US by Maple Vail

Contents

A Note on Bibliographical Sources

Lenin's texts are reprinted from: V. I. Lenin, *Collected Works*, 4th English edition, 42 volumes, Moscow: Progress Publishers 1964.

1 "Letters from Afar", vol. 23, pp. 295–342. Written March 7–26 1917. Translated from the Russian by M. S. Levin, Joe Fineberg and others. Edited by M. S. Levin.
2 "The Tasks of the Proletariat in the Present Revolution (April Theses)", vol. 24, pp. 21–9. First published in *Pravda* no. 26, 7 April 1917. Translated from the Russian and edited by Bernard Isaacs.
3 "On Slogans", vol. 25, pp. 185–92. Written in mid-July 1917. First published in pamphlet form in 1917. Translated from the Russian and edited by Stephan Apresyan and Jim Riordan.
4 "The Impending Catastrophe and How to Combat It", vol. 25, pp. 323–69. First published at the end of October 1917 in pamphlet form. Translated from the Russian and edited by Stephan Apresyan and Jim Riordan.
5 "One of the Fundamental Questions of the Revolution", vol. 25, pp. 370–77. First published on 27 September 1917. Translated from the Russian and edited by Stephan Apresyan and Jim Riordan.
6 "The Bolsheviks Must Assume Power", vol. 26, pp. 19–21. Written 25–27 September 1917, first published in 1921. Translated from the Russian by Yuri Sodobnikov and George Hanna. Edited by George Hanna.
7 "Marxism and Insurrection", vol. 26, pp. 22–7. Written 26–27 September 1917, first published in 1921. Translated from the Russian by Yuri Sodobnikov and George Hanna. Edited by George Hanna.
8 "The Tasks of the Revolution", vol. 26, pp. 59–68. First published in *Rabochy Put* nos 20 and 21, 9 and 10 October 1917. Translated from the Russian by Yuri Sodobnikov and George Hanna. Edited by George Hanna.

9 "The Crisis Has Matured", vol. 26, pp. 74–85. Sections I–III and V first published on 9 October 1917 in *Rabochy Put* no. 20, sections IV and VI first published in 1924. Translated from the Russian by Yuri Sodobnikov and George Hanna. Edited by George Hanna.

10 "Advice of an Onlooker", vol. 26, pp. 179–81. Written 21 October 1917, first published in *Pravda* on 7 November 1920, signed An Onlooker. Translated from the Russian by Yuri Sodobnikov and George Hanna. Edited by George Hanna.

11 "Letter to Comrades", vol. 26, pp. 195–215. First published in *Rabochy Put* nos 40, 41, and 42, 1, 2 and 3 November 1917. Translated from the Russian by Yuri Sodobnikov and George Hanna. Edited by George Hanna.

12 "Meeting of the Petrograd Soviet of Workers' and Soldiers' Deputies", vol. 26, pp. 239–41. First published in *Izvestia* no. 207, 26 October 1917. Translated from the Russian by Yuri Sodobnikov and George Hanna. Edited by George Hanna.

The numbered footnotes are editorial; all other footnotes are Lenin's own.

Introduction

Introduction: Between the
Two Revolutions

Slavoj Žižek

The first public reaction to the idea of reactualizing Lenin is, of course, an outburst of sarcastic laughter. Marx is OK – today, even on Wall Street, there are people who still love him: Marx the poet of commodities, who provided perfect descriptions of the capitalist dynamic; Marx of Cultural Studies, who portrayed the alienation and reification of our daily lives. But Lenin – no, you can't be serious! Doesn't Lenin stand precisely for the *failure* to put Marxism into practice, for the big catastrophe which left its mark on the whole of twentieth-century world politics, for the Real Socialist experiment which culminated in an economically inefficient dictatorship? So, if there is a consensus among (whatever remains of) today's radical Left, it is that, in order to resuscitate the radical political project, we should leave the Leninist legacy behind: the ruthless focusing on the class struggle, the Party as the privileged form of organization, the violent revolutionary seizure of power, the ensuing "dictatorship of the proletariat" . . . are all these not "zombie-concepts" to be abandoned if the Left is to have any chance in the conditions of "post-industrial" late capitalism?

The problem with this apparently convincing argument is that it endorses all too easily the inherited image of Lenin the wise revolutionary Leader who, after formulating the basic co-ordinates of his thought and practice in *What Is to Be Done?*, simply ruthlessly pursued them thereafter. What if there is another story to be told about Lenin? It is true that today's Left is undergoing the shattering experience of the end of an entire epoch for the progressive movement, an experience which compels it to reinvent the very basic co-ordinates of its project – however, it was an exactly homologous experience that gave birth to Leninism. Recall Lenin's shock when, in autumn 1914, all European Social Democratic parties (with the honourable exception of the Russian Bolsheviks and the Serb Social Democrats) adopted the "patriotic line" – Lenin even thought that the issue of *Vorwärts*, the daily newspaper of the German Social Democrats, which reported how

Social Democrats in the Reichstag voted for military credits, was a forgery by the Russian secret police destined to deceive the Russian workers. In that era of the military conflict that cut the European continent in half, how difficult it was to reject the notion that one should take sides in this conflict, and to fight against the "patriotic fervour" in one's own country! How many great minds (including Freud) succumbed to the nationalist temptation, even if only for a couple of weeks!

This shock of 1914 was – to put it in Alain Badiou's terms – a *désastre*, a catastrophe in which an entire world disappeared: not only the idyllic bourgeois faith in progress, but also the socialist movement which accompanied it. Lenin himself (the Lenin of *What Is to Be Done?*) lost the ground under his feet – in his desperate reaction there is no satisfaction, no "I told you so!". This moment of *Verzweiflung*, this catastrophe, cleared the ground for the Leninist event, for breaking the evolutionary historicism of the Second International – and Lenin was the only one who realized this, the only one who articulated the Truth of the catastrophe. Through this moment of despair, the Lenin who, via a close reading of Hegel's *Logic*, was able to discern the unique chance for revolution, was born.[1]

It is crucial to emphasize this relevance of "high theory" for the most concrete political struggle *today*, when even such an engaged intellectual as Noam Chomsky likes to underscore how unimportant theoretical knowledge is for progressive political struggle: of what help is studying great philosophical and social-theoretical texts in today's struggle against the neoliberal model of globalization? Is it not that we are dealing either with obvious facts (which simply have to be made public, as Chomsky is doing in his numerous political texts), or with such an incomprehensible complexity that we cannot understand anything? If we wish to argue against this anti-theoretical temptation, it is not enough to draw attention to numerous theoretical presuppositions about freedom, power and society, which also abound in Chomsky's political texts; what is arguably more important is how, today, perhaps for the first time in the history of humankind, our daily experience (of biogenetics, ecology, cyberspace and Virtual Reality) compels *all* of us to confront basic philosophical issues of the nature of freedom and human identity, and so on.

Back to Lenin: his *State and Revolution* is strictly relevant to that shattering experience of 1914 – Lenin's full subjective engagement in it is clear from this famous letter to Kamenev written in July 1917:

---

[1] This passage draws on conversations with Sebastian Budgen and Eustache Kouvélakis.

Entre nous: If they kill me, I ask you to publish my notebook "Marxism & the State" (stuck in Stockholm). It is bound in a blue cover. It is a collection of all the quotations from Marx & Engels, likewise from Kautsky against Pannekoek. There is a series of remarks & notes, formulations. I think with a week's work it could be published. I consider it imp. for not only Plekhanov but also Kautsky got it wrong. Condition: all this is *entre nous*.[2]

The existential engagement is extreme here, and the kernel of the Leninist "utopia" arises from the ashes of the catastrophe of 1914, in his settling of the accounts with the Second International orthodoxy: the radical imperative to smash the bourgeois state, which means the state *as such*, and to invent a new communal social form without a standing army, police or bureaucracy, in which all could take part in the administration of social matters. For Lenin, this was not a theoretical project for some distant future – in October 1917 he claimed: "We can at once set in motion a state apparatus constituting of ten if not twenty million people."[3] *This urge of the moment is the true utopia.* What we should stick to is the *madness* (in the strict Kierkegaardian sense) of this Leninist utopia – and, if anything, Stalinism stands for a return to the realistic "common sense". It is impossible to overestimate the explosive potential of *The State and Revolution* – in this book, "the vocabulary and grammar of the Western tradition of politics was abruptly dispensed with".[4]

What then followed can be called – borrowing the title of Althusser's text on Machiavelli – *la solitude de Lénine*: the time when he basically stood alone, struggling against the current in his own party. When, in his "April Theses" (1917), Lenin discerned the *Augenblick*, the unique chance for a revolution, his proposals were first met with stupor or contempt by a large majority of his party colleagues. No prominent leader within the Bolshevik Party supported his call to revolution, and *Pravda* took the extraordinary step of dissociating the Party, and the editorial board as a whole, from Lenin's "April Theses" – Lenin was far from being an opportunist flattering and exploiting the prevailing mood of the populace; his views were highly idiosyncratic. Bogdanov characterized the "April Theses" as "the delirium of a madman",[5] and Nadezhda Krupskaya herself concluded: "I am afraid it looks as if Lenin has gone crazy."[6]

---

[2] V. I. Lenin, *Collected Works*, Moscow: Progress Publishers 1965, vol. 42, p. 67.
[3] Quoted from Neil Harding, *Leninism*, Durham, NC: Duke University Press 1996, p. 309.
[4] Ibid., p. 152.
[5] Ibid., p. 87.
[6] Ibid.

This is the Lenin from whom we still have something to learn. The greatness of Lenin was that in this catastrophic situation, *he wasn't afraid to succeed* – in contrast to the negative pathos discernible in Rosa Luxemburg and Adorno, for whom the ultimate authentic act is the admission of the failure which brings the truth of the situation to light. In 1917, instead of waiting until the time was ripe, Lenin organized a pre-emptive strike; in 1920, as the leader of the party of the working class with no working class (most of it being decimated in the civil war), he went on organizing a state, fully accepting the paradox of the party which has to organize – even re-create – its own base, its working class.

Nowhere is this greatness more evident than in Lenin's writings which cover the time span from February 1917, when the first revolution abolished tsarism and installed a democratic regime, to the second revolution in October. The opening text of the present volume ("Letters from Afar") reveals Lenin's initial grasp of the unique revolutionary chance, while the last text (the minutes of the "Meeting of the Petrograd Soviet of Workers' and Soldiers' Deputies") declares the Bolshevik seizure of power. Everything is here, from "Lenin the ingenious revolutionary strategist" to "Lenin of the enacted utopia" (of the immediate abolishing of the state apparatuses). To refer again to Kierkegaard: what we are allowed to perceive in these writings is *Lenin-in-becoming*: not yet "Lenin the Soviet institution", but Lenin thrown into an open situation. Are we, within our late capitalist closure of the "end of history", still able to experience the shattering impact of such an authentic historical opening?

In February 1917 Lenin was an almost anonymous political emigrant, stranded in Zurich, with no reliable contacts to Russia, mostly learning about the events from the Swiss press; in October 1917 he led the first successful socialist revolution – so what happened in between? In February, Lenin immediately perceived the revolutionary chance, the result of unique contingent circumstances – if the moment was not seized, the chance for the revolution would be forfeited, perhaps for decades. In his stubborn insistence that one should take the risk and go on to the next stage – that is, repeat the revolution – he was alone, ridiculed by the majority of the Central Committee members of his own party; this selection of his texts endeavours to provide a glimpse into the obstinate, patient – and often frustrating – revolutionary work through which Lenin imposed his vision. Indispensable as Lenin's personal intervention was, however, we should not change the story of the October Revolution into the story of the lone genius confronted with the disorientated masses and gradually imposing his vision. Lenin succeeded because his appeal, while bypassing the Party *nomenkla-*

tura, found an echo in what I am tempted to call revolutionary micropolitics: the incredible explosion of grass-roots democracy, of local committees sprouting up all around Russia's big cities and, ignoring the authority of the "legitimate" government, taking matters into their own hands. This is the untold story of the October Revolution, the obverse of the myth of the tiny group of ruthless dedicated revolutionaries which accomplished a *coup d'état*.

The first thing that strikes today's reader is how directly *readable* Lenin's texts from 1917 are: there is no need for long explanatory notes – even if the strange-sounding names are unknown to us, we immediately get what was at stake. From today's distance, the texts display an almost classical clarity in tracing the contours of the struggle in which they participate. Lenin is fully aware of the paradox of the situation: in spring 1917, after the February Revolution which toppled the tsarist regime, Russia was the most democratic country in the whole of Europe, with an unprecedented degree of mass mobilization, freedom of organization and freedom of the press – yet this freedom made the situation non-transparent, thoroughly ambiguous. If there is a common thread running through all Lenin's texts written between the two revolutions (the February one and the October one), it is his insistence on the gap which separates the "explicit" formal contours of the political struggle between the multitude of parties and other political subjects from its actual social stakes (immediate peace, the distribution of land, and, of course, "all the power to the soviets", that is, the dismantling of the existing state apparatus and its replacement with the new commune-like forms of social management). This gap is the gap between revolution *qua* the imaginary explosion of freedom in sublime enthusiasm, the magic moment of universal solidarity when "everything seems possible", and the hard *work* of social reconstruction which is to be performed if this enthusiastic explosion is to leave its traces in the inertia of the social edifice itself.

This gap – a repetition of the gap between 1789 and 1793 in the French Revolution – is the very space of Lenin's unique intervention: the fundamental lesson of revolutionary *materialism* is that revolution must strike twice, and for essential reasons. The gap is not simply the gap between form and content: what the "first revolution" misses is not the content, but *the form itself* – it remains stuck in the old form, thinking that freedom and justice can be accomplished if we simply put the existing state apparatus and its democratic mechanisms to use. What if the "good" party wins the free elections and "legally" implements socialist transformation? (The clearest expression of this illusion, bordering on the ridiculous, is Karl Kautsky's thesis, formulated in the 1920s, that the logical political form of the first stage of socialism, of the passage from capitalism to socialism, is the parliamentary coalition of bourgeois and proletarian parties.) Here there is a perfect parallel with the era of early modernity, in which opposition to the Church ideological hegemony first articulated itself in the very form of another religious ideology, as a *heresy*: along the same lines, the partisans of the "first revolution" want to subvert capitalist domination in the very political form of capitalist democracy. This is the Hegelian "negation of negation": first the old order is negated within its own ideologico-political form; then this form itself has to be negated. Those who oscillate, those who are afraid to take the second step of overcoming this form itself, are those who (to repeat Robespierre) want a "revolution without revolution" – and Lenin displays all the strength of his "hermeneutics of suspicion" in discerning the different forms of this retreat.

In his 1917 writings, Lenin saves his most acerbic irony for those who engage in the endless search for some kind of "guarantee" for the revolution; this guarantee assumes two main forms: either the reified notion of social Necessity (one should not risk the revolution too early; one has to wait for the right moment, when the time is "ripe" with regard to the laws of historical development: "It is too early for the Socialist revolution, the working class is not yet mature") or normative ("democratic") legitimacy ("The majority of the population are not on our side, so the revolution would not really be democratic") – as Lenin repeatedly puts it: as if, before the revolutionary agent risks the seizure of state power, it should get permission from some figure of the big Other (organize a referendum which will ascertain that the majority support the revolution). With Lenin, as with Lacan, the point is that the revolution *ne s'autorise que d'elle-même*: we should venture the revolutionary *act* not covered by the big Other – the fear of taking power "prematurely", the search for the guarantee, is the fear of the abyss of the act. That is the ultimate dimension of what Lenin incessantly denounces as "opportunism", and his premiss is that "opportunism" is a position which is in itself, inherently, false, masking a fear of accomplishing the act with the protective screen of "objective" facts, laws or norms, which is why the first step in combating it is to *announce* it clearly: "What, then, is to be done? We must *aussprechen was ist*, 'state the facts', admit the truth that there is a tendency, or an opinion, in our Central Committee . . ."[7]

Lenin's answer is not the reference to a different set of "objective facts",

[7] V. I. Lenin, "The Crisis Has Matured", see the present volume, p. 139.

but the repetition of the argument made a decade ago by Rosa Luxemburg against Kautsky: those who wait for the objective conditions of the revolution to arrive will wait for ever – such a position of the objective observer (and not of an engaged agent) is itself the main obstacle to the revolution. Lenin's counterargument against the formal-democratic critics of the second step is that this "pure democratic" option is itself utopian: in the concrete Russian circumstances, the bourgeois-democratic state has no chance of survival – the only "realistic" way to protect the true gains of the February Revolution (freedom of organization and the press, etc.) is to move on to the Socialist revolution, otherwise the tsarist reactionaries will win.

The basic lesson of the psychoanalytic notion of temporality is that there are things one has to do in order to learn that they are superfluous: in the course of the treatment, one loses months on false moves before "it clicks" and one finds the right formula – although they retroactively appear superfluous, these detours were necessary. And does the same not go also for the revolution? What, then, happened when, in his last years, Lenin became fully aware of the limitations of Bolshevik power? It is here that we should oppose Lenin and Stalin: from Lenin's very last writings, long after he renounced the utopia of his *State and Revolution*, we can discern the contours of a modest "realistic" project of what Bolshevik power should do. Because of the economic underdevelopment and cultural backwardness of the Russian masses, there is no way for Russia to "pass directly to Socialism"; all that Soviet power can do is to combine the moderate politics of "state capitalism" with the intense cultural education of the inert peasant masses – not "Communist propaganda" brainwashing, simply a patient, gradual imposition of developed civilized standards. Facts and figures reveal "what a vast amount of urgent spadework we still have to do to reach the standard of an ordinary West European civilized country. . . . We must bear in mind the semi-Asiatic ignorance from which we have not yet extricated ourselves."[8] So Lenin warns repeatedly against any kind of direct "implantation of Communism":

> Under no circumstances must this be understood [in the sense] that we should immediately propagate purely in strictly communist ideas in the countryside. As long as our countryside lacks the material basis for communism, it will be, I should say, harmful, in fact, I should say, fatal, for communism to do so.[9]

[8] V. I. Lenin, "Pages from a Diary", in *Collected Works*, Moscow: Progress Publishers 1966, vol. 33, p. 463.
[9] Ibid., p. 465.

His recurrent theme is: "The most harmful thing here would be haste."[10] Against this stance of "cultural revolution", Stalin opted for the thoroughly anti-Leninist notion of "building Socialism in one state".

Does this mean, then, that Lenin silently adopted the standard Menshevik criticism of Bolshevik utopianism, their idea that revolution must follow the preordained necessary stages (it can occur only once its material conditions are in place)? It is here that we can observe Lenin's refined dialectical sense at work: he is fully aware that, now, in the early 1920s, the main task of Bolshevik power is to execute the tasks of the progressive bourgeois regime (general education, etc.); however, the very fact that it is a proletarian revolutionary power which is doing this changes the situation fundamentally – there is a unique chance that these "civilizing" measures will be implemented in such a way that they will be deprived of their limited bourgeois ideological framework (general education will be really general education serving the people, not an ideological mask for propagating narrow bourgeois class interest, etc.). The properly dialectical paradox is thus that it is the very *hopelessness* of the Russian situation (the backwardness that compels the proletarian power to fulfil the bourgeois civilizing mission) which can be turned into a unique advantage:

> What if the complete hopelessness of the situation, by stimulating the efforts of the workers and peasants tenfold, offered us the opportunity to create the fundamental requisites of civilization in a different way from that of the West European countries?[11]

Here we have two models, two incompatible logics, of the revolution: those who wait for the ripe teleological moment of the final crisis when revolution will explode "at its own proper time" according to the necessity of the historical evolution; and those who are aware that revolution has no "proper time", those who perceive the revolutionary chance as something that emerges and has to be seized in the very detours of "normal" historical development. Lenin is not a voluntarist "subjectivist" – what he insists on is that the exception (the extraordinary set of circumstances, like those in Russia in 1917) offers a way to undermine the norm itself.

Is this line of argumentation, this fundamental stance, not more apposite than ever today? Do not we, also, live in an era when the state and its apparatuses, including its political agents, are simply less and less able to articulate the key issues – as none other than John le Carré put it recently,

[10] V. I. Lenin, "Better Fewer, but Better", in *Collected Works*, vol. 33, p. 488.
[11] V. I. Lenin, "Our Revolution", in *Collected Works*, vol. 33, p. 479.

"Politicians are ignoring the real problems of the world" (by which he meant ecology, deteriorating healthcare, poverty, the role of multinationals, etc.). Le Carré was not simply making a point about the shortsightedness of some politicians – if we take what he said seriously, the only logical conclusion is that we urgently need a new *form of politicization* which will directly "socialize" these crucial issues. The illusion of 1917 that the pressing problems which faced Russia (peace, land distribution, etc.) could be solved through "legal" parliamentary means is the same as today's illusion that the ecological threat, for instance, could be avoided by expanding the market logic to ecology (making polluters pay for the damage they cause).

"Lenin" is not the nostalgic name for old dogmatic certainty; quite the contrary, *the* Lenin who is to be retrieved is the Lenin whose fundamental experience was that of being thrown into a catastrophic new constellation in which the old co-ordinates proved useless, and who was thus compelled to reinvent Marxism – take his acerbic remark apropos of some new problem: "About this, Marx and Engels said not a word." The idea is not to return to Lenin, but to *repeat* him in the Kierkegaardian sense: to retrieve the same impulse in today's constellation. The return to Lenin aims neither at nostalgically *re-enacting* the "good old revolutionary times", nor at an opportunistic-pragmatic *adjustment* of the old programme to "new conditions", but at *repeating*, in the present worldwide conditions, the Leninist gesture of reinventing the revolutionary project in the conditions of imperialism and colonialism – more precisely: after the politico-ideological collapse of the long era of progressivism in the catastrophe of 1914. Eric Hobsbawm has defined the concept of the twentieth century as the time between 1914, the end of the long peaceful expansion of capitalism, and 1990, the emergence of the new form of global capitalism after the collapse of Really Existing Socialism.[12] What Lenin did for 1914, we should do for 1990. "Lenin" stands for the compelling freedom to suspend the stale existing (post-)ideological co-ordinates, the debilitating *Denkverbot* (prohibition on thinking) in which we live – it simply means that we are allowed to think again.

So what role should Lenin's *personality* play in our assessment of his contribution? Are we not, in fact, reducing him to a pure symbol of a certain revolutionary stance? In a letter to Engels written on 30 July 1862, Marx designated Ferdinand Lassalle – co-founder of German Social Democracy, and his competitor for influence in it – not only as "a greasy Jew

---

[12] See Eric Hobsbawm, *The Age of Extremes*, New York: Vintage 1996.

disguised under brilliantine and cheap jewels", but, even more brutally, as "the Jewish Nigger": "It is now perfectly clear to me that, as the shape of his head and the growth of his hair indicate, he is descended from the Negroes who joined in Moses' flight from Egypt (unless his mother or grandmother on the father's side was crossed with a nigger)."[13] Instead of reading such statements as proof of the Eurocentric bias of Marx's theory, we should simply dismiss them as fundamentally *irrelevant*; their only positive significance is that they prevent us from indulging in any kind of hagiography of Marx, since they clearly reveal the irreducible gap between Marx as a person and his theory which, precisely, provides the tools for an analysis and a criticism of such racist outbursts. And, of course, the same goes for Lenin: his alleged "ruthlessness" has exactly the same status as his love of cats and little children in the Stalinist hagiography.

After the Hungarian rebellion of 1956 was crushed by the Russian tanks, Georg Lukács (who participated in the Imre Nagy government) was taken prisoner; when a KGB officer asked him if he had a weapon, Lukács calmly reached into his pocket and handed over his pen.[14] Does not the implication of this gesture hold even more for Lenin's texts collected here? If ever a pen was a weapon, it was the pen which wrote Lenin's 1917 texts.

[13] *Marx-Engels-Werke*, Berlin (GDR): Dietz Verlag 1968, vol. XXX, p. 259.
[14] Arpad Kadarkay, *Georg Lukács*, Oxford: Blackwell 1991, p. 434.

Revolution at the Gates

1

Letters from Afar

(March 7–26, 1917)[1]

First Letter

The first stage of the first revolution[2]

The first revolution engendered by the imperialist world war has broken out. The first revolution but certainly not the last.

[1] The first four *Letters from Afar* were written between March 7 and 12 (20 and 25); the fifth, unfinished letter was written on the eve of Lenin's departure from Switzerland, on March 26 (April 8) 1917.

As soon as the first news reached him of the revolutionary events in Russia and the composition of the bourgeois Provisional Government and the Executive Committee of the Petrograd Soviet, Lenin began work on an article for *Pravda* – he regarded the press as an important vehicle of propaganda and organisation. "The press is now the main thing," he wrote to Alexandra Kollontai on March 3 (16). "I cannot deliver lectures or attend meetings, for I must write daily for *Pravda*," he wrote to V. A. Karpinsky on March 8 (21), in reply to the latter's invitation to deliver a lecture on the tasks of the Party in the revolution to Russian émigrés and Swiss socialists in Geneva.

The first and second "Letters from Afar" were sent to Alexandra Kollontai in Oslo on March 9 (22) for forwarding to Petrograd. On March 17 (30) Lenin asked J. S. Hanecki whether the first four letters had reached *Pravda* in Petrograd, adding that if they had not, he would send copies. The letters were brought to Petrograd by Alexandra Kollontai, who handed them over to *Pravda* on March 19 (April 1).

The first letter appeared in Nos 14 and 15 of *Pravda*, March 21 and 22 (April 3 and 4), with considerable abridgements and certain changes by the editorial board, which, beginning with mid-March, included L. B. Kamenev and J. V. Stalin. The second, third and fourth letters were not published in 1917.

[2] The *Pravda* editors deleted about one fifth of the first letter. The cuts concern chiefly Lenin's characterisation of the Menshevik and Socialist-Revolutionary leaders as conciliators and flunkeys of the bourgeoisie, their attempts to hide from the people the fact that representatives of the British and French governments helped the Cadets and Octobrists secure the abdication of Nicholas II, and also Lenin's exposure of the monarchist and imperialist proclivities of the Provisional Government, which was determined to continue the predatory war.

Judging by the scanty information available in Switzerland, the first stage of this first revolution, namely, of the *Russian* revolution of March 1, 1917, has ended. This first stage of our revolution will certainly not be the last.

How could such a "miracle" have happened, that in only eight days – the period indicated by Mr Milyukov in his boastful telegram to all Russia's representatives abroad – a monarchy collapsed that had maintained itself for centuries, and that in spite of everything had managed to maintain itself throughout the three years of the tremendous, nation-wide class battles of 1905–07?

There are no miracles in nature or history, but every abrupt turn in history, and this applies to every revolution, presents such a wealth of content, unfolds such unexpected and specific combinations of forms of struggle and alignment of forces of the contestants, that to the lay mind there is much that must appear miraculous.

The combination of a number of factors of world-historic importance was required for the tsarist monarchy to have collapsed in a few days. We shall mention the chief of them.

Without the tremendous class battles and the revolutionary energy displayed by the Russian proletariat during the three years 1905–07, the second revolution could not possibly have been so rapid in the sense that its *initial stage* was completed in a few days. The first revolution (1905) deeply ploughed the soil, uprooted age-old prejudices, awakened millions of workers and tens of millions of peasants to political life and political struggle and revealed to each other – and to the world – *all* classes (and all the principal parties) of Russian society in their true character and in the true alignment of their interests, their forces, their modes of action, and their immediate and ultimate aims. This first revolution, and the succeeding period of counter-revolution (1907–14), laid bare the very essence of the tsarist monarchy, brought it to the "utmost limit", exposed all the rottenness and infamy, the cynicism and corruption of the tsar's clique, dominated by that monster, Rasputin. It exposed all the bestiality of the Romanov family – those pogrom-mongers who drenched Russia in the blood of Jews, workers and revolutionaries, those *landlords*, "first among peers", *who own millions* of dessiatines of land and are prepared to stoop to any brutality, to any crime, to ruin and strangle any number of citizens in order to preserve the "sacred right of property" for themselves *and their class*.

Without the Revolution of 1905–07 and the counter-revolution of 1907–14, there could not have been that clear "self-determination" of all classes of the Russian people and of the nations inhabiting Russia, that determination of the relation of these classes to each other and to the tsarist monarchy, which manifested itself during the eight days of the February–March Revolution of 1917. This eight-day revolution was "performed", if we may use a metaphorical expression, as though after a dozen major and minor rehearsals; the "actors" knew each other, their parts, their places and their setting in every detail, through and through, down to every more or less important shade of political trend and mode of action.

For the first great Revolution of 1905, which the Guchkovs and Milyukovs and their hangers-on denounced as a "great rebellion", led, after the lapse of twelve years, to the "brilliant", the "glorious" Revolution of 1917 – the Guchkovs and Milyukovs have proclaimed it "glorious" because it has put them in power (*for the time being*). But this required a great, mighty and all-powerful "stage manager", capable, on the one hand, of vastly accelerating the course of world history, and, on the other, of engendering world-wide crises of unparalleled intensity – economic, political, national and international. Apart from an extraordinary acceleration of world history, it was also necessary that history make particularly abrupt turns, in order that at one such turn the filthy and blood-stained cart of the Romanov monarchy should be overturned *at one stroke*.

This all-powerful "stage manager", this mighty accelerator, was the imperialist world war.

That it is a world war is now indisputable, for the United States and China are already half-involved today, and will be fully involved tomorrow.

That it is an imperialist war on *both* sides is now likewise indisputable. Only the capitalists and their hangers-on, the social-patriots and social-chauvinists, or – if instead of general critical definitions we use political names familiar in Russia – only the Guchkovs and Lvovs, Milyukovs and Shingaryovs on the one hand, and only the Gvozdyovs, Potresovs, Chkhenkelis, Kerenskys and Chkheidzes on the other, can deny or gloss over this fact. *Both* the German and the Anglo-French bourgeoisie are waging the war for the plunder of foreign countries and the strangling of small nations, for financial world supremacy and the division and redivision of colonies, and in order to save the tottering capitalist regime by misleading and dividing the workers of the various countries.

The imperialist war was bound, with objective inevitability, immensely to accelerate and intensify to an unprecedented degree the class struggle of the proletariat against the bourgeoisie; it was bound to turn into a civil war between the hostile classes.

This *transformation has been started* by the February–March Revolution of 1917, the first stage of which has been marked, firstly, by a joint blow at tsarism struck by two forces: one, the whole of bourgeois and landlord

Russia, with all her unconscious hangers-on and all her conscious leaders, the British and French ambassadors and capitalists, and the other, *the Soviet of Workers' Deputies*, which has begun to win over the soldiers' and peasants' deputies.[3]

[3] Lenin here refers to the Petrograd Soviet of Workers' Deputies, which emerged in the very early days of the February Revolution. Elections to the Soviet began spontaneously at individual factories and within a few days spread to all the factories in the capital. On February 27 (March 12), before the Soviet had assembled for its first meeting, the Menshevik liquidators K. A. Gvozdyov and B. O. Bogdanov, and Duma members N. S. Chkheidze, M. I. Skobelev and others proclaimed themselves the Provisional Executive Committee of the Soviet in an attempt to bring it under their complete control. At its first meeting in the evening of the same day, the Soviet formed a Presidium composed of Chkheidze, Kerensky and Skobelev who, together with A. G. Shlyapnikov, N. N. Sukhanov and Y. M. Steklov, made up the Executive Committee. Provision was made for inclusion of representatives of the central and Petrograd committees of the socialist parties. The Socialist-Revolutionaries were at first opposed to the organisation of the Soviet, but subsequently delegated their representatives, V. A. Alexandrovich, V. M. Zenzinov and others.

The Soviet proclaimed itself the organ of the workers and soldiers, and up to the first Congress of Soviets (June 1917) was factually an all-Russian centre. On March 1 (14) the Executive Committee was extended to include soldiers' deputies, among them F. F. Linde. A. I. Paderin and A. D. Sadovsky.

The Bureau of the Executive Committee was composed, among others, of N. S. Chkheidze, Y. M. Steklov, B. O. Bogdanov, P. I. Stucka, P. A. Krasikov, K. A. Gvozdyov. N. S. Chkheidze and A. F. Kerensky were delegated to represent the Soviet on the Duma Committee.

On February 28 (March 13), the Soviet issued its Manifesto to the Population of Petrograd and Russia. It called on the people to rally around the Soviet and take over the administration of local affairs. On March 3 (14), the Soviet appointed several commissions – on food, military affairs, public order and the press. The latter commission provided the first editorial board of *Izvestia*, composed of N. D. Sokolov, Y. M. Steklov, N. N. Sukhanov and K. S. Grinevich; V. A. Bazarov and B. V. Avilov were added somewhat later.

Meetings of the Executive Committee were attended, in a consultative capacity, by the Social-Democratic members of all the four State Dumas, five representatives of the Soldiers' Commission, two representatives of the Central Trade Union Bureau, representatives of the district Soviets, the *Izvestia* editorial board, and other organisations.

The Soviet appointed special delegates to organise district Soviets and began the formation of a militia (100 volunteers for every 1,000 workers).

Though leadership of the Soviet was in the hands of compromising elements, the pressure of the militant workers and soldiers compelled it to take a number of revolutionary measures – the arrest of tsarist officials, release of political prisoners, etc.

On March 1 (14), the Soviet issued its "Order No. 1 to the Petrograd Garrison". It played a very big part in revolutionising the army. Henceforth all military units were to be guided in their political actions solely by the Soviet, all weapons were to be placed at the disposal and under the control of company and battalion soldiers' committees,

These three political camps, these three fundamental political forces – (1) the tsarist monarchy, the head of the feudal landlords, of the old bureaucracy and the military caste; (2) bourgeois and landlord-Octobrist-Cadet Russia, behind which trailed the petty bourgeoisie (of which Kerensky and Chkheidze are the principal representatives); (3) the Soviet of Workers' Deputies, which is seeking to make the entire proletariat and the entire mass of the poorest part of the population its allies – these three *fundamental* political forces fully and clearly revealed themselves even in the eight days of the "first stage" and even to an observer so remote from the scene of events as the present writer, who is obliged to content himself with the meagre foreign press dispatches.

But before dealing with this in greater detail, I must return to the part of my letter devoted to a factor of prime importance, namely, the imperialist world war.

The war shackled the belligerent powers, the belligerent groups of capitalists, the "bosses" of the capitalist system, the slave-owners of the capitalist slave system, to each other with *chains of iron. One bloody clot* – such is the social and political life of the present moment in history.

The socialists who deserted to the bourgeoisie on the outbreak of the war – all these Davids and Scheidemanns in Germany and the Plekhanovs, Potresovs, Gvozdyovs and Co. in Russia – clamoured loud and long against the "illusions" of the revolutionaries, against the "illusions" of the Basle Manifesto, against the "farcical dream" of turning the imperialist war into a civil war. They sang praises in every key to the strength, tenacity and adaptability allegedly revealed by capitalism – *they*, who had aided the capitalists to "adapt", tame, mislead and divide the working classes of the various countries!

But "he who laughs last laughs best". The bourgeoisie has been unable to delay for long the revolutionary crisis engendered by the war. That crisis is growing with irresistible force in all countries, beginning with Germany, which, according to an observer who recently visited that country, is suffering "brilliantly organised famine", and ending with England and

---

orders issued by the Provisional Committee of the State Duma were to be obeyed only if they did not conflict with the orders of the Soviet, etc.

But at the crucial moment, on the night following March 1 (14) the compromising leaders of the Soviet Executive voluntarily turned over power to the bourgeoisie: they endorsed the Provisional Government composed of representatives of the bourgeoisie and landlords. This was not known abroad, since papers standing to the left of the Cadets were not allowed out of the country. Lenin learned of the surrender of power only when he returned to Russia.

France, where *famine is also* looming, but where organisation is far less "brilliant".

It was natural that the revolutionary crisis should have broken out *first of all* in tsarist Russia, where the disorganisation was most appalling and the proletariat most revolutionary (not by virtue of any special qualities, but because of the living traditions of 1905). This crisis was precipitated by the series of extremely severe defeats sustained by Russia and her allies. They shook up the old machinery of government and the old order and roused the anger of *all* classes of the population against them; they embittered the army, wiped out a very large part of the old commanding personnel, composed of die-hard aristocrats and exceptionally corrupt bureaucratic elements, and replaced it by a young, fresh, mainly bourgeois, commoner, petty-bourgeois personnel. Those who, grovelling to the bourgeoisie or simply lacking backbone, howled and wailed about "defeatism", are now faced by the fact of the historical connection between the defeat of the most backward and barbarous tsarist monarchy and the *beginning* of the revolutionary conflagration.

But while the defeats early in the war were a negative factor that precipitated the upheaval, the *connection* between Anglo-French finance capital, Anglo-French imperialism, and Russian Octobrist-Cadet capital was a factor that hastened this crisis by the direct *organisation of a plot* against Nicholas Romanov.

This highly important aspect of the situation is, for obvious reasons, hushed up by the Anglo-French press and maliciously emphasised by the German. We Marxists must soberly face the truth and not allow ourselves to be confused either by the lies, the official sugary diplomatic and ministerial lies, of the first group of imperialist belligerents, or by the sniggering and smirking of their financial and military rivals of the other belligerent group. The whole course of events in the February–March Revolution clearly shows that the British and French embassies, with their agents and "connections", who had long been making the most desperate efforts to prevent "separate" agreements and a separate peace between Nicholas II (and last, we hope, and we will endeavour to make him that) and Wilhelm II, directly organised a plot in conjunction with the Octobrists and Cadets, in conjunction with a section of the generals and army and St Petersburg garrison officers, with the express object of *deposing* Nicholas Romanov.

Let us not harbour any illusions. Let us not make the mistake of those who – like certain OC supporters or Mensheviks who are oscillating between Gvozdyov–Potresov policy and internationalism and only too often slip into petty-bourgeois pacifism – are now ready to extol "agreement" between the workers' party and the Cadets, "support" of the latter by the former, etc. In conformity with the old (and by no means Marxist) doctrine that they have learned by rote, they are trying to veil the plot of the Anglo-French imperialists and the Guchkovs and Milyukovs aimed at deposing the "chief warrior", Nicholas Romanov, and putting more energetic, fresh and more capable *warriors* in his place.

That the revolution succeeded so quickly and – seemingly, at the first superficial glance – so radically, is only due to the fact that, as a result of an extremely unique historical situation, *absolutely dissimilar currents, absolutely heterogeneous* class interests, *absolutely contrary* political and social strivings have merged, and in a strikingly "harmonious" manner. Namely, the conspiracy of the Anglo-French imperialists, who impelled Milyukov, Guchkov and Co. to seize power *for the purpose of continuing the imperialist war*, for the purpose of conducting the war still more ferociously and obstinately, for the purpose of *slaughtering fresh millions* of Russian workers and peasants in order that the Guchkovs might obtain Constantinople, the French capitalists Syria, the British capitalists Mesopotamia, and so on. This on the one hand. On the other, there was a profound proletarian and mass popular movement of a revolutionary character (a movement of the entire poorest section of the population of town and country) for *bread*, for *peace*, for *real freedom*.

It would simply be foolish to speak of the revolutionary proletariat of Russia "supporting" the Cadet-Octobrist imperialism, which has been "patched up" with English money and is as abominable as tsarist imperialism. The revolutionary workers were destroying, have already destroyed to a considerable degree and will destroy to its foundations the infamous tsarist *monarchy*. They are neither elated nor dismayed by the fact that at certain brief and exceptional historical conjunctures *they were aided* by the struggle of Buchanan, Guchkov, Milyukov and Co. to *replace* one monarch by *another monarch*, also preferably a Romanov!

Such, and only such, is the way the situation developed. Such, and only such, in the view that can be taken by a politician who does not fear the truth, who soberly weighs the balance of social forces in the revolution, who appraises every "current situation" not only from the standpoint of all its present, current peculiarities, but also from the standpoint of the more fundamental motivations, the deeper interest-relationship of the proletariat and the bourgeoisie, both in Russia and throughout the world.

The workers of Petrograd, like the workers of the whole of Russia, self-sacrificingly fought the tsarist monarchy – fought for freedom, land for the peasants, and *for peace*, against the imperialist slaughter. To continue and intensify that slaughter, Anglo-French imperialist capital hatched Court intrigues, conspired with the officers of the Guards, incited and encouraged the Guchkovs and Milyukov, and fixed up a *complete new government*, which in fact *did seize power* immediately the proletarian struggle had struck the first blows at tsarism.

This new government, in which Lvov and Guchkov of the Octobrists and Peaceful Renovation Party,[4] yesterday's abettors of Stolypin the Hangman, control *really important* posts, vital posts, decisive posts, the army and the bureaucracy – this government, in which Milyukov and the other Cadets[5] are more than anything decorations, a signboard – they are there to deliver

---

[4] Octobrists – members of the Union of October Seventeen, a counter-revolutionary party formed after promulgation of the tsar's Manifesto of October 17 (30) 1905. It represented and upheld the interests of the big bourgeoisie and of the landlords who ran their estates on capitalist lines. Its leaders were A. I. Guchkov, a big Moscow manufacturer and real estate owner, and M. V. Rodzyanko, a rich landlord. The Octobrists gave their full support to the tsar's home and foreign policy, and in the First World War joined the "Progressist bloc", a sham opposition group demanding responsible government – in other words, a government that would enjoy the confidence of the bourgeoisie and landlords. The Octobrists became the ruling party after the February Revolution, and did everything they could to ward off socialist revolution. Their leader, Guchkov, was War Minister in the First Provisional Government. Following the Great October Socialist Revolution, the party became one of the main forces in the battle against Soviet power.

The party of Peaceful Renovation was a constitutional-monarchist organisation of the big bourgeoisie and landlords. It took final shape in 1906 following the dissolution of the First Duma. It united the "Left" Octobrists and "Right" Cadets, and its chief leaders were P. A. Heiden, N. N. Lvov, P. P. Ryabushinsky, M. A. Stakhovich, Y. N. and G. N. Trubetskoi, D. N. Shipov. Like the Octobrists, it sought to safeguard and promote the interests of the industrial and commercial bourgeoisie and of the landlords who ran their estates along capitalist lines. In the Third Duma the party joined with the so-called Party of Democratic Reforms to form the Progressist group.

[5] Cadets – the name derives from the Constitutional-Democratic Party, the chief party of the Russian liberal-monarchist bourgeoisie. Founded in October 1905, it was composed chiefly of capitalists, Zemstvo leaders, landlords and bourgeois intellectuals. Prominent in the leadership were P. N. Milyukov, S. A. Muromtsev, V. A. Maklakov, A. I. Shingaryov, P. B. Struve and F. I. Rodichev. The Cadets became the party of the imperialist bourgeoisie, and in the First World War actively supported the tsarist government's predatory policies, and in the February Revolution tried to save the monarchy. The dominant force in the Provisional Government, they followed a counter-revolutionary policy inimical to the people but advantageous to US, British and French imperialism. Implacable enemies of Soviet power, the Cadets had an active part in all the armed counter-revolutionary actions and foreign intervention campaigns. Most of their leaders emigrated after the defeat of the counter-revolutionary forces and continued their anti-Soviet and counter-revolutionary work abroad.

sentimental professorial speeches – and in which the Trudovik[6] Kerensky is a balalaika on which they play to deceive the workers and peasants – this government is not a fortuitous assemblage of persons.

They are representatives of the new class that has risen to political power in Russia, the class of capitalist landlords and bourgeoisie which has long been *ruling* our country economically, and which during the Revolution of 1905–07, the counter-revolutionary period of 1907–14, and finally – and with especial rapidity – the war period of 1914–17, was quick to organise itself politically, taking over control of the local government bodies, public education, congresses of various types, the Duma, the war industries committees, etc. This new class was already "almost completely" *in* power by 1917, and therefore it needed only the first blows to bring tsarism to the ground and clear the way for the bourgeoisie. The imperialist war, which required an incredible exertion of effort, so accelerated the course of backward Russia's development that we have "at one blow" (*seemingly* at one blow) *caught up* with Italy, England, and almost with France. We have obtained a "coalition", a "national" (i.e. adapted for carrying on the imperialist slaughter and for fooling the people) "parliamentary" government.

Side by side with this government – which as regards the *present* war is but the agent of the billion-dollar "firm" "England and France" – there has arisen the chief, unofficial, as yet undeveloped and comparatively weak *workers' government*, which expresses the interests of the proletariat and of the entire poor section of the urban and rural population. This is the *Soviet of Workers' Deputies* in Petrograd, which is seeking connections with the soldiers and peasants, and also with the agricultural workers – with the latter particularly and primarily, of course, more than with the peasants.

Such is the *actual* political situation, which we must first endeavour to define with the greatest possible objective precision, in order that Marxist tactics may be based upon the only possible solid foundation – the foundation of *facts*.

---

[6] Trudovik – member of the Trudovik group in the State Dumas formed in April 1906 by petty-bourgeois democrats – peasants and intellectuals of the Narodnik persuasion. The group wavered between the Cadets and the revolutionary Social-Democrats, and in the First World War most of its members adopted a social-chauvinist position.

The Trudoviks spoke for the rich peasants, the kulaks, and after the February Revolution actively supported the Provisional Government. One of their representatives, Zarudny, became Minister of Justice following the July events, and directed the police campaign against the Bolsheviks. After the October Revolution the Trudoviks sided with the counter-revolutionary forces.

The tsarist monarchy has been smashed, but not finally destroyed.

The Octobrist-Cadet bourgeois government, which wants to fight the imperialist war "to a finish", and which in reality is the agent of the financial arm "England and France", is *obliged to promise* the people the maximum of liberties and sops compatible with the maintenance of its power over the people and the possibility of continuing the imperialist slaughter.

The Soviet of Workers' Deputies is an organisation of the workers, the embryo of a workers' government, the representative of the interests of the entire mass of the *poor* section of the population, i.e. of nine-tenths of the population, which is striving for *peace*, *bread* and *freedom*.

The conflict of these three forces determines the situation that has now arisen, a situation that is *transitional* from the first stage of the revolution to the second.

The antagonism between the first and second force is *not* profound, it is temporary, the result *solely* of the present conjuncture of circumstances, of the abrupt turn of events in the imperialist war. The *whole* of the new government is monarchist, for Kerensky's *verbal* republicanism simply cannot be taken seriously, is not worthy of a statesman and, *objectively*, is political chicanery. The new government, which has not dealt the tsarist monarchy the final blow, has already *begun to strike a bargain* with the landlord Romanov dynasty. The bourgeoisie of the Octobrist-Cadet type *needs* a monarchy to serve as the head of the bureaucracy and the army in order to protect the privileges of capital against the working people.

He who says that the workers must support the new government in the interests of the struggle against tsarist reaction (and apparently this is being said by the Potresovs, Gvozdyovs, Chkhenkelis and also, all *evasiveness* notwithstanding, by *Chkheidze*) is a traitor to the workers, a traitor to the cause of the proletariat, to the cause of peace and freedom. For actually, *precisely* this new government is *already* bound hand and foot by imperialist capital, by the imperialist policy of *war* and plunder, has *already* begun to strike a bargain (without consulting the people!) with the dynasty, *is already working to restore the tsarist monarchy*, is already soliciting the candidature of Mikhail Romanov as the new kinglet, is already taking measures to prop up the throne, to substitute for the legitimate (lawful, ruling by virtue of the old law) monarchy a Bonapartist, plebiscite monarchy (ruling by virtue of a fraudulent plebiscite).

No, if there is to be a real struggle against the tsarist monarchy, if freedom is to be guaranteed in fact and not merely in words, in the glib promises of Milyukov and Kerensky, the workers must not support the new government; the government must "support" the workers! For the only guarantee of freedom and of the complete destruction of tsarism lies in *arming the proletariat*, in strengthening, extending and developing the role, significance and power of the Soviet of Workers' Deputies.

All the rest is mere phrase-mongering and lies, self-deception on the part of the politicians of the liberal and radical camp, fraudulent trickery.

Help, or at least do not hinder, the arming of the workers, and freedom in Russia will be invincible, the monarchy irrestorable, the republic secure.

Otherwise the Guchkovs and Milyukovs will restore the monarchy and grant *none*, absolutely none of the "liberties" they promised. All bourgeois politicians in *all* bourgeois revolutions "fed" the people and fooled the workers with promises.

Ours is a bourgeois revolution, *therefore*, the workers must support the bourgeoisie, say the Potresovs, Gvozdyovs and Chkheidzes, as Plekhanov said yesterday.

Ours is a bourgeois revolution, we Marxists say, *therefore* the workers must open the eyes of the people to the deception practised by the bourgeois politicians, teach them to put no faith in words, to depend entirely on their *own* strength, their *own* organisation, their *own* unity, and their *own* weapons.

The government of the Octobrists and Cadets, of the Guchkovs and Milyukovs, *cannot*, even if it sincerely wanted to (only infants can think that Guchkov and Lvov are sincere), *cannot* give the people either *peace*, *bread*, or *freedom*.

It cannot give peace because it is a war government, a government for the continuation of the imperialist slaughter, a government of *plunder*, out to plunder Armenia, Galicia and Turkey, annex Constantinople, reconquer Poland, Courland, Lithuania, etc. It is a government bound hand and foot by Anglo-French imperialist capital. Russian capital is merely a branch of the world-wide "firm" which manipulates *hundreds of billions* of rubles and is called "England and France".

It cannot give bread because it is a bourgeois government. *At best*, it can give the people "brilliantly organised famine", as Germany has done. But the people will not accept famine. They will learn, and probably very soon, that there is bread and that it can be obtained, but only by methods that *do not respect the sanctity of capital and land ownership*.

It cannot give freedom because it is a landlord and capitalist government which fears the people and has already begun to strike a bargain with the Romanov dynasty.

The tactical problems of our immediate attitude towards this government will be dealt with in another article. In it, we shall explain the peculiarity of the present situation, which is a *transition* from the first stage of the revolution to the second, and why the slogan, the "task of the day", at *this* moment must be: *Workers, you have performed miracles of proletarian heroism, the heroism of the people, in the civil war against tsarism. You must perform miracles of organisation, organisation of the proletariat and of the whole people, to prepare the way for your victory in the second stage of the revolution.*

Confining ourselves for the *present* to an analysis of the class struggle and the alignment of class forces at this stage of the revolution, we have still to put the question: who are the proletariat's *allies* in *this* revolution?

It has *two* allies: first, the broad mass of the semi-proletarian and partly also of the small-peasant population, who number scores of millions and constitute the overwhelming majority of the population of Russia. For this mass peace, bread, freedom and land are *essential*. It is inevitable that to a certain extent this mass will be under the influence of the bourgeoisie, particularly of the petty bourgeoisie, to which it is most akin in its conditions of life, vacillating between the bourgeoisie and the proletariat. The cruel lessons of war, and they will be the *more* cruel the more vigorously the war is prosecuted by Guchkov, Lvov, Milyukov and Co., will *inevitably* push this mass towards the proletariat, compel it to follow the proletariat. We must now take advantage of the relative freedom of the new order and of the Soviets of Workers' Deputies to *enlighten* and *organise* this mass first of all and above all. Soviets of Peasants' Deputies and Soviets of Agricultural Workers – that is one of our most urgent tasks. In this connection we shall strive not only for the agricultural workers to establish their own separate Soviets, but also for the propertyless and poorest peasants to organise *separately* from the well-to-do peasants. The special tasks and special forms of organisation urgently needed at the present time will be dealt with in the next letter.

Second, the ally of the Russian proletariat is the proletariat of all the belligerent countries and of all countries in general. At present this ally is to a large degree repressed by the war, and all too often the European social-chauvinists speak in its name – men who, like Plekhanov, Gvozdyov and Potresov in Russia, have deserted to the bourgeoisie. But the liberation of the proletariat from their influence has progressed with every month of the imperialist war, and the Russian revolution will *inevitably* immensely hasten this process.

With these two allies, the proletariat, *utilising the peculiarities* of the present transition situation, can and will proceed, first, to the achievement of a democratic republic and complete victory of the peasantry over the landlords, instead of the Guchkov–Milyukov semi-monarchy, and then to *socialism*, which alone can give the war-weary people *peace*, *bread* and *freedom*.

Second Letter

The new government and the proletariat

The principal document I have at my disposal at today's date (March 8/21) is a copy of that most conservative and bourgeois English newspaper *The Times* of March 16, containing a batch of reports about the revolution in Russia. Clearly, a source more favourably inclined – to put it mildly – towards the Guchkov and Milyukov government it would not be easy to find.

This newspaper's correspondent reports from St Petersburg on Wednesday, March 1 (14), when the *first* Provisional government still existed, i.e. the thirteen-member Duma Executive Committee,[7] headed by Rodzyanko and including two "socialists", as the newspaper puts it, Kerensky and Chkheidze:

"A group of 22 elected members of the Upper House [State Council] including M. Guchkov, M. Stakhovich, Prince Trubetskoi, and Professor Vassiliev, Grimm, and Vernadsky, yesterday addressed a telegram to the Tsar" imploring him in order to save the "dynasty", etc., etc., to convoke the Duma and to name as the head of the government someone who enjoys the "confidence of the nation". "What the Emperor may decide to do on

---

[7] The first Provisional Government, or the Provisional Committee of the State Duma, was formed on February 27 (March 12), 1917. On that day the Duma Council of Doyens sent a telegram to the tsar drawing his attention to the critical situation in the capital and urging immediate measures "to save the fatherland and the dynasty". The tsar replied by sending the Duma President, M. V. Rodzyanko, a decree dissolving the Duma. By this time the insurgent people had surrounded the Duma building, the Taurida Palace, where Duma members were meeting in private conference, and blocked all the streets leading to it. Soldiers and armed workers were in occupation of the building. In this situation the Duma hastened to elect a Provisional Commitlee to "maintain order in Petrograd and for communication with various institutions and individuals".

The Provisional Committee was composed of V. V. Shulgin and V. N. Lvov, both of the extreme Right, Octobrists S. I. Shidlovsky. I. I. Dmitryukov, M. V. Rodzyanko (chairman), Progressists V. A. Rzhevsky and A. I. Konovalov, Cadets P. N. Milyukov and N. V. Nekrasov, the Trudovik A. F. Kerensky, and the Menshevik N. S. Chkheidze.

his arrival today is unknown at the hour of telegraphing," writes the correspondent, "but one thing is quite certain. Unless His Majesty immediately complies with the wishes of the most moderate elements among his loyal subjects, the influence at present exercised by the Provisional Committee of the Imperial Duma will pass wholesale into the hands of the socialists, who want to see a republic established, but who are unable to institute any kind of orderly government and would inevitably precipitate the country into anarchy within and disaster without. . . ."

What political sagacity and clarity this reveals. How well this Englishman, who thinks like (if he does not guide) the Guchkovs and Milyukovs, understands the alignment of class forces and interests! "The most moderate elements among his loyal subjects", i.e. the monarchist landlords and capitalists, want to take power into their hands, fully realising that otherwise "influence" will pass into the hands of the "socialists". Why the "socialists" and not somebody else? Because the English Guchkovite is fully aware that there is *no* other social force in the political arena, *nor can there be*. The revolution was made by the proletariat. It displayed heroism; it shed its blood; it swept along with it the broadest masses of the toilers and the poor; it is demanding bread, peace and freedom; it is demanding a republic; it sympathises with socialism. But the handful of landlords and capitalists headed by the Guchkovs and Milyukovs want to betray the will, or strivings, of the vast majority and conclude *a deal with the loitering monarchy*, bolster it up, save it: appoint Lvov and Guchkov, Your Majesty, and we will be with the monarchy against the people. Such is the entire meaning, the sum and substance of the new government's policy!

But how to justify the deception, the fooling of the people, the violation of the will of the overwhelming majority of the population?

By slandering the people – the old but eternally new method of the bourgeoisie. And the English Guchkovite slanders, scolds, spits and splutters: "anarchy within and disaster without", no "orderly government"!!

That is not true, Mr Guchkovite! The workers want a republic; and a republic represents far more "orderly" government than monarchy does. What guarantee have the people that the second Romanov will not get himself a second Rasputin? Disaster will be brought on precisely by continuation of the war, i.e. precisely by the new government. Only a proletarian republic, backed by the rural workers and the poorest section of the peasants and town dwellers, can secure peace, provide bread, order and freedom.

All the shouts about anarchy are merely a screen to conceal the selfish interests of the capitalists, who want to make profit out of the war, out of war loans, who want to restore the monarchy *against* the people.

"Yesterday," continues the correspondent, "the Social-Democratic Party issued a proclamation of a most seditious character, which was spread broadcast throughout the city. They [i.e. the Social-Democratic Party] are mere doctrinaires, but their power for mischief is enormous at a time like the present. M. Kerensky and M. Chkheidze, who realise that without the support of the officers and the more moderate elements of the people they cannot hope to avoid anarchy, have to reckon with their less prudent associates, and are insensibly driven to take up an attitude which complicates the task of the Provisional Committee. . . ."

O great English, Guchkovite diplomat! How "imprudently" you have blurted out the truth!

"The Social-Democratic Party" and "their less prudent associates", with whom Kerenskv and Chkheidze "have to reckon", evidently mean the Central or the St Petersburg Committee of our Party, which was restored at the January 1912 Conference,[8] those very same Bolsheviks at whom the bourgeoisie always hurl the abusive term "doctrinaires", because of their faithfulness to the "doctrine", i.e. the fundamentals, the principles, teachings, aims of *socialism*. Obviously, the English Guchkovite hurls the abusive terms seditious and doctrinaire at the manifesto[9] and at the conduct of our Party in urging a fight for a republic, peace, complete destruction of the tsarist monarchy, bread for the people.

---

[8] The composition of the CC Bureau in Russia on March 9 (22), 1917 was as follows: A. I. Yelizarova, K. S. Yeremeyev, V. N. Zalezhsky, P. A. Zalutsky, M. I. Kalinin, V. M. Molotov, M. S. Olminsky, A. M. Smirnov, Y. D. Stasova, M. I. Ulyanova, M. I. Khakharev, K. M. Shvedchikov, A. C. Shlyapnikov and K. I. Shutko. On March 12 (25), G. I. Bokii and M. K. Muranov were added, also J. V. Stalin, with voice but no vote.

The Petrograd Committee of the RSDLP was formed at a meeting on March 2 (15), 1917, and was composed of all those who had served on the illegal committees and newly co-opted members. The composition was: B. V. Avilov, N. K. Antipov, B. A. Zhemchuzhin, V. N. Zalezhsky, M. I. Kalinin, N. P. Komarov, L. M. Mikhailov, V. M. Molotov, K. Orlov, N. I. Podvoisky, P. I. Stucka, V. V. Schmidt, K. I. Shutko and A. G. Shlyapnikov, representing the Central Committee Bureau.

[9] This refers to the *Manifesto of the Russian Social-Democratic Labour Party to All Citizens of Russia*, issued by the Central Committee and published as a supplement to *Izvestia* of February 28 (March 13), 1917 (No. 1). Lenin learned of the Manifesto from an abridged version in the morning edition of the *Frankfurter Zeitung*, March 9 (22), 1917. On the following day he wired *Pravda* in Petrograd via Oslo: "Have just read excerpts from the Central Committee Manifesto. Best wishes. Long live the proletarian militia, harbinger of peace and socialism!"

Bread for the people and peace – that's sedition, but ministerial posts for Guchkov and Milyukov – that's "order". Old and familiar talk!

What, then, are the tactics of Kerensky and Chkheidze as characterised by the English Guchkovite?

Vacillation: on the one hand, the Guchkovite praises them: they "realise" (Good boys! Clever boys!) that without the "support" of the army officers and the more moderate elements, anarchy cannot be avoided (we, however, have always thought, in keeping with our doctrine, with our socialist teachings, that it is the capitalists who introduce anarchy and war into human society, that only the transfer of *all* political power to the proletariat and the poorest people can rid us of war, of anarchy and starvation!). On the other hand, they "have to reckon with their less prudent associates", i.e. the Bolsheviks, the Russian Social-Democratic Labour Party, restored and united by the Central Committee.

What is the force that compels Kerensky and Chkheidze to "reckon" with the Bolshevik Party to which they have never belonged, which they, or their literary representatives (Socialist-Revolutionaries, Popular Socialists,[10] the

[10] Socialist-Revolutionaries – members of the Socialist-Revolutionary Party, a petty-bourgeois party in Russia, which arose at the end of 1901 and beginning of 1902 as a result of the merger of various Narodnik groups and circles. The Socialist-Revolutionaries were oblivious to the class differences between the proletariat and petty proprietors, glossed over the class differentiation and contradictions within the peasantry, and negated the leading role of the proletariat in the revolution. The views of the Socialist-Revolutionaries were an eclectic mixture of the ideas of Narodism and revisionism. The Bolshevik Party exposed their attempts to masquerade as socialists, carried out a determined struggle against them for influence over the peasantry, and showed the danger to the working-class movement of their tactics of individual terrorism.

The fact that the peasantry, to which the Socialist-Revolutionaries appealed, was not a homogeneous class determined their political and ideological instability and organisational disunity, and their constant wavering between the liberal bourgeoisie and the proletariat. As early as the first Russian revolution (1905–07) the Right wing of the Socialist-Revolutionary Party broke away and formed the legal Trudovik Popular Socialist Party, whose outlook was close to that of the Cadets, and the Left wing formed the semi-anarchist League of Maximalists. The majority of Socialist-Revolutionaries adopted a social-chauvinist position during the First World War.

The Organising Committee – the leading Menshevik centre, inaugurated at the August 1912 Conference of liquidators. In the First World War the Organising Committee followed a social-chauvinist policy, justified tsarist Russia's part in the war and carried on jingoist propaganda. It published a magazine, *Nasha Zarya* (*Our Dawn*) and, after its closure, *Nashe Dyelo* (*Our Cause*), later renamed *Dyelo*, and the newspaper *Rabocheye Utro* (*Workers' Morning*), later renamed *Utro*. The OC functioned up to the elections of the Menshevik Central Committee in August 1917. Besides the OC which operated inside Russia, there was a Secretariat Abroad composed of five secretaries –

Menshevik OC supporters, and so forth), have always abused, condemned, denounced as an insignificant underground circle, a sect of doctrinaires, and so forth? Where and when has it ever happened that in time of revolution, at a time of predominantly *mass* action, sane-minded politicians should "reckon" with "doctrinaires"??

He is all mixed up, our poor English Guchkovite; he has failed to produce a logical argument, has failed to tell either a whole lie or the whole truth, he has merely given himself away.

Kerensky and Chkheidze are compelled to reckon with the Social-Democratic Party of the Central Committee by the influence it exerts on the proletariat, on the masses. Our Party was found to be with the masses, with the revolutionary proletariat, *in spite of* the arrest and deportation of our Duma deputies to Siberia, as far back as 1914; in spite of the fierce persecution and arrests to which the St Petersburg Committee was subjected for its underground activities during the war, *against* the war and against tsarism.

"Facts are stubborn things," as the English proverb has it. Let me remind you of it, most esteemed English Guchkovite! That our Party guided, or at least rendered devoted assistance to, the St Petersburg workers in the great days of revolution is a fact the English Guchkovite "*himself*" was *obliged* to admit. And he was equally obliged to admit the fact that Kerensky and Chkheidze are oscillating *between* the bourgeoisie and the proletariat. The Gvozdyovites, the "defencists", i.e. the social-chauvinists, i.e. the defenders of the imperialist, predatory war, are now completely following the bourgeoisie; Kerensky, by entering the ministry, i.e. the second Provisional Government, has also completely deserted to the bourgeoisie; Chkheidze has not; he continues to *oscillate* between the Provisional Government of the bourgeoisie, the Guchkovs and Milyukovs, and the "provisional government" of the proletariat and the poorest masses of the people, the Soviet of Workers' Deputies and the Russian Social-Democratic Labour Party united by the Central Committee.

Consequently, the revolution has confirmed what we especially insisted on when we urged the workers clearly to realise the class difference between the principal parties and principal trends in the working-class movement and among the petty bourgeoisie – what we wrote, for example, in the

P. B. Axelrod, I. S. Astrov-Poves, Y. O. Martov, A. S. Martynov and S. Y. Semkovsky. It followed a pro-Centrist line and used internationalist phraseology to cover up its support of the Russian social-chauvinists. The Secretariat Abroad published a newspaper, *Izvestia* (*News*), which appeared from February 1915 to March 1917.

Geneva *Sotsial-Demokrat* No. 41, nearly eighteen months ago, on Octobor 13, 1915:

> As hitherto, we consider it admissible for Social-Democrats to join a provisional revolutionary government together with the democratic petty bourgeoisie, but *not* with the revolutionary chauvinists. By revolutionary chauvinists we mean those who want a victory over tsarism so as to achieve victory over Germany – plunder other countries – consolidate Great-Russian rule over the other peoples of Russia, etc. Revolutionary chauvinism is based on the class position of the petty bourgeoisie. The latter always vacillates between the bourgeoisie and the proletariat. At present it is vacillating between chauvinism (which prevents it from being consistently revolutionary, even in the meaning of a democratic revolution) and proletarian internationalism. At the moment the Trudoviks, the Socialist-Revolutionaries, *Nasha Zarya* (now *Dyelo*), Chkheidze's Duma group, the Organising Committee, Mr Plekhanov and the like are political spokesmen for this petty bourgeoisie in Russia. If the revolutionary chauvinists won in Russia, we would be opposed to a defence of *their* "fatherland" in the present war. Our slogan is: against the chauvinists, even if they are revolutionary and republican – *against* them and *for* an alliance of the international proletariat for the socialist revolution.

But let us return to the English Guchkovite.

"The Provisional Committee of the Imperial Duma," he continues, "appreciating the dangers ahead, have purposely refrained from carrying out the original intention of arresting Ministers, although they could have done so yesterday without the slightest difficulty. The door is thus left open for negotiations, thanks to which we ["we" = British finance capital and imperialism] may obtain all the benefits of the new regime without passing through the dread ordeal of the Commune and the anarchy of civil war. . . ."

The Guchkovites were *for* a civil war from which *they* would benefit; but they are *against* a civil war from which the people, i.e. the actual majority of the working people, would benefit.

> The relations between the Provisional Committee of the Duma, which represents the whole nation [imagine saying this about the committee of the landlord and capitalist Fourth Duma!], and the Council of Labour Deputies, representing purely class interests [this is the language of a diplomat who has heard learned words with one ear and wants to conceal the fact that the Soviet of Workers' Deputies represents the proletariat and the poor, i.e. nine-tenths of the population], but in a crisis like the present wielding enormous power, have aroused no small misgivings among reasonable men regarding the possibility

of a conflict between them – the results of which might be too terrible to describe.

Happily this danger has been averted, at least for the present [note the "at least"!], thanks to the influence of M. Kerensky, a young lawyer of much oratorical ability, who clearly realises [unlike Chkheidze, who also "realised", but evidently less clearly in the opinion of the Guchkovite?] the necessity of working with the Committee in the interests of his Labour constituents [i.e. to catch the workers' votes, to flirt with them]. A satisfactory Agreement[11] was concluded today [Wednesday, March 1/14], whereby all unnecessary friction will be avoided.

What this agreement was, whether it was concluded with the *whole* of the Soviet of Workers' Deputies and on what terms, we do not know. On this *chief* point, the English Guchkovite says nothing at all this time. And no wonder! It is not to the advantage of the bourgeoisie to have these terms made clear, precise and known to all, for it would then be more difficult for it to violate them!

The preceding lines were already written when I read two very important communications. First, in that most conservative and bourgeois Paris newspaper *Le Temps*[12] of March 20, the text of the Soviet of Workers' Deputies manifesto appealing for "support" of the new government;[13] second,

---

[11] Reference is to the agreement concluded on the night following March 1 (14), 1917 between the Duma Provisional Committee and the Socialist-Revolutionary and Menshevik leaders of the Petrograd Soviet Executive Committee. The latter voluntarily surrendered power to the bourgeoisie, and authorised the Duma Provisional Committee to form a Provisional Government of its own choice.

[12] *Le Temps* – a daily paper published in Paris from 1861 to 1942. It spoke for the ruling element, and was the factual organ of the French Foreign Ministry.

[13] The Manifesto of the Executive Committee of the Soviet of Workers' and Soldiers' Deputies was published in *Izvestia* on March 3 (16), 1917 (No. 4), simultaneously with the announcement of the formation of a Provisional Government under Prince Lvov. Drawn up by the Socialist-Revolutionary and Menshevik members of the Executive Committee, it declared that the democratic forces would support the new government "to the extent that it carries out its undertakings and wages a determined struggle against the old regime".

The Manifesto did not mention the fact that the Soviet had authorised Kerensky to join the new government, inasmuch as on March 1 (14) the Executive Committee had decided "not to delegate democratic representatives to the government". *Le Temps* reported this in a dispatch from its correspondent. On March 2 (15) the Soviet, "defying the protest of the minority", approved Kerensky's entry into the government as Minister of Justice.

excerpts from Skobelev's speech in the State Duma on March 1 (14), reproduced in a Zurich newspaper (*Neue Zürcher Zeitung*, 1 Mit.-bl., March 21) from a Berlin newspaper (*National-Zeitung*).[14]

The manifesto of the Soviet of Workers' Deputies, if the text has not been distorted by the French imperialists, is a most remarkable document. It shows that the St Petersburg proletariat, at least at the time the manifesto was issued, was under the predominating influence of petty-bourgeois politicians. You will recall that in this category of politicians I include, as has been already mentioned above, people of the type of Kerensky and Chkheidze.

In the manifesto we find two political ideas, and two slogans corresponding to them:

Firstly. The manifesto says that the government (the new one) consists of "moderate elements". A strange description, by no means complete, of a purely liberal, not of a Marxist character. I too am prepared to agree that in a certain sense – in my next letter I will show in precisely what sense – now, with the first stage of the revolution completed, every government must be "moderate". But it is absolutely impermissible to conceal from ourselves and from the people that this government wants to continue the imperialist war, that it is an agent of British capital, that it wants to restore the monarchy and strengthen the rule of the landlords and capitalists.

The manifesto declares that all democrats must "support" the new government, and that the Soviet of Workers' Deputies requests and authorises Kerensky to enter the Provisional Government. The conditions – implementation of the promised reforms already during the war, guarantees for the "free cultural" (only??) development of the nationalities (a purely Cadet, wretchedly liberal programme), and the establishment of a special committee consisting of members of the Soviet of Workers' Deputies and of "military men"[15] to supervise the activities of the Provisional Government.

[14] *Neue Zürcher Zeitung* – founded in Zurich in 1780 and until 1821 published under the name *Zürcher Zeitung*, now the most influential paper in Switzerland.

National-Zeitung – published in Berlin from 1848 to 1938; from 1914 onwards appeared under the name *Acht-Uhr Abendblatt*.

[15] The foreign press reported the appointment by the Petrograd Soviet of a special body to keep a check on the Provisional Government. On the basis of this report, Lenin at first welcomed the organisation of this control body, pointing out, however, that only experience would show whether it would live up to expectations. Actually, this so-called Contact Committee, appointed by the Executive on March 8 (21) to "influence" and "control" the work of the Provisional Government, only helped the latter exploit the prestige of the Soviet as a cover for its counter-revolutionary policy. The Contact Committee consisted of M. I. Skobelev, Y. M. Steklov, N. N. Sukhanov,

This Supervising Committee, which comes within the second category of ideas and slogans, we will discuss separately further on.

The appointment of the Russian Louis Blanc, Kerensky, and the appeal to support the new government is, one may say, a classical example of betrayal of the cause of the revolution and the cause of the proletariat, a betrayal which doomed a number of nineteenth-century revolutions, irrespective of how sincere and devoted to socialism the leaders and supporters of such a policy may have been.

The proletariat cannot and must not support a war government, a restoration government. To fight reaction, to rebuff all possible and probable attempts by the Romanovs and their friends to restore the monarchy and muster a counter-revolutionary army, it is necessary not to support Guchkov and Co., but to *organise*, expand and strengthen a *proletarian* militia, to arm the people under the leadership of the workers. Without this principal, fundamental, radical measure, there can be no question either of offering serious resistance to the restoration of the monarchy and attempts to rescind or curtail the promised freedoms, or of firmly taking the road that will give the people bread, *peace* and freedom.

If it is true that Chkheidze, who, with Kerensky, was a member of the first Provisional Government (the Duma committee of thirteen), refrained from entering the second Provisional Government out of principled considerations of the above-mentioned or similar character, then that does him credit. That must be said frankly. Unfortunately, such an interpretation is contradicted by the facts, and primarily by the speech delivered by Skobelev, who has always gone hand in hand with Chkheidze.

Skobelev said, if the above-mentioned source is to be trusted, that "the social [? evidently the Social-Democratic] group and the workers are only slightly in touch (have little contact) with the aims of the Provisional Government", that the workers are demanding peace, and that if the war is continued there will be disaster in the spring anyhow, that "the workers have concluded with society [liberal society] a temporary agreement [*eine vorläufige Waffenfreundschaft*], although their political aims are as far removed from the aims of society as heaven is from earth", that "the liberals must abandon the senseless [*unsinnige*] aims of the war", etc.

This speech is a sample of what we called above, in the excerpt from

---

V. N. Filippovsky, N. S. Chkheidze and, later, V. M. Chernov and I. G. Tsereteli. It helped keep the masses from active revolutionary struggle for the transfer of power to the Soviets. The committee was dissolved in April 1917, when its functions were taken over by the Petrograd Soviet Executive Committee Bureau.

Sotsial-Demokrat, "oscillation" between the bourgeoisie and the proletariat. The liberals, while remaining liberals, *cannot* "abandon" the "senseless" aims of the war, which, incidentally, are not determined by them alone, but by Anglo-French finance capital, a world-mighty force measured by hundreds of billions. The task is not to "coax" the liberals, but to *explain* to the workers why the liberals find themselves in a blind alley, why *they* are bound hand and foot, why they *conceal* both the treaties tsarism concluded with England and other countries and the deals between Russian and Anglo-French capital, and so forth.

If Skobelev says that the workers have concluded an agreement with liberal society, no matter of what character, and since he does not protest against it, does not explain from the Duma rostrum how harmful it is for the workers, he thereby *approves* of the agreement. And that is exactly what he should not do.

Skobelev's direct or indirect, clearly expressed or tacit, approval of the agreement between the Soviet of Workers' Deputies and the Provisional Government is Skobelev's swing towards the bourgeoisie. Skobelev's statement that the workers are demanding peace, that their aims are as far removed from the liberals' aims as heaven is from earth, is Skobelev's swing towards the proletariat.

Purely proletarian, truly revolutionary and profoundly correct in design is the second political idea in the manifesto of the Soviet of Workers' Deputies that we are studying, namely, the idea of establishing a "Supervising Committee" (I do not know whether this is what it is called in Russian; I am translating freely from the French), of proletarian-soldier supervision over the Provisional Government.

Now, that's something real! It is worthy of the workers who have shed their blood for freedom, peace, bread for the people! It is a *real step* towards *real guarantees* against tsarism, against a monarchy and against the monarchists Guchkov, Lvov and Co.! It is a sign that the Russian proletariat, in spite of everything, has made progress compared with the French proletariat in 1848, when it "authorised" Louis Blanc! It is proof that the instinct and mind of the proletarian masses are not satisfied with declamations, exclamations, promises of reforms and freedoms, with the title of "minister authorised by the workers", and similar tinsel, but are seeking support *only* where it is to be found, in the *armed* masses of the people organised and led by the proletariat, the class-conscious workers.

It is a step along the right road, but *only* the first step.

If this "Supervising Committee" remains a purely political-type parliamentary institution, a committee that will "put questions" to the Provisional

Government and receive answers from it, then it will remain a plaything, will amount to nothing.

If, on the other hand, it leads, immediately and despite all obstacles, to the formation of a *workers' militia*, or *workers' home guard*, extending to the whole people, to all men and women, which would not only replace the exterminated and dissolved police force, not only make the latter's restoration *impossible* by *any* government, constitutional-monarchist or democratic-republican, *either* in St Petersburg *or* anywhere else in Russia – then the advanced workers of Russia will really take the road towards new and great victories, the road to victory over war, to the realisation of the slogan which, as the newspapers report, adorned the colours of the cavalry troops that demonstrated in St Petersburg, in the square outside the State Duma:

"Long Live Socialist Republics in All Countries!"

I will set out my ideas about this workers' militia in my next letter.

In it I will try to show, on the one hand, that the formation of a militia embracing the entire people and led by the workers is the correct slogan of the day, one that corresponds to the tactical tasks of the peculiar transitional moment through which the Russian revolution (and the world revolution) is passing; and, on the other hand, that to be successful, this workers' militia must, firstly, embrace the entire people, must be a mass organisation to the degree of being *universal*, must really embrace the *entire* able-bodied population of both sexes; secondly, it must proceed to combine not only purely police, but general state functions with military functions and with the control of social production and distribution.

N. Lenin

Zurich, March 22 (9), 1917
PS I forgot to date my previous letter March 20 (7).

Third Letter

Concerning a proletarian militia

The conclusion I drew yesterday about Chkheidze's vacillating tactics has been fully confirmed today, March 10 (23), by two documents. First – a telegraphic report from Stockholm in the *Frankfurter Zeitung*[16] containing

---

[16] *Frankfurter Zeitung* – published in Frankfurt-on-Main, from 1856 to 1943. Resumed publication in 1949 under the name *Frankfurter Allgemeine Zeitung*.

excerpts from the manifesto of the Central Committee of our Party, the Russian Social-Democratic Labour Party, in St Petersburg. In this document there is not a word about either supporting the Guchkov government or overthrowing it; the workers and soldiers are called upon to organise around the Soviet of Workers' Deputies, to elect representatives to it for the fight against tsarism and for a republic, for an eight-hour day, for the confiscation of the landed estates and grain stocks, and chiefly, for an end to the predatory war. Particularly important and particularly urgent in this connection is our Central Committee's absolutely correct idea that to obtain peace, relations must be established with *the proletarians of all the belligerent countries.*

To expect peace from negotiations and relations between the bourgeois governments would be self-deception and deception of the people.

The second document is a Stockholm report, also by telegraph, to another German newspaper (*Vossische Zeitung*[17]) about a conference between the Chkheidze group in the Duma, the workers' group (*Arbeiterfraktion*) and representatives of fifteen workers' unions on March 2 (15) and a manifesto published the next day. Of the eleven points of this manifesto, the telegram reports only three; the first, the demand for a republic; the seventh, the demand for peace and immediate peace negotiations; and the third, the demand for "adequate participation in the government of representatives of the Russian working class".

If this point is correctly reported, I can understand why the bourgeoisie is praising Chkheidze. I can understand why the praise of the English Guchkovites in *The Times* which I quoted elsewhere has been supplemented by the praise of the French Guchkovites in *Le Temps*. This newspaper of the French millionaires and imperialists writes on March 22: "The leaders of the workers' parties, particularly M. Chkheidze, are exercising all their influence to moderate the wishes of the working classes."

Indeed, to demand workers' "participation" in the Guchkov–Milyukov government is a theoretical and political absurdity: to participate as a minority would mean serving as a pawn; to participate on an "equal footing" is impossible, because the demand to continue the war cannot be reconciled with the demand to conclude an armistice and start peace negotiations; to "participate" as a majority requires the strength to *overthrow* the Guchkov–Milyukov government. In practice, the demand for "participation" is the worst sort of Louis Blanc-ism, i.e. oblivion to the

[17] *Vossische Zeitung* – a moderate liberal newspaper published in Berlin from 1704 to 1934.

class struggle and the actual conditions under which it is being waged, infatuation with a most hollow-sounding phrase, spreading illusions among the workers, loss, in negotiations with Milyukov or Kerensky, of *precious* time which must be used to create a *real* class and revolutionary force, a proletarian militia that will *enjoy the confidence of all* the poor strata of the population, and they constitute the vast majority, and will *help them to organise*, help *them* to fight for bread, peace, freedom.

This mistake in the manifesto issued by Chkheidze and his group (I am not speaking of the OC, Organising Committee *party*, because in the sources available to me there is not a word about the OC) – this mistake is all the more strange considering that at the March 2 (15) conference, Chkheidze's closest collaborator, Skobelev, said, according to the newspapers: "Russia is on the eve of a second, real [*wirklich*] revolution."

Now that is the truth, from which Skobelev and Chkheidze have forgotten to draw the practical conclusions. I cannot judge from here, from my accursed afar, how near this second revolution is. Being on the spot, Skobelev can see things better. Therefore, I am not raising for myself problems for the solution of which I have not and cannot have the necessary concrete data. I am merely emphasising the confirmation by Skobelev, an "outside witness", i.e. one who does not belong to our Party, of the *factual* conclusion I drew in my first letter, namely: that the February–March Revolution was merely the *first stage* of the revolution. Russia is passing through a peculiar historical moment of *transition* to the next stage of the revolution, or, to use Skobelev's expression, to a "second revolution".

If we want to be Marxists and learn from the experience of revolution in the whole world, we must strive to understand in what, precisely, lies the *peculiarity* of this *transitional* moment, and what tactics follow from its objective specific features.

The peculiarity of the situation lies in that the Guchkov–Milyukov government gained the first victory with extraordinary ease due to the following three major circumstances: (1) assistance from Anglo-French finance capital and its agents; (2) assistance from part of the top ranks of the army; (3) the already existing organisation of the entire Russian bourgeoisie in the shape of the rural and urban local government institutions, the State Duma, the war industries committees, and so forth.

The Guchkov government is held in a vice: bound by the interests of capital, it is compelled to strive to continue the predatory, robber war, to protect the monstrous profits of capital and the landlords, to restore the monarchy. Bound by its revolutionary origin and by the need for an abrupt change from tsarism to democracy, pressed by the bread-hungry and peace-hungry masses, the government is compelled to lie, to wriggle, to play for time, to "proclaim" and promise (promises are the only things that are very cheap even at a time of madly rocketing prices) as much as possible and do as little as possible, to make concessions with one hand and to withdraw them with the other.

Under certain circumstances, the new government can at best postpone its collapse somewhat by leaning on all the organising ability of the entire Russian bourgeoisie and bourgeois intelligentsia. But even in that case it is *unable* to avoid collapse, because it is *impossible* to escape from the claws of the terrible monster of imperialist war and famine nurtured by world capitalism unless one renounces bourgeois relationships, passes to revolutionary measures, appeals to the supreme historic heroism of both the Russian and world proletariat.

Hence the conclusion: we cannot overthrow the new government at one stroke, or, if we can (in revolutionary times the limits of what is possible expand a thousandfold), we will not be able to maintain power *unless we counter* the magnificent organisation of the entire Russian bourgeoisie and the entire bourgeois intelligentsia with an equally magnificent *organisation of the proletariat*, which must lead the entire vast mass of urban and rural poor, the semi-proletariat and small proprietors.

Irrespective of whether the "second revolution" has already broken out in St Petersburg (I have said that it would be absolutely absurd to think that it is possible from abroad to assess the actual tempo at which it is maturing), whether it has been postponed for some time, or whether it has already begun in individual areas (of which some signs are evident) – in *any* case, the slogan of the moment on the eve of the new revolution, during it, and on the morrow of it, must be *proletarian organisation*.

Comrade workers! You performed miracles of proletarian heroism yesterday in overthrowing the tsarist monarchy. In the more or less near future (perhaps even now, as these lines are being written) you will again have to perform the same miracles of heroism to overthrow the rule of the landlords and capitalists, who are waging the imperialist war. You will not achieve *durable victory* in this next "real" revolution if you do not perform *miracles of proletarian organisation*!

Organisation is the slogan of the moment. But to confine oneself to that is to say nothing, for, on the one hand, organisation is *always* needed; hence, mere reference to the necessity of "organising the masses" explains absolutely nothing. On the other hand, he who confines himself solely to this becomes an abettor of the liberals, for the *very thing* the *liberals* want in order to strengthen their rule is that the workers *should not go beyond their ordinary* "legal" (from the standpoint of "normal" bourgeois society) organisations, i.e. that they should *only* join their party, their trade union, their co-operative society, etc., etc.

Guided by their class instinct, the workers have realised that in revolutionary times they need *not only* ordinary, but an entirely different organisation. They have rightly taken the path indicated by the experience of our 1905 Revolution and of the 1871 Paris Commune; they have set up a *Soviet of Workers' Deputies*; they have begun to develop, expand and strengthen it by drawing in soldiers' deputies, and, undoubtedly, deputies from rural *wage*-workers, and then (in one form or another) from the entire peasant poor.

The prime and most important task, and one that brooks no delay, is to set up organisations of this kind in all parts of Russia without exception, for all trades and strata of the proletarian and semi-proletarian population without exception, i.e. for all the working and exploited people, to use a less economically exact but more popular term. Running ahead somewhat, I shall mention that for the entire mass of the peasantry our Party (its *special* role in the new type of proletarian organisations I hope to discuss in one of my next letters) should especially recommend Soviets of wage-workers and Soviets of small tillers who do not sell grain, to be formed *separately* from the well-to-do peasants. Without this, it will be impossible either to conduct a truly proletarian policy in general,[*] or correctly to approach the extremely important practical question which is a matter of life and death for millions of people: the proper distribution of *grain*, increasing its production, etc.

It might be asked: What should be the function of the Soviets of Workers' Deputies? They "must be regarded as organs of insurrection, of revolutionary rule", we wrote in No. 47 of the Geneva *Sotsial-Demokrat*, of October 13, 1915.

This theoretical proposition, deduced from the experience of the Commune of 1871 and of the Russian Revolution of 1905, must be explained and concretely developed on the basis of the practical experience of precisely the present stage of the present revolution in Russia.

We need revolutionary *government*, we need (for a certain transitional period) a *state*. This is what distinguishes us from the anarchists. The

---

* In the rural districts a struggle will now develop for the small and, partly, middle peasants. The landlords, leaning on the well-to-do peasants, will try to lead them into subordination to the bourgeoisie. Leaning on the rural wage-workers and rural poor, we must lead them into the closest alliance with the urban proletariat.

difference between the revolutionary Marxists and the anarchists is not only that the former stand for centralised, large-scale communist production, while the latter stand for disconnected small production. The difference between us precisely on the question of government, of the state, is that we are *for*, and the anarchists *against*, utilising revolutionary forms of the state in a revolutionary way for the struggle for socialism.

We need a state. But *not the kind* of state the bourgeoisie has created everywhere, from constitutional monarchies to the most democratic republics. And in this we differ from the opportunists and Kautskyites of the old, and decaying, socialist parties, who have distorted, or have forgotten, the lessons of the Paris Commune and the analysis of these lessons made by Marx and Engels.[*]

We need a state, but not the kind the bourgeoisie needs, with organs of government in the shape of a police force, an army and a bureaucracy (officialdom) separate from and opposed to the people. All bourgeois revolutions merely perfected *this* state machine, merely transferred *it* from the hands of one party to those of another.

The proletariat, on the other hand, if it wants to uphold the gains of the present revolution and proceed further, to win peace, bread and freedom, must "*smash*", to use Marx's expression, this "ready-made" state machine and substitute a new one for it by *merging* the police force, the army and the bureaucracy with the *entire armed people*. Following the path indicated by the experience of the Paris Commune of 1871 and the Russian Revolution of 1905, the proletariat must organise and arm *all* the poor, exploited sections of the population in order that they *themselves* should take the organs of state power directly into their own hands, in order that *they themselves should constitute* these organs of state power.

And the workers of Russia have already taken this path in the first stage of the first revolution, in February–March 1917. The whole task now is clearly to understand what this new path is, to proceed along it further, boldly, firmly and perseveringly.

The Anglo-French and Russian capitalists wanted "only" to remove, or only to "frighten", Nicholas II, and to leave intact the old state machine, the police force, the army and the bureaucracy.

---

* In one of my next letters, or in a special article, I will deal in detail with this analysis, given in particular in Marx's *The Civil War in France*, in Engels's preface to the third edition of that work, in the letters: Marx's of April 12, 1871, and Engels's of March 18–28, 1875, and also with the utter distortion of Marxism by Kautsky in his controversy with Pannekoek in 1912 on the question of the so-called "destruction of the state".

The workers went further and smashed it. And now, not only the Anglo-French, but also the German capitalists are *howling* with rage and horror as they see, for example, Russian soldiers shooting their officers, as in the case of Admiral Nepenin, that supporter of Guchkov and Milyukov.

I said that the workers have smashed the old state machine. It would be more correct to say: *have begun* to smash it.

In St Petersburg and in many other places the police force has been partly wiped out and partly dissolved. The Guchkov–Milyukov government *cannot* either restore the monarchy or, in general, maintain power *without restoring* the police force as a special organisation of armed men under the command of the bourgeoisie, separate from and opposed to the people. That is as clear as daylight.

On the other hand, the new government must reckon with the revolutionary people, must feed them with half-concessions and promises, must play for time. That is why it resorts to half-measures: it establishes a "people's militia" with elected officials (this sounds awfully respectable, awfully democratic, revolutionary and beautiful!) – *but* . . . *but*, firstly, it places this militia under the control of the rural and urban local government bodies, i.e. under the command of landlords and capitalists who have been elected in conformity with laws passed by Nicholas the Bloody and Stolypin the Hangman!! Secondly, although it calls it a "people's militia" in order to throw dust in the eyes of the "people", it does *not* call upon the *entire* people to join this militia, *and does not compel* the employers and capitalists to *pay* workers and office employees their ordinary wages *for the hours and days* they spend in the *public service*, i.e. in the militia.

That's their trick. That is how the landlord and capitalist government of the Guchkovs and Milyukovs manages to have a "people's militia" on paper, while in reality it is restoring, gradually and on the quiet, the *bourgeois*, anti-people's militia. At first it is to consist of "eight thousand students and professors" (as foreign newspapers describe the present St Petersburg militia) – an obvious plaything! – and will gradually be built up of the old and new *police force*.

Prevent restoration of the police force! Do not let the local government bodies slip out of your hands! Set up a militia that will really embrace the entire people, be really universal, and be led by the proletariat! – such is the task of the day, such is the slogan of the moment which equally conforms with the properly understood interests of furthering the class struggle, furthering the revolutionary movement, and the democratic instinct of every worker, of every peasant, of every exploited toiler who cannot help hating the policemen, the rural police patrols, the village constables, the command of landlords and capitalists over armed men with power over the people.

What kind of police force do *they* need, the Guchkovs and Milyukovs, the landlords and capitalists? The same kind as existed under the tsarist monarchy. After the briefest revolutionary periods, *all* the bourgeois and bourgeois-democratic republics in the world set up or restored *precisely such* a police force, a special organisation of armed men subordinate to the bourgeoisie in one way or another, separate from and opposed to the people.

What kind of militia do we need, the proletariat, all the toiling people? A genuine *people's* militia, i.e. one that, first, consists of the *entire* population, of all adult citizens of *both* sexes; and, second, one that combines the functions of a people's army with police functions, with the functions of the chief and fundamental organ of public order and public administration.

To make these propositions more comprehensible I will take a purely schematic example. Needless to say, it would be absurd to think of drawing up any kind of a "plan" for a proletarian militia: when the workers and the entire people set about it practically, on a truly mass scale, they will work it out and organise it a hundred times better than any theoretician. I am not offering a "plan", I only want to illustrate my idea.

St Petersburg has a population of about two million. Of these, more than half are between the ages of 15 and 65. Take half – one million. Let us even subtract an entire fourth as physically unfit, etc., taking no part in public service at the present moment for justifiable reasons. There remain 750,000 who, serving in the militia, say, one day in fifteen (and receiving their pay for this time from their employers), would form an army of 50,000.

That's the type of "state" we need!

That's the kind of militia that would be a "people's militia" in deed and not only in words.

That is how we must proceed in order to *prevent* the restoration either of a special police force, or of a special army separate from the people.

Such a militia, 95 hundredths of which would consist of workers and peasants, would express the *real* mind and will, the strength and power of the vast majority of the people. Such a militia would really arm, and provide military training for, the entire people, would be a safeguard, but *not* of the Guchkov or Milyukov type, against all attempts to restore reaction, against all the designs of tsarist agents. Such a militia would be the executive organ of the Soviets of Workers' and Soldiers' Deputies, it would enjoy the *boundless* respect and confidence of the people, for it itself would be an organisation of the entire people. Such a militia would transform democracy from a beautiful signboard, which covers up the enslavement and torment of the people by the capitalists, into a means of actually *training the masses* for participation in *all* affairs of state. Such a militia would draw the young people into political life and teach them not only by words, but also by action, by *work*. Such a militia would develop those functions which, speaking in scientific language, come within the purview of the "welfare police", sanitary inspection, and so forth, and would enlist for such work all adult women. If women are not drawn into public service, into the militia, into political life, if women are not torn out of their stupefying house and kitchen environment, it will be *impossible* to guarantee real freedom, it will be *impossible* to build even democracy, let alone socialism.

Such a militia would be a proletarian militia, for the industrial and urban workers would exert a guiding influence on the masses of the poor as naturally and inevitably as they came to hold the leading place in the people's revolutionary struggle both in 1905–07 and in 1917.

Such a militia would ensure absolute order and devotedly observed comradely discipline. At the same time, in the severe crisis that all the belligerent countries are experiencing, it would make it possible to combat this crisis in a very democratic way, properly and rapidly to distribute grain and other supplies, introduce "universal labour service", which the French now call "civilian mobilisation" and the Germans "civilian service", and without which *it is impossible – it has proved to be impossible* – to heal the wounds that have been and are being inflicted by the predatory and horrible war.

Has the proletariat of Russia shed its blood only in order to receive fine promises of political democratic reforms, and nothing more? Can it be that it will not demand, and secure, that *every* toiler should *forthwith* see and feel some improvement in his life? That every family should have bread? That every child should have a bottle of good milk, and that not a single adult in a rich family should dare take extra milk until children are provided for? That the palaces and rich apartments abandoned by the tsar and the aristocracy should not remain vacant, but provide shelter for the homeless and the destitute? Who can carry out these measures except a people's militia, to which women must belong equally with men?

These measures *do not yet* constitute socialism. They concern the distribution of consumption, not the reorganisation of production. They would not yet constitute the "dictatorship of the proletariat", only the "revolutionary-democratic dictatorship of the proletariat and the poor peasantry". It is not a matter of finding a theoretical classification. We would be committing a great mistake if we attempted to force the complete, urgent, rapidly developing practical tasks of the revolution into the Procrustean bed of narrowly conceived "theory", instead of regarding theory primarily and predominantly as a *guide to action*.

Do the masses of the Russian workers possess sufficient class-consciousness, fortitude and heroism to perform "miracles of proletarian organisation" after they have performed miracles of daring, initiative and self-sacrifice in the direct revolutionary struggle? That we do not know, and it would be idle to indulge in guessing, for practice *alone* furnishes the answers to such questions.

What we do know definitely – and what we, as a party, must explain to the masses – is, on the one hand, the immense power of the locomotive of history that is engendering an unprecedented crisis, starvation and incalculable hardship. That locomotive is the war, waged for predatory aims by the capitalists of *both* belligerent camps. This "locomotive" has brought a number of the richest, freest and most enlightened nations to the brink of doom. It is *forcing* the peoples to strain to the utmost all their energies, placing them in unbearable conditions, putting on the order of the day not the application of certain "theories" (an illusion against which Marx always warned socialists), but implementation of the most extreme practical measures; for *without* extreme measures, death – immediate and certain death from starvation – awaits millions of people.

That the revolutionary enthusiasm of the advanced class can do a *great deal* when the objective situation *demands* extreme measures from the entire people, needs no proof. *This* aspect is clearly seen and *felt* by everybody in Russia.

It is important to realise that in revolutionary times the objective situation changes with the same swiftness and abruptness as the current of life in general. And we must *be able to adapt* our tactics and immediate tasks to the *specific features* of every given situation. Before February 1917, the immediate task was to conduct bold revolutionary internationalist propaganda, summon the masses to fight, rouse them. The February–March days required the heroism of devoted struggle to crush the immediate enemy – tsarism. Now we are in *transition* from that first stage of the revolution to the second, from "coming to grips" with tsarism to "coming to grips" with Guchkov–Milyukov landlord and capitalist imperialism. The immediate task is *organisation*, not only in the stereotyped sense of working to form stereotyped organisations, but in the sense of drawing unprecedentedly broad masses of the oppressed classes into an organisation that would take over the military, political and economic functions of the state.

The proletariat has approached, and will approach, this singular task in different ways. In some parts of Russia the February–March Revolution puts nearly complete power in its hands. In others the proletariat may, perhaps, in a "usurpatory" manner, begin to form and develop a proletarian militia. In still others, it will probably strive for immediate elections of urban and rural local government bodies on the basis of universal, etc., suffrage, in order to turn them into revolutionary centres, etc., until the growth of proletarian organisation, the coming together of the soldiers with the workers, the movement among the peasantry and the disillusionment of very many in the war-imperialist government of Guchkov and Milyukov, bring near the hour when this government will be replaced by the "government" of the Soviet of Workers' Deputies.

Nor ought we to forget that close to St Petersburg we have one of the most advanced, factually republican countries, namely, Finland, which, from 1905 to 1917, shielded by the revolutionary battles of Russia, has in a relatively peaceful way developed democracy, and has won the *majority* of the people for socialism. The Russian proletariat will guarantee the Finnish Republic complete freedom, including freedom to secede (it is doubtful now whether a single Social-Democrat will waver on this point when the Cadet Rodichev is so meanly haggling in Helsingfors for bits of privileges for the Great Russians[18]) – and, precisely in this way, will win the *complete* confidence and comradely assistance of the Finnish workers for the all-Russian proletarian cause. In a difficult and big undertaking, mistakes are inevitable, nor will we avoid them. The Finnish workers are better organisers, they will help us in this sphere, they will, *in their own way*, push forward the establishment of the socialist republic.

[18] Soon after its formation, the Provisional Government appointed the Octobrist M. A. Stakhovich Governor-General of Finland and the Cadet F. I. Rodichev Minister (or Commissioner) for Finnish Affairs. On March 8 (21), the Provisional Government issued its Manifesto "On Approval and Enforcement of the Constitution of the Grand Duchy of Finland". Under this, Finland was allowed autonomy, with the proviso that laws promulgated by the Finnish Diet would be subject to confirmation by the Russian Government. Laws that ran counter to Finnish legislation were to remain in force for the duration of the war.

The Provisional Government wanted the Finnish Diet to amend the Constitution to give "Russian citizens equal rights with Finnish citizens in commerce and industry", for under the tsarist government such equality was imposed in defiance of Finnish laws. At the same time, the Provisional Government refused to discuss self-determination for Finland "pending convocation of the constituent assembly". This led to a sharp conflict, resolved only after the Great October Socialist Revolution when, on December 18 (31), 1917, the Soviet Government granted Finland full independence.

Revolutionary victories in Russia proper – peaceful organisational successes in Finland shielded by these victories – the Russian workers' transition to revolutionary organisational tasks on a new scale – capture of power by the proletariat and poorest strata of the population – encouragement and development of the socialist revolution in the West – this is the road that will lead us to *peace* and *socialism*.

N. Lenin

Zurich, March 11 (24), 1917

Fourth Letter

How to achieve peace

I have just (March 12/25) read in the *Neue Zürcher Zeitung* (No. 517 of March 24) the following telegraphic dispatch from Berlin:

> It is reported from Sweden that Maxim Gorky has sent the government and the Executive Committee greetings couched in enthusiastic terms. He greets the people's victory over the lords of reaction and calls upon all Russia's sons to help erect the edifice of the new Russian state. At the same time he urges the government to crown the cause of emancipation by concluding peace. It must not, he says, be peace at any price; Russia now has less reason than ever to strive for peace at any price. It must be a peace that will enable Russia to live in honour among the other nations of the earth. Mankind has shed much blood; the new government would render not only Russia, but all mankind, the greatest service if it succeeded in concluding an early peace.

That is how Maxim Gorky's letter is reported.

It is with deep chagrin that one reads this letter, impregnated through and through with stock philistine prejudices. The author of these lines has had many occasions, in meetings with Gorky in Capri, to warn and reproach him for his political mistakes. Gorky parried these reproaches with his inimitable charming smile and with the ingenuous remark: "I know I am a bad Marxist. And besides, we artists are all somewhat irresponsible." It is not easy to argue against that.

There can be no doubt that Gorky's is an enormous artistic talent which has been, and will be, of great benefit to the world proletarian movement.

But why should Gorky meddle in politics?

In my opinion, Gorky's letter expresses prejudices that are exceedingly widespread not only among the petty bourgeoisie, but also among a section of the workers under its influence. *All* the energies of our Party, all the efforts of the class-conscious workers, must be concentrated on a persistent, persevering, all-round struggle against these prejudices.

The tsarist government began and waged the present war as an *imperialist*, predatory war to rob and strangle weak nations. The government of the Guchkovs and Milyukovs, which is a landlord and capitalist government, is forced to continue, and wants to continue, *this very same kind* of war. To urge that government to conclude a democratic peace is like preaching virtue to brothel keepers.

Let me explain what is meant.

What is imperialism?

In my *Imperialism, the Highest Stage of Capitalism*, the manuscript of which was delivered to Parus Publishers some time before the revolution, was accepted by them and announced in the magazine *Letopis*,[19] I answered this question as follows:

"Imperialism is capitalism at that stage of development at which the dominance of monopolies and finance capital is established; in which the export of capital has acquired pronounced importance; in which the division of the world among the international trusts has begun; in which the division of all territories of the globe among the biggest capitalist powers has been completed" (Chapter VII of the above-mentioned book, the publication of

[19] *Imperialism, the Highest Stage of Capitalism* was written in the first half of 1916, and on June 19 (July 2) was sent to Petrograd via Paris. It was to have been published by the Parus publishing house which, on Maxim Gorky's initiative, was putting out a series of popular surveys of West European countries involved in the war. Lenin maintained contact with the publishers through the editor of the series, M. N. Pokrovsky. On September 29, 1916, Gorky wrote Pokrovsky in Paris that Lenin's book was "really excellent", and would be put out in addition to the regular series. However, the Parus editors strongly objected to Lenin's criticism of Kautsky's renegade position and substantially altered the text, deleting all criticism of Kautsky's theory of ultra-imperialism and distorting a number of Lenin's formulations. The book was finally published in mid-1917 with a preface by Lenin, dated April 26.

Parus (Sail) and *Letopis* (Annals) – the names of the publishing house and magazine founded by Gorky in Petrograd.

Letopis – a magazine of literature, science and politics whose contributors included former Bolsheviks (the Machists V. A. Bazarov and A. A. Bogdanov) and Mensheviks. Gorky was literary editor, and among the other prominent writers contributing to *Letopis* were Alexander Blok, Valeri Bryusov, Fyodor Gladkov, Sergei Yesenin, A. V. Lunacharsky, Vladimir Mayakovsky, Vyacheslav Shishkov and A. Chaplygin. *Letopis* appeared from December 1915 to December 1917. The Parus publishing house existed from 1915 through 1918.

which was announced in *Letopis*, when the censorship still existed, under the title: "Modern Capitalism", by V. Ilyin).

The whole thing hinges on the fact that capital has grown to huge dimensions. Associations of a small number of the biggest capitalists (cartels, syndicates, trusts) manipulate billions, and divide the whole world among themselves.

The world has been *completely* divided up. The war was brought on by the clash of the two most powerful groups of multimillionaires, Anglo-French and German, for the *redivision* of the world.

The Anglo-French group of capitalists wants first to rob Germany, deprive her of her colonies (nearly all of which have already been seized), and then to rob Turkey.

The German group of capitalists wants to seize Turkey for itself and to compensate *itself* for the loss of its colonies by seizing neighbouring small states (Belgium, Serbia, Romania).

This is the real truth; it is being concealed by all sorts of bourgeois lies about a "liberating", "national" war, a "war for right and justice", and similar jingles with which the capitalists always fool the common people.

Russia is waging this war with foreign money. Russian capital is a *partner* of Anglo-French capital. Russia is waging the war in order to rob Armenia, Turkey, Galicia.

Guchkov, Lvov and Milyukov, our present ministers, are not chance comers. They are the representatives and leaders of the entire landlord and capitalist class. They are *bound* by the interests of capital. The capitalists can no more renounce their interests than a man can lift himself by his bootstraps.

Secondly, Guchkov–Milyukov and Co. are *bound* by Anglo-French capital. They have waged, and are still waging, the war with foreign money. They have borrowed billions, promising to pay *hundreds of millions* in interest *every year*, and to squeeze this *tribute* out of the Russian workers and Russian peasants.

Thirdly, Guchkov–Milyukov and Co. are *bound* to England, France, Italy, Japan and other groups of robber capitalists by direct *treaties* concerning the predatory aims of this war. These treaties were concluded by *Tsar Nicholas II*. Guchkov–Milyukov and Co. took advantage of the workers' struggle against the tsarist monarchy to seize power, and *they have confirmed the treaties* concluded by the tsar.

This was done by the whole of the Guchkov–Milyukov government in a Manifesto which the St Petersburg Telegraph Agency circulated on March 7 (20): "The government [of Guchkov and Milyukov] will faithfully abide by all the treaties that bind us with other powers," says the Manifesto. Milyukov, the new Minister for Foreign Affairs, said the same thing in his telegram of March 5 (18), 1917 to all Russian representatives abroad.

These are all *secret* treaties, and Milyukov and Co. *refuse* to make them public for two reasons: (1) they fear the people, who are opposed to the predatory war; (2) they are bound by Anglo-French capital, which insists that the treaties remain secret. But every newspaper reader who has followed events knows that these treaties envisage the robbery of China by Japan; of Persia, Armenia, Turkey (especially Constantinople) and Galicia by Russia; of Albania by Italy; of Turkey and the German colonies by France and England, etc.

This is how things stand.

Hence, to urge the Guchkov–Milyukov government to conclude a speedy, honest, democratic and good-neighbourly peace is like the good village priest urging the landlords and the merchants to "walk in the way of God", to love their neighbours and to turn the other cheek. The land-lords and merchants listen to these sermons, continue to oppress and rob the people, and praise the priest for his ability to console and pacify the "muzhiks".

Exactly the same role is played – consciously or unconsciously – by all those who, in the present imperialist war, address pious peace appeals to the bourgeois governments. The bourgeois governments either refuse to listen to such appeals, and even prohibit them, or they allow them to be made, and assure all and sundry that they are fighting only to conclude the speediest and "justest" peace, and that all the blame lies with the enemy. Actually, talking peace *to bourgeois* governments turns out to be *deception of the people.*

The groups of capitalists who have drenched the world in blood for the sake of dividing territories, markets and concessions cannot conclude an "honourable" peace. They can conclude only a shameful peace, a peace based on the division of the spoils, on the partition of Turkey and the colonies. Moreover, the Guchkov–Milyukov government is in general opposed to peace at the present moment, because the "*only*" "loot" it would get now would be Armenia and part of Galicia, whereas it *also* wants to get Constantinople *and* regain from the Germans Poland, which tsarism has always so inhumanly and shamelessly oppressed.

Further, the Guchkov–Milyukov government is, in essence, only the agent of Anglo-French capital, which wants to retain the colonies it has wrested from Germany and, *on top of that*, compel Germany to hand back Belgium and part of France. Anglo-French capital helped the Guchkovs and

Milyukovs to remove Nicholas II in order that they might help it to "vanquish" Germany.

What, then, is to be done?

To achieve peace (and still more to achieve a really democratic, a really honourable peace), it is necessary that political power be in the hands of *the workers and poorest peasants*, not the landlords and capitalists. The latter represent an insignificant minority of the population, and the capitalists, as everybody knows, are making fantastic profits out of the war.

The workers and poorest peasants are the *vast* majority of the population. They are not making profit out of the war; on the contrary, they are being reduced to ruin and starvation. They are bound neither by capital nor by the treaties between the predatory groups of capitalists; they can and sincerely want to end the war.

If political power in Russia were in the hands of the *Soviets* of Workers', Soldiers' and Peasants' Deputies, these Soviets, and the *All-Russia Soviet* elected by them, could, and no doubt would, agree to carry out the peace programme which our Party (the Russian Social-Democratic Labour Party) outlined as early as October 13, 1915, in No. 47 of its Central Organ, *Sotsial-Demokrat* (then published in Geneva because of the draconic tsarist censorship).

This programme would probably be the following:

(1) The All-Russia Soviet of Workers', Soldiers' and Peasants' Deputies (or the St Petersburg Soviet temporarily acting for it) would forthwith declare that it is not bound by *any* treaties concluded *either* by the tsarist monarchy *or* by the bourgeois governments.

(2) It would forthwith publish *all* these treaties in order to hold up to public shame the predatory aims of the tsarist monarchy and of *all* the bourgeois governments without exception.

(3) It would forthwith publicly call upon *all* the belligerent powers to conclude an *immediate armistice*.

(4) It would immediately bring to the knowledge of all the people our, the workers' and peasants' peace *terms*: liberation of *all* colonies; liberation of *all* dependent, oppressed and unequal nations.

(5) It would declare that it expects nothing good from the bourgeois governments, and calls upon the workers of all countries to overthrow them and to transfer all political power to Soviets of Workers' Deputies.

(6) It would declare that the *capitalist gentry themselves* can repay the billions of debts contracted by the bourgeois governments to wage this criminal, predatory war, and that the workers and peasants *refuse to recognise* these debts. To pay the interest on these loans would mean paying

the capitalists *tribute* for many years for having graciously allowed the workers to kill one another in order that the capitalists might divide the spoils.

Workers and peasants! – the Soviet of Workers' Deputies would say – Are you willing to pay these gentry, the capitalists, *hundreds of millions* of roubles *every year* for a war waged for the division of the African colonies, Turkey, etc.?

For *these* peace terms the Soviet of Workers' Deputies would, in my opinion, agree to *wage war* against *any* bourgeois government and against *all* the bourgeois governments of the world, because this would really be a just war, because *all* the workers and toilers in *all* countries would *work for its success*.

The German worker now sees that the bellicose monarchy in Russia is being replaced by a bellicose republic, a republic of capitalists who want to continue the imperialist war, and who have confirmed the predatory treaties of the tsarist monarchy.

Judge for yourselves: can the German worker trust *such* a republic?

Judge for yourselves: can the war continue, can the capitalist domination continue on earth, if the Russian people, always sustained by the living memories of the great Revolution of 1905, win complete freedom and transfer all political power to the Soviets of Workers' and Peasants' Deputies?

N. Lenin

Zurich, March 12 (25), 1917

Fifth Letter

The tasks involved in the building of the revolutionary proletarian state

In the preceding letters, the immediate tasks of the revolutionary proletariat in Russia were formulated as follows: (1) to find the surest road to the next stage of the revolution, or to the second revolution, which (2) must transfer political power from the government of the landlords and capitalists (the Guchkovs, Lvovs, Milyukovs, Kerenskys) to a government of the workers and poorest peasants. (3) This latter government must be organised on the model of the Soviets of Workers' and Peasants' Deputies, namely, (4) it must smash, completely eliminate, the old state machine, the army, the police force and bureaucracy (officialdom) that is common to *all* bourgeois states, and substitute for this machine (5) not only a mass organisation, but a universal organisation of the entire armed people. (6) *Only* such a government, of "such" a class composition ("revolutionary-democratic dictatorship of the proletariat and peasantry"), and such organs of government ("proletarian militia") *will be capable* of successfully carrying out the extremely difficult and absolutely urgent *chief* task of the moment, namely: to achieve *peace* – not an imperialist peace, not a deal between the imperialist powers concerning the division of the booty by the capitalists and their governments, but a really lasting and democratic peace, which cannot be achieved without a proletarian revolution in a number of countries. (7) In Russia, the victory of the proletariat can be achieved in the very near future *only* if, from the very first step, the workers are supported by the vast majority of the peasants fighting for the confiscation of the landed estates (and for the nationalisation of all the land, if we assume that the agrarian programme of the "104" is still essentially the agrarian programme of the *peasantry*[20]). (8) In connection with such a peasant revolution, and on its basis, the proletariat can and must, in alliance with the *poorest* section of the peasantry, take further steps towards *control* of the production and distribution of the basic products, towards the introduction of "universal labour service", etc. These steps are dictated, with absolute inevitability, by the conditions created by the war, which in many respects will become still more acute in the post-war period. In their entirety and in their development these steps will mark the *transition to socialism*, which cannot be achieved in Russia directly, at one stroke, without transitional measures, but is quite achievable and urgently necessary as a result of such transitional measures. (9) In this connection, the task of immediately organising special Soviets of Workers' Deputies in the *rural districts*, i.e. Soviets of agricultural *wage*-workers *separate* from the Soviets of the other peasant deputies, comes to the forefront with extreme urgency.

Such, briefly, is the programme we have outlined, based on an appraisal of the class forces in the Russian and world revolution, and also on the experience of 1871 and 1905.

---

[20] The agrarian programme of the "104" – the land reform bill the Trudovik members submitted to the 13th meeting of the First State Duma on May 23 (June 5) 1906. The land would belong to the entire people, and farmlands would be allowed only to those tilling them by their own labour. The Trudoviks advocated organisation of a "national land fund" that would include all state, crown, monastery and church lands, also part of privately owned lands, which were to be alienated if the size of the holding exceeded the labour by local committees elected by universal, direct and equal suffrage and by secret ballot.

Let us now attempt a general survey of this programme as a whole and, in passing, deal with the way the subject was approached by K. Kautsky, the chief theoretician of the "Second" (1889–1914) International and most prominent representative of the "Centre", "marsh" trend that is now to be observed in all countries, the trend that oscillates between the social-chauvinists and the revolutionary internationalists. Kautsky discussed this subject in his magazine *Die Neue Zeit* of April 6, 1917 (new style) in an article entitled "The Prospects of the Russian Revolution".

"First of all," writes Kautsky, "we must ascertain what tasks confront the revolutionary proletarian regime" (state system).

"Two things", continues the author, "are urgently needed by the proletariat: democracy and socialism."

Unfortunately, Kautsky advances this absolutely incontestable thesis in an exceedingly general form, so that in essence he says nothing and explains nothing. Milyukov and Kerensky, members of a bourgeois and imperialist government, would readily subscribe to this general thesis – one to the first part, and the other to the second. . . .[21]

[21] The manuscript breaks off here. – *Ed.*

2

The Tasks of the Proletariat in the Present Revolution ("April Theses")

I did not arrive in Petrograd until the night of April 3, and therefore at the meeting on April 4 I could, of course, deliver the report on the tasks of the revolutionary proletariat only on my own behalf, and with reservations as to insufficient preparation.[1]

The only thing I could do to make things easier for myself – and for *honest* opponents – was to prepare the theses *in writing*. I read them out, and gave the text to Comrade Tsereteli. I read them *twice* very slowly: first at a meeting of Bolsheviks and then at a meeting of both Bolsheviks and Mensheviks. I publish these personal theses of mine with only the briefest explanatory notes, which were developed in far greater detail in the report.

Theses

(1) In our attitude towards the war, which under the now government of Lvov and Co. unquestionably remains on Russia's part a predatory imperialist war owing to the capitalist nature of that government, not the slightest concession to "revolutionary defencism" is permissible.

The class-conscious proletariat can give its consent to a revolutionary war, which would really justify revolutionary defencism, only on condition: (a) that the power pass to the proletariat and the poorest sections of the

---

[1] Published in *Pravda* No. 26, for April 7, 1917, over the signature *N. Lenin*, this article contains Lenin's famous April Theses read by him at two meetings held at the Taurida Palace on April 4 (17), 1917 (at a meeting of Bolsheviks and at a joint meeting of Bolshevik and Menshevik delegates to the All-Russia Conference of Soviets of Workers' and Soldiers' Deputies). The article was reprinted in the Bolshevik newspapers *Sotsial-Demokrat* (Moscow), *Proletary* (Kharkov), *Krasnoyarsky Rabochy* (Krasnoyarsk), *Vperyod* (Ufa), *Bakinsky Rabochy* (Baku), *Kavkazsky Rabochy* (Tinis) and others.

peasants aligned with the proletariat; (b) that all annexations be renounced in deed and not in word; (c) that a complete break with all capitalist interests be effected in actual fact.

In view of the undoubted honesty of those broad sections of the mass believers in revolutionary defencism who accept the war only as a necessity, and not as a means of conquest, in view of the fact that they are being deceived by the bourgeoisie, it is necessary with particular thoroughness, persistence and patience to explain their error to them, to explain the inseparable connection existing between capital and the imperialist war, and to prove that without overthrowing capital *it is impossible* to end the war by a truly democratic peace, a peace not imposed by violence.

The most widespread campaign for this view must be organised in the army at the front.

Fraternisation.

(2) The specific feature of the present situation in Russia is that the country is *passing* from the first stage of the revolution – which, owing to the insufficient class-consciousness and organisation of the proletariat, placed power in the hands of the bourgeoisie – to its *second* stage, which must place power in the hands of the proletariat and the poorest sections of the peasants.

This transition is characterised, on the one hand, by a maximum of legally recognised rights (Russia is *now* the freest of all the belligerent countries in the world); on the other, by the absence of violence towards the masses, and, finally, by their unreasoning trust in the government of capitalists, those worst enemies of peace and socialism.

This peculiar situation demands of us an ability to adapt ourselves to the *special* conditions of Party work among unprecedentedly large masses of proletarians who have just awakened to political life.

(3) No support for the Provisional Government; the utter falsity of all its promises should be made clear, particularly of those relating to the renunciation of annexations. Exposure in place of the impermissible, illusion-breeding "demand" that *this* government, a government of capitalists, should cease to be an imperialist government.

(4) Recognition of the fact that in most of the Soviets of Workers' Deputies our Party is in a minority, so far a small minority, as against *a bloc of all* the petty-bourgeois opportunist elements, from the Popular Socialists and the Socialist-Revolutionaries down to the Organising Committee[2]

---

[2] Socialist-Revolutionaries (SRs) – a petty-bourgeois party formed in Russia at the end of 1901 and beginning of 1902 through the amalgamation of various Narodnik groups

(Chkheidze, Tsereteli, etc.), Steklov, etc., etc., who have yielded to the influence of the bourgeoisie and spread that influence among the proletariat.

The masses must be made to see that the Soviets of Workers' Deputies are the *only possible* form of revolutionary government, and that therefore our task is, as long as *this* government yields to the influence of the bourgeoisie, to present a patient, systematic, and persistent *explanation* of the errors of their tactics, an explanation especially adapted to the practical needs of the masses.

---

and circles (the Union of Socialist-Revolutionaries, the Party of Socialist-Revolutionaries, and others). The views of the SRs were an eclectic medley of Narodism and revisionism – they tried, as Lenin put it, to "patch up the rents in the Narodnik ideas with bits of fashionable opportunist 'criticism' of Marxism" (see Lenin, *Collected Works*, fourth edition, vol. 9, p. 310). The First World War found most of the SRs taking a social-chauvinist stand.

After the victory of the bourgeois-democratic revolution of February 1917, the SRs, together with the Mensheviks and Cadets, were the mainstay of the counter-revolutionary Provisional Government of the bourgeoisie and landowners, and the leaders of the party (Kerensky, Avksentyev, Chernov) were members of that government. The SR Party refused to support the peasants' demand for the abolition of the landed estates and in effect stood for private property in land; the SR ministers in the Provisional Government sent punitive expeditions against the peasants who had seized landed estates. On the eve of the October armed uprising, this party openly sided with the counter-revolutionary bourgeoisie in defence of the capitalist system, and found itself isolated from the mass of the revolutionary people.

At the end of November 1917 the Left wing of the party founded a separate Left Socialist-Revolutionary Party. In an endeavour to maintain their influence among the peasant masses, the Left SRs formally recognised the Soviet Government and entered into an agreement with the Bolsheviks, but very soon turned against the Soviet power.

Popular Socialists – members of the petty-bourgeois Labour Popular Socialist Party, which separated from the Right wing of the Socialist-Revolutionary Party in 1906. The PSs stood for a bloc with the Cadets. Lenin called them "Social-Cadets", "petty-bourgeois opportunists", and "Socialist-Revolutionary Mensheviks" who vacillated between the Cadets and the SRs, and he emphasised that this party "differs very little from the Cadets, for it deletes from its programme both the republicanism and the demand for all the land". The party's leaders were A. V. Peshekhonov, N. F. Annensky, V. A. Myakotin, and others. During the First World War the PSs took a social-chauvinist stand. After the bourgeois-democratic revolution of February 1917, the Popular Socialist Party merged with the Trudoviks and actively supported the bourgeois Provisional Government, in which it was represented.

The Organising Committee (OC) was set up in 1912 at the August conference of the liquidators. During World War I the OC justified the war on the part of tsarism, and advocated the ideas of nationalism and chauvinism. The OC published the journal *Nasha Zarya*, and when this was closed down, *Nashe Dyelo*, then *Dyelo*, and the newspapers *Rabocheye Utro*, then *Utro*. The OC functioned up to the time of the election of the Central Committee of the Menshevik Party in August 1917.

As long as we are in the minority we carry on the work of criticising and exposing errors, and at the same time we preach the necessity of transferring the entire state power to the Soviets of Workers' Deputies, so that the people may overcome their mistakes by experience.

(5) Not a parliamentary republic – to return to a parliamentary republic from the Soviets of Workers' Deputies would be a retrograde step – but a republic of Soviets of Workers', Agricultural Labourers' and Peasants' Deputies throughout the country, from top to bottom.

Abolition of the police, the army and the bureaucracy.[*]

The salaries of all officials, all of whom are elective and displaceable at any time, not to exceed the average wage of a competent worker.

(6) The weight of emphasis in the agrarian programme to be shifted to the Soviets of Agricultural Labourers' Deputies.

Confiscation of all landed estates.

Nationalisation of *all* lands in the country, the land to be disposed of by the local Soviets of Agricultural Labourers' and Peasants' Deputies. The organisation of separate Soviets of Deputies of Poor Peasants. The setting up of a model farm on each of the large estates (ranging in size from 100 to 300 dessiatines, according to local and other conditions, and to the decisions of the local bodies) under the control of the Soviets of Agricultural Labourers' Deputies and for the public account.

(7) The immediate amalgamation of all banks in the country into a single national bank, and the institution of control over it by the Soviet of Workers' Deputies.

(8) It is not our *immediate* task to "introduce" socialism, but only to bring social production and the distribution of products at once under the control of the Soviets of Workers' Deputies.

(9) Party tasks:

   (a) Immediate convocation of a Party congress;

   (b) Alteration of the Party Programme, mainly:

      (i) On the question of imperialism and the imperialist war;

      (ii) On our attitude towards the state and our demand for a "commune state";[†]

      (iii) Amendment of our out-of-date minimum programme.

   (c) Change of the Party's name.[‡]

---

* That is, the standing army to be replaced by the arming of the whole people.

† That is, a state of which the Paris Commune was the prototype.

‡ Instead of "Social-Democracy", whose official leaders *throughout* the world have betrayed socialism and deserted to the bourgeoisie (the "defencists" and the vacillating "Kautskyites"), we must call ourselves the Communist Party.

(10) A new International.

We must take the initiative in creating a revolutionary International, an International against the *social-chauvinists* and against the "Centre".[*]

In order that the reader may understand why I had especially to emphasise as a rare exception the "case" of honest opponents, I invite him to compare the above theses with the following objection by Mr Goldellberg: Lenin, he said, "has planted the banner of civil war in the midst of revolutionary democracy" (quoted in No. 5 of Mr Plekhanov's *Yedinstvo*[3]).

Isn't it a gem?

I write, announce and elaborately explain: "In view of the undoubted honesty of those *broad* sections of the *mass* believers in revolutionary defencism . . . in view of the fact that they are being deceived by the bourgeoisie, it is necessary with particular thoroughness, persistence and patience to explain their error to them. . . ."

Yet the bourgeois gentlemen who call themselves Social-Democrats, who do not belong either to the *broad* sections or to the mass believers in defencism, with serene brow present my views thus: "The banner [!][†] of civil war" (of which there is not a word in the theses and not a word in my speech!) has been planted(!) "in the midst [!!] of revolutionary democracy . . .".

What does this mean? In what way does this differ from riot-inciting agitation, from *Russkaya Volya*?[4]

I write, announce and elaborately explain: "The Soviets of Workers' Deputies are the *only possible* form of revolutionary government, and therefore our task is to present a patient, systematic, and persistent *explanation* of the errors of their tactics, an explanation especially adapted to the practical needs of the masses."

---

* The "Centre" in the international Social-Democratic movement is the trend which vacillates between the chauvinists (= "defencists") and internationalists, i.e. Kautsky and Co. in Germany, Longuet and Co. in France, Chkheidze and Co. in Russia, Turati and Co. in Italy, MacDonald and Co. in Britain, etc.

[3] *Yedinstvo* (*Unity*) – a daily published in Petrograd from March to November 1917, and then under another name from December 1917 to January 1918. Edited by G. V. Plekhanov. United the extreme Right of the Menshevik defencists and gave unqualified support to the Provisional Government. Carried on a fierce struggle against the Bolshevik Party.

† Interpolations in square brackets (within passages quoted by Lenin) have been introduced by Lenin, unless otherwise indicated. – *Ed.*

[4] *Russkaya Volya* (*Russian Freedom*) – a daily founded and run by the big banks. Carried on a riot-provoking campaign against the Bolsheviks. Appeared in Petrograd from December 1916 to October 1917.

Yet opponents of a certain brand present my views as a call to "civil war in the midst of revolutionary democracy"!

I attacked the Provisional Government for *not* having appointed an early date, or any date at all, for the convocation of the Constituent Assembly, and for confining itself to promises. I argued that *without* the Soviets of Workers' and Soldiers' Deputies the convocation of the Constituent Assembly is not guaranteed and its success is impossible.

And the view is attributed to me that I am opposed to the speedy convocation of the Constituent Assembly!

I would call this "raving", had not decades of political struggle taught me to regard honesty in opponents as a rare exception.

Mr Plekhanov, in his paper, called my speech "raving". Very good, Mr Plekhanov! But look how awkward, uncouth, and slow-witted you are in your polemics. If I delivered a raving speech for two hours, how is it that an audience of hundreds tolerated this "raving"? Further, why does your paper devote a whole column to an account of the "raving"? Inconsistent, highly inconsistent!

It is, of course, much easier to shout, abuse, and howl than to attempt to relate, to explain, to recall *what* Marx and Engels said in 1871, 1872 and 1875 about the experience of the Paris Commune and about the kind of state the proletariat needs.

Ex-Marxist Mr Plekhanov evidently does not care to recall Marxism.

I quoted the words of Rosa Luxemburg, who on August 4, 1914, called *German* Social-Democracy a "stinking corpse". And the Plekhanovs, Goldenbergs and Co. feel "offended". On whose behalf? On behalf of the *German* chauvinists, because they were called chauvinists!

They have got themselves in a mess, these poor Russian social-chauvinists – socialists in word and chauvinists in deed.

3

On Slogans

Too often has it happened that, when history has taken a sharp turn, even progressive parties have for some time been unable to adapt themselves to the new situation and have repeated slogans which had formerly been correct but had now lost all meaning – lost it as "suddenly" as the sharp turn in history was "sudden".

Something of the sort seems likely to recur in connection with the slogan calling for the transfer of all state power to the Soviets. That slogan was correct during a period of our revolution – say, from February 27 to July 4 – that has now passed irrevocably. It has patently ceased to be correct now. Unless this is understood, it is impossible to understand anything of the urgent questions of the day. Every particular slogan must be deduced from the totality of specific features of a definite political situation. And the political situation in Russia now, after July 4, differs radically from the situation between February 27 and July 4.

During that period of the revolution now past, the so-called "dual power" existed in the country, which both materially and formally expressed the indefinite and transitional condition of state power. Let us not forget that the issue of power is the fundamental issue of every revolution.

At that time state power was unstable. It was shared, by voluntary agreement, between the Provisional Government and the Soviets. The Soviets were delegations from the mass of free – i.e. not subject to external coercion – and armed workers and soldiers. What *really mattered* was that arms were in the hands of the people, and that there was no coercion of the people from without. That is what opened up and ensured a peaceful path for the progress of the revolution. The slogan "All Power Must Be Transferred to the Soviets" was a slogan for the next step, the immediately feasible step, on that peaceful path of development. It was a slogan for the peaceful development of the revolution, which was possible and, of course, most desirable between February 27 and July 4, but which is now absolutely impossible.

Apparently, not all the supporters of the slogan "All Power Must Be Transferred to the Soviets" have given adequate thought to the fact that it was a slogan for peaceful progress of the revolution – peaceful not only in the sense that nobody, no class, no force of any importance, would then (between February 27 and July 4) have been able to resist and prevent the transfer of power to the Soviets. That is not all. Peaceful development would then have been possible, even in the sense that the struggle of classes and parties *within* the Soviets could have assumed a most peaceful and painless form, provided full state power had passed to the Soviets in good time.

The latter aspect of the matter has similarly not yet received adequate attention. In their class composition, the Soviets were organs of the movement of the workers and peasants, a ready-made form of their dictatorship. Had they possessed full state power, the main shortcoming of the petty-bourgeois groups, their chief sin, that of trusting the capitalists, really would have been overcome, would have been criticised by the experience of their own measures. The change of classes and parties in power could have proceeded peacefully within the Soviets, provided the latter wielded exclusive and undivided power. The contact between all the Soviet parties and the people could have remained stable and unimpaired. One must not forget for a single moment that only such a close contact between the Soviet parties and the people, freely growing in extent and depth, could have helped peacefully to get rid of the illusion of petty-bourgeois compromise with the bourgeoisie. The transfer of power to the Soviets would not, and could not, in itself have changed the correlation of classes; it would in no way have changed the petty-bourgeois nature of the peasants. But it would have taken a big and timely step towards separating the peasants from the bourgeoisie, towards bringing them closer to, and then uniting them with, the workers.

This is what might have happened had power passed to the Soviets at the proper time. That would have been the easiest and the most advantageous course for the people. This course would have been the least painful, and it was therefore necessary to fight for it most energetically. Now, however, this struggle, the struggle for the timely transfer of power to the Soviets, has ended. A peaceful course of development has become impossible. A non-peaceful and most painful course has begun.

The turning point of July 4 was precisely a drastic change in the objective situation. The unstable condition of state power has come to an end. At the decisive point, power has passed into the hands of the counter-revolution. The development of the parties on the basis of the collaboration of the petty-bourgeois Socialist-Revolutionary and Menshevik parties and the counter-revolutionary Cadets has brought about a situation in which both these petty-bourgeois parties have virtually become participants in and abettors of counter-revolutionary butchery. As the struggle between parties developed, the unreasoning trust which the petty bourgeoisie put in the capitalists led to their deliberate support of the counter-revolutionaries. The development of party relations has completed its cycle. On February 27, all classes found themselves united against the monarchy. After July 4, the counter-revolutionary bourgeoisie, working hand in glove with the monarchists and the Black Hundreds,[1] secured the support of the petty-bourgeois Socialist-Revolutionaries and Mensheviks, partly by intimidating them, and handed over real state power to the Cavaignacs, the military gang, who are shooting insubordinate soldiers at the front and smashing the Bolsheviks in Petrograd.

The slogan calling for the transfer of state power to the Soviets would now sound quixotic or mocking. Objectively it would be deceiving the people; it would be fostering in them the delusion that even now it is enough for the Soviets to want to take power, or to pass such a decision, for power to be theirs, that there are still parties in the Soviets which have not been tainted by abetting the butchers, that it is possible to undo what has been done.

It would be a profound error to think that the revolutionary proletariat is capable of "refusing" to support the Socialist-Revolutionaries and Mensheviks against the counter-revolution by way of "revenge", so to speak, for the support they gave in smashing the Bolsheviks, in shooting down soldiers at the front and in disarming the workers. First, this would be applying philistine conceptions of morality to the proletariat (since, *for the good of the cause*, the proletariat will always support not only the vacillating petty bourgeoisie but even the big bourgeoisie); second – and that is the important thing – it would be a philistine attempt to obscure the political substance of the situation by "moralising".

And the political substance is that power can no longer be taken peacefully. It can be obtained only by winning a decisive struggle against those actually in power at the moment, namely, the military gang, the Cavaignacs, who are relying for support on the reactionary troops brought to Petrograd, and on the Cadets and monarchists.

---

[1] The Black Hundreds – monarchist gangs formed by the tsarist police to fight against the revolutionary movement. They assassinated revolutionaries, attacked progressive intellectuals and organised anti-Jewish pogroms.

The substance of the situation is that these new holders of state power can be defeated only by the revolutionary masses, who, to be brought into motion, must not only be led by the proletariat, but must also turn their backs on the Socialist-Revolutionary and Menshevik parties, which have betrayed the cause of the revolution.

Those who introduce philistine morals into politics reason as follows: let us assume that the Socialist-Revolutionaries and Mensheviks did commit an "error" in supporting the Cavaignacs, who are disarming the proletariat and the revolutionary regiments; still, they must be given a chance to "rectify" their "error"; the rectification of the "error" "should not be made difficult" for them; the swing of the petty bourgeoisie towards the workers should be facilitated. Such reasoning would be childishly naive or simply stupid, if not a new deception of the workers. For the swing of the petty-bourgeois masses towards the workers would mean, and could only mean, that these masses had turned their backs upon the Socialist-Revolutionaries and Mensheviks. The Socialist-Revolutionary and Menshevik parties could now rectify their "error" only by denouncing Tsereteli, Chernov, Dan and Rakitnikov as the butchers' aides. We are wholly and unconditionally in favour of their "error" being "rectified" in this way. . . .

We said that the fundamental issue of revolution is the issue of power. We must add that it is revolutions that show us at every step how the question of where actual power lies is obscured, and reveal the divergence between formal and real power. That is one of the chief characteristics of every revolutionary period. It was not clear in March and April 1917 whether real power was in the hands of the government or the Soviet.

Now, however, it is particularly important for class-conscious workers to soberly face the fundamental issue of revolution, namely, who holds state power at the moment? Consider its material manifestations, do not mistake words for deeds, and you will have no difficulty in finding the answer.

Frederick Engels once wrote that the state is primarily contingents of armed men with material adjuncts, such as prisons. Now it is the military cadets and the reactionary Cossacks, who have been specially brought to Petrograd, those who are keeping Kamenev and the others in prison, who closed down *Pravda*, who disarmed the workers and a certain section of the soldiers, who are shooting down an equally certain section of the soldiers, who are shooting down an equally certain section of troops in the army. These butchers are the real power. The Tseretelis and Chernovs are ministers without power, puppet ministers, leaders of parties that support the butchery. That is a fact. And the fact is no less true because Tsereteli and Chernov themselves probably "do not approve" of the butchery, or because their papers timidly dissociate themselves from it. Such changes of political garb change nothing in substance.

The newspaper of 150,000 Petrograd voters has been closed down. On July 6 the military cadets killed the worker Voinov for carrying *Listok "Pravdy"*[2] out of the printers'. Isn't that butchery? Isn't that the handiwork of Cavaignacs? But neither the government nor the Soviets are to "blame" for this, they may tell us.

So much the worse for the government and the Soviets, we reply; for that means that they are mere figureheads, puppets, and that real power is not in their hands.

Primarily, and above all, the people must know the truth – they must know who actually wields state power. The people must be told the whole truth, namely, that power is in the hands of a military clique of Cavaignacs (Kerensky, certain generals, officers, etc.), who are supported by the bourgeois class headed by the Cadet Party, and by all the monarchists, acting through the Black Hundred papers *Novoye Vremya*, *Zhivoye Slovo*, etc., etc.

That power must be overthrown. Unless this is done, all talk of fighting the counter-revolution is so much phrase-mongering, "self-deception and deception of the people".

That power now has the support both of the Tseretelis and Chernovs in the Cabinet, and of their parties. We must explain to the people the butcher's role they are playing, and the fact that such a "finale" for these parties was inevitable after their "errors" of April 21, May 5, June 9 and July 4, and after their approval of the policy of an offensive, a policy which went nine-tenths of the way to predetermining the victory of the Cavaignacs in July.

All agitational work among the people must be reorganised to ensure that it takes account of the specific experience of the present revolution, and particularly of the July days – i.e. that it clearly points to the real enemy of the people, the military clique, the Cadets and the Black Hundreds, and that it definitely unmasks the petty-bourgeois parties, the Socialist-Revolutionary and Menshevik parties, which played and are playing the part of butcher's aides.

All agitational work among the people must be reorganised so as to make clear that it is absolutely hopeless to expect the peasants to obtain land as long as the power of the military clique has not been overthrown, and as

---

[2] *Listok "Pravdy"* (*Pravda's Newssheet*) – one of the names of the legal Bolshevik daily newspaper *Pravda*.

long as the Socialist-Revolutionary and Menshevik parties have not been exposed and deprived of the people's trust. That would be a very long and arduous process under the "normal" conditions of capitalist development, but both the war and economic disruption will tremendously accelerate it. These are "accelerators" that may make a month, or even a week, equal to a year.

Two objections may perhaps be advanced against what has been said above: first, that to speak now of a decisive struggle is to encourage sporadic action, which would only benefit the counter-revolutionaries; second, that their overthrow would still mean transferring power to the Soviets.

In answer to the first objection, we say: the workers of Russia are already class-conscious enough not to yield to provocation at a moment which is obviously unfavourable to them. It is indisputable that for them to take action and offer resistance at the moment would mean aiding the counter-revolutionaries. It is also indisputable that a decisive struggle will be possible only in the event of a new revolutionary upsurge in the very depths of the masses. But it is not enough to speak in general terms of a revolutionary upsurge, of the rising tide of revolution, of aid by the West European workers, and so forth; we must draw a definite conclusion from our past, from the lessons we have been given. And that will lead us to the slogan of a decisive struggle against the counter-revolutionaries, who have seized power.

The second objection also amounts to a substitution of arguments of too general a character for concrete realities. No one, no force, can overthrow the bourgeois counter-revolutionaries except the revolutionary proletariat. Now, after the experience of July 1917, it is the revolutionary proletariat that must independently take over state power. Without that, the victory of the revolution is *impossible*. The only solution is for power to be in the hands of the proletariat, and for the latter to be supported by the poor peasants or semi-proletarians. And we have already indicated the factors that can enormously accelerate this solution.

Soviets may appear in this new revolution, and indeed are bound to, but *not* the present Soviets, not organs collaborating with the bourgeoisie, but organs of revolutionary struggle against the bourgeoisie. It is true that even then we shall be in favour of building the whole state on the model of the Soviets. It is not a question of Soviets in general, but of combating the *present* counter-revolution and the treachery of the *present* Soviets.

The substitution of the abstract for the concrete is one of the greatest and most dangerous sins in a revolution. The present Soviets have failed, have suffered complete defeat, because they are dominated by the Socialist-

Revolutionary and Menshevik parties. At the moment these Soviets are like sheep brought to the slaughterhouse and bleating pitifully under the knife. The Soviets *at present* are powerless and helpless against the triumphant and triumphing counter-revolution. The slogan calling for the transfer of power to the Soviets might be construed as a "simple" appeal for the transfer of power to the present Soviets, and to say that, to appeal for it, would now mean deceiving the people. Nothing is more dangerous than deceit.

The cycle of development of the class and party struggle in Russia from February 27 to July 4 is complete. A new cycle is beginning, one that involves not the old classes, not the old parties, not the old Soviets, but classes, parties and Soviets rejuvenated in the fire of struggle, tempered, schooled and refashioned by the process of the struggle. We must look forward, not backward. We must operate not with the old, but with the new, post-July, class and party categories. We must, at the beginning of the new cycle, proceed from the triumphant bourgeois counter-revolution, which triumphed because the Socialist-Revolutionaries and Mensheviks compromised with it, and which can be defeated only by the revolutionary proletariat. Of course, in this new cycle there will be many and various stages, both before the complete victory of the counter-revolution and the complete defeat (without a struggle) of the Socialist Revolutionaries and Mensheviks, and before a new upsurge of a new revolution. But it will be possible to speak of this only later, as each of these stages is reached.

4

The Impending Catastrophe and How to Combat It

Famine is Approaching

Unavoidable catastrophe is threatening Russia. The railways are incredibly disorganised, and the disorganisation is progressing. The railways will come to a standstill. The delivery of raw materials and coal to the factories will cease. The delivery of grain will cease. The capitalists are deliberately and unremittingly sabotaging (damaging, stopping, disrupting, hampering) production, hoping that an unparalleled catastrophe will mean the collapse of the republic and democracy, and of the Soviets and proletarian and peasant associations generally, thus facilitating the return to a monarchy and the restoration of the unlimited power of the bourgeoisie and the landowners.

The danger of a great catastrophe and of famine is imminent. All the newspapers have written about this time and again. A tremendous number of resolutions have been adopted by the parties and by the Soviets of Workers', Soldiers' and Peasants' Deputies – resolutions which admit that a catastrophe is unavoidable, that it is very close, that extreme measures are necessary to combat it, that "heroic efforts" by the people are necessary to avert ruin, and so on.

Everybody says this. Everybody admits it. Everybody has decided it is so.

Yet nothing is being done.

Six months of revolution have elapsed. The catastrophe is even closer. Unemployment has assumed a mass scale. To think that there is a shortage of goods in the country, the country is perishing from a shortage of food and labour, although there is a sufficient quantity of grain and raw materials, and yet in such a country, at so critical a moment, there is mass unemployment! What better evidence is needed to show that after six months of revolution (which some call a great revolution, but which so far it would perhaps be fairer to call a rotten revolution), in a democratic republic, with an abundance of unions, organs and institutions which proudly call themselves "revolutionary democratic", absolutely *nothing* of any importance has actually been done to avert catastrophe, to avert famine? We are nearing ruin with increasing speed. The war will not wait, and is causing increasing dislocation in every sphere of national life.

Yet the slightest attention and thought will suffice to satisfy anyone that the ways of combating catastrophe and famine are available, that the measures required to combat them are quite clear, simple, perfectly feasible, and fully within reach of the people's forces, and that these measures are not being adopted *only* because – *exclusively* because – their realisation would affect the fabulous profits of a handful of landowners and capitalists.

And, indeed, it is safe to say that every single speech, every single article in a newspaper of any trend, every single resolution passed by any meeting or institution quite clearly and explicitly recognises the chief and principal measure of combating, of averting, catastrophe and famine. This measure is control, supervision, accounting, regulation by the state, introduction of a proper distribution of labour-power in the production and distribution of goods, husbanding of the people's forces, the elimination of all wasteful effort, economy of effort. Control, supervision and accounting are the prime requisites for combating catastrophe and famine. This is indisputable and universally recognised. And it is just what *is not being done* from fear of encroaching on the supremacy of the landowners and capitalists, on their immense, fantastic and scandalous profits, profits derived from high prices and war contracts (and, directly or indirectly, nearly everybody is now "working" for the war), profits about which everybody knows and which everybody sees, and over which everybody is sighing and groaning.

And absolutely nothing is being done to introduce such control, accounting and supervision by the state as would be in the least effective.

Complete Government Inactivity

There is a universal, systematic and persistent sabotage of every kind of control, supervision and accounting, and of all state attempts to institute them. And one must be incredibly naive not to understand – one must be an utter hypocrite to pretend not to understand – where this sabotage comes from, and by what means it is being carried on. For this sabotage by the bankers and capitalists, their *frustration* of every kind of control, supervision and accounting, is being adapted to the state forms of a democratic republic, to the existence of "revolutionary-democratic" institutions. The capitalist gentlemen have learnt very well a fact which all supporters of scientific socialism profess to recognise but which the Mensheviks and Socialist-Revolutionaries tried to forget as soon as their friends had secured cushy jobs as ministers, deputy ministers, etc. That fact is that the economic substance of capitalist exploitation is in no wise affected by the substitution of republican-democratic forms of government for monarchist forms, and that, consequently, the reverse is also true – only the *form* of the struggle for the inviolability and sanctity of capitalist profits need be changed in order to uphold them under a democratic republic as effectively as under an absolute monarchy.

The present, modern republican-democratic sabotage of every kind of control, accounting and supervision consists in the capitalists "eagerly" accepting in words the "principle" of control and the necessity for control (as, of course, do all Mensheviks and Socialist-Revolutionaries), insisting only that this control be introduced "gradually", methodically and in a "state-regulated" way. In practice, however, these specious catchwords serve to conceal the *frustration* of control, its nullification, its reduction to a fiction, the mere playing at control, the delay of all business-like and practically effective measures, the creation of extraordinarily complicated, cumbersome and bureaucratically lifeless institutions of control which are hopelessly dependent on the capitalists, and which do absolutely nothing and cannot do anything.

So as not to trot out bald statements, let us cite witnesses from among the Mensheviks and Socialist-Revolutionaries, i.e. the very people who had the majority in the Soviets during the first six months of revolution, who took part in the "coalition government" and who are therefore politically responsible to the Russian workers and peasants for winking at the capitalists and allowing them to frustrate all control.

Izvestia (i.e. the newspaper of the Central Executive Committee of the All-Russia Congress of Soviets of Workers', Soldiers' and Peasants' Deputies), the official organ of the highest of the so-called "fully authorised" (no joke!) bodies of "revolutionary" democracy, in issue No. 164, of September 7, 1917, printed a *resolution* by a special control organisation created and run by these very Mensheviks and Socialist-Revolutionaries. This special institution is the Economic Department of the Central Executive Committee. Its resolution officially records as a fact "*the complete inactivity of the central bodies set up under the government for the regulation of economic life*".

Now, how could one imagine any more eloquent testimony to the collapse of the Menshevik and Socialist-Revolutionary policy than this statement signed by the Mensheviks and Socialist-Revolutionaries themselves?

The need for the regulation of economic life was already recognised under tsarism, and certain institutions were set up for the purpose. But under tsarism, economic chaos steadily grew and reached monstrous proportions. It was at once recognised that it was the task of the republican, revolutionary government to adopt effective and resolute measures to put an end to the economic chaos. When the "coalition" government was formed, with the Mensheviks and Socialist-Revolutionaries participating, it promised and undertook, in its most solemn public declaration of May 6, to introduce state control and regulation. The Tseretelis and Chernovs, like all the Menshevik and Socialist-Revolutionary leaders, vowed and swore that not only were they responsible for the government, but that the "authorised bodies of revolutionary democracy" under their control actually kept an eye on the work of the government and verified its activities.

Four months have passed since May 6, four long months, in which Russia has sacrificed the lives of hundreds of thousands of soldiers for the sake of the absurd imperialist "offensive", in which chaos and disaster have been advancing in seven-league strides, in which the summer season afforded an exceptional opportunity to do a great deal in the matter of water transport, agriculture, prospecting for minerals, and so on and so forth – and after four months the Mensheviks and Socialist-Revolutionaries have been obliged officially to admit the "complete inactivity" of the control institutions set up under the government!!

And these Mensheviks and Socialist-Revolutionaries, with the serious mien of statesmen, now prate (I am writing this on the very eve of the Democratic Conference of September 12[1]) that matters can be furthered by replacing the coalition with the Cadets by a coalition with commercial and

---

[1] The All-Russia Democratic Conference was held in Petrograd between September 14 and 22 (September 27–October 5), 1917. It was called by the Mensheviks and Socialist-Revolutionaries to stem the rising tide of the revolution. The delegates represented petty-bourgeois parties, the compromising Soviets, the trade unions, Zemstvos, commercial and industrial circles, and troop units. The Bolsheviks attended with the aim of exposing the designs of the Mensheviks and SRs. The conference elected a pre-parliament (Provisional Council of the Republic) through which the Mensheviks and SRs hoped to check the revolution and divert the country on to the track of a bourgeois parliamentary system.

On Lenin's proposal, the Central Committee of the Party decided that the Bolsheviks should withdraw from the pre-parliament. Only Kamenev, Rykov and Ryazanov, who were against the Party's course for the socialist revolution, insisted on participation in the pre-parliament.

industrial Kit Kityches,[2] the Ryabushinskys, Bublikovs, Tereshchenkos and Co.

How, one may ask, are we to explain this astonishing blindness of the Mensheviks and Socialist-Revolutionaries? Are we to regard them as political babes in the wood who, in their extreme foolishness and naivety, do not realise what they are doing, and err in good faith? Or does the abundance of posts they occupy as ministers, deputy ministers, governors-general, commissars, and the like have the property of engendering a special kind of "political" blindness?

Control Measures Are Known to All and Easy to Take

One may ask: aren't methods and measures of control extremely complex, difficult, untried, and even unknown? Isn't the delay due to the fact that although the statesmen of the Cadet Party, the merchant and industrial class, and the Menshevik and Socialist-Revolutionary parties have for six months been toiling in the sweat of their brow, investigating, studying and discovering measures and methods of control, still the problem is incredibly difficult and has not yet been solved?

Unfortunately, this is how they are trying to present matters to hoodwink the ignorant, illiterate and downtrodden muzhiks and the Simple Simons who believe everything and never look into things. In reality, however, even tsarism, even the "old regime", when it set up the War Industries Committees,[3] *knew* the principal measure, the chief method and way

---

[2] Kit Kitych (literally, Whale Whaleson) – nickname of Tit Titych, a rich merchant in Alexander Ostrovsky's comedy *Shouldering Another's Troubles*. Lenin applies the nickname to capitalist tycoons.

[3] The War Industries Committees, which came into being in May 1915, were formed by Russia's big imperialist bourgeoisie to help the tsarist regime with the war. The chairman of the Central War Industries Committee was the Octobrist leader A. I. Guchkov, a big capitalist. Among its members were the manufacturer A. I. Konovalov and the banker and sugar manufacturer M. I. Tereshchenko. In an effort to bring the workers under its sway and inspire them with defencist sentiments, the bourgeoisie decided to form "workers' groups" under the committees, and thereby to show that "class peace" had been established between the bourgeoisie and the proletariat of Russia. The Bolsheviks declared a boycott of the committees, and maintained it with support from the majority of the workers.

As a result of the Bolsheviks' explanatory work, elections to the "workers' groups" took place only in 70 out of the 239 regional and local War Industries Committees, workers' representatives being elected to only 36 Committees.

to introduce control, namely, by uniting the population according to profession, purpose of work, branch of labour, etc. But tsarism *feared* the union of the population, and therefore did its best to restrict and artificially hinder this generally known, very easy and quite practical method and way of control.

All the belligerent countries, suffering as they are from the extreme burdens and hardships of the war, suffering – in one degree or another – from economic chaos and famine, have long ago outlined, determined, applied and tested a *whole series* of control measures, which consist almost invariably in uniting the population and in setting up or encouraging unions of various kinds, in which state representatives participate, which are under the supervision of the state, etc. All these measures of control are known to all, much has been said and written about them, and the laws passed by the advanced belligerent powers relating to control have been translated into Russian or expounded in detail in the Russian press.

If our state really *wanted* to exercise control in a business-like and earnest fashion, if its institutions had not condemned themselves to "complete inactivity" by their servility to the capitalists, all the state would have to do would be to draw freely on the rich store of control measures which are already known and have been used in the past. The only obstacle to this – an obstacle concealed from the eyes of the people by the Cadets, Socialist-Revolutionaries and Mensheviks – was, and still is, that control would bring to light the fabulous profits of the capitalists, and would cut the ground from under these profits.

To explain this most important question more clearly (a question which is essentially equivalent to that of the programme of *any* truly revolutionary government that would wish to save Russia from war and famine), let us enumerate these principal measures of control, and examine each of them.

We shall see that all a government would have had to do, if its name of revolutionary-democratic government were not merely a joke, would have been to decree, in the very first week of its existence, the adoption of the principal measures of control, to provide for strict and severe punishment to be meted out to capitalists who fraudulently evaded control, and to call upon the population itself to exercise supervision over the capitalists and see to it that they scrupulously observed the regulations on control – and control would have been introduced in Russia long ago. These principal measures are:

(1) Amalgamation of all banks into a single bank, and state control over its operations, or nationalisation of the banks.

(2) Nationalisation of the syndicates, i.e. the largest, monopolistic capitalist associations (sugar, oil, coal, iron and steel, and other syndicates).

(3) Abolition of commercial secrecy.

(4) Compulsory syndication (i.e. compulsory amalgamation into associations) of industrialists, merchants and employers generally.

(5) Compulsory organisation of the population into consumers' societies, or encouragement of such organisation, and the exercise of control over it.

Let us see what the significance of each of these measures would be if carried out in a revolutionary-democratic way.

Nationalisation of the Banks

The banks, as we know, are centres of modern economic life, the principal nerve centres of the whole capitalist economic system. To talk about "regulating economic life", yet evade the question of the nationalisation of the banks, means either betraying the most profound ignorance or deceiving the "common people" by florid words and grandiloquent promises with the deliberate intention of not fulfilling these promises.

It is absurd to control and regulate deliveries of grain, or the production and distribution of goods generally, without controlling and regulating bank operations. It is like trying to snatch at odd kopeks and closing one's eyes to millions of roubles. Banks nowadays are so closely and intimately bound up with trade (in grain and everything else) and with industry that without "laying hands" on the banks, nothing of any value, nothing "revolutionary-democratic", can be accomplished.

But perhaps for the state to "lay hands" on the banks is a very difficult and complicated operation? They usually try to scare philistines with this very idea – that is, the capitalists and their defenders try it, because it is to their advantage to do so.

In reality, however, nationalisation of the banks, which would not deprive any "owner" of a single kopek, presents absolutely no technical or cultural difficulties, and is being delayed *exclusively* because of the vile greed of an insignificant handful of rich people. If nationalisation of the banks is so often confused with the confiscation of private property, it is the bourgeois press, which has an interest in deceiving the public, that is to blame for this widespread confusion.

The ownership of the capital wielded by and concentrated in the banks is certified by printed and written certificates called shares, bonds, bills, receipts, etc. Not a single one of these certificates would be invalidated or altered if the banks were nationalised, i.e. if all the banks were amalgamated into a single state bank. Anyone who owned fifteen roubles on a savings account would continue to be the owner of fifteen roubles after the nationalisation of the banks; and anyone who had fifteen million roubles would continue after the nationalisation of the banks to have fifteen million roubles in the form of shares, bonds, bills, commercial certificates, and so on.

What, then, is the significance of nationalisation of the banks?

It is that no effective control of any kind over the individual banks and their operations is possible (even if commercial secrecy, etc., were abolished), because it is impossible to keep track of the extremely complex, involved and wily tricks that are used in drawing up balance sheets, founding fictitious enterprises and subsidiaries, enlisting the services of figureheads, and so on and so forth. Only the amalgamation of all banks into one – which in itself would imply no change whatever in respect of ownership and which, we repeat, would not deprive any owner of a single kopek – would make it *possible* to exercise real control – provided, of course, all the other measures indicated above were carried out. Only by nationalising the banks *can* the state *put itself in a position* to know where and how, whence and when, millions and billions of roubles flow. And only control over the banks, over the centre, over the pivot and chief mechanism of capitalist circulation, would make it possible to organise real and not fictitious control over all economic life, over the production and distribution of staple goods, and organise that "regulation of economic life" which otherwise is inevitably doomed to remain a ministerial phrase designed to fool the common people. Only control over banking operations, provided they were concentrated in a single state bank, would make it possible, if certain other easily practicable measures were adopted, to organise the effective collection of income tax in such a way as to prevent the concealment of property and incomes; for at present income tax is very largely a fiction.

Nationalisation of the banks has only to be decreed and it would be carried out by the directors and employees themselves. No special machinery, no special preparatory steps on the part of the state, would be required, for this is a measure that can be effected by a single decree, "at a single stroke". It was made economically feasible by capitalism itself once it had developed to the stage of bills, shares, bonds, and so on. All that is required is to *unify accountancy*. And if the revolutionary-democratic government were to decide that immediately, by telegraph, meetings of managers and employees should be called in every city, and conferences in every region and in the country as a whole, for the immediate amalgamation of all banks into a single state bank, this reform could be carried out in a few weeks. Of course, it would be the managers and the higher bank officials who would offer resistance, who would try to deceive the state, delay matters, and so on, for these gentlemen would lose their highly remunerative posts and the opportunity of performing highly profitable fraudulent operations. *That is the heart of the matter.* But there is not the slightest technical difficulty in the way of the amalgamation of the banks; and if the state power were revolutionary not only in word (i.e. if it did not fear to do away with inertia and routine), if it were democratic not only in word (i.e. if it acted in the interests of the majority of the people, not those of a handful of rich men), it would be enough to decree confiscation of property and imprisonment as the penalty for managers, board members and big shareholders for the slightest delay, or for attempting to conceal documents and accounts. It would be enough, for example, to organise the poorer employees *separately*, and to reward them for detecting fraud and delay on the part of the rich, for nationalisation of the banks to be effected as smoothly and rapidly as can be.

The advantages accruing to the whole people from nationalisation of the banks – *not* to the workers especially (for the workers have little to do with banks) but to the mass of peasants and small industrialists – would be enormous. The saving in labour would be gigantic, and, assuming that the state would retain the former number of bank employees, nationalisation would be a highly important step towards making the use of the banks universal, towards increasing the number of their branches, putting their operations within easier reach, etc., etc. The availability of credit on easy terms for the *small* owners, for the peasants, would increase immensely. As for the state, it would for the first time be in a position first to *review* all the chief monetary operations, which would be unconcealed, then to *control* them, then to *regulate* economic life, and finally to *obtain* millions and billions for major state transactions, without paying the capitalist gentlemen sky-high "commissions" for their "services". That is the reason – and the only reason – why all the capitalists, all the bourgeois professors, all the bourgeoisie, and all the Plekhanovs, Potresovs and Co., who serve them, are prepared to fight tooth and nail against nationalisation of the banks, and invent thousands of excuses to prevent the adoption of this very easy and very pressing measure, although even from the standpoint of the "defence" of the country – i.e. from the military standpoint – this measure would provide a gigantic advantage, and would tremendously enhance the "military might" of the country.

The following objection might be raised: why do such advanced states as Germany and the USA "regulate economic life" so magnificently without even thinking of nationalising the banks?

Because, we reply, *both* these states are not merely capitalist, but also imperialist states, although one of them is a monarchy and the other a republic. As such, they carry out the reforms they need by reactionary-bureaucratic methods, whereas we are speaking here of revolutionary-democratic methods.

This "little difference" is of major importance. In most cases it is "not the custom" to think of it. The term "revolutionary democracy" has become with us (especially among the Socialist-Revolutionaries and Mensheviks) almost a conventional phrase, like the expression "thank God", which is also used by people who are not so ignorant as to believe in God; or the expression "honourable citizen", which is sometimes used even in addressing staff members of *Dyen* or *Yedinstvo*, although nearly everybody guesses that these newspapers have been founded and are maintained by the capitalists in the interests of the capitalists, and that there is therefore very little "honourable" about the pseudo-socialists who contribute to these newspapers.

If we do not employ the phrase "revolutionary democracy" as a stereotyped ceremonial phrase, as a conventional epithet, but *reflect* on its meaning, we find that to be a democrat means reckoning in reality with the interests of the majority of the people, not the minority, and that to be a revolutionary means destroying everything harmful and obsolete in the most resolute and ruthless manner.

Neither in America nor in Germany, as far as we know, is any claim laid by either the government or the ruling classes to the name "revolutionary democrats", to which our Socialist-Revolutionaries and Mensheviks lay claim (and which they prostitute).

In Germany there are only four very large private banks of national importance. In America there are only *two*. It is easier, more convenient, more profitable for the financial magnates of those banks to unite privately, surreptitiously, in a reactionary and not a revolutionary way, in a bureaucratic and not a democratic way, bribing government officials (this is the general rule both in America and *in Germany*) and preserving the private character of the banks in order to preserve secrecy of operations, to milk the state of millions upon millions in "super-profits", and to make financial frauds possible.

Both America and Germany "regulate economic life" in such a way as to create conditions of *war-time penal servitude* for the workers (and partly for the peasants) and a *paradise* for the bankers and capitalists. Their regulation consists in "squeezing" the workers to the point of starvation, while the capitalists are guaranteed (surreptitiously, in a reactionary-bureaucratic fashion) profits *higher* than before the war.

Such a course is quite possible in republican-imperialist Russia, too. Indeed, it is the course being followed not only by the Milyukovs and Shingaryovs, but also by Kerensky in partnership with Tereshchenko, Nekrasov, Bernatsky, Prokopovich and Co., who *also uphold*, in a reactionary-bureaucratic manner, the "inviolability" of the banks and their sacred right to fabulous profits. So we had better tell the *truth*, namely, that in republican Russia they want to regulate economic life in a reactionary-bureaucratic manner, but "often" find it difficult to do so owing to the existence of the "Soviets", which Kornilov No. 1 did not manage to disband, but which Kornilov No. 2 will try to disband.

That would be the truth. And this simple – if bitter – truth is more useful for the enlightenment of the people than the honeyed lies about "our", "great", "revolutionary" democracy.

Nationalisation of the banks would greatly facilitate the simultaneous nationalisation of the insurance business, i.e. the amalgamation of all the insurance companies into one, the centralisation of their operations, and state control over them. Here, too, congresses of insurance company employees could carry out this amalgamation immediately and without any great effort, provided a revolutionary-democratic government decreed this, ordered directors and big shareholders to effect the amalgamation without the slightest delay, and held every one of them strictly accountable for it. The capitalists have invested hundreds of millions of roubles in the insurance business; the work is all done by the employees. The amalgamation of this business would lead to lower insurance premiums, would provide a host of facilities and conveniences for the insured, and would make it possible to increase their number without increasing expenditure of effort and funds. Absolutely nothing but the inertia, routine and self-interest of a handful of holders of remunerative jobs are delaying this reform, which, among other things, would enhance the country's defence potential by economising national labour and creating a number of highly important opportunities to "regulate economic life" not in word, but in deed.

Nationalisation of the syndicates

Capitalism differs from the old, pre-capitalistic systems of economy in having created the closest interconnection and interdependence of the various branches of the economy. Were this not so, incidentally, no steps towards socialism would be technically feasible. Modern capitalism, under which the banks dominate production, has carried this interdependence of the various branches of the economy to the utmost. The banks and the more important branches of industry and commerce have become inseparably merged. This means, on the one hand, that it is impossible to nationalise the banks alone, without proceeding to create a state monopoly of commercial and industrial syndicates (sugar, coal, iron, oil, etc.), and without nationalising them. It means, on the other hand, that if it were carried out in earnest, the regulation of economic activity would demand the simultaneous nationalisation of the banks and the syndicates.

Let us take the sugar syndicate as an example. It came into being under tsarism, and at that time developed into a huge capitalist combine of splendidly equipped refineries. And, of course, this combine, thoroughly imbued with the most reactionary and bureaucratic spirit, secured scandalously high profits for the capitalists, and reduced its employees to the status of humiliated and downtrodden slaves lacking any rights. Even at that time the state controlled and regulated production – in the interests of the rich, the magnates.

All that remains to be done here is to transform reactionary-bureaucratic regulation into revolutionary-democratic regulation by simple decrees providing for the summoning of a congress of employees, engineers, directors and shareholders, for the introduction of uniform accountancy, for control by the workers' unions, etc. This is an exceedingly simple thing, yet it has not been done! Under what is a democratic republic, the regulation of the sugar industry *actually* remains reactionary-bureaucratic; everything remains as of old – the dissipation of national labour, routine and stagnation, and the enrichment of the Bobrinskys and Tereshchenkos. Democrats and not bureaucrats, the workers and other employees and not the "sugar barons", should be called upon to exercise independent initiative – and this could and should be done in a few days, at a single stroke, if only the Socialist-Revolutionaries and Mensheviks did not befog the minds of the people by plans for "association" with these very sugar barons, for the very association with the wealthy from which the "complete inaction" of the government in the matter of regulating economic life follows with absolute inevitability, and of which it is a consequence.[*]

Take the oil business. It was to a vast extent "socialised" by the earlier development of capitalism. Just a couple of oil barons wield millions and hundreds of millions of roubles, clipping coupons and raking in fabulous profits from a "business" which is *already* actually, technically and socially organised on a national scale, and is *already* being conducted by hundreds and thousands of employees, engineers, etc. Nationalisation of the oil industry could be effected *at once* by – and is imperative for   a revolutionary-democratic state, especially when the latter suffers from an acute crisis, and when it is essential to economise national labour and to increase the output of fuel at all costs. It is clear that here bureaucratic control can achieve nothing, can change nothing, for the "oil barons" can cope with the Tereshchenkoc, the Kerenskys, the Avksentyevs and the Skobelevs as easily as they coped with the tsar's ministers – by means of delays, excuses and promises, and by bribing the bourgeois press directly or indirectly (this is called "public opinion", and the Kerenskys and Avksentyevs "reckon" with it), by bribing officials (left by the Kerenskys and Avksentyevs in their old jobs in the old state machinery which remains intact).

If anything real is to be done, bureaucracy must be abandoned for democracy, and in a truly revolutionary way, i.e. war must be declared on the oil barons and shareholders, the confiscation of their property and punishment by imprisonment must be decreed for delaying nationalisation of the oil business, for concealing incomes or accounts, for sabotaging production, and for failing to take steps to increase production. The initiative of the workers and other employees must be drawn on; *they* must be immediately summoned to conferences and congresses; a certain proportion of the profits must be assigned to *them*, provided they institute overall control and increase production. Had these revolutionary-democratic steps been taken at once, immediately, in April 1917, Russia, which is one of the richest countries in the world in deposits of liquid fuel, could, using water transport, have done a very great deal during this summer to supply the people with the necessary quantities of fuel.

Neither the bourgeois nor the coalition Socialist-Revolutionary–Menshevik-Cadet government has done anything at all. Both have confined themselves

---

* These lines had already been written when I learnt from the newspapers that the Kerensky government is introducing a sugar monopoly, and, of course, is introducing it in a reactionary-bureaucratic way, without congresses of workers and other employees, without publicity, and without curbing the capitalists!

to a bureaucratic playing at reforms. They have not dared to take a single revolutionary-democratic step. Everything has remained as it was under the tsars – the oil barons, the stagnation, the hatred of the workers and other employees for their exploiters, the resulting chaos, and the dissipation of national labour – only the *letterheads* on the incoming and outgoing papers in the "republican" offices have been changed!

Take the coal industry. It is technically and culturally no less "ripe" for nationalisation, and is being no less shamelessly managed by the robbers of the people, the coal barons, and there are a number of most striking *facts* of direct sabotage, direct *damage* to and stoppage of production by the industrialists. Even the ministerial *Rabochaya Gazeta* of the Mensheviks has admitted these facts. And what do we find? Absolutely nothing has been done, except to call the old, reactionary-bureaucratic meetings "on a half-and-half basis" – an equal number of workers and bandits from the coal syndicate! Not a single revolutionary-democratic step has been taken, not a shadow of an attempt has been made to establish the only control which is real – control from *below*, through the employees' union, through the workers, and by using terror against the coal industrialists who are ruining the country and bringing production to a standstill! How can this be done when we are "all" in favour of the "coalition" – if not with the Cadets, then with commercial and industrial circles. And coalition means leaving power in the hands of the capitalists, letting them go unpunished, allowing them to hamper affairs, to blame everything on the workers, to intensify the chaos and *thus* pave the way for a new Kornilov revolt!

Abolition of commercial secrecy

Unless commercial secrecy is abolished, either control over production and distribution will remain an empty promise – only needed by the Cadets to fool the Socialist-Revolutionaries and Mensheviks, and by the Socialist-Revolutionaries and Mensheviks to fool the working classes – or control can be exercised only by reactionary-bureaucratic methods and means. Although this is obvious to every unprejudiced person, and although *Pravda* persistently demanded the abolition of commercial secrecy (and was suppressed largely for this reason by the Kerensky government, which is subservient to capital), neither our republican government nor the "authorised bodies of revolutionary democracy" have even thought of this *first step* to real control.

This is the very key to all control. Here we have the most sensitive spot of capital, which is robbing the people and sabotaging production. And this is exactly why the Socialist-Revolutionaries and Mensheviks are afraid to do anything about it.

The usual argument of the capitalists, one reiterated by the petty bourgeoisie without reflection, is that in a capitalist economy the abolition of commercial secrecy is in general absolutely impossible, for private ownership of the means of production, and the dependence of the individual undertakings on the market, render essential the "sanctity" of commercial books and commercial operations – including, of course, banking operations.

Those who, in one form or another, repeat this or similar arguments allow themselves to be deceived, and themselves deceive the people, by shutting their eyes to two fundamental, highly important and generally known facts of modern economic activity. The first fact is the existence of large-scale capitalism, i.e. the peculiar features of the economic system of banks, syndicates, large factories, etc. The second fact is the war.

It is modern large-scale capitalism, which is everywhere becoming mono-poly capitalism, that deprives commercial secrecy of every shadow of reasonableness, turns it into hypocrisy and into an instrument exclusively for concealing financial swindles and the fantastically high profits of big capital. Large-scale capitalist economy, by its very technical nature, is socialised economy, that is, it both operates for millions of people and, directly or indirectly, unites by its operations hundreds, thousands and tens of thousands of families. It is not like the economy of the small handicrafts-man or the middle peasant, who keep no commercial books at all, and would therefore not be affected by the abolition of commercial secrecy!

As it is, the operations conducted in large-scale business are known to hundreds or more people. Here the law protecting commercial secrecy does not serve the interests of production or exchange, but those of speculation and profit-seeking in their crudest form, and of direct fraud, which, as we know, in the case of joint-stock companies is particularly widespread and very skilfully concealed by reports and balance-sheets, so compiled as to deceive the public.

While commercial secrecy is unavoidable in small commodity production – i.e. among the small peasants and handicraftsmen, where production itself is not socialised but scattered and disunited – in large-scale capitalist production, the protection of commercial secrecy means protection of the privileges and profits of literally a handful of people *against* the interest of the whole people. This has already been recognised by the law, inasmuch as provision is made for the publication of the accounts of joint-stock companies. But *this* control – which has already been introduced in all advanced countries, as well as in Russia – is a reactionary-bureaucratic control which does not open the eyes of the *people*, and *does not allow the whole truth* about the operations of joint-stock companies to become known.

To act in a revolutionary-democratic way, it would be necessary immediately to pass another law abolishing commercial secrecy, compelling the big undertakings and the wealthy to render the fullest possible accounts, and investing every group of citizens of substantial democratic numerical strength (1,000 or 10,000 voters, let us say) with the right to examine *all* the records of any large undertaking. Such a measure could be fully and easily effected by a simple decree. It *alone* would allow full scope for *popular* initiative in control, through the office employees' unions, the workers' unions and all the political parties, and it alone would make control effective and democratic.

Add to this the war. The vast majority of commercial and industrial establishments are now working not for the "free market", but *for the government*, for the war. This is why I have already stated in *Pravda* that people who counter us with the argument that socialism cannot be introduced are liars, and barefaced liars at that, because it is not a question of introducing socialism now, directly, overnight, but of *exposing plunder of the state*.

Capitalist "war" economy (i.e. economy directly or indirectly connected with war contracts) is systematic and legalised *plunder*, and the Cadet gentry – who, together with the Mensheviks and Socialist-Revolutionaries, are opposing the abolition of commercial secrecy – are nothing but *assistants and abettors of plunder*.

The war is now costing Russia fifty million roubles *a day*. These fifty million go mostly to army contractors. Of these fifty, at least five million *daily*, and probably ten million or more, constitute the "honest income" of the capitalists, and of the officials who are in collusion with them in one way or another. The very large firms and banks which lend money for war contracts transactions thereby make fantastic profits, and do so by plundering the state, for no other epithet can be applied to this defrauding and plundering of the people "on the occasion of" the hardships of war, "on the occasion of" the deaths of hundreds of thousands and millions of people.

"Everybody" knows about these scandalous profits made on war contracts, about the "letters of guarantee" which are concealed by the banks, about who benefits from the rising cost of living. They are smiled on in "society". Quite a number of precise references are made to them *even* in the bourgeois press, which as a general rule keeps silent about "unpleasant" facts and avoids "ticklish" questions. Everybody knows about them, yet everybody keeps silent, everybody tolerates them, everybody puts up with the government, which prates eloquently about "control" and "regulation"!!

The revolutionary democrats, were they real revolutionaries and democrats, would immediately pass a law abolishing commercial secrecy, compelling contractors and merchants to make accounts public, forbidding them to abandon their field of activity without the permission of the authorities, imposing the penalty of confiscation of property and shooting* for concealment and for deceiving the people, organising verification and control *from below*, democratically, by the people themselves, by unions of workers and other employees, consumers, etc.

Our Socialist-Revolutionaries and Mensheviks fully deserve to be called scared democrats, for on this question they repeat what is said by all the scared philistines, namely, that the capitalists will "run away" if "too severe" measures are adopted, that "we" shall be unable to get along without the capitalists, that the British and French millionaires – who are, of course, "supporting" us – will most likely be "offended" in their turn, and so on. It might be thought that the Bolsheviks were proposing something unknown to history, something that has never been tried before, something "utopian", while, as a matter of fact, even 125 years ago, in France, people who were real "revolutionary democrats", who were really convinced of the just and defensive character of the war they were waging, who really had popular support and were sincerely convinced of this, were able to establish *revolutionary* control over the rich, and to achieve results which earned the admiration of the world. And in the century and a quarter that have since elapsed, the development of capitalism, which resulted in the creation of banks, syndicates, railways, and so forth, has greatly facilitated and simplified the adoption of measures of really democratic control by the workers and peasants over the exploiters, the landowners and capitalists.

In point of fact, the whole question of control boils down to who controls whom, i.e. which class is in control and which is being controlled. In our

---

* I have already had occasion to point out in the Bolshevik press that it is right to argue against the death penalty only when it is applied by the exploiters against the *mass* of the working people with the purpose of maintaining exploitation. It is hardly likely that any revolutionary government whatever could do without applying the death penalty to the *exploiters* (i.e. the landowners and capitalists).

country, in republican Russia, with the help of the "authorised bodies" of supposedly revolutionary democracy, it is the landowners and capitalists who are still recognised to be, and still are, the controllers. The inevitable result is the capitalist robbery that arouses universal indignation among the people, and the economic chaos that is being artificially kept up by the capitalists. We must resolutely and irrevocably – not fearing to break with the old, not fearing boldly to build the new – pass to control over the landowners and capitalists by the workers and peasants. And this is what our Socialist-Revolutionaries and Mensheviks fear worse than the plague.

Compulsory association

Compulsory syndication – i.e. compulsory association – of the industrialists, for example, is already being practised in Germany. Nor is there anything new in it. Here, too, through the fault of the Socialist-Revolutionaries and Mensheviks, we see the utter stagnation of republican Russia, whom these none-too-respectable parties "entertain" by dancing a quadrille with the Cadets, or with the Bublikovs, or with Tereshchenko and Kerensky.

Compulsory syndication is, on the one hand, a means whereby the state, as it were, expedites capitalist development, which everywhere leads to the organisation of the class struggle and to a growth in the number, variety and importance of unions. On the other hand, compulsory "unionisation" is an indispensable precondition for any kind of effective control and for all economy of national labour.

The German law, for instance, binds the leather manufacturers of a given locality or of the whole country to form an association, on the board of which there is a representative of the state for the purpose of control. A law of this kind does not directly, i.e. in itself, affect property relations in any way; it does not deprive any owner of a single kopek and does not predetermine whether the control is to be exercised in a reactionary-bureaucratic or a revolutionary-democratic form, direction or spirit.

Such laws can and should be passed in our country immediately, without wasting a single week of precious time; it should be left to *social conditions themselves* to determine the more specific forms of enforcing the law, the speed with which it is to be enforced, the methods of supervision over its enforcement, etc. In this case, the state requires no special machinery, no special investigation, nor preliminary enquiries for the passing of such a law. All that is required is the determination to break with certain private interests of the capitalists, who are "not accustomed" to such interference and have no desire to forfeit the super-profits which are ensured by the old methods of management and the absence of control.

No machinery and no "statistics" (which Chernov wanted to substitute for the revolutionary initiative of the peasants) are required to *pass* such a law, inasmuch as its implementation must be made the duty of the manufacturers or industrialists themselves, of the *available* public forces, under the control of the available public (i.e. non-government, non-bureaucratic) forces too, which, however, must consist by all means of the so-called "lower estates", i.e. of the oppressed and exploited classes, which in history have always proved to be immensely *superior* to the exploiters in their capacity for heroism, self-sacrifice and comradely discipline.

Let us assume that we have a really revolutionary-democratic government, and that it decides that the manufacturers and industrialists in every branch of production who employ, let us say, not fewer than two workers shall immediately amalgamate into uyezd and gubernia associations. Responsibility for the strict observance of the law is laid in the first place on the manufacturers, directors, board members, and big shareholders (for they are the real leaders of modern industry, its real masters). They shall be regarded as deserters from military service, and punished as such, if they do not work for the immediate implementation of the law, and shall bear mutual responsibility, one answering for all, and all for one, with the whole of their property. Responsibility shall next be laid on all office employees, who shall also form *one* union, and on all workers and their trade union. The purpose of "unionisation" is to institute the fullest, strictest and most detailed accountancy, but chiefly to *combine operations* in the purchase of raw materials, the sale of products, and the *economy* of national funds and forces. When the separate establishments are amalgamated into a single syndicate, this economy can attain tremendous proportions, as economic science teaches us and as is shown by the example of all syndicates, cartels and trusts. And it must be repeated that this unionisation will not in itself alter property relations one iota and will not deprive any owner of a single kopek. This circumstance must be strongly stressed, for the bourgeois press constantly "frightens" small and medium proprietors by asserting that socialists in general, and the Bolsheviks in particular, want to "expropriate" them – a deliberately false assertion, as socialists do not intend to, cannot and will not expropriate the small peasant *even if there is a fully socialist* revolution. All the time we are speaking *only* of the immediate and urgent measures, which have already been introduced in Western Europe and which a democracy that is at all consistent ought to introduce immediately in our country to combat the impending and inevitable catastrophe.

Serious difficulties, both technical and cultural, would be encountered in amalgamating the small and very small proprietors into associations, owing to the extremely small proportions and technical primitiveness of their enterprises and the illiteracy or lack of education of the owners. But precisely such enterprises could be exempted from the law (as was pointed out above in our hypothetical example). Their non-amalgamation, let alone their belated amalgamation, could create no serious obstacle, for the part played by the huge number of small enterprises in the sum total of production and their importance to the economy as a whole are *negligible*, and, moreover, they are often in one way or another dependent on the big enterprises.

Only the big enterprises are of decisive importance; and here the technical and cultural means and forces for "unionisation" *do exist*; what is lacking is the firm, determined initiative of a *revolutionary* government which should be ruthlessly severe towards the exploiters to set these forces and means in motion.

The poorer a country is in technically trained forces, and in intellectual forces generally, the more *urgent* it is to decree compulsory association as early and as resolutely as possible, and to begin with the bigger and biggest enterprises when putting the decree into effect, for it is association that will *economise* intellectual forces and make it possible to use them *to the full* and to distribute them more correctly. If, after 1905, even the Russian peasants in their out-of-the-way districts, under the tsarist government, in face of the thousands of obstacles raised by that government, were able to make a tremendous forward stride in the creation of all kinds of associations, it is clear that the amalgamation of large- and medium-scale industry and trade could be effected in several months, if not earlier, provided compulsion to this end were exercised by a really revolutionary-democratic government relying on the support, participation, interest and advantage of the "lower ranks", the democracy, the workers and other employees, and calling upon *them* to exercise control.

Regulation of consumption

The war has compelled all the belligerent and many of the neutral countries to resort to the regulation of consumption. Bread cards have been issued and have become customary, and this has led to the appearance of other ration cards. Russia is no exception, and has also introduced bread cards.

Using this as an example, we can draw, perhaps, the most striking comparison of all between reactionary-bureaucratic methods of combating a catastrophe, which are confined to minimum reforms, and revolutionary-democratic methods, which, to justify their name, must directly aim at a violent rupture with the old, obsolete system and at the achievement of the speediest possible progress.

The bread card – this typical example of how consumption is regulated in modern capitalist countries – aims at, and achieves (at best), one thing only, namely, distributing available supplies of grain to give everybody his share. A maximum limit to consumption is established, not for all foodstuffs by far, but only for principal foodstuffs, those of "popular" consumption. And that is all. There is no intention of doing anything else. Available supplies of grain are calculated in a bureaucratic way, then divided on a per capita basis, a ration is fixed and introduced, and there the matter ends. Luxury articles are not affected, for they are "anyway" scarce and "anyway" so dear as to be beyond the reach of the "people". And so, in *all* the belligerent countries without exception, *even* in Germany, which evidently, without fear of contradiction, may be said to be a model of the most careful, pedantic and strict regulation of consumption – *even* in Germany we find that the rich constantly *get around* all "rationing". This, too, "everybody" knows and "everybody" talks about with a smile; and in the German socialist papers, and sometimes even in the bourgeois papers, despite the fierce military stringency of the German censorship, we constantly find items and reports about the "menus" of the rich, saying how the wealthy can obtain white bread in any quantity at a certain health resort (visited, on the plea of illness, by everybody who has plenty of money), and how the wealthy substitute choice and rare articles of luxury for articles of popular consumption.

A reactionary capitalist state which *fears* to undermine the pillars of capitalism, of wage slavery, of the economic supremacy of the rich, which *fears* to encourage the initiative of the workers and the working people generally, which *fears* to provoke them to a more exacting attitude – *such* a state will be quite content with bread cards. Such a state does not for a moment, in any measure it adopts, lose sight of the *reactionary* aim of strengthening capitalism, preventing its being undermined, and confining the "regulation of economic life" in general, and the regulation of consumption in particular, to such measures as are absolutely essential to feed the people, *and makes no attempt* whatsoever at real regulation of consumption by exercising *control over the rich* and laying the *greater part* of the burden in war-time on those who are better off, who are privileged, well fed and overfed in peace-time.

The reactionary-bureaucratic solution to the problem with which the war has confronted the peoples confines itself to bread cards, to the equal distribution of "popular" foodstuffs, of those absolutely essential to feed the people, without retreating one little bit from bureaucratic and reactionary ideas, that is, from the aim of *not* encouraging the initiative of the poor, the proletariat, the mass of the people ("demos"), of *not* allowing *them* to exercise control over the rich, and of leaving *as many* loopholes *as possible* for the rich to compensate themselves with articles of luxury. And a great number of loopholes are left in *all* countries, we repeat, even in Germany – not to speak of Russia; the "common people" starve while the rich visit health resorts, supplement the meagre official ration by all sorts of "extras" obtained on the side, and do *not* allow *themselves* to be controlled.

In Russia, which has only just made a revolution against the tsarist regime in the name of liberty and equality, in Russia, which, as far as its actual political institutions are concerned, has at once become a democratic republic, what particularly strikes the people, what particularly arouses popular discontent, irritation, anger and indignation is that *everybody* sees the easy way in which the wealthy get around the bread cards. They do it very easily indeed. "From under the counter", and for a very high price, especially if one has *"pull"* (which only the rich have), one can obtain anything, and in large quantities, too. It is the people who are starving. The regulation of consumption is confined within the narrowest bureaucratic-reactionary limits. The government has not the slightest intention of putting regulation on a really revolutionary-democratic footing, is not in the least concerned about doing so.

"Everybody" is suffering from the queues, but – but the rich send their servants to stand in the queues, and even engage special servants for the purpose! And that is "democracy"!

At a time when the country is suffering untold calamities, a revolutionary-democratic policy would not confine itself to bread cards to combat the impending catastrophe but would add, firstly, the compulsory organisation of the whole population in consumers' societies, for otherwise control over consumption cannot be fully exercised; secondly, labour service for the rich, making them perform without pay secretarial and similar duties for these consumers' societies; thirdly, the equal distribution among the population of absolutely all consumer goods, so as really to distribute the burdens of the war equitably; fourthly, the organisation of control in such a way as to have the poorer classes of the population exercise control over the consumption of the rich.

The establishment of real democracy in this sphere and the display of a real revolutionary spirit in the organisation of control by the most needy classes of the people would be a very great stimulus to the employment of all available intellectual forces and to the development of the truly revolutionary energies of the entire people. Yet now the ministers of republican and revolutionary-democratic Russia, exactly like their colleagues in all other imperialist countries, make pompous speeches about "working in common for the good of the people" and about "exerting every effort", but the people see, feel and sense the hypocrisy of this talk.

The result is that no progress is being made, chaos is spreading irresistibly, and a catastrophe is approaching, for our government cannot introduce war-time penal servitude for the workers in the Kornilov, Hindenburg, general imperialist way – the traditions, memories, vestiges, habits and institutions of the *revolution* are still too much alive among the people; our government does not want to take any really serious steps in a revolutionary-democratic direction, for it is thoroughly infected and thoroughly enmeshed by its dependence on the bourgeoisie, its "coalition" with the bourgeoisie, and its fear to encroach on their real privileges.

Government Disruption of the Work of the Democratic Organisations

We have examined various ways and means of combating catastrophe and famine. We have seen everywhere that the contradictions between the democrats, on the one hand, and the government and the bloc of the Socialist-Revolutionaries and Mensheviks which is supporting it, on the other, are irreconcilable. To prove that these contradictions exist in reality, and not merely in our exposition, and that their irreconcilability is *actually* borne out by conflicts affecting the people as a whole, we have only to recall two very typical "results" and lessons of the six months' history of our revolution.

The history of the "reign" of Palchinsky is one lesson. The history of the "reign" and fall of Peshekhonov is the other.

The measures to combat catastrophe and hunger described above boil down to the all-round encouragement (even to the extent of compulsion) of "unionisation" of the population, and primarily the democrats, i.e. the majority of the population, or, above all, the oppressed classes, the workers and peasants, especially the poor peasants. And this is the path which the population itself spontaneously began to adopt in order to cope with the unparalleled difficulties, burdens and hardships of the war.

Tsarism did everything to hamper the free and independent "unionisation" of the population. But after the fall of the tsarist monarchy, democratic organisations began to spring up and grow rapidly all over Russia. The struggle against the catastrophe began to be waged by spontaneously arising democratic organisations – by all sorts of committees of supply, food committees, fuel councils, and so on and so forth.

And the most remarkable thing in the whole six months' history of our revolution, as far as the question we are examining is concerned, is that a government which calls itself republican and revolutionary, and which is supported by the Mensheviks and Socialist-Revolutionaries in the name of the "authorised bodies of revolutionary democracy", fought the democratic organisations and *defeated them*!!

By this fight, Palchinsky earned extremely wide and very sad notoriety all over Russia. He acted behind the government's back, without coming out publicly (just as the Cadets generally preferred to act, willingly pushing forward Tsereteli "for the people", while they themselves arranged all the important business on the quiet). Palchinsky hampered and thwarted every serious measure taken by the spontaneously created democratic organisations, for no serious measure could be taken without "injuring" the excessive profits and wilfulness of the Kit Kityches. And Palchinsky was in fact a loyal defender and servant of the Kit Kityches. Palchinsky went so far – and this fact was reported in the newspapers – as simply to *annul* the orders of the spontaneously created democratic organisations!

The whole history of Palchinsky's "reign" – and he "reigned" for many months, and just when Tsereteli, Skobelev and Chernov were "ministers" – was a monstrous scandal from beginning to end; the will of the people and the decisions of the democrats were frustrated to *please* the capitalists and meet their filthy greed. Of course, only a negligible part of Palchinsky's "feats" could find its way into the press, and a full investigation of the manner in which he *hindered* the struggle against famine can be made only by a truly democratic government of the proletariat when it gains power and submits all the actions of Palchinsky and his like, without concealing anything, *to the judgement* of the people.

It will perhaps be argued that Palchinsky was an exception, and that after all he was removed. But the fact is that Palchinsky was not the exception but the *rule*, that the situation has in no way improved with his removal, that his place has been taken by the same kind of Palchinskys with different names, and that all the "*influence*" of the capitalists, and the entire policy of *frustrating the struggle against hunger to please the capitalists*, has remained intact. For Kerensky and Co. are only a screen for defence of the interests of the capitalists.

The most striking proof of this is the resignation of Peshekhonov, the Food Minister. As we know, Peshekhonov is a very, very moderate Narodnik. But in the organisation of food supply he wanted to work honestly, in contact with and supported by the democratic organisations. The *experience* of Peshekhonov's work and his *resignation* are all the more interesting because this extremely moderate Narodnik, this member of the Popular Socialist Party, who was ready to accept any compromise with the bourgeoisie, was nevertheless compelled to resign! For the Kerensky government, to please the capitalists, landowners and kulaks, had *raised* the fixed prices of grain!

This is how M. Smith describes this "step" and its significance in the newspaper *Svobodnaya Zhizn*[4] No. 1, of September 2:

> Several days before the government decided to raise the fixed prices, the following scene was enacted in the national Food Committee: Rolovich, a Right-winger, a stubborn defender of the interests of private trade and a ruthless opponent of the grain monopoly and state interference in economic affairs, publicly announced with a smug smile that he understood the fixed grain prices would shortly be raised.
>
> The representative of the Soviet of Workers' and Soldiers' Deputies replied by declaring that he knew nothing of the kind, that as long as the revolution in Russia lasted such an act could not take place, and that at any rate the government could not take such a step without first consulting the authorised democratic bodies – the Economic Council and the national Food Committee. This statement was supported by the representative of the Soviet of Peasants' Deputies.
>
> But, alas, reality introduced a very harsh amendment to this counter-version! It was the representative of the wealthy elements and not the representatives of the democrats who turned out to be right. He proved to be excellently informed of the preparations for an attack on democratic rights, although the democratic representatives indignantly denied the very possibility of such an attack.

And so, both the representative of the workers and the representative of the peasants explicitly state their opinion in the name of the vast majority of the people, yet the Kerensky government acts contrary to that opinion, in the interests of the capitalists!

Rolovich, a representative of the capitalists, turned out to be excellently informed behind the backs of the democrats – just as we have always

[4] *Svobodnaya Zhizn* (*Free Life*) – a newspaper with a Menshevik trend published in Petrograd from September 2–8 (15–21), 1917, instead of the suspended *Novaya Zhizn*.

observed, and now observe, that the bourgeois newspapers, *Rech* and *Birzhevka*, are best informed of the doings in the Kerensky government.

What does this possession of excellent information show? Obviously, that the capitalists have their "channels" and *virtually* hold power in their own hands. Kerensky is a figurehead which they use as and when they find necessary. The interests of tens of millions of workers and peasants turn out to have been sacrificed to the profits of a handful of the rich.

And how do our Socialist-Revolutionaries and Mensheviks react to this outrage to the people? Did they address an appeal to the workers and peasants, saying that after this, prison was the only place for Kerensky and his colleagues?

God forbid! The Socialist-Revolutionaries and Mensheviks, through their Economic Department, confined themselves to adopting the impressive resolution to which we have already referred! In this resolution they declare that the raising of grain prices by the Kerensky government is "a *ruinous* measure which deals a *severe blow* both at the food supply and at the whole economic life of the country", and that these ruinous measures have been taken in direct "*violation*" of the law!!

Such are the results of the policy of compromise, of flirting with Kerensky and desiring to "spare" him!

The government violates the law by adopting, in the interests of the rich, the landowners and capitalists, a measure which *ruins* the whole business of control, food supply and the stabilisation of the extremely shaky finances, yet the Socialist-Revolutionaries and Mensheviks continue to talk about an understanding with commercial and industrial circles, continue to attend conferences with Tereshchenko and to spare Kerensky, and confine themselves to a paper resolution of protest, which the government very calmly pigeonholes!!

This reveals with great clarity the fact that the Socialist-Revolutionaries and Mensheviks have betrayed the people and the revolution, and that the Bolsheviks are becoming the real leaders of the masses, *even* of the Socialist-Revolutionary and Menshevik masses.

For only the winning of power by the proletariat, headed by the Bolshevik Party, can put an end to the outrageous actions of Kerensky and Co. and *restore* the work of democratic food distribution, supply and other organisations, which Kerensky and his government are *frustrating*.

The Bolsheviks are acting – and this can be very clearly seen from the above example – as the representatives of the interests of the *whole* people, which are to ensure food distribution and supply and meet the most urgent needs of the workers *and peasants*, despite the vacillating, irresolute and truly treacherous policy of the Socialist-Revolutionaries and Mensheviks, a policy which has brought the country to an act as shameful as this raising of grain prices!

Financial Collapse and Measures to Combat It

There is another side to the problem of raising the fixed grain prices. This raising of prices involves a new chaotic increase in the issuing of paper money, a further increase in the cost of living, increased financial disorganisation and the approach of financial collapse. Everybody admits that the issuing of paper money constitutes the worst form of compulsory loan, that it most of all affects the conditions of the workers, of the poorest section of the population, and that it is the chief evil engendered by financial disorder.

And it is to this measure that the Kerensky government, supported by the Socialist-Revolutionaries and Mensheviks, is resorting!

There is no way of effectively combating financial disorganisation and inevitable financial collapse except that of revolutionary rupture with the interests of capital and that of the organisation of really democratic control, i.e. control from "below", control by the workers and the poor peasants *over* the capitalists, a way to which we referred throughout the earlier part of this exposition.

Large issues of paper money encourage profiteering, enable the capitalists to make millions of roubles, and place tremendous difficulties in the way of a very necessary expansion of production, for the already high cost of materials, machinery, etc., is rising further by leaps and bounds. What can be done about it when the wealth acquired by the rich through profiteering is being concealed?

An income tax with progressive and very high rates for larger and very large incomes might be introduced. Our government has introduced one, following the example of other imperialist governments. But it is largely a fiction, a dead letter, for, firstly, the value of money is falling faster and faster, and, secondly, the more incomes are derived from profiteering and the more securely commercial secrecy is maintained, the greater their concealment.

Real and not nominal control is required to make the tax real and not fictitious. But control over the capitalists is impossible if it remains bureaucratic, for the bureaucracy is itself bound to and interwoven with the bourgeoisie by thousands of threads. That is why in the West-European imperialist states, monarchies and republics alike, financial order is obtained solely by the introduction of "labour service", which creates *war-time penal servitude or war-time slavery* for the workers.

Reactionary-bureaucratic control is the only method known to imperialist states – not excluding the democratic republics of France and America – of foisting the burdens of the war on to the proletariat and the working people.

The basic contradiction in the policy of our government is that, in order not to quarrel with the bourgeoisie, not to destroy the "coalition" with them, the government has to introduce reactionary-bureaucratic control, which it calls "revolutionary-democratic" control, deceiving the people at every step and irritating and angering the masses who have just overthrown tsarism.

Yet only revolutionary-democratic measures, only the organisation of the oppressed classes, the workers and peasants, the masses, into unions would make it possible to establish a most effective control *over the rich* and wage a most successful fight against the concealment of incomes.

An attempt is being made to encourage the use of cheques as a means of avoiding excessive issue of paper money. This measure is of no significance as far as the poor are concerned, for anyway they live from hand to mouth, complete their "economic cycle" in one week and return to the capitalists the few meagre coppers they manage to earn. The use of cheques might have great significance as far as the rich are concerned. It would enable the state, especially in conjunction with such measures as nationalisation of the banks and abolition of commercial secrecy, *really to control* the incomes of the capitalists, really to impose taxation on them, and really to "democratise" (and at the same time bring order into) the financial system.

But this is hampered by the fear of infringing the privileges of the bourgeoisie and destroying the "coalition" with them. For unless truly revolutionary measures are adopted and compulsion is very seriously resorted to, the capitalists will not submit to any control, will not make known their budgets, and will not surrender their stocks of paper money for the democratic state to "keep account" of.

The workers and peasants, organised in unions, by nationalising the banks, making the use of cheques legally compulsory for all rich persons, abolishing commercial secrecy, imposing confiscation of property as a penalty for concealment of incomes, etc., might with extreme ease make control both effective and universal – control, that is, over the rich, and such control as would *secure the return* of paper money *from those* who have it, *from those* who conceal it, *to the Treasury, which issues* it.

This requires a revolutionary dictatorship of the democracy, headed by the revolutionary proletariat; that is, it requires that the democracy should become revolutionary *in fact*. That is the crux of the matter. But that is just what is not wanted by our Socialist-Revolutionaries and Mensheviks, who are deceiving the people by displaying the *flag* of "revolutionary democracy" while they are in fact supporting the reactionary-bureaucratic policy of the bourgeoisie, who, as always, are guided by the rule: "*Après nous le déluge*" – after us the deluge!

We usually do not even notice how thoroughly we are permeated by anti-democratic habits and prejudices regarding the "sanctity" of bourgeois property. When an engineer or banker publishes the income and expenditure of a worker, information about his wages and the productivity of his labour, this is regarded as absolutely legitimate and fair. Nobody thinks of seeing it as an intrusion into the "private life" of the worker, as "spying or informing" on the part of the engineer. Bourgeois society regards the labour and earnings of a wage-worker as *its* open book, any bourgeois being entitled to peer into it at any moment, and at any moment to expose the "luxurious living" of the worker, his supposed "laziness", etc.

Well, and what about reverse control? What if the unions of employees, clerks and *domestic servants* were invited by a *democratic* state to verify the income and expenditure of capitalists, to publish information on the subject and to assist the government in combating concealment of incomes?

What a furious howl against "spying" and "informing" would be raised by the bourgeoisie! When "masters" control servants, or when capitalists control workers, this is considered to be in the nature of things; the private life of the working and exploited people is *not* considered inviolable. The bourgeoisie are entitled to call to account any "wage slave" and at any time to make public his income and expenditure. But if the oppressed attempt to control the oppressor, to show up *his* income and expenditure, to expose his luxurious living even in war-time, when *his* luxurious living is directly responsible for armies at the front starving and perishing – oh, no, the bourgeoisie will not tolerate "spying" and "informing"!

It all boils down to the same thing: the rule of the bourgeoisie *is irreconcilable* with truly revolutionary true democracy. We cannot be revolutionary democrats in the twentieth century and in a capitalist country *if we fear* to advance towards socialism.

Can We Go Forward If We Fear to Advance towards Socialism?

What has been said so far may easily arouse the following objection on the part of a reader who has been brought up on the current opportunist ideas of the Socialist-Revolutionaries and Mensheviks. Most measures described here, he may say, are *already* in effect socialist and not democratic measures!

This current objection, one that is usually raised (in one form or another) in the bourgeois, Socialist-Revolutionary and Menshevik press, is a reactionary defence of backward capitalism, a defence decked out in a Struvean garb. It seems to say that we are not ripe for socialism, that it is too early to "introduce" socialism, that our revolution is a bourgeois revolution and therefore we must be the menials of the bourgeoisie (although the great bourgeois revolutionaries in France 125 years ago made their revolution a great revolution by exercising *terror* against all oppressors, landowners and capitalists alike!).

The pseudo-Marxist lackeys of the bourgeoisie, who have been joined by the Socialist-Revolutionaries and who argue in this way, do not understand (as an examination of the theoretical basis of their opinion shows) what imperialism is, what capitalist monopoly is, what the state is, and what revolutionary democracy is. For anyone who understands this is bound to admit that there can be no advance except towards socialism.

Everybody talks about imperialism. But imperialism is merely monopoly capitalism.

That capitalism in Russia has also become monopoly capitalism is sufficiently attested by the examples of the Produgol, the Prodamet, the Sugar Syndicate, etc. This Sugar Syndicate is an object-lesson in the way monopoly capitalism develops into state-monopoly capitalism.

And what is the state? It is an organisation of the ruling class – in Germany, for instance, of the Junkers and capitalists. And therefore what the German Plekhanovs (Scheidemann, Lensch, and others) call "war-time socialism" is in fact war-time state-monopoly capitalism, or, to put it more simply and clearly, war-time penal servitude for the workers and war-time protection for capitalist profits.

Now try to *substitute* for the Junker-capitalist state, for the landowner-capitalist state, a *revolutionary-democratic* state, i.e. a state which in a revolutionary way abolishes *all* privileges and does not fear to introduce the fullest democracy in a revolutionary way. You will find that, given a really revolutionary-democratic state, state-monopoly capitalism inevitably and unavoidably implies a step, and more than one step, towards socialism!

For if a huge capitalist undertaking becomes a monopoly, it means that it serves the whole nation. If it has become a state monopoly, it means that the state (i.e. the armed organisation of the population, the workers and peasants above all, provided there is *revolutionary* democracy) directs the whole undertaking. In whose interest?

Either in the interest of the landowners and capitalists, in which case we have not a revolutionary-democratic, but a reactionary-bureaucratic state, an imperialist republic.

Or in the interest of revolutionary democracy – and then *it is a step towards socialism.*

For socialism is merely the next step forward from state-capitalist monopoly. Or, in other words, socialism is merely state-capitalist monopoly *which is made to serve the interests of the whole people,* and has to that extent *ceased* to be capitalist monopoly.

There is no middle course here. The objective process of development is such that it is *impossible* to advance from *monopolies* (and the war has magnified their number, role and importance tenfold) without advancing towards socialism.

Either we have to be revolutionary democrats in fact, in which case we must not fear to take steps towards socialism. Or we fear to take steps towards socialism, condemn them in the Plekhanov, Dan or Chernov way, by arguing that our revolution is a bourgeois revolution, that socialism cannot be "introduced", etc., in which case we inevitably sink to the level of Kerensky, Milyukov and Kornilov, i.e. we in a *reactionary-bureaucratic* way suppress the "revolutionary-democratic" aspirations of the workers and peasants.

There is no middle course.

And therein lies the fundamental contradiction of our revolution.

It is impossible to stand still in history in general, and in war-time in particular. We must either advance or retreat. It is *impossible* in twentieth-century Russia, which has won a republic and democracy in a revolutionary way, to go forward without *advancing* towards socialism, without taking steps towards it (steps conditioned and determined by the level of technology and culture: large-scale machine production cannot be "introduced" in peasant agriculture nor abolished in the sugar industry).

But to fear to advance *means* retreating – which the Kerenskys, to the delight of the Milyukovs and Plekhanovs, and with the foolish assistance of the Tseretelis and Chernovs, are actually doing.

The dialectics of history is such that the war, by extraordinarily expediting the transformation of monopoly capitalism into state-monopoly capitalism, has *thereby* extraordinarily advanced mankind towards socialism.

Imperialist war is the eve of socialist revolution. And this not only because the horrors of the war give rise to proletarian revolt – no revolt can bring about socialism unless the economic conditions for socialism are ripe – but because state-monopoly capitalism is a complete *material* preparation for socialism, the *threshold* of socialism, a rung on the ladder of history between which and the rung called socialism *there are no intermediate rungs*.

Our Socialist-Revolutionaries and Mensheviks approach the question of socialism in a doctrinaire way, from the standpoint of a doctrine learnt by heart but poorly understood. They picture socialism as some remote, unknown and dim future.

But socialism is now gazing at us from all the windows of modern capitalism; socialism is outlined directly, *practically*, by every important measure that constitutes a forward step on the basis of this modern capitalism.

What is universal labour conscription?

It is a step forward on the basis of modern monopoly capitalism, a step towards the regulation of economic life as a whole, in accordance with a certain general plan, a step towards the economy of national labour and towards the prevention of its senseless wastage by capitalism.

In Germany it is the Junkers (landowners) and capitalists who are introducing universal labour conscription, and therefore it inevitably becomes war-time penal servitude for the workers.

But take the same institution and think over its significance in a revolutionary-democratic state. Universal labour conscription, introduced, regulated and directed by the Soviets of Workers', Soldiers' and Peasants' Deputies, will *still not* be socialism, but it will *no longer* be capitalism. It will be a tremendous *step towards* socialism, a step from which, if complete democracy is preserved, there can no longer be any retreat back to capitalism, without unparalleled violence being committed against the masses.

The Struggle against Economic Chaos – and the War

A consideration of the measures to avert the impending catastrophe brings us to another supremely important question, namely, the connection between home and foreign policy, or, in other words, the relation between a war of conquest, an imperialist war, and a revolutionary, proletarian war, between a criminal predatory war and a just democratic war.

All the measures to avert catastrophe we have described would, as we have already stated, greatly enhance the defence potential, or, in other words, the military might of the country. That, on the one hand. On the other hand, these measures cannot be put into effect without turning the war of conquest into a just war, turning the war waged by the capitalists in the interests of the capitalists into a war waged by the proletariat in the interests of all the working and exploited people.

And, indeed, nationalisation of the banks and syndicates, taken in conjunction with the abolition of commercial secrecy and the establishment of workers' control over the capitalists, would not only imply a tremendous saving of national labour, the possibility of economising forces and means, but would also imply an improvement in the conditions of the working *masses*, of the majority of the population. As everybody knows, economic organisation is of decisive importance in modern warfare. Russia has enough grain, coal, oil and iron; in this respect, we are in a better position than any of the belligerent European countries. And given a struggle against economic chaos by the measures indicated above, enlisting popular initiative in this struggle, improving the people's conditions, and nationalising the banks and syndicates, Russia could use her revolution and her democracy to raise the whole country to an incomparably higher level of economic organisation.

If instead of the "coalition" with the bourgeoisie, which is hampering every measure of control and sabotaging production, the Socialist-Revolutionaries and Mensheviks had in April effected the transfer of power to the Soviets and had directed their efforts not to playing at "ministerial leapfrog", not to bureaucratically occupying, side by side with the Cadets, ministerial, deputy-ministerial and similar posts, but to guiding the workers and peasants in *their* control *over* the capitalists, in their *war against* the capitalists, Russia would now be a country completely transformed economically, with the land in the hands of the peasants, and with the banks nationalised, i.e. would *to that extent* (and these are extremely important economic bases of modern life) be *superior* to all other capitalist countries.

The defence potential, the military might, of a country whose banks have been nationalised is *superior* to that of a country whose banks remain in private hands. The military might of a peasant country whose land is in the hands of peasant committees is *superior* to that of a country whose land is in the hands of landowners.

Reference is constantly being made to the heroic patriotism and the miracles of military valour performed by the French in 1792–93. But the material, historical economic conditions which alone made such miracles possible are forgotten. The suppression of obsolete feudalism in a really revolutionary way, and the introduction throughout the country of a superior mode of production and free peasant land tenure, effected, moreover, with truly revolutionary democratic speed, determination, energy and devotion – such were the material, economic conditions which with "miraculous" speed saved France by *regenerating* and *renovating* her economic foundation.

The example of France shows one thing, and one thing only, namely, that to render Russia capable of self-defence, to obtain in Russia, too, "miracles" of mass heroism, all that is obsolete must be swept away with "Jacobin" ruthlessness, and Russia renovated and regenerated *economically*. And in the twentieth century this cannot be done merely by sweeping tsarism away (France did not confine herself to this 125 years ago). It cannot be done even by the mere revolutionary abolition of the landed estates (we have not even done that, for the Socialist-Revolutionaries and Mensheviks have betrayed the peasants), by the mere transfer of the land to the peasants. For we are living in the twentieth century, and mastery over the land *without mastery over the banks* cannot regenerate and renovate the life of the people.

The material, industrial renovation of France at the end of the eighteenth century was associated with a political and spiritual renovation, with the dictatorship of revolutionary democrats and the revolutionary proletariat (from which the democrats had not dissociated themselves and with which they were still almost fused), and with a ruthless war declared on everything reactionary. The whole people, and especially the masses, i.e. the *oppressed* classes, were swept up by boundless revolutionary enthusiasm; *everybody* considered the war a just war of defence, as it *actually was*. Revolutionary France was defending herself against reactionary monarchist Europe. It was not in 1792–93, but many years later, *after* the victory of reaction within the country, that the counter-revolutionary dictatorship of Napoleon turned France's wars from defensive wars into wars of conquest.

And what about Russia? We continue to wage an imperialist war in the interests of the capitalists, in alliance with the imperialists and in accordance with the secret treaties the *tsar* concluded with the capitalists of Britain and other countries, promising the Russian capitalists in these treaties the spoliation of foreign lands, of Constantinople, Lvov, Armenia, etc.

The war will remain an unjust, reactionary and predatory war on Russia's part as long as she does not propose a just peace and does not break with imperialism. The social character of the war, its true meaning, is not determined by the position of the enemy troops (as the Socialist-Revolutionaries and Mensheviks think, stooping to the vulgarity of an ignorant yokel). What determines this character is the *policy* of which the war is a continuation ("war is the continuation of politics"), the *class* that is waging the war, and the aims for which it is waging this war.

You cannot lead the people into a predatory war in accordance with secret treaties and expect them to be enthusiastic. The foremost class in revolutionary Russia, the proletariat, is becoming increasingly aware of the criminal character of the war, and not only have the bourgeoisie been unable to shatter this popular conviction, but, on the contrary, awareness of the criminal character of the war is growing. The proletariat of *both metropolitan cities* of Russia has definitely become internationalist!

How, then, can you expect mass enthusiasm for the war!

One is inseparable from the other – home policy is inseparable from foreign policy. The country cannot be made capable of self-defence without the supreme heroism of the people in boldly and resolutely carrying out great economic transformations. And it is impossible to arouse popular heroism without breaking with imperialism, without proposing a democratic peace to all nations, and without thus turning the war from a criminal war of conquest and plunder into a just, revolutionary war of defence.

Only a thorough and consistent break with the capitalists in both home and foreign policy can save our revolution and our country, which is gripped in the iron vice of imperialism.

The Revolutionary Democrats and the Revolutionary Proletariat

To be really revolutionary, the democrats of Russia today must march in very close alliance with the proletariat, supporting it in its struggle as the only thoroughly revolutionary class.

Such is the conclusion prompted by an analysis of the means of combating an impending catastrophe of unparalleled dimensions.

The war has created such an immense crisis, has so strained the material and moral forces of the people, has dealt such blows at the entire modern social organisation, that humanity must now choose between perishing or entrusting its fate to the most revolutionary class for the swiftest and most radical transition to a superior mode of production.

Owing to a number of historical causes – the greater backwardness of Russia, the unusual hardships brought upon her by the war, the utter rottenness of tsarism and the extreme tenacity of the traditions of 1905 – the revolution broke out in Russia earlier than in other countries. The revolution has resulted in Russia catching up with the advanced countries in a few months, as far as her *political* system is concerned.

But that is not enough. The war is inexorable; it puts the alternative with ruthless severity: either perish or overtake and outstrip the advanced countries *economically as well.*

That is possible, for we have before us the experience of a large number of advanced countries, the fruits of their technology and culture. We are receiving moral support from the war protest that is growing in Europe, from the atmosphere of the mounting world-wide workers' revolution. We are being inspired and encouraged by a revolutionary-democratic freedom which is extremely rare in time of imperialist war.

Perish or forge full steam ahead. That is the alternative put by history.

And the attitude of the proletariat to the peasants in such a situation confirms the old Bolshevik concept, correspondingly modifying it, that the peasants must be wrested from the influence of the bourgeosie. That is the sole guarantee of salvation for the revolution.

And the peasants are the most numerous section of the entire petty-bourgeois mass.

Our Socialist-Revolutionaries and Mensheviks have assumed the reactionary function of keeping the peasants under the influence of the bourgeoisie and leading them to a coalition with the bourgeoisie, and not with the proletariat.

The masses are learning rapidly from the experience of the revolution. And the reactionary policy of the Socialist-Revolutionaries and Mensheviks is meeting with failure: they have been beaten in the Soviets of both Petrograd and Moscow. A "Left" opposition is growing in both petty-bourgeois-democratic parties. On September 10, 1917, a city conference of the Socialist-Revolutionaries held in Petrograd gave a two-thirds majority to the *Left* Socialist-Revolutionaries, who incline towards an alliance with the proletariat and reject an alliance (coalition) with the bourgeoisie.

The Socialist-Revolutionaries and Mensheviks repeat a favourite bourgeois comparison – bourgeoisie and democracy. But, in essence, such a comparison is as meaningless as comparing pounds with yards.

There is such a thing as a democratic bourgeoisie, and there is such a thing as bourgeois democracy; one would have to be completely ignorant of both history and political economy to deny this.

The Socialist-Revolutionaries and Mensheviks needed a false comparison to *conceal* the indisputable fact that between the bourgeoisie and the proletariat stand the *petty bourgeoisie*. By virtue of their economic class status, the latter inevitably vacillate between the bourgeoisie and the proletariat.

The Socialist-Revolutionaries and Mensheviks are trying to draw the petty bourgeoisie into an alliance with the bourgeoisie. That is the whole meaning of their "coalition", of the coalition cabinet, and of the whole policy of Kerensky, a typical semi-Cadet. In the six months of the revolution this policy has suffered a complete fiasco.

The Cadets are full of malicious glee. The revolution, they say, has suffered a fiasco; the revolution has been *unable* to cope either with the war or with economic dislocation.

That is not true. It is the *Cadets*, and the *Socialist-Revolutionaries and Mensheviks* who have suffered a fiasco, for this alliance has ruled Russia for six months, only to increase economic dislocation and confuse and aggravate the military situation.

The more complete the fiasco of the *alliance* of the bourgeoisie and the *Socialist-Revolutionaries and Mensheviks*, the sooner the people will *learn their lesson* and the more easily they will find the *correct* way out, namely, the alliance of the peasant poor, i.e. the majority of the peasants, and the proletariat.

September 10–14, 1917

5

One of the Fundamental Questions
of the Revolution

The key question of every revolution is undoubtedly the question of state power. Which class holds power decides everything. When *Dyelo Naroda*, the paper of the chief governing party in Russia, recently complained (No. 147) that, owing to the controversies over power, both the question of the Constituent Assembly and that of bread are being forgotten, the Socialist-Revolutionaries should have been answered, "Blame yourselves. For it is the wavering and indecision of *your* party that are mostly to blame for 'ministerial leapfrog', the interminable postponements of the Constituent Assembly, and the undermining by the capitalists of the planned and agreed measures of a grain monopoly and of providing the country with bread."

The question of power cannot be evaded or brushed aside, because it is the key question determining *everything* in a revolution's development, and in its foreign and domestic policies. It is an undisputed fact that our revolution has "wasted" six months in wavering over the system of power; it is a fact resulting from the wavering policy of the Socialist-Revolutionaries and Mensheviks. In the long run, these parties' wavering policy was determined by the class position of the petty bourgeoisie, by their economic instability in the struggle between capital and labour.

The whole issue at present is whether the petty-bourgeois democrats have learned anything during these great, exceptionally eventful six months. If not, then the revolution is lost, and only a victorious uprising of the proletariat can save it. If they have learned something, the establishment of a stable, unwavering power must be begun immediately. Only if power is based, obviously and unconditionally, *on a majority* of the population can it be stable during a popular revolution, i.e. a revolution which rouses the people, the majority of the workers and peasants, to action. Up to now state power in Russia has *virtually* remained in the hands of the *bourgeoisie*, who are compelled to make only particular concessions (only to begin withdrawing them the following day), to hand out promises (only to fail to carry them out), to search for all sorts of excuses to cover their domination (only to fool the people by a show of "honest coalition"), etc., etc. In words it claims to be a popular, democratic, revolutionary government, but in deeds it is an anti-popular, undemocratic, counter-revolutionary, bourgeois government. This is the contradiction which has existed so far and which has been a source of the complete instability and inconsistency of power, of that "ministerial leapfrog" in which the SRs and Mensheviks have been engaged with such unfortunate (for the people) enthusiasm.

In early June 1917 I told the All-Russia Congress of Soviets that either the Soviets would be dispersed and die an inglorious death, or all power must be transferred to them. The events of July and August very convincingly bore out these words. No matter what lies the lackeys of the bourgeoisie – Potresov, Plekhanov and others, who designate as "broadening the base" of power its virtual transfer to a tiny minority of the people, to the bourgeoisie, the exploiters – may resort to, only the power of the Soviets can be stable, obviously based on a majority of the people.

Only Soviet power could be stable and not be overthrown even in the stormiest moments of the stormiest revolution. Only this power could assure a continuous and broad development of the revolution, a peaceful struggle of parties within the Soviets. Until this power is created, there will inevitably be indecision, instability, vacillation, endless "crises of power", a constant farce of ministerial leapfrog, outbreaks on the Right and on the Left.

The slogan "Power to the Soviets", however, is very often, if not in most cases, taken quite incorrectly to mean a "Cabinet of the parties of the Soviet majority". We would like to go into more detail on this very false notion.

A "Cabinet of the parties of the Soviet majority" means a change of individual ministers, with the entire old government apparatus left intact – a thoroughly bureaucratic and thoroughly undemocratic apparatus incapable of carrying out serious reforms, such as are contained even in the SR and Menshevik programmes.

"Power to the Soviets" means radically reshaping the entire old state apparatus, that bureaucratic apparatus which hampers everything democratic. It means removing this apparatus and substituting for it a new, popular one, i.e. a truly democratic apparatus of Soviets, i.e. the organised and armed majority of the people – the workers, soldiers and peasants. It means allowing the majority of the people initiative and independence not only in the election of deputies, but also in state administration, in effecting reforms and various other changes.

To make this difference clearer and more comprehensible, it is worth recalling a valuable admission made some time ago by the paper of the governing party of the SRs, *Dyelo Naroda*. It wrote that *even* in those ministries which were in the hands of socialist Ministers (this was written during the notorious coalition with the Cadets, when some Mensheviks and SRs were ministers), the entire administrative apparatus had remained unchanged, and hampered work.

This is quite understandable. The entire history of the bourgeois-parliamentary – and also, to a considerable extent, of the bourgeois-constitutional – countries shows that a change of ministers means very little, for the real work of administration is in the hands of an enormous army of officials. This army, however, is undemocratic through and through, it is connected by thousands and millions of threads with the landowners and the bourgeoisie and is completely dependent on them. This army is surrounded by an atmosphere of bourgeois relations, and breathes nothing but this atmosphere. It is set in its ways, petrified, stagnant, and is powerless to break free of this atmosphere. It can only think, feel, or act in the old way. This army is bound by servility to rank, by certain privileges of "Civil" Service; the upper ranks of this army are, through the medium of shares and banks, entirely enslaved by finance capital, being to a certain extent its agent and a vehicle of its interests and influence.

It is the greatest delusion, the greatest self-deception, and a deception of the people, to attempt, by means of *this* state apparatus, to carry out such reforms as the abolition of landed estates without compensation, or the grain monopoly, etc. This apparatus *can* serve a republican bourgeoisie, creating a republic in the shape of a "monarchy without a monarch", like the French Third Republic, but it is absolutely incapable of carrying out reforms which would even seriously curtail or limit the rights of capital, the rights of "sacred private property", much less abolish those rights. That is why it always happens, under all sorts of "coalition" Cabinets that include "socialists", that these socialists, even when individuals among them are perfectly honest, in reality turn out to be either a useless ornament of or a screen for the bourgeois government, a sort of lightning conductor to divert the people's indignation from the government, a tool for the government to deceive the people. This was the case with Louis Blanc in 1848, and dozens of times in Britain and France, when socialists participated in Cabinets. This is also the case with the Chernovs and Tseretelis in 1917. So it has been and so it will be as long as the bourgeois system exists and as long as the old bourgeois, bureaucratic state apparatus remains intact.

The Soviets of Workers', Soldiers' and Peasants' Deputies are particularly valuable because they represent a new *type* of state apparatus, which is immeasurably higher, incomparably more democratic. The SRs and Mensheviks have done everything, the possible and the impossible, to turn the Soviets (particularly the Petrograd Soviet and the All-Russia Soviet, i.e. the Central Executive Committee) into useless talking shops which, under the guise of "control", merely adopted useless resolutions and suggestions which the government shelved with the most polite and kindly smile. The "fresh breeze" of the Kornilov affair,[1] however, which promised a real storm, was enough for all that was musty in the Soviet to blow away for a while, and for the initiative of the revolutionary people to begin expressing itself as something majestic, powerful and invincible.

Let all sceptics learn from this example from history. Let those who say: "We have no apparatus to replace the old one, which inevitably gravitates towards the defence of the bourgeoisie," be ashamed of themselves. For this apparatus *exists*. It is the Soviets. Don't be afraid of the people's initiative and independence. Put your faith in their revolutionary organisations, and you will see *in all* realms of state affairs the same strength, majesty and invincibility of the workers and peasants as were displayed in their unity and their fury against Kornilov.

Lack of faith in the people, fear of their initiative and independence, trepidation before their revolutionary energy instead of all-round and unqualified support for it – this is where the SR and Menshevik leaders

---

[1] The counter-revolutionary revolt of the bourgeoisie and the landowners in August 1917, which was headed by the Commander-in-Chief of the Army, the tsarist General Kornilov. The plotters planned to take Petrograd, destroy the Bolshevik Party, disperse the Soviets and set up a military dictatorship with a view to restoring the monarchy. Kerensky, the head of the Provisional Government, took part in the plot, but when the revolt got under way he realised that he would be swept away with Kornilov, and washed his hands of the whole business: be declared the revolt was aimed against the Provisional Government.

It broke out on August 25 (September 7), with Kornilov sending the Third Cavalry Corps against Petrograd, where counter-revolutionary organisations were itching to go into action.

The mass struggle against Kornilov was led by the Bolshevik Party, which continued, as Lenin demanded, to expose the Provisional Government and its Socialist-Revolutionary and Menshevik accomplices. The Central Committee of the Bolshevik Party rallied the workers of Petrograd, and the revolutionary soldiers and sailors, to struggle against the mutineers. Petrograd workers swiftly organised Red Guard units, and revolutionary committees were set up in several places. The advance of the Kornilov troops was stopped and their morale undermined by Bolshevik agitators.

The Kornilov revolt was crushed by the workers and peasants led by the Bolshevik Party. Under the pressure of the masses, the Provisional Government was forced to order the arrest and prosecution of Kornilov and his accomplices on charges of organising the revolt.

have sinned most of all. This is where we find one of the deepest roots of their indecision, their vacillation, their infinite and infinitely fruitless attempts to pour new wine into the old bottles of the old, bureaucratic state apparatus.

Take the history of the democratisation of the army in the 1917 Russian revolution, the history of the Chernov Ministry, of Palchinsky's "reign", and of Peshekhonov's resignation – you will find what we have said above strikingly borne out at every step. Because there was no full confidence in the elected soldiers' organisations and no absolute observance of the principle of soldiers electing their commanding officers, the Kornilovs, Kaledins and counter-revolutionary officers came to be at the head of the army. This is a fact. Without deliberately closing one's eyes, one cannot fail to see that *after* the Kornilov affair Kerensky's government is *leaving everything as before*, that *in fact it is bringing back the Kornilov affair*. The appointment of Alexeyev, the "peace" with the Klembovskys, Gagarins, Bagrations and other Kornilov men, and leniency in the treatment of Kornilov and Kaledin all very clearly prove that Kerensky is in fact bringing back the Kornilov affair.

There is no middle course. This has been shown by experience. Either all power goes to the Soviets and the army is made fully democratic, or another Kornilov affair occurs.

And what about the history of the Chernov Ministry? Didn't it prove that every more or less serious step towards actually satisfying the peasants' needs, every step showing confidence in the peasants and in their mass organisations and actions, evoked very great enthusiasm among them? Chernov, however, had to spend almost four months "haggling" with the Cadets and bureaucrats, who by endless delays and intrigues finally forced him to resign without having accomplished anything. For and during these four months the landowners and capitalists "won the game" – they saved the landed estates, delayed the convocation of the Constituent Assembly, and even started a number of repressions against the land committees.

There is no middle course. This has been shown by experience. Either all power goes to the Soviets both centrally and locally, and all land is given to the peasants *immediately*, pending the Constituent Assembly's decision, or the landowners and capitalists obstruct every step, restore the landowners' power, drive the peasants into a rage and carry things to an exceedingly violent peasant revolt.

The same thing happened when the capitalists (with the aid of Palchinsky) crushed every more or less serious attempt to supervise production, when the merchants thwarted the grain monopoly and broke up the regulated democratic distribution of grain and other foodstuffs just begun by Peshekhonov.

What is now necessary in Russia is not to invent "new reforms", not to make "plans" for "comprehensive" changes. Nothing of the kind. This is how the situation is depicted – deliberately depicted in a false light – by the capitalists, the Potresovs, the Plekhanovs, who shout against "introducing socialism" and against the "dictatorship of the proletariat". The situation in Russia in fact is such that the unprecedented burdens and hardships of the war, the unparalleled and very real danger of economic dislocation and famine, have of themselves suggested the way out, have of themselves not only pointed out, but advanced reforms and other changes as absolutely necessary. These changes must be the grain monopoly, control over production and distribution, restriction of the issue of paper money, a fair exchange of grain for manufactured goods, etc.

Everyone recognises measures of this kind and in this direction as inevitable, and in many places they have already been launched from the most diverse sides. *They have already been launched*, but they have been and are being obstructed everywhere by the resistance of the landowners and the capitalists, which is being put up through the Kerensky government (an utterly bourgeois and Bonapartist government *in reality*), through the old bureaucratic state apparatus, and through the direct and indirect pressure of Russian and "Allied" finance capital.

Not so long ago I. Prilezhayev, lamenting the resignation of Peshekhonov and the collapse of the fixed prices and the grain monopoly, wrote in *Dyelo Naroda* (No. 147): "Courage and resolve are what our governments of all compositions have lacked. . . . The revolutionary democrats must not wait; they must themselves show initiative, and intervene in the economic chaos in a planned way. . . . If anywhere, it is here that a firm course and a determined government are necessary."

That goes without saying. Words of gold. The only trouble is that the author forgot that the question of the firm course to take, of courage and resolve, is not a personal matter, but a question of which *class* is capable of manifesting courage and resolve. The only class capable of this is the proletariat. A courageous and resolute government steering a firm course is nothing but the dictatorship of the proletariat and the poor peasants. I. Prilezhayev unwittingly longs for *this dictatorship*.

What would such a dictatorship mean in practice? It would mean nothing but the fact that the resistance of the Kornilov men would be broken and the democratisation of the army restored and completed. Two days after its creation ninety-nine per cent of the army would be enthusiastic supporters of this dictatorship. This dictatorship would give land to the peasants and full power to the local peasant committees. How can anyone in his right senses doubt that the peasants would support this dictatorship? What Peshekhonov only *promised* ("the resistance of the capitalists has been broken" was what Peshekhonov actually said in his famous speech before the Congress of Soviets), this dictatorship would put into effect, would translate into reality. At the same time the democratic organisations of food supply, control, etc., that have already begun to form would in no way be eliminated. They would, on the contrary, be supported and developed, and all obstacles in the way of their work would be removed.

Only the dictatorship of the proletariat and the poor peasants is capable of smashing the resistance of the capitalists, of displaying truly supreme courage and determination in the exercise of power, and of securing the enthusiastic, selfless and truly heroic support of the masses both in the army and among the peasants.

Power to the Soviets – this is the only way to make further progress gradual, peaceful and smooth, keeping perfect pace with the political awareness and resolve of the majority of the people and with their own experience. Power to the Soviets means the complete transfer of the country's administration and economic control into the hands of the workers and peasants, to whom *nobody* would dare offer resistance and who, through practice, through their own experience, *would soon learn* how to distribute the land, products and grain properly.

6

The Bolsheviks Must Assume Power

A Letter to the Central Committee and the Petrograd and Moscow Committees of the RSDLP (B)

The Bolsheviks, having obtained a majority in the Soviets of Workers' and Soldiers' Deputies of both capitals, can and must take state power into their own hands.[1]

They can because the active majority of revolutionary elements in the two chief cities is large enough to carry the people with it, to overcome the opponent's resistance, to smash him, and to gain and retain power. For the Bolsheviks, by immediately proposing a democratic peace, by immediately giving the land to the peasants and by re-establishing the democratic institutions and liberties which have been mangled and shattered by Kerensky, will form a government which *nobody* will be able to overthrow.

The majority of the people are *on our side*. This was proved by the long and painful course of events from May 6 to August 31 and to September 12.[2] The majority gained in the Soviets of the metropolitan cities *resulted* from the people coming over *to our side*. The wavering of the Socialist-

---

[1] The letters were discussed by the Central Committee on September 15 (28), 1917, which decided to call a meeting shortly to discuss tactics. The following question was put to the vote: preservation of only one copy of Lenin's letters. The vote was six in favour, four against and six abstentions.

[2] May 6: announcement of the first coalition Provisional Government; August 31: the Petrograd Soviet of Workers' and Soldiers' Deputies passed a Bolshevik resolution calling for the establishment of a Soviet Government; September 12: the date set by the Central Executive Committee of the Soviets of Workers' and Soldiers' Deputies and the Executive Committee of the All-Russia Soviet of Peasants' Deputies, both dominated by Socialist-Revolutionaries and Mensheviks, for the convocation of a Democratic Conference. The Democratic Conference took place in Petrograd September 14–22 (September 27–October 5), 1917.

Revolutionaries[3] and Mensheviks and the increase in the number of internationalists within their ranks prove the same thing.

The Democratic Conference[4] represents not a majority of the revolutionary people, but *only the compromising upper strata of the petty bourgeoisie.*
We must not be deceived by the election figures; elections prove nothing.
Compare the elections to the city councils of Petrograd and Moscow with
the elections to the Soviets. Compare the elections in Moscow with the
Moscow strike of August 12. Those are objective facts regarding that
majority of revolutionary elements that are leading the people.

The Democratic Conference is deceiving the peasants; it is giving them
neither peace nor land.

A Bolshevik government alone will satisfy the demands of the peasants.

Why must the Bolsheviks assume power *at this very moment*?

Because the impending surrender of Petrograd will make our chances a
hundred times less favourable.

[3] Socialist-Revolutionaries – a petty-bourgeois party founded in late 1901 and early
1902 through the merger of various Narodnik groups and circles (League of Socialist-
Revolutionaries, Socialist-Revolutionary Party, etc.) which professed a hotch-potch of
Narodnik and revisionist ideas. During the First World War, most of its members held
social-chauvinist views.

[4] The All-Russia Democratic Conference was called by the Central Executive Committee of the Soviets, which was dominated by Mensheviks and Socialist-Revolutionaries,
to decide on the question of state power, but its actual purpose was to switch the
attention of the masses away from the mounting revolutionary movement. It was first
set for September 12 (25), and later postponed to September 14–22 (September 27–
October 5), 1917, when it was held in Petrograd and attended by more than 1,500
delegates. The Menshevik and Socialist-Revolutionary leaders did their utmost to reduce
the number of workers' and peasants' delegates and increase those of various petty-
bourgeois and bourgeois groups, thereby securing a majority.

The Central Committee of the RSDLP (B) met on September 3 (16) and decided to
take part. It circulated a letter among local Party organisations instructing them to "do
their utmost to build up the largest possible well-knit group of delegates from among
our Party members". The Bolsheviks decided to attend in order to expose the Mensheviks
and the Socialist-Revolutionaries.

The Democratic Conference adopted a resolution on the establishment of a Pre-
parliament (Caretaker Council of the Republic), which was an attempt to create the
impression that Russia now had a parliamentary system. Actually, according to the
Provisional Government's ordinance, the Pre-parliament was to be a consultative body
under the Government.

A meeting of the Bolshevik delegates to the Democratic Conference called by the
Central Committee decided, by a vote of 77 to 50, to take part in the Pre-parliament.

And it is *not in our power* to prevent the surrender of Petrograd while the army is headed by Kerensky and Co.

Nor can we "wait" for the Constituent Assembly, for by surrendering Petrograd, Kerensky and Co. *can* always *frustrate* its convocation. Our Party alone, on taking power, can secure the Constituent Assembly's convocation; it will then accuse the other parties of procrastination, and will be able to substantiate its accusations.[5]

A separate peace between the British and German imperialists must and can be prevented, but only by quick action.

The people are tired of the waverings of the Mensheviks and Socialist-Revolutionaries. It is only our victory in the metropolitan cities that will carry the peasants with us.

We are concerned now not with the "day", or "moment" of insurrection in the narrow sense of the word. That will be decided only by the common voice of those who are *in contact* with the workers and soldiers, with *the masses*.

The point is that now, at the Democratic Conference our Party has virtually *its own congress*, and this congress (whether it wishes to or not) *must* decide the *fate of the revolution*.

The point is to make the *task* clear to the Party. The present task must be an *armed uprising* in Petrograd and Moscow (with its region), the seizing of power and the overthrow of the government. We must consider *how* to agitate for this without expressly saying as much in the press.

[5] The Provisional Government announced the convocation of the Constituent Assembly in its declaration of March 2 (15), 1917. On June 14 (27) it adopted a decision setting the election for September 17 (30), but in August postponed the date to November 12 (25).

The election was actually held after the October Socialist Revolution at the appointed time and on party lists drawn up before the revolution, in accordance with a Provisional Government ordinance. At the time of the election the bulk of the people had not yet realised the full implications of the socialist revolution, a fact which the Right Socialist-Revolutionaries used to win a majority in the areas remote from the capital and the industrial centres. The Constituent Assembly was called by the Soviet Government and opened in Petrograd on January 5 (18), 1918. Its counter-revolutionary majority rejected the Declaration of Rights of the Working and Exploited People, which was placed before it by the All-Russia Central Executive Committee, and refused to recognise Soviet power. It was dissolved by a decree of the Central Executive Committee on January 6 (19).

We must remember and weigh Marx's words about insurrection, "*Insurrection is an art*",[6] etc.

It would be naive to wait for a "formal" majority for the Bolsheviks. No revolution ever waits for *that*. Kerensky and Co. are not waiting either, and are preparing to surrender Petrograd. It is the wretched waverings of the Democratic Conference that are bound to exhaust the patience of the workers of Petrograd and Moscow! History will not forgive us if we do not assume power now.

There is no apparatus? There is an apparatus – the Soviets and the democratic organisations. The international situation *right* now, on *the eve* of the conclusion of a separate peace between the British and the Germans, is *in our favour*. To propose peace to the nations right now means *to win*.

By taking power both in Moscow and in Petrograd at once (it doesn't matter which comes first; Moscow may possibly begin), we shall win *absolutely and unquestionably*.

N. Lenin

---

[6] See Engels's *Revolution and Counter-Revolution in Germany*, which was published in instalments in the *New York Daily Tribune* in 1851 and 1852. It bore the signature of Marx, who had intended to write the work but was too busy with his economic studies and asked Engels to do it. Engels consulted Marx on various points, and submitted the articles for his perusal before dispatching them to the paper. The fact that the work was written by Engels came out later with the publication of their correspondence.

7

Marxism and Insurrection

A Letter to the Central Committee of the RSDLP (B)

One of the most vicious and probably most widespread distortions of Marxism resorted to by the dominant "socialist" parties is the opportunist lie that preparation for insurrection, and generally the treatment of insurrection as an art, is "Blanquism".[1]

Bernstein, the leader of opportunism, has already earned himself unfortunate fame by accusing Marxism of Blanquism, and when our present-day opportunists cry Blanquism they do not improve on or "enrich" the meagre "ideas" of Bernstein one little bit.

Marxists are accused of Blanquism for treating insurrection as an art! Can there be a more flagrant perversion of the truth, when not a single Marxist will deny that it was Marx who expressed himself on this score in the most definite, precise and categorical manner, referring to insurrection specifically as an *art*, saying that it must be treated as an art, that you must *win* the first success and then proceed from success to success, never ceasing the *offensive* against the enemy, taking advantage of his confusion, etc., etc.?

To be successful, insurrection must rely not upon conspiracy and not upon a party, but upon the advanced class. That is the first point. Insurrection must rely upon a *revolutionary upsurge of the people*. That is the second point. Insurrection must rely upon that *turning-point* in the history of the growing revolution when the activity of the advanced ranks of the people is at its height, and when the *vacillations* in the ranks of the enemy and *in the ranks of the weak, half-hearted and irresolute friends of the*

---

[1] Blanquism – a trend within the French socialist movement led by Louis Auguste Blanqui (1805–81), an outstanding utopian communist. Blanquism expects that mankind will be emancipated from wage slavery, not by the proletarian class struggle, but through a conspiracy hatched by a small minority of intellectuals.

revolution are strongest. That is the third point. And these three conditions for raising the question of insurrection distinguish *Marxism from Blanquism*.

Once these conditions exist, however, to refuse to treat insurrection as an art is a betrayal of Marxism and a betrayal of the revolution.

To show that it is precisely the present moment that the Party *must* recognise as the one in which the entire course of events has objectively placed *insurrection* on the order of the day, and that insurrection must be treated as an art, it will perhaps be best to use the method of comparison, and to draw a parallel between July 3–4[2] and the September days.

---

[2] What Lenin has in mind are the mass demonstrations which took place in Petrograd on July 3–4 (16–17), 1917. It was a movement of soldiers, sailors and workers, who were incensed at the Provisional Government for sending troops into a patently hopeless offensive which proved a fiasco. It started on July 3 (16) with a demonstration by the First Machine-Gun Regiment in the Vyborg District, and threatened to develop into an armed revolt against the Provisional Government.

The Bolshevik Party was opposed to insurrection at that time because it believed that the revolutionary crisis had not yet come to a head. The Central Committee, meeting at 4.00 p.m. on July 3 (16), decided to refrain from taking action, and a similar decision was adopted by the Second Petrograd City Conference of Bolsheviks which was just then in session. Its delegates went to the factories and the districts to stop the masses from going into action, but the movement had already got under way and nothing could be done to stop it.

Late that night, the Central Committee, together with the Petrograd Committee and the Military Organisation, took account of the mood of the masses and decided to take part in the demonstration to lend it a peaceful and organised character. Lenin was away on a short holiday after an exhausting stretch of work. Being informed of the events, he returned to Petrograd on the morning of July 4 (17) and assumed leadership.

More than 500,000 people took part in the demonstration on July 4 (17). The demonstrators carried Bolshevik slogans, such as "All Power to the Soviets", and demanded that the All-Russia Central Executive Committee of the Soviet should take power. But the Socialist-Revolutionary and Menshevik leaders refused to do so. The Provisional Government, with the knowledge and consent of the Central Executive Committee, which was dominated by the Mensheviks and Socialist-Revolutionaries, sent detachments of officer cadets and Cossacks to attack and shoot down the peaceful demonstrators. Counter-revolutionary troops were brought in from the front to disperse the demonstrations.

That night, Lenin presided at a meeting of members of the Central Committee and the Petrograd Committee, which adopted a decision to stop the demonstrations in an organised manner. This was a wise step, for it helped to save the main revolutionary force from defeat. The Mensheviks and Socialist-Revolutionaries acted in a manner which helped the counter-revolutionaries: they joined the bourgeoisie in attacking the Bolshevik Party. The Bolshevik newspapers *Pravda*, *Soldatskaya Pravda* (*Soldiers' Truth*) and others were closed down by the Provisional Government, while the *Trud* Printing

On July 3–4 it could have been argued, without violating the truth, that the correct thing to do was to take power, for our enemies would in any case have accused us of insurrection and ruthlessly treated us as rebels. However, to have decided on this account in favour of taking power at that time would have been wrong, because the objective conditions for the victory of the insurrection did not exist.

(1) We still lacked the support of the class which is the vanguard of the revolution.

We still did not have a majority among the workers and soldiers of Petrograd and Moscow. Now we have a majority in both Soviets. It was created *solely* by the history of July and August, by the experience of the "ruthless treatment" meted out to the Bolsheviks, and by the experience of the Kornilov revolt.

(2) There was no country-wide revolutionary upsurge at that time. There is now, after the Kornilov revolt; the situation in the provinces and assumption of power by the Soviets in many localities prove this.

(3) At that time there was no *vacillation* on any serious political scale among our enemies and among the irresolute petty bourgeoisie. Now the vacillation is enormous. Our main enemy, Allied and world imperialism (for world imperialism is headed by the "Allies"), *has begun to waver* between a war to a victorious finish and a separate peace directed against Russia. Our petty-bourgeois democrats, having clearly lost their majority among the people, have begun to vacillate enormously, and have rejected a bloc, i.e. a coalition, with the Cadets.[3]

House, operated on funds donated by the workers, was destroyed. The workers were disarmed and arrested, and searches and persecution were started. The revolutionary units of the Petrograd garrison were withdrawn from the capital and sent to the front.

After the July events, power in the country passed into the hands of the counter-revolutionary Provisional Government, with the Soviet an impotent appendage. The period of dual power was at an end, and so was the revolution's peaceful stage. The Bolsheviks were faced with the task of preparing an armed insurrection to overthrow the Provisional Government.

[3] Cadets (Constitutional-Democratic Party) – the leading party of the liberal-monarchist bourgeoisie in Russia, set up in October 1905. Its membership was made up of capitalists, landowners serving on local councils, and bourgeois intellectuals. Among its more prominent members were P. N. Milyukov, S. A. Muromtsev, V. A. Maklakov, A. I. Shingaryov, and P. B. Struve. The Cadets eventually developed into a party of the imperialist bourgeoisie. During the First World War they actively supported the tsarist government's foreign policy of aggrandisement. During the bourgeois-democratic revolution of February 1917, they tried to save the monarchy; playing a key part in the bourgeois Provisional Government; they conducted a counter-revolutionary policy opposed to the people's interests.

(4) Therefore, an insurrection on July 3–4 would have been a mistake; we could not have retained power either physically or politically. We could not have retained it physically even though Petrograd was at times in our hands, because at that time our workers and soldiers would not have *fought and died* for Petrograd. There was not at the time that "savageness", or fierce hatred *both* of the Kerenskys and of the Tseretelis and Chernovs. Our people had still not been tempered by the experience of the persecution of the Bolsheviks in which the Socialist-Revolutionaries and Mensheviks participated.

We could not have retained power politically on July 3–4 because, *before the Kornilov revolt*, the army and the provinces could and would have marched against Petrograd.

Now the picture is entirely different.

We have the following of the majority of a *class*, the vanguard of the revolution, the vanguard of the people, which is capable of carrying the masses with it.

We have the following of the *majority* of the people, because Chernov's resignation, while by no means the only symptom, is the most striking and obvious symptom that the peasants *will not receive land* from the Socialist-Revolutionaries' bloc (or from the Socialist-Revolutionaries themselves). And that is the chief reason for the popular character of the revolution.

We are in the advantageous position of a party that knows for certain which way to go at a time when *imperialism as a whole* and the Menshevik and Socialist-Revolutionary bloc as a whole are vacillating in an incredible fashion.

Our victory is assured, for the people are close to desperation, and we are showing the entire people a sure way out; we demonstrated to the entire people during the "Kornilov days" the value of our leadership, and then *proposed* to the politicians of the bloc a compromise, *which they rejected*, although there is no let-up in their vacillations.

It would be a great mistake to think that our offer of a compromise had not *yet* been rejected, and that the Democratic Conference may *still* accept it. The compromise was proposed by a *party* to *parties*; it could not have been proposed in any other way. It was rejected by *parties*. The Democratic Conference is a conference, and nothing more. One thing must not be forgotten, namely, that the *majority* of the revolutionary people, the poor, embittered peasants, are not represented in it. It is a conference of *a minority of the people* – this obvious truth must not be forgotten. It would be a big mistake, sheer parliamentary cretinism on our part, if we were to regard the Democratic Conference as a parliament; for even *if it were* to proclaim itself a permanent and sovereign parliament of the revolution, it would nevertheless *decide nothing*. The power of decision lies *outside* it in the working-class quarters of Petrograd and Moscow.

All the objective conditions exist for a successful insurrection. We have the exceptional advantage of a situation in which *only* our victory in the insurrection can put an end to that most painful thing on earth, vacillation, which has worn the people out; in which only our victory in the insurrection will give the peasants land immediately; a situation in which *only our victory* in the insurrection can *foil* the game of a separate peace directed against the revolution – foil it by publicly proposing a fuller, more just and earlier peace, a peace that will *benefit* the revolution.

Finally, our Party alone *can*, by a victorious insurrection, save Petrograd; for if our proposal for peace is rejected, if we do not secure even an armistice, then we shall become "defencists", we shall place ourselves *at the head of the war parties*, we shall be the *war party par excellence*, and we shall conduct the war in a truly revolutionary manner. We shall take away all the bread and boots from the capitalists. We shall leave them only crusts and dress them in bast shoes. We shall send all the bread and footwear to the front.

And then we shall save Petrograd.

The resources, both material and spiritual, for a truly revolutionary war in Russia are still immense; the chances are a hundred to one that the Germans will grant us at least an armistice. And to secure an armistice now would in itself mean to win the *whole world*.

Having recognised the absolute necessity for an insurrection of the workers of Petrograd and Moscow in order to save the revolution and to save Russia from a "separate" partition by the imperialists of both groups, we must first adapt our political tactics at the Conference to the conditions of the growing insurrection; secondly, we must show that it is not only in words that we accept Marx's idea that insurrection must be treated as an art.

At the Conference we must immediately cement the Bolshevik group, without striving after numbers, and without fearing to leave the waverers in the waverers' camp. They are more useful to the cause of the revolution *there* than in the camp of the resolute and devoted fighters.

We must draw up a brief declaration from the Bolsheviks, emphasising in no uncertain manner the irrelevance of long speeches and of "speeches" in general, the necessity for immediate action to save the revolution, the absolute necessity for a complete break with the bourgeoisie, for the removal of the present government, in its entirety, for a complete rupture with the Anglo-French imperialists, who are preparing a "separate" partition of Russia, and for the immediate transfer of all power to *revolutionary democrats, headed by the revolutionary proletariat.*

Our declaration must give the briefest and most trenchant formulation of this conclusion in connection with the programme proposals of peace for the peoples, land for the peasants, confiscation of scandalous profits, and a check on the scandalous sabotage of production by the capitalists.

The briefer and more trenchant the declaration, the better. Only two other highly important points must be clearly indicated in it, namely, that the people are worn out by the vacillations, that they are fed up with the irresolution of the Socialist-Revolutionaries and Mensheviks; and that we are definitely breaking with these *parties* because they have betrayed the revolution.

And another thing. By immediately proposing a peace without annexations, by immediately breaking with the Allied imperialists and with all imperialists, either we shall at once obtain an armistice, or the entire revolutionary proletariat will rally to the defence of the country, and a really just, really revolutionary war will then be waged by revolutionary democrats under the leadership of the proletariat.

Having read this declaration, and having appealed for *decisions* and not talk, for *action* and not resolution-writing, we must *dispatch* our entire group to the *factories and the barracks*. Their place is there, the pulse of life is there, there is the source of salvation for our revolution, and there is the motive force of the Democratic Conference.

There, in ardent and impassioned speeches, we must explain our programme and put the alternative: either the Conference adopts it *in its entirety*, or else insurrection. There is no middle course. Delay is impossible. The revolution is dying.

By putting the question in this way, by concentrating our entire group in the factories and barracks, *we shall be able to determine the right moment to start the insurrection.*

In order to treat insurrection in a Marxist way, i.e. as an art, we must at the same time, without losing a single moment, organise a *headquarters* of the insurgent detachments, distribute our forces, move the reliable regiments to the most important points, surround the Alexandrinsky Theatre, occupy the Peter and Paul Fortress,[4] arrest the General Staff and the government, and move against the officer cadets and the Savage Division[5] those detachments which would rather die than allow the enemy to approach the strategic points of the city. We must mobilise the armed workers and call them to fight the last desperate fight, occupy the telegraph and the telephone exchange at once, move *our* insurrection headquarters to the central telephone exchange, and connect it by telephone with all the factories, all the regiments, all the points of armed fighting, etc.

Of course, this is all by way of example, only to *illustrate* the fact that at the present moment it is impossible to remain loyal to Marxism, to remain loyal to the revolution, *unless insurrection is treated as an art.*

N. Lenin

[4] The Alexandrinsky Theatre in Petrograd was the place where the Democratic Conference was convened.

The Peter and Paul Fortress on the Neva opposite the Winter Palace, served as a state prison for the tsar's political opponents. Now a museum, it had a large arsenal and was strategically situated.

[5] The Savage Division – formed during World War I from volunteer mountaineers of the North Caucasus. General Kornilov tried to use it as a battering ram in his assault on revolutionary Petrograd.

8

The Tasks of the Revolution

Russia is a country of the petty bourgeoisie, by far the greater part of the population belonging to this class. Its vacillations between the bourgeoisie and the proletariat are inevitable, and only when it joins the proletariat is the victory of the revolution, of the cause of peace, freedom, and land for the working people, assured easily, peacefully, quickly, and smoothly.

The course of our revolution shows us these vacillations in practice. Let us then not harbour any illusions about the Socialist-Revolutionary and Menshevik parties; let us stick firmly to the path of our proletarian class. The poverty of the poor peasants, the horrors of the war, the horrors of hunger – all these are showing the masses more and more clearly the correctness of the proletarian path, the need to support the proletarian revolution.

The "peaceful" hopes of the petty bourgeoisie that there might be a "coalition" with the bourgeoisie and agreements with them, that it will be possible to wait "calmly" for the "speedy" convocation of the Constituent Assembly, etc., have been mercilessly, cruelly, implacably destroyed by the course of the revolution. The Kornilov revolt was the last cruel lesson, a lesson on a grand scale, supplementing thousands upon thousands of small lessons in which workers and peasants were deceived by local capitalists and landowners, in which soldiers were deceived by the officers, etc., etc.

Discontent, indignation and wrath are growing in the army, among the peasantry and among the workers. The "coalition" of the Socialist-Revolutionaries and Mensheviks with the bourgeoisie, promising everything and fulfilling nothing, is irritating the masses, is opening their eyes, is pushing them towards insurrection.

There is a growing Left opposition among the Socialist-Revolutionaries (Spiridonova and others) and among the Mensheviks (Martov and others), which has already reached forty per cent of the Council and Congress of those parties. And down *below*, among the proletariat and the peasantry, particularly the poorest sections, the *majority* of the Socialist-Revolutionaries and Mensheviks belong to the *Lefts*.

The Kornilov revolt is instructive, and has proved a good lesson.

It is impossible to know whether the Soviets will be able to go farther than the leaders of the Socialist-Revolutionaries and Mensheviks, and thus ensure a peaceful development of the revolution, or whether they will continue to mark time, thus making a proletarian uprising inevitable.

We cannot know this.

Our business is to help get everything possible done to make sure the "last" chance for a peaceful development of the revolution, to help by the presentation of our programme, by making clear its national character, its absolute accord with the interests and demands of a vast majority of the population.

The following lines are an essay in the presentation of such a programme.

Let us take it more to those down below, to the masses, to the office employees, to the workers, to the peasants, not only to our supporters, but particularly to those who follow the Socialist-Revolutionaries, to the non-party elements, to the ignorant. Let us lift them up so that they can pass an independent judgement, make their own decisions, send *their own* delegations to the Conference, to the Soviets, to the government, and our work will not have been in vain, *no matter what* the outcome of the Conference. This will then prove useful for the Conference, for the elections to the Constituent Assembly, and for all other political activity in general.

Experience teaches us that the Bolshevik programme and tactics are correct. So little time passed, so much happened from April 20 to the Kornilov revolt.

The experience of the *masses*, the experience of *oppressed* classes taught them very, very much in that time; the leaders of the Socialist-Revolutionaries and Mensheviks have completely cut adrift from the masses. This will most certainly be revealed in the discussion of our concrete programme in so far as we are able to bring it to the notice of the masses.

Agreements with the Capitalists are Disastrous

1. To leave in power the representatives of the bourgeoisie, even a small number of them, to leave in power such notorious Kornilovites as Generals Alexeyev, Klembovsky, Bagration, Gagarin, and others, or such as have proved their complete powerlessness in face of the bourgeoisie, and their ability of acting Bonaparte-fashion like Kerensky, is, on the one hand,

merely opening the door wide to famine and the inevitable economic catastrophe which the capitalists are purposely accelerating and intensifying; on the other hand, it will lead to a military catastrophe, since the army hates the General Staff and cannot enthusiastically participate in the imperialist war. Besides, there is no doubt that Kornilovite generals and officers remaining in power will *deliberately open the front to the Germans*, as they have done in Galicia and Riga. This can be prevented only by the formation of a new government on a new basis, as expounded below. To continue any kind of agreements with the bourgeoisie after all that we have gone through since April 20 would be, on the part of the Socialist-Revolutionaries and Mensheviks, not only an error but a direct betrayal of the people and of the revolution.

Power to the Soviets

2. All power in the country must pass exclusively to the representatives of the Soviets of Workers', Soldiers' and Peasants' Deputies on the basis of a definite programme and under the condition of the government being fully responsible to the Soviets. New elections to the Soviets must be held immediately, both to record the experience of the people during the recent weeks of the revolution, which have been particularly eventful, and to eliminate crying injustices (lack of proportional representation, unequal elections, etc.) which in some cases still remain.

All power locally, wherever there are not yet any democratically elected institutions, and also in the army, must be taken over exclusively by the local Soviets and by commissars and other institutions elected by them, but only those that have been properly elected. Workers and revolutionary troops, i.e. those who have in practice shown their ability to suppress the Kornilovites, must everywhere be armed, and this must be done with the full support of the state.

Peace to the Peoples

3. The Soviet Government must *straight away* offer to *all* the belligerent peoples (i.e. simultaneously both to their governments and to the worker and peasant masses) to conclude an immediate general peace on democratic terms, and also to conclude an immediate armistice (even if only for three months).

The main condition for a democratic peace is the renunciation of annexations (seizures) – not in the incorrect sense that all powers get back what they have lost, but in the only correct sense that *every* nationality without any exception, both in Europe and in the colonies, shall obtain its freedom and the possibility to decide for itself whether it is to form a *separate* state or whether it is to enter into the composition of some other state.

In offering the peace terms, the Soviet Government must itself immediately take steps towards their fulfilment, i.e. it must publish and repudiate the secret treaties by which we have been bound up to the present time, those which were concluded by the tsar and which give Russian capitalists the promise of the pillaging of Turkey, Austria, etc. Then we must immediately satisfy the demands of the Ukrainians and the Finns, ensure them, as well as all other non-Russian nationalities in Russia, full freedom, including freedom of secession, applying the same *to all* Armenia, undertaking to evacuate that country as well as the Turkish lands occupied by us, etc.

Such peace terms will not meet with the approval of the capitalists, but they will meet with such tremendous sympathy on the part of all the peoples and will cause such a great world-wide outburst of enthusiasm and of general indignation against the continuation of the predatory war that it is extremely probable that we shall at once obtain a truce and a consent to open peace negotiations. For the workers' revolution against the war is irresistibly growing everywhere, and it can be spurred on, not by phrases about peace (with which the workers and peasants have been deceived by *all* the imperialist governments including our own Kerensky government), but by a break with the capitalists and by the offer of peace.

If the least probable thing happens, i.e. if not a single belligerent state accepts even a truce, then as far as we are concerned the war becomes truly forced upon us, it becomes a truly just war of defence. If this is understood by the proletariat and the poor peasantry, Russia will become many times stronger even in the military sense, especially after a complete break with the capitalists who are robbing the people; furthermore, under such conditions it would, as far as we are concerned, be a war in league with the oppressed classes of all countries, a war in league with the oppressed peoples of the whole world, not in word, but in deed.

The people must be particularly cautioned against the capitalists' assertion which sometimes influences the petty bourgeoisie and others who are frightened, namely, that the British and other capitalists are capable of doing serious damage to the Russian revolution if we break the present predatory alliance with them. Such an assertion is false through and through, for "Allied financial aid" enriches the bankers and "supports" the

Russian workers and peasants in exactly the same way as a rope supports a man who has been hanged. There is plenty of bread, coal, oil and iron in Russia; for these products to be properly distributed it is only necessary for us to rid ourselves of the landowners and capitalists who are robbing the people. As to the possibility of the Russian people being threatened with war by their present Allies, it is obviously absurd to assume that the French and Italians could unite their armies with those of the Germans and move them against Russia, who offers a just peace. As to Britain, America, and Japan, even if they were to declare war against Russia (which for them is extremely difficult, both because of the extreme unpopularity of such a war among the masses and because of the divergence of material interests of the capitalists of those countries over the partitioning of Asia, especially over the plunder of China), they could not cause Russia one-hundredth part of the damage and misery which the war with Germany, Austria, and Turkey is causing her.

Land to Those Who Till It

4. The Soviet Government must immediately declare the abolition of private landed estates without compensation and place all these estates under the management of the peasant committees pending the solution of the problem by the Constituent Assembly. These peasant committees are also to take over all the landowners' stock and implements, with the proviso that they be placed primarily at the disposal of the poor peasants for their use free of charge.

Such measures, which have long been demanded by an immense majority of the peasantry, both in the resolutions of congresses and in hundreds of mandates from local peasants (as may be seen, for instance, from a summary of 242 mandates published by *Izvestia Soveta Krestyanskikh Deputatov*[1]), are absolutely and urgently necessary. There must be no further procrastination like that from which the peasantry suffered so much at the time of the "coalition" government.

Any government that hesitates to introduce these measures should be regarded as a government *hostile to the people* that should be overthrown

[1] *Izvestia Vserossiiskogo Soveta Krestyanskikh Deputatov* (*News of the All-Russia Soviet of Peasants' Deputies*) – a daily, the official organ of the All-Russia Soviet of Peasants' Deputies, published in Petrograd from May 9 (22) to December 1917. It expressed the views of the Right wing of the Socialist-Revolutionary Party.

and crushed by an uprising of the workers and peasants. On the other hand, only a government that realises these measures will be a government of all the people.

Struggle against Famine and Economic Ruin

5. The Soviet Government must immediately introduce workers' control of production and distribution on a nation-wide scale. Experience since May 6 has shown that in the absence of such control all the promises of reforms and attempts to introduce them are powerless, and famine, accompanied by unprecedented catastrophe, is becoming a greater menace to the whole country week by week.

It is necessary to nationalise the banks and the insurance business immediately, and also the most important branches of industry (oil, coal, metallurgy, sugar, etc.), and at the same time, to abolish commercial secrets and to establish unrelaxing supervision by the workers and peasants over the negligible minority of capitalists who wax rich on government contracts and evade accounting and just taxation of their profits and property.

Such measures, which do not deprive either the middle peasants, the Cossacks or the small handicraftsmen of a single kopek, are urgently needed for the struggle against famine, and are absolutely just because they distribute the burdens of the war equitably. Only after capitalist plunder has been curbed and the deliberate sabotage of production has been stopped will it be possible to work for an improvement in labour productivity, introduce universal labour conscription and the proper exchange of grain for manufactured goods, and return to the Treasury thousands of millions in paper money now being hoarded by the rich.

Without such measures, the abolition of the landed estates without compensation is also impossible, for the major part of the estates is mortgaged to the banks, so that the interests of the landowners and capitalists are inseparably linked up.

The latest resolution of the Economic Department of the All-Russia Central Executive Committee of Soviets of Workers' and Soldiers' Deputies (*Rabochaya Gazeta* No. 152) recognises not only the "*harm*" caused by the government's measures (like the raising of grain prices for the enrichment of the landowners and kulaks), not only "the fact of the *complete inactivity* on the part of the central organs set up by the government for the regulation of economic life", but even the "contravention of the laws" by this government. This admission on the part of the ruling parties, the Socialist-

Revolutionaries and Mensheviks, proves once more the criminal nature of the policy of conciliation with the bourgeoisie.

Struggle against the Counter-revolution of the Landowners and Capitalists

6. The Kornilov and Kaledin revolt was supported by the entire class of the landowners and capitalists, with the party of the Cadets ("people's freedom" party) at their head. This has already been fully proved by the facts published in *Izvestia* of the Central Executive Committee.

However, nothing has been done either to suppress this counter-revolution completely or even to investigate it, and nothing serious can be done without the transfer of power to the Soviets. No commission can conduct a full investigation, or arrest the guilty, etc., unless it holds state power. Only a Soviet government can do this, and must do it. Only a Soviet government can make Russia secure against the otherwise inevitable repetition of "Kornilov" attempts by arresting the Kornilovite generals and the ring-leaders of the bourgeois counter-revolution (Guchkov, Milyukov, Rya-bushinsky, Maklakov and Co.), by disbanding the counter-revolutionary associations (the State Duma, the officers' unions, etc.), by placing their members under the surveillance of the local Soviets and by disbanding counter-revolutionary armed units.

This government alone can set up a commission to make a full and public investigation of the Kornilov case and all the other cases, even those started by the bourgeoisie; and the party of the Bolsheviks, in its turn, would appeal to the workers to give full co-operation and to submit only to such a commission.

Only a Soviet government could successfully combat such a flagrant injustice as the capitalists' seizure of the largest printing presses and most of the papers with the aid of millions squeezed out of the people. It is necessary to suppress the bourgeois counter-revolutionary papers (*Rech*, *Russkoye Slovo*,[2] etc.), to confiscate their printing presses, to declare private advertisements in the papers a state monopoly, to transfer them to the paper published by the Soviets, the paper that tells the peasants the truth. Only in

[2] *Russkoye Slovo* (*Russian Word*) – a daily published in Moscow from 1895 (a pilot issue was published in 1894). Ostensibly independent, it took a moderately liberal attitude in the interests of the Russian bourgeoisie. In 1917, the paper sided with the bourgeois Provisional Government and bitterly attacked Lenin and the Bolshevik Party.

this way can and must the bourgeoisie be deprived of its powerful weapon of lying and slandering, deceiving the people with impunity, misleading the peasantry, and preparing a counter-revolution.

Peaceful Development of the Revolution

7. A possibility very seldom to be met with in the history of revolutions now faces the democracy of Russia, the Soviets and the Socialist-Revolutionary and Menshevik parties – the possibility of convening the Constituent Assembly at the appointed date without further delays, of making the country secure against a military and economic catastrophe, and of ensuring the peaceful development of the revolution.

If the Soviets now take full state power exclusively into their own hands for the purpose of carrying out the programme set forth above, they will not only obtain the support of nine-tenths of the population of Russia, the working class and an overwhelming majority of the peasantry; they will also be assured of the greatest revolutionary enthusiasm on the part of the army and the majority of the people, an enthusiasm without which victory over famine and war is impossible.

There could be no question of any resistance to the Soviets if the Soviets themselves did not waver. No class will dare start an uprising against the Soviets, and the landowners and capitalists, taught a lesson by the experience of the Kornilov revolt, will give up their power peacefully and yield to the ultimatum of the Soviets. To overcome the capitalists' resistance to the programme of the Soviets, supervision over the exploiters by workers and peasants and such measures of punishing the recalcitrants as confiscation of their entire property coupled with a short term of arrest will be sufficient.

By seizing full power, the Soviets could still today – and this is probably their last chance – ensure the peaceful development of the revolution, peaceful elections of deputies by the people, and a peaceful struggle of parties inside the Soviets; they could test the programmes of the various parties in practice and power could pass peacefully from one party to another.

The entire course of development of the revolution, from the movement of April 20 to the Kornilov revolt, shows that there is bound to be the bitterest civil war between the bourgeoisie and the proletariat if this opportunity is missed. Inevitable catastrophe will bring this war nearer. It must end, as all data and considerations accessible to human reason go to prove, in the full victory of the working class, in that class, supported by the poor peasantry, carrying out the above programme; it may, however, prove very difficult and bloody, and may cost the lives of tens of thousands of landowners, capitalists, and officers who sympathise with them. The proletariat will not hesitate to make every sacrifice to save the revolution, which is possible only by implementing the programme set forth above. On the other hand, the proletariat would support the Soviets in every way if they were to make use of their last chance to secure a peaceful development of the revolution.

9

The Crisis has Matured[1]

The end of September undoubtedly marked a great turning-point in the history of the Russian revolution and, to all appearances, of the world revolution as well.

The world working-class revolution began with the action of individuals, whose boundless courage represented everything honest that remained of that decayed official "socialism" which is in reality social-chauvinism. Liebknecht in Germany, Adler in Austria, MacLean in Britain – these are the best-known names of the isolated heroes who have taken upon themselves the arduous role of forerunners of the world revolution.

The second stage in the historical preparation for this revolution was a widespread mass discontent, expressing itself in the split of the official parties, in illegal publications and in street demonstrations. The protest against the war became stronger, and the number of victims of government persecution increased. The prisons of countries famed for their observance of law, and even for their freedom – Germany, France, Italy and Britain – became filled with tens and hundreds of internationalists, opponents of the war and advocates of a working-class revolution.

The third stage has now begun. This stage may be called the eve of revolution. Mass arrests of party leaders in free Italy, and particularly the

[1] Written in Vyborg. It consisted of six chapters, the last not being intended for publication but for circulation among members of the Central Committee, the Petrograd and Moscow Committees and the Soviets. Only the manuscript of the last two chapters has come down to us. The article was first published in four chapters in *Rabochy Put* No. 30 of October 20 (7), 1917; a comparison of the newspaper text and the manuscript shows that one of the chapters was omitted, and Chapter V was headed as Chapter IV.

The article was widely carried by Bolshevik periodicals.

beginning of mutinies in the German army,[2] are indisputable symptoms that a great turning-point is at hand, that we are on the eve of a world-wide revolution.

Even before this there were, no doubt, individual cases of mutiny among the troops in Germany, but they were so small, so weak and isolated that it was possible to hush them up – and that was the chief way of checking the *mass contagion* of seditious action. Finally, there developed such a movement in the navy that it was *impossible* to hush it up, despite all the severity of the German regime of military servitude, severity elaborated with amazing minuteness of detail and observed with incredible pedantry.

Doubt is out of the question. We are on the threshold of a world proletarian revolution. And since of all the proletarian internationalists in all countries, only we Russian Bolsheviks enjoy a measure of freedom – we have a legal party and a score or so of papers, we have the Soviets of Workers' and Soldiers' Deputies of both capitals on our side, and we have the support of a *majority* of the people in a time of revolution – to us the saying, "To whom much has been given, of him much shall be required" in all justice can and must be applied.

II
The crucial point of the revolution in Russia has undoubtedly arrived

In a peasant country, and under a revolutionary, republican government which enjoys the support of the Socialist-Revolutionary and Menshevik parties that only yesterday dominated petty-bourgeois democracy, a *peasant revolt* is developing.

Incredible as this is, it is a fact.

---

[2] The reference is to the revolutionary action by German sailors in August 1917, who were led by a revolutionary sailors' organisation numbering 4,000 members (late July 1917). It was led by seamen Max Reichpietsch and Albin Köbis of the *Friedrich der Große*. The organisation decided to fight for a democratic peace and prepare for an uprising. Manifestations broke out in the navy in early August. Sailors of the warship *Prinzregenten Luitpold*, which was at Wilhelmshaven, took absence without leave to fight for the release of their comrades who had earlier been arrested for staging a strike; on August 16, the firemen of the *Westphalia* refused to work; at the same time the crew of the cruiser *Nürnberg*, which was out at sea, staged an uprising. The sailors' movement spread to the ships of several squadrons at Wilhelmshaven. These manifestations were put down with great savagery. Reichpietsch and Köbis were shot, and other active participants were sentenced to long terms of hard labour.

We Bolsheviks are not surprised by this fact. We have always said that the government of the notorious "coalition" with the bourgeoisie is a government that *betrays* democracy and the revolution, that it is a government of *imperialist* slaughter, a government that *protects* the capitalists and landowners *from* the people.

Owing to the deception practised by the Socialist-Revolutionaries and the Mensheviks, there still exists in Russia, under a republic and in a time of revolution, a government of capitalists and landowners side by side with the Soviets. This is the bitter and sinister reality. Is it then surprising, in view of the incredible hardship inflicted on the people by prolonging the imperialist war and by its consequences, that a peasant revolt has begun and is spreading in Russia?

Is it then surprising that the enemies of the Bolsheviks, the leaders of the *official* Socialist-Revolutionary Party, the very party that supported the "coalition" all along, the party that until the last few days or weeks had the majority of the people on its side, the party that continues to harry and abuse the "new" Socialist-Revolutionaries, who have realised that the policy of coalition is a betrayal of the interests of the peasants – is it surprising that these leaders of the official Socialist-Revolutionary Party wrote the following in an editorial in their official organ, *Dyelo Naroda*, of September 29:

> So far practically nothing has been done to put an end to the relations of bondage that still prevail in the villages of central Russia. . . . The bill for the regulation of land relations in the countryside, which was introduced in the Provisional Government long ago, and which has even passed through such a purgatory as the Judicial Conference, has got hopelessly stuck in some office. . . . Are we not right in asserting that our republican government is still a long way from having rid itself of the old habits of the tsarist administration, and that the dead hand of Stolypin is still making itself strongly felt in the methods of the revolutionary ministers?

This is written by the official Socialist-Revolutionaries! Just think: the supporters of the coalition are *forced* to admit that in a peasant country, after seven months of revolution, "practically nothing has been done to put an end to the bondage" of the peasants, to their enslavement by the landowners! These Socialist-Revolutionaries are *forced* to give the name of *Stolypins* to their colleague, Kerensky, and his gang of ministers.

Could we get more eloquent testimony than this from the camp of our opponents, not only to the effect that the coalition has collapsed and that the official Socialist-Revolutionaries who tolerate Kerensky have become an *anti-popular*, *anti-peasant* and *counter-revolutionary* party, but also that the whole Russian revolution has reached a turning-point?

A peasant revolt in a peasant country against the government of the Socialist-Revolutionary Kerensky, the Mensheviks Nikitin and Gvozdyov, and other ministers who represent capital and the interests of the landowners! The crushing of this revolt by *military measures* by a republican government!

In the face of such facts, can one remain a conscientious champion of the proletariat and yet deny that a crisis has matured, that the revolution is passing through an extremely critical moment, that the government's victory over the peasant revolt would now sound the death knell of the revolution, would be the final triumph of the Kornilov revolt?

III

It is obvious that if in a peasant country, after seven months of a democratic republic, matters could come to a peasant revolt, it irrefutably proves that the revolution is suffering nation-wide collapse, that it is experiencing a crisis of unprecedented severity, and that the forces of counter-revolution have gone the *limit*.

That is obvious. In the face of such a fact as a peasant revolt all other political symptoms, even were they to contradict the fact that a nation-wide crisis is maturing, would have no significance whatsoever.

But on the contrary, all the symptoms do indicate that a nation-wide crisis has matured.

Next to the agrarian question, the most important question in Russia's state affairs is the national question, particularly for the petty-bourgeois masses of the population. And at the "Democratic" Conference, which was fixed by Mr Tsereteli and Co., we find that the "national" curia takes second place for radicalism, yielding only to the trade unions, and *exceeding* the curia of the Soviets of Workers' and Soldiers' Deputies in the percentage of votes cast *against* the coalition (40 out of 55). The Kerensky government – a government suppressing the peasant revolt – is withdrawing the revolutionary troops from Finland in order to strengthen the reactionary Finnish bourgeoisie. In the Ukraine, the conflicts of the Ukrainians in general, and of the Ukrainian troops in particular, with the government are becoming more and more frequent.

Furthermore, let us take the army, which in war-time plays an exceptionally big role in all state affairs. We find that the army in Finland and the fleet in the Baltic have completely *parted ways* with the government. We have the testimony of the officer Dubasov, a non-Bolshevik, who speaks in the name of the whole front and declares in a manner more revolutionary than that of any Bolsheviks that the soldiers will not fight any longer.[3] We have governmental reports stating that the soldiers are in a state of "agitation", and that it is impossible to guarantee the maintenance of "order" (i.e. participation of these troops in the suppression of the peasant revolt). We have, finally, the voting in Moscow, where fourteen thousand out of seventeen thousand soldiers voted for the Bolsheviks.

This vote in the elections to the district councils in Moscow is in general one of the most striking symptoms of the profound change which has taken place in the mood of the whole nation. It is generally known that Moscow is more petty bourgeois than Petrograd. It is a fact frequently corroborated and indisputable that the Moscow proletariat has an incomparably greater number of connections with the countryside, that it has greater sympathy for the peasant and is closer to the sentiments of the peasant.

In Moscow the vote cast for the Socialist-Revolutionaries and the Mensheviks nevertheless dropped from 70 per cent in June to 18 per cent. There can be no doubt that the petty bourgeoisie and the people have turned away from the coalition. The Cadets have increased their strength from 17 to 30 per cent, but they remain a minority, a hopeless minority, despite the fact that they have obviously been joined by the "Right" Socialist-Revolutionaries, and the "Right" Mensheviks. *Russkiye Vedomosti*[4] states that the *absolute* number of votes cast for the Cadets fell from *67,000* to *62,000*. Only the votes cast for the Bolsheviks increased – from 34,000 to 82,000. They received 47 per cent of the total vote. There can be no shadow of doubt that we, together with the Left Socialist-Revolutionaries, now have a majority in the Soviets, in the army, and *in the country*.

Among the symptoms that have not only a symptomatic, but also a very real significance is the fact that the armies of railway and postal employees, who are of immense importance from the general economic, political and military point of view, continue to be in sharp conflict with the government,[5]

---

[3] The reference is to what an officer, Dubasov, said at a meeting of the Petrograd Soviet on September 21 (October 4), 1917. He had just returned from the front, and declared: "Whatever you may say over here, the soldiers will not fight."

[4] *Russkiye Vedomosti* (*Russian Recorder*) – a daily published in Moscow from 1863, expressing the views of moderate liberal intellectuals. From 1905 the paper was an organ of the Right wing of the Cadet Party.

[5] The reference is to the nation-wide strike of railwaymen for higher wages. It started on the night of September 23 (October 6), 1917, and threw the Provisional Government into a panic.

even the Menshevik defencists are dissatisfied with "their" Minister, Nikitin, and the official Socialist-Revolutionaries call Kerensky and Co. "Stolypins". Is it not clear that if such "support" of the government by the Mensheviks and Socialist-Revolutionaries has any value at all it can be only a negative value?

IV

. . .

V

Yes, the leaders of the Central Executive Committee are pursuing the correct tactics of defending the bourgeoisie and the landowners. And there is not the slightest doubt that if the Bolsheviks allowed themselves to be caught in the trap of constitutional illusions, "faith" in the Congress of Soviets and in the convocation of the Constituent Assembly, "waiting" for the Congress of Soviets, and so forth – these Bolsheviks would most certainly be *miserable traitors* to the proletarian cause.

They would be traitors to the cause, for by their conduct they would be betraying the German revolutionary workers who have started a revolt in the navy. To "wait" for the Congress of Soviets and so forth under such circumstances would be a *betrayal of internationalism*, a betrayal of the cause of the world socialist revolution.

For internationalism consists of *deeds* and not phrases, not expressions of solidarity, not resolutions.

The Bolsheviks would be traitors to the *peasants*, for to tolerate the suppression of the peasant revolt by a government which *even Dyelo Naroda* compares with the Stolypin government would be *to ruin* the whole revolution, to ruin it for good. An outcry is raised about anarchy and about the increasing indifference of the people, but what else can the people be but indifferent to the elections, when the peasants have been *driven to revolt* while the so-called "revolutionary democrats" are patiently tolerating its suppression by military force!

The Bolsheviks would be traitors to democracy and to freedom, for to tolerate the suppression of the peasant revolt at such a moment would *mean* allowing the elections to the Constituent Assembly to be fixed *in exactly the same* way as the Democratic Conference and the "Pre-parliament" were fixed, only even worse and more crudely.

The crisis has matured. The whole future of the Russian revolution is at stake. The honour of the Bolshevik Party is in question. The whole future of the international workers' revolution for socialism is at stake.

The crisis has matured. . . .

September 29, 1917

Everything to this point may be published, but what follows is *to be distributed* among the members of the *Central Committee, the Petrograd Committee, the Moscow Committee, and the Soviets.*

VI

What, then, is to be done? We must *aussprechen was ist*, "state the facts", admit the truth that there is a tendency, or an opinion, in our Central Committee and among the leaders of our Party which favours *waiting* for the Congress of Soviets, and is *opposed* to taking power immediately, is *opposed* to an immediate insurrection. That tendency, or opinion, must be *overcome.*

Otherwise, the Bolsheviks will cover themselves with eternal *shame* and *destroy themselves* as a party.

For to miss such a moment and to "wait" for the Congress of Soviets would be *utter idiocy*, or *sheer treachery.*

It would be sheer treachery to the German workers. Surely we should not wait until their revolution begins. In that case even the Lieberdans would be in favour of "supporting" it. But it *cannot* begin as long as Kerensky, Kishkin and Co. are in power.

It would be sheer treachery to the peasants. To allow the peasant revolt to be suppressed when we control the Soviets of both *capitals* would be to *lose*, and *justly lose*, every ounce of the peasants' confidence. In the eyes of the peasants we would be putting ourselves on a level with the Lieberdans and other scoundrels.

To "wait" for the Congress of Soviets would be utter idiocy, for it would mean losing *weeks* at a time when weeks and even days decide *everything.* It would mean faint-heartedly *renouncing* power, for on November 1–2 it will have become impossible to take power (both politically and technically, since the Cossacks would be mobilised for the day of the insurrection so foolishly "appointed"[*]).

To "wait" for the Congress of Soviets is idiocy, for the Congress will *give nothing, and can give nothing*!

"Moral" importance? Strange indeed, to talk of the "importance" of resolutions and conversations with the Lieberdans when we know that the Soviets *support* the peasants and that the peasant revolt is *being suppressed*! We would be reducing the *Soviets* to the status of wretched debating parlours. First defeat Kerensky, then call the Congress.

The Bolsheviks are now *guaranteed* the success of the insurrection: (1) we can[†] (if we do not "wait" for the Soviet Congress) launch a *surprise* attack from three points – from Petrograd, from Moscow and from the Baltic fleet; (2) we have slogans that guarantee us support – down with the government that is suppressing the revolt of the peasants against the landowners! (3) we have a majority *in the country*; (4) the disorganisation among the Mensheviks and the Socialist-Revolutionaries is complete; (5) we are technically in a position to take power in Moscow (where the start might even be made, so as to catch the enemy unawares); (6) we have *thousands* of armed workers and soldiers in Petrograd who could *at once* seize the Winter Palace, the General Staff building, the telephone exchange and the large printing presses. Nothing will be able to drive us out, while agitational work in the *army* will be such as to make it *impossible* to combat this government of peace, of land for the peasants, and so forth.

If we were to attack at once, suddenly, from three points, Petrograd, Moscow and the Baltic fleet, the chances are a hundred to one that we would succeed with smaller sacrifices than on July 3–5, because *the troops will not advance* against a government of peace. Even though Kerensky *already* has "loyal" cavalry, etc., in Petrograd, if we were to attack from two sides, he would be compelled to *surrender* since *we* enjoy the sympathy of the army. If with such chances as we have at present we do not take power, then all talk of transferring the power to the Soviets becomes *a lie*.

To refrain from taking power now, to "wait", to indulge in talk in the Central Executive Committee, to confine ourselves to "fighting for the

---

* To "convene" the Congress of Soviets for October 20 in order to decide upon "taking power" – how does that differ from foolishly "appointing" an insurrection? It is possible to take power now, whereas on October 20–29 you will not be given a chance to.

† What has the Party done to *study* the disposition of the troops, etc.? What has it done to conduct the insurrection as an art? Mere talk in the Central Executive Committee, and so on!

organ" (of the Soviet), "fighting for the Congress", is *to doom the revolution to failure*.

In view of the fact that the Central Committee has *even left unanswered* the persistent demands I have been making for such a policy ever since the beginning of the Democratic Conference, in view of the fact that the Central Organ is *deleting* from my articles all references to such glaring errors on the part of the Bolsheviks as the shameful decision to participate in the Pre-parliament, the admission of Mensheviks to the Presidium of the Soviet, etc., etc. – I am compelled to regard this as a "subtle" hint at the unwillingness of the Central Committee even to consider this question, a subtle hint that I should keep my mouth shut, and as a proposal for me to retire.

I am compelled to *tender my resignation from the Central Committee*, which I hereby do, reserving for myself freedom to campaign among the *rank and file* of the Party and at the Party Congress.

For it is my profound conviction that if we "wait" for the Congress of Soviets and let the present moment pass, we shall *ruin* the revolution.

N. Lenin

September 29

PS There are a number of facts which serve to prove that even the Cossack troops will not go against a government of peace! And how many are there? Where are they? And will not the entire army dispatch units *for our support*?

10

Advice of an Onlooker

I am writing these lines on October 8 and have little hope that they will reach Petrograd comrades by the 9th. It is possible that they will arrive too late, since the Congress of the Northern Soviets has been fixed for October 10. Nevertheless, I shall try to give my "Advice of an Onlooker" in the event that the probable action of the workers and soldiers of Petrograd and of the whole "region" will take place soon but has not yet taken place.

It is clear that all power must pass to the Soviets. It should be equally indisputable for every Bolshevik that proletarian revolutionary power (or Bolshevik power – which is now one and the same thing) is assured of the utmost sympathy and unreserved support of all the working and exploited people all over the world in general, in the belligerent countries in particular, and among the Russian peasants especially. There is no need to dwell on these all too well known and long established truths.

What must be dealt with is something that is probably not quite clear to all comrades, namely, that in practice the transfer of power to the Soviets now means armed uprising. This would seem obvious, but not everyone has given or is giving thought to the point. To repudiate armed uprising now would mean to repudiate the key slogan of Bolshevism (All Power to the Soviets) and proletarian revolutionary internationalism in general.

But armed uprising is a *special* form of political struggle, one subject to special laws to which attentive thought must be given. Karl Marx expressed this truth with remarkable clarity when he wrote that "*insurrection is an art quite as much as war*".

Of the principal rules of this art, Marx noted the following:

(1) *Never play* with insurrection, but when beginning it realise firmly that you must *go all the way*.
(2) Concentrate a *great superiority of forces* at the decisive point and at the

decisive moment, otherwise the enemy, who has the advantage of better preparation and organisation, will destroy the insurgents.

(3) Once the insurrection has begun, you must act with the greatest *determination*, and by all means, without fail, take the *offensive*. "The defensive is the death of every armed rising."

(4) You must try to take the enemy by surprise and seize the moment when his forces are scattered.

(5) You must strive for *daily* successes, however small (one might say hourly, if it is the case of one town), and at all costs retain "*moral superiority*".

Marx summed up the lessons of all revolutions in respect to armed uprising in the words of "Danton, the greatest master of revolutionary policy yet known: *de l'audace, de l'audace, encore de l'audace*".

Applied to Russia and to October 1917, this means: a simultaneous offensive on Petrograd, as sudden and as rapid as possible, which must without fail be carried out from within and from without, from the working-class quarters and from Finland, from Revel and from Kronstadt, an offensive of the *entire* navy, the concentration of a *gigantic superiority* of forces over the 15,000 or 20,000 (perhaps more) of our "bourgeois guard" (the officers' schools), our "Vendée troops" (part of the Cossacks), etc.

Our *three* main forces – the fleet, the workers, and the army units – must be so combined as to occupy without fail and to hold *at any cost*: (a) the telephone exchange; (b) the telegraph office; (c) the railway stations; (d) and above all, the bridges.

The *most determined* elements (our "shock forces" and *young workers*, as well as the best of the sailors) must be formed into small detachments to occupy all the more important points and to *take part* everywhere in all important operations, for example: to encircle and cut off Petrograd; to seize it by a combined attack of the sailors, the workers, and the troops – a task which requires *art and triple audacity*; to form detachments from the best workers, armed with rifles and bombs, for the purpose of attacking and surrounding the enemy's "centres" (the officers' schools, the telegraph office, the telephone exchange, etc.). Their watch-word must be: "*Better die to a man than let the enemy pass!*"

Let us hope that if action is decided on, the leaders will successfully apply the great precepts of Danton and Marx.

The success of both the Russian and the world revolution depends on two or three days' fighting.

11

Letter to Comrades

Comrades,

We are living in a time that is so critical, events are moving at such incredible speed that a publicist, placed by the will of fate somewhat aside from the mainstream of history, constantly runs the risk either of being late or proving uninformed, especially if some time elapses before his writings appear in print. Although I fully realise this, I must nevertheless address this letter to the Bolsheviks, even at the risk of its not being published at all, for the vacillations against which I deem it my duty to warn in the most decisive manner are of an unprecedented nature and may have a disastrous effect on the Party, the movement of the international proletariat, and the revolution. As for the danger of being too late, I will prevent it by indicating the nature and date of the information I possess.

It was not until Monday morning, October 16, that I saw a comrade who had on the previous day participated in a very important Bolshevik gathering in Petrograd, and who informed me in detail of the discussion.[1] The subject of discussion was that same question of the uprising discussed by the Sunday papers of all political trends. The gathering represented all that is most influential in all branches of Bolshevik work in the capital. Only a most insignificant minority of the gathering, namely, all in all two comrades, took a negative stand. The arguments which those comrades advanced are so weak, they are a manifestation of such an astounding confusion, timidity, and collapse of all the fundamental ideas of Bolshevism and proletarian revolutionary internationalism that it is not easy to discover an explanation for such shameful vacillations. The fact, however,

---

[1] A reference to the enlarged Central Committee meeting on October 16 (29), 1917. Lenin remained in hiding in Petrograd and changed the date of the meeting to October 15 (28) in order to conceal his presence at the meeting; for reasons of secrecy he referred to a comrade who had allegedly informed him of the meeting.

remains, and since the revolutionary party has no right to tolerate vacillations on such a serious question, and since this pair of comrades, who have scattered their principles to the winds, might cause some confusion, it is necessary to analyse their arguments, to expose their vacillations, and to show how shameful they are. The following lines are an attempt to do this.

"We have no majority among the people, and without this condition the uprising is hopeless. . . ."

People who can say this are either distorters of the truth or pedants who want an advance guarantee that throughout the whole country the Bolshevik Party has received exactly one-half of the votes plus one, this they want at all events, without taking the least account of the real circumstances of the revolution. History has never given such a guarantee, and is quite unable to give it in any revolution. To make such a demand is jeering at the audience, and is nothing but a cover to hide one's own *flight* from reality.

For reality shows us clearly that it was after the July days that the majority of the people began quickly to go over to the side of the Bolsheviks. This was demonstrated first by the August 20 elections in Petrograd, even before the Kornilov revolt, when the Bolshevik vote rose from 20 to 33 per cent in the city not including the suburbs, and then by the district council elections in Moscow in September, when the Bolshevik vote rose from 11 to 49.3 per cent (one Moscow comrade, whom I saw recently, told me that the correct figure is 51 per cent). This was proved by the new elections to the Soviets. It was proved by the fact that a majority of the peasant Soviets, their "Aksentyev" central Soviet notwithstanding, has expressed itself *against* the coalition. To be against the coalition means *in practice* to follow the Bolsheviks. Furthermore, reports from the front prove more frequently and more definitely that the soldiers are passing *en masse* over to the side of the Bolsheviks with ever greater determination, in spite of the malicious slanders and attacks by the Socialist-Revolutionary and Menshevik leaders, officers, deputies, etc., etc.

Last, but not least, the most outstanding fact of present-day Russian life is *the revolt of the peasantry*. This shows objectively, not by words but by deeds, that the people are going over to the side of the Bolsheviks. But the fact remains, notwithstanding the lies of the bourgeois press and its miserable yes-men of the "vacillating" *Novaya Zhizn* crowd, who shout about riots and anarchy. The peasant movement in Tambov

Gubernia[2] was an uprising both in the physical and political sense, an uprising that has yielded such splendid political results as, in the first place, agreement to transfer the land to the peasants. It is not for nothing that the Socialist-Revolutionary rabble, including *Dyelo Naroda*, who are frightened by the uprising, now *scream* about the need to transfer the land to the peasants. Here is a *practical* demonstration of the correctness of Bolshevism, and of its success. It proved to be impossible to "teach" the Bonapartists and their lackeys in the Pre-parliament otherwise than by an uprising.

This is a fact, and facts are stubborn things. And such a factual "argument" *in favour* of an uprising is stronger than thousands of "pessimistic" evasions on the part of confused and frightened politicians.

If the peasant uprising were not an event of nation-wide political import, the Socialist-Revolutionary lackeys from the Pre-parliament would not be shouting about the need to hand over the land to the peasants.

Another splendid political and revolutionary consequence of the peasant uprising, as already noted in *Rabochy Put*, is the delivery of grain to the railway stations in Tambov Gubernia. Here is another "argument" for you, confused gentlemen, an argument in favour of the uprising as the only means to save the country from the famine that is knocking at our door, and from a crisis of unheard-of dimensions. While the Socialist-Revolutionary and Menshevik betrayers of the people are grumbling, threatening, writing resolutions, promising to feed the hungry by convening the Constituent Assembly, the people are beginning to solve the bread problem *Bolshevik-fashion*, *by rebelling* against the landowners, capitalists, and speculators.

Even the *bourgeois* press, even *Russkaya Volya*, was compelled to admit the wonderful results of *such* a solution (the only real solution) of the bread problem, by publishing information to the effect that the railway stations in Tambov Gubernia were swamped with grain. . . . *And this after the peasants had revolted!*

---

[2] The peasant movement in Tambov Gubernia in September 1917 assumed great proportions: the peasants seized tracts of landed estates, destroyed and burned landowners' mansions and confiscated grain stocks. In September, 82 landowners' estates were destroyed in 68 gubernias and regions, including 32 in Tambov Gubernia. Altogether there is a record of 166 peasant manifestations in the gubernia, especially in Kozlov Uyezd. The frightened landowners took their grain to the railway stations in an effort to sell it, so that the railway junctions were literally swamped with grain. The commanding officer of the Moscow Military District sent military units to Tambov Gubernia to crush the peasant uprising, and imposed martial law, but the peasants' revolutionary struggle for land continued to grow in scope.

To doubt now that the majority of the people are following and will follow the Bolsheviks is shameful vacillation and in practice is the abandoning of *all* the principles of proletarian revolutionism, the complete renunciation of Bolshevism.

"We are not strong enough to seize power, and the bourgeoisie is not strong enough to hinder the convening of the Constituent Assembly."

The first part of this argument is a simple paraphrase of the preceding one. It does not gain in strength or power of conviction, when the confusion of its authors and their fear of the bourgeoisie are expressed in terms of pessimism in respect of the workers and optimism in respect of the bourgeoisie. If the officer cadets and the Cossacks say that they will fight against the Bolsheviks to the last drop of blood, this deserves full credence; if, however, the workers and soldiers at hundreds of meetings express full confidence in the Bolsheviks and affirm their readiness to defend the transfer of power to the Soviets, then it is "timely" to recall that voting is one thing and fighting another!

If you argue like that, of course, you "refute" the possibility of an uprising. But, we may ask, in what way does this peculiarly orientated "pessimism", with its peculiar urge, differ from a political shift to the side of the bourgeoisie?

Look at the facts. Remember the Bolshevik declarations, repeated thousands of times and now "forgotten" by our pessimists. We have said thousands of times that the Soviets of Workers' and Soldiers' Deputies are a force, that they are the vanguard of the revolution, that they *can* take power. Thousands of times have we upbraided the Mensheviks and Socialist-Revolutionaries for phrase-mongering about the "plenipotentiary organs of democracy" accompanied by *fear* to transfer power to the Soviets.

And what has the Kornilov revolt proved? It has proved that the Soviets are a real force.

And, now, after this has been proved by experience, by facts, we are expected to repudiate Bolshevism, deny ourselves, and say that we are not strong enough (although the Soviets of Petrograd and Moscow and a majority of the provincial Soviets are on the side of the Bolsheviks)! Are these not shameful vacillations? As a matter of fact, our "pessimists" are abandoning the slogan of "All Power to the Soviets", though they *are afraid* to admit it.

How can it be proved that the bourgeoisie are not strong enough to hinder the calling of the Constituent Assembly?

If the Soviets *have not the strength* to overthrow the bourgeoisie, this *means* the latter are strong enough to prevent the convocation of the Constituent Assembly, for there is nobody else to stop them. To trust the promises of Kerensky and Co., to trust the resolutions of the servile Pre-parliament – is this worthy of a member of a proletarian party and a revolutionary?

Not only has the bourgeoisie *enough strength* to hinder the convocation of the Constituent Assembly if the present government is not overthrown, but it can also achieve this result *indirectly* by surrendering Petrograd to the Germans, laying open the front, increasing lockouts, and sabotaging deliveries of foodstuffs. It has been proved by *facts* that the bourgeoisie have already been partly doing this, which means that they are capable of doing it *to the full extent*, if the workers and soldiers do not overthrow them.

"The Soviets must be a revolver pointed at the head of the government with the demand to convene the Constituent Assembly and stop all Kornilovite plots."

This is how far one of the two sad pessimists has gone.

He had to go that far, for to reject the uprising is *the same as* rejecting the slogan "All Power to the Soviets".

Of course, a slogan is "not sacred"; we all agree to that. But then why has *no one* raised the question of changing this slogan (in the same way as I raised the question after the July days)? Why be *afraid* to say it openly, when the Party, since September, has been discussing the question of the uprising, which is now *the only way* to realise the slogan "All Power to the Soviets"?

There is no way for our sad pessimists to turn. A renunciation of the uprising is a renunciation of the transfer of power to the Soviets, and implies a "transfer" of all hopes and expectations to the kind bourgeoisie, which has "promised" to convoke the Constituent Assembly.

Is it so difficult to understand that once *power* is in the hands of the Soviets, the Constituent Assembly and its success are *guaranteed*? The Bolsheviks have said so thousands of times, and *no one* has ever attempted to refute it. Everybody has recognised this "combined type", but to smuggle in a renunciation of the transfer of power to the Soviets under cover of the words "combined type", to smuggle it in *secretly* while *fearing* to renounce our slogan openly, is a matter for wonder. Is there any parliamentary term to describe it?

Someone has very pointedly retorted to our pessimist: "Is it a revolver with no cartridges?" If so, it means going over directly to the Lieberdans, who have declared the Soviets a "revolver" thousands of times, and have deceived the people thousands of times. For *while they were in control*, the Soviets proved to be worthless.

If, however, it is to be a revolver "with cartridges", this cannot mean anything but *technical* preparation for an uprising; the cartridges have to be procured, the revolver has to be loaded – and cartridges alone will not be enough.

Either go over to the side of the Lieberdans and *openly* renounce the slogan "All Power to the Soviets", or start the uprising.

There is no middle course.

"The bourgeoisie cannot surrender Petrograd to the Germans, although Rodzyanko wants to, for the fighting is done not by the bourgeoisie, but by our heroic sailors."

This argument again reduces itself to the same "optimism" *in respect of the bourgeoisie* which is fatally manifested at every step by those who are pessimistic about the revolutionary forces and capabilities of the proletariat.

The fighting is done by the heroic sailors, *but* this did not prevent *two* admirals from *disappearing* before the capture of Esel!

That is a fact, and facts are stubborn things. The facts prove that admirals *are capable* of treachery no less than Kornilov. It is an undisputed fact that Field Headquarters has not been reformed, and that the commanding staff is Kornilovite in composition.

If the Kornilovites (with Kerensky at their head, for he is also a Kornilovite) *want* to surrender Petrograd, they can do it in two or even in three ways.

First, they can, through an act of treachery on the part of the Kornilovite officers, open the northern land front.

Second, they can "agree" on freedom of action for the entire German navy, which is *stronger* than we are; they can agree both with the German and with the British imperialists. Moreover, the admirals who have disappeared may have delivered the *plans* to the Germans *as well*.

Third, they can, by means of lockouts, and by sabotaging the delivery of food, bring our troops to complete *desperation* and impotence.

Not a single one of these three ways can be denied. The facts have proved that the bourgeois-Cossack party of Russia has already knocked at all three doors and has tried to force open each of them.

What follows? It follows that we have no right to *wait* until the bourgeoisie strangle the revolution.

Experience has proved that Rodzyanko's wishes are no trifle. Rodzyanko is a man of affairs. Rodzyanko is backed by *capital*. This is beyond dispute. Capital is tremendous strength as long as the proletariat does not have power. *For decades*, Rodzyanko has faithfully and truly carried out the policies of capital.

What follows? It follows that to vacillate on the question of an uprising as the only means to save the revolution means to sink into that cowardly credulity in the bourgeoisie which is half-Lieberdan, Socialist-Revolutionary-Menshevik and half "peasant-like" unquestioning credulity, against which the Bolsheviks have been battling most of all.

Either fold your idle arms on your empty chest, wait and swear "faith" in the Constituent Assembly until Rodzyanko and Co. have surrendered Petrograd and strangled the revolution or start an uprising. There is no middle course.

Even the convocation of the Constituent Assembly does not, in itself, change anything, for no "constituting", no voting by any arch-sovereign assembly will have any effect on the famine, or on Wilhelm. Both the convocation and the *success* of the Constituent Assembly depend upon the transfer of power to the Soviets. This old Bolshevik truth is being proved by reality ever more strikingly and ever more *cruelly*.

"We are becoming stronger every day. We can enter the Constituent Assembly as a strong opposition; why should we stake everything? . . ."

This is the argument of a philistine who has "read" that the Constituent Assembly is being called, and who trustingly acquiesces in the most legal, most loyal, most constitutional course.

It is a pity, however, that *waiting* for the Constituent Assembly does not solve either the question of famine or the question of surrendering Petrograd. This "trifle" is forgotten by the confused or by those who have allowed themselves to be frightened.

The famine will not wait. The peasant uprising did not wait. The war will not wait. The admirals who have disappeared did not wait.

Will the famine agree to wait, because we Bolsheviks *proclaim* faith in the convocation of the Constituent Assembly? Will the admirals who have disappeared agree to wait? Will the Maklakovs and Rodzyankos agree to stop the lockouts and the sabotaging of grain deliveries, or to denounce the secret treaties with the British and the German imperialists?

This is what the arguments of the heroes of "constitutional illusions" and parliamentary cretinism amount to. The living reality disappears, and what remains is only a *paper* dealing with the convocation of the Constituent Assembly; there is nothing left but to hold elections.

And blind people are still wondering why hungry people and soldiers betrayed by generals and admirals are indifferent to the elections! Oh, wiseacres!

"Were the Kornilovites to start again, we would show them! But why should we take risks and start?"

This is extraordinarily convincing and revolutionary. History does not repeat itself, but if we turn our *backs* on it, contemplate the first Kornilov revolt and repeat: "If only the Kornilovites would start" – if we do that, what excellent revolutionary strategy it would be! How much like a waiting game it is! Maybe the Kornilovites will start again at an inopportune time. Isn't this a "weighty" argument? What kind of an earnest foundation for a proletarian policy is this?

And what if the Kornilovites of the second draft will have learned a thing or two? What if they *wait* for the hunger riots to begin, for the front to be broken through, for Petrograd to be surrendered, *before they begin*? What then?

It is proposed that we build the tactics of the proletarian party on the possibility of the Kornilovites' repeating one of their old errors!

Let us forget all that was being and *has been demonstrated* by the Bolsheviks a hundred times, all that the six months' history of our revolution has proved, namely, that there is *no* way out, that there is no objective way out and can be none *except* a dictatorship of the Kornilovites or a dictatorship of the proletariat. Let us forget this, let us renounce all this and wait! Wait for what? Wait for a miracle, for the tempestuous and catastrophic course of events from April 20 to August 29 to be succeeded (due to the prolongation of the war and the spread of famine) by a peaceful, quiet, smooth, legal convocation of the Constituent Assembly and by a fulfilment of its most lawful decisions. Here you have the "Marxist" tactics! Wait, ye hungry! Kerensky has promised to convene the Constituent Assembly.

"There is really nothing in the international situation that makes it obligatory for us to act immediately; we would be more likely to damage the cause of a socialist revolution in the West, if we were to allow ourselves to be shot. . . ."

This argument is truly magnificent: Scheidemann "himself", Renaudel[3] "himself" would not be able to "manipulate" more cleverly the workers' sympathies for the international socialist revolution!

Just think of it: under devilishly difficult conditions, having but *one* Liebknecht (and he in prison), with no newspapers, with no freedom of assembly, with no Soviets, with *all* classes of the population, including every well-to-do peasant, incredibly hostile to the idea of internationalism, with the imperialist big, middle, and petty bourgeoisie splendidly organised – the Germans, i.e. the German revolutionary internationalists, the German workers dressed in sailors' jackets, started a mutiny in the navy with one chance in a hundred of winning.

But we, with dozens of papers at our disposal, freedom of assembly, a *majority* in the Soviets, we, the best-situated proletarian internationalists in the world, should refuse to support the German revolutionaries by our uprising. We ought to reason, like the Scheidemanns and Renaudels, that it is most prudent not to revolt, for if we are shot, then the world will lose such excellent, reasonable, ideal internationalists!

Let us prove how reasonable we are. Let us pass a resolution of sympathy with the *German insurrectionists*, and let us renounce the *insurrection* in Russia. This would be genuine, reasonable internationalism. Imagine how fast world internationalism would blossom forth, if the same wise policy were to triumph *everywhere*!

The war has fatigued and tormented the workers of all countries to the utmost. Outbursts are becoming frequent in Italy, Germany and Austria. We *alone* have Soviets of Workers' and Soldiers' Deputies. Let us then *keep on waiting*. Let us betray the German internationalists as we are betraying the Russian peasants, who, not by words but by deeds, by their uprising against the landowners, appeal to us to rise against Kerensky's government. . . .

Let the clouds of the imperialist conspiracy of the capitalists of all countries who are ready to strangle the Russian revolution gather – we shall wait patiently until we are strangled *by the rouble*! Instead of attacking the conspirators and breaking their ranks by a victory of the Soviets of Workers' and Soldiers' Deputies, let us wait for the Constituent Assembly, where all international plots will be vanquished by *voting*, provided Kerensky and

[3] Scheidemann, Philip (1865–1939) – a leader of the Right-wing section of German Social-Democracy.
Renaudel, Pierre (1871–1935) – a reformist leader of the French Socialist Party.

Rodzyanko conscientiously convene the Constituent Assembly. Have we any right to doubt the honesty of Kerensky and Rodzyanko?

"But 'everyone' is against us! We are isolated; the Central Executive Committee, the Menshevik internationalists, the *Novaya Zhizn* people, and the Left Socialist-Revolutionaries have been issuing and will continue to issue appeals against us!"

A crushing argument. Up to now we have been mercilessly scourging the vacillators for their vacillations. *By so doing*, we have won the sympathies of the people. *By so doing*, we have won over the Soviets, without which the uprising could not be safe, quick, and sure. Now let us use the Soviets which we have won over in order *to move into the camp of the vacillators*. What a splendid career for Bolshevism!

The whole essence of the policy of the Lieberdans and Chernovs, and also of the Left Socialist-Revolutionaries and Mensheviks, consists in *vacillations*. The Left Socialist-Revolutionaries and Menshevik internationalists have tremendous political importance as an *indication* of the fact that the *masses are moving to the left*. Two such facts as the passing of some 40 per cent of both Mensheviks and Socialist-Revolutionaries into the camp of the Left, on the one hand, and the peasant uprising, on the other, are clearly and obviously interconnected.

But it is the very character of this connection that reveals the abysmal spinelessness of those who have now undertaken to whimper over the fact that the Central Executive Committee, which has rotted away, or the vacillating Left Socialist-Revolutionaries and Co., have come out against us. For *these* vacillations of the petty-bourgeois leaders – the Martovs, Kamkovs, Sukhanovs and Co. – have to be compared to the *uprising* of the peasants. Here is a *realistic* political comparison. With whom shall we go? Should it be with the vacillating handfuls of Petrograd leaders, who have expressed *indirectly* the *leftward swing* of the masses, but who, at *every* political turn, have shamefully whimpered, vacillated, run to ask forgiveness of the Lieberdans, Avksentyevs and Co., *or with those masses that have moved to the left*?

Thus, and only thus, can the question be presented.

Because the peasant uprising has been betrayed by the Martovs, Kamkovs, and Sukhanovs, we, the workers' party of revolutionary internationalists, are asked to betray it, too. This is what the policy of blaming the Left Socialist-Revolutionaries and Menshevik internationalists reduces itself to.

But we have said that to help the vacillating, we must stop vacillating ourselves. Have those "nice" Left petty-bourgeois democrats not "vacillated" in favour of the coalition? In the long run we succeeded in making them follow us because we ourselves did not vacillate. Events have shown we are right.

These gentlemen, by their vacillations, have always held back the revolution; we alone have saved it. Shall we now give up, when the famine is knocking at the gates of Petrograd, and Rodzyanko and Co. are preparing to surrender the city?!

"But we do not even have firm connections with the railwaymen and the postal employees. Their official representatives are the Plansons.[4] And can we win without the post office and without railways?"

Yes, yes, the Plansons here, the Lieberdans there. What confidence have the *masses* shown them? Have we not always shown that those leaders betrayed the *masses*? Did the masses not turn away from those leaders *towards us*, both at the elections in Moscow and at the elections to the Soviets? Or perhaps the mass of railway and postal employees are not starving! Or do not strike against Kerensky and Co.?

"Did we have connections with these unions before February 28?", one comrade asked a pessimist. The latter replied by pointing out that the two revolutions could not be compared. But this reply only *strengthens* the position of the one who asked the question. For it is the Bolsheviks who have spoken thousands of times about prolonged preparation for the *proletarian* revolution *against the bourgeoisie* (and they have not spoken about it in order to forget their words when the decisive moment is at hand). The political and economic life of the unions of postal and telegraph employees and railwaymen is characterised by the very *separation* of the proletarian elements of the masses from the petty-bourgeois and bourgeois upper layer. It is not absolutely necessary to secure "connections" with one or the other union beforehand; what matters is that only a victory of a proletarian and peasant uprising *can* satisfy the *masses* both of the army of railwaymen and of postal and telegraph employees.

---

[4] Planson, A. A. – a Popular Socialist, and member of the Central Executive Committee (First Convocation). A leader of Vikzhel – the All-Russia Executive Committee of the Railwaymen's Trade Union, an organisation run by the compromisers.

"There is only enough bread in Petrograd for two or three days. Can we give bread to the insurrectionists?"

This is one of a thousand sceptical remarks (the sceptics can *always* "doubt", and cannot be refuted by anything but experience), one of those remarks that put the blame on the wrong shoulders.

It is Rodzyanko and Co., it is the bourgeoisie, that are preparing the famine and speculating on strangling the revolution by famine. There is no escaping the famine, and *there can be none* except by an uprising of the peasants against the landowners in the countryside, and by a victory of the workers over the capitalists in the cities and Petrograd and Moscow. There is *no other way* to get grain from the rich, or to transport it despite their sabotage, or to break the resistance of the corrupt employees and the capitalist profiteers, or to establish strict accounting. The history of the supply organisations and of the food difficulties of the "democracy", with its millions of *complaints* against the sabotage of the capitalists, with its *whimpering* and *supplication*, is proof of this.

There is no power on earth, apart from the power of a victorious proletarian revolution, that would advance from complaints and begging and tears to *revolutionary action*. And the longer the proletarian revolution is delayed, the longer it is put off by events or by the vacillations of the wavering and confused, the more victims it will claim and the more difficult it will be to *organise* the transportation and distribution of food.

"In insurrection delay is fatal" – this is our answer to those having the sad "courage" to look at the growing economic ruin, at the approaching famine, and still *dissuade* the workers from the uprising (*that is, persuade them to wait and place confidence in the bourgeoisie for some further time*).

"There is not yet any danger at the front either. Even if the soldiers conclude an armistice themselves, it is still not a calamity."

But the soldiers will not conclude an armistice. For this state power is necessary, and that cannot be obtained without an uprising. The soldiers will simply *desert*. Reports from the front tell that. We must not wait, because of the risk of aiding collusion between Rodzyanko and Wilhelm and the risk of *complete* economic ruin, with the soldiers deserting in masses, once they (*being already close to desperation*) sink into absolute despair and leave everything to the mercy of fate.

*

"But if we take power, and obtain neither an armistice nor a democratic peace, the soldiers may not be willing to fight a revolutionary war. What then?"

An argument which brings to mind the saying: one fool can ask ten times more questions than ten wise men can answer.

We have never denied the difficulties of *those in power* during an imperialist war. Nevertheless, we have always *preached* the dictatorship of the proletariat and the poor peasantry. Shall we renounce this, when the moment to act has arrived?

We have always said that the dictatorship of the proletariat in one country creates gigantic changes in the international situation, in the economic life of the country, in the condition of the army and in its mood – shall we now "forget" all this, and allow ourselves to be frightened by the "difficulties" of the revolution?

"As everybody reports, the masses are not in a mood that would drive them into the streets. Among the signs justifying pessimism may be mentioned the greatly increasing circulation of the pogromist and Black-Hundred press."

When people allow themselves to be frightened by the bourgeoisie, all objects and phenomena naturally appear yellow to them. First, they substitute an impressionist, intellectualist criterion for the Marxist criterion of the movement; they *substitute* subjective impressions of moods *for* a political analysis of the development of the class struggle and of the course of events in the entire country against the entire international background. They "conveniently" forget, of course, that a firm party line, its unyielding resolve, is also a mood-creating *factor*, particularly at the sharpest revolutionary moments. It is sometimes very "convenient" for people to forget that the responsible leaders, by their vacillations and by their readiness to burn their yesterday's idols, cause the most unbecoming vacillations in the mood of certain strata of the masses.

Secondly – and this is at present the main thing – in speaking about the mood of the masses, the spineless people forget to add:

that "everybody" reports it as a tense and expectant mood;

that "everybody" agrees that, called upon by the Soviets for the defence of the Soviets, the workers will rise to a man;

that "everybody" agrees that the workers are greatly dissatisfied with the indecision of the centres concerning the "last decisive struggle", the inevitability of which they clearly recognise;

that "everybody" unanimously characterises the mood of the broadest masses as close to desperation and points to the anarchy developing therefrom;

that "everybody" also recognises that there is among the class-conscious workers a definite unwillingness to go out into the streets *only* for demonstrations, *only* for partial struggles, since a general and not a partial struggle is in the air, while the hopelessness of individual strikes, demonstrations and acts to influence the authorities has been seen and is fully realised.

And so forth.

If we approach this characterisation of the mass mood from the point of view of the entire development of the class and political struggle and of the entire course of events during the six months of our revolution, it will become clear to us how people frightened by the bourgeoisie are distorting the question. Things are not as they were before April 20–21, June 9, July 3, for then it was a matter of *spontaneous excitement* which we, as a party, either failed to comprehend (April 20) or held back and shaped into a peaceful demonstration (June 9 and July 3), for we knew very well at that time that the Soviets were *not yet* ours, that the peasants *still* trusted the Lieberdan–Chernov and not the Bolshevik course (uprising), that consequently we could not have the majority of the people behind us, and that consequently the uprising would be premature.

At that time the majority of the class-conscious workers did not raise the question of the last decisive struggle at all; *not* one of all our Party units would have raised it at that time. As for the unenlightened and very broad masses, there was neither a concerted effort nor the resolve born out of despair; there was only a spontaneous *excitement* with the naive hope of "influencing" Kerensky and the bourgeoisie by "action", by a demonstration pure and simple.

What is needed for an uprising is not this, but, on the one hand, a conscious, firm and unswerving resolve on the part of the class-conscious elements to fight to the end; and on the other, a mood of despair among the broad masses who *feel* that nothing can now be saved by half-measures; that you cannot "influence" anybody; that the hungry will "smash everything, destroy everything, even anarchically", *if* the Bolsheviks are not able to lead them in a decisive battle.

The development of the revolution has in practice brought *both* the workers *and* the peasantry to precisely this combination of a tense mood resulting from experience among the class-conscious and a mood of hatred towards those using the lockout weapon and the capitalists that is close to despair among the broadest masses.

We can also understand the "success" on this very soil of the scoundrels of the reactionary press who imitate Bolshevism. The malicious glee of the reactionaries at the approach of a decisive battle between the bourgeoisie and the proletariat has been observed in all revolutions without exception; it has always been so, and it is absolutely unavoidable. And if you allow yourselves to be frightened by *this* circumstance, then you have to renounce not only the uprising but the proletarian revolution in general. For in a capitalist society, this revolution *cannot* mature *without* being accompanied by malicious glee on the part of the reactionaries and by hopes that they would be able to feather their nest in this way.

The class-conscious workers know perfectly well that the Black Hundreds work hand in hand with the bourgeoisie, and that a decisive victory of the workers (in which the petty bourgeoisie do not believe, which the capitalists are afraid of, which the Black Hundreds sometimes wish for out of sheer malice, convinced as they are that the Bolsheviks cannot retain power) – that this victory will completely *crush* the Black Hundreds, that the Bolsheviks *will be able* to retain power firmly and to the greatest advantage of all humanity tortured and tormented by the war.

Indeed, is there anybody in his senses who can doubt that the *Rodzyankos* and Suvorins are acting in concert, that the roles have been distributed among them?

Has it not been proved by facts that Kerensky acts on Rodzyanko's orders, while the State Printing Press of the Russian Republic (don't laugh!) prints the Black-Hundred speeches of reactionaries in the "Duma" at the expense of the state. Has not this fact been exposed *even* by the lackeys from *Dyelo Naroda*, who serve "their own mannikin"? Has not the experience of *all* elections proved that the Cadet lists were fully supported by *Novoye Vremya*, which is a venal paper controlled by the "interests" of the tsarist landowners?[5]

Did we not read yesterday that commercial and industrial capitalists (non-partisan capitalists, of course; oh, non-partisan capitalists, to be sure, for the Vikhlayevs and Rakitnikovs, the Gvozdyovs and Nikitins, are in coalition not with the Cadets – God forbid – but with *non-partisan* commercial and industrial circles!) have donated the goodly sum of 300,000 roubles to the Cadets?

---

[5] *Novoye Vremya* (*New Times*) – a daily published in Petersburg from 1868 to 1917, by various publishers. It changed political colours a number of times, and from 1905 became the organ of the Black Hundreds. After the bourgeois-democratic revolution of February 1917, it took a counter-revolutionary attitude and conducted a rabid campaign against the Bolsheviks. Closed down by the Revolutionary Military Committee of the Petrograd Soviet on October 26 (November 8), 1917.

The whole Black-Hundred press, if we look at things from a class and not a sentimental point of view, is a *branch* of the firm "Ryabushinsky, Milyukov, and Co.". Capitalists buy, on the one hand, the Milyukovs, Zaslavskys, Potresovs, and so on; on the other, the Black Hundreds.

The *victory of the proletariat* is the only means of putting an end to this most hideous poisoning of the people by the cheap Black-Hundred venom.

Is it any wonder that the crowd, tired out and made wretched by hunger and the prolongation of the war, clutches at the Black-Hundred poison? Can one imagine a capitalist society on the eve of collapse in which the oppressed masses are *not* desperate? Is there any doubt that the desperation of the masses, a large part of whom are still ignorant, *will* express itself in the increased consumption of all sorts of poison?

Those who, in arguing about the mood of the masses, blame the masses for their own personal spinelessness, are in a hopeless position. The masses are divided into those who are consciously biding their time and those who unconsciously are ready to sink into despair; but the masses of the oppressed and the hungry are *not* spineless.

"On the other hand, the Marxist party cannot reduce the question of an uprising to that of a military conspiracy. . . ."

Marxism is an extremely profound and many-sided doctrine. It is, therefore, no wonder that scraps of quotations from Marx – especially when the quotations are made inappropriately – can always be found among the "arguments" of those who break with Marxism. Military conspiracy is Blanquism, *if* it is organised not by a party of a definite class, *if* its organisers have not analysed the political moment in general and the international situation in particular, *if* the party has not on its side the sympathy of the majority of the people, as proved by objective facts, *if* the development of revolutionary events has not brought about a practical refutation of the conciliatory illusions of the petty bourgeoisie, *if* the majority of the Soviet-type organs of revolutionary struggle that have been recognised as authoritative or have shown themselves to be such in practice have not been won over, *if* there has not matured a sentiment in the army (if in war-time) against the government that protracts the unjust war against the will of the whole people, *if* the slogans of the uprising (like "All Power to the Soviets", "Land to the peasants", or "Immediate offer of a democratic peace to all the belligerent nations, with an immediate abrogation of all secret treaties and secret diplomacy", etc.) have not become widely known and popular, *if* the advanced workers are not sure of the desperate situation of the masses and of the support of the countryside, a support proved by a serious peasant movement or by an uprising against the landowners and the government that defends the landowners, *if* the country's economic situation inspires earnest hopes for a favourable solution of the crisis by peaceful and parliamentary means.

This is probably enough.

In my pamphlet entitled: *Can the Bolsheviks Retain State Power?* (I hope it will appear in a day or two), there is a quotation from Marx which really bears upon the question of insurrection, and enumerates the features of insurrection as an "art".

I am ready to wager that if we were to propose to all those chatterers in Russia who are now shouting against a military conspiracy, to open their mouths and explain the difference between the "art" of an insurrection and a military conspiracy that deserves condemnation, they would either repeat what was quoted above or would cover themselves with shame, and would call forth the general ridicule of the workers. Why not try, my dear would-be Marxists! Sing us a song *against* "military conspiracy"!

Postscript

The above lines had been written when I received, at eight o'clock Tuesday evening, the morning Petrograd papers; there was an article by Mr V. Bazarov in *Novaya Zhizn*. Mr V. Bazarov asserts that "a handwritten manifesto was distributed in the city, in which arguments were presented in the name of two eminent Bolsheviks, against immediate action".

If this is true, I beg the comrades, whom this letter cannot reach earlier than Wednesday noon, to *publish it* as quickly as possible.

I did not write it for the press; I wanted to talk to the members of our Party by letter. But we cannot remain silent when the heroes of *Novaya Zhizn*, who do not belong to the Party and who have been ridiculed by it a thousand times for their contemptible spinelessness (they voted for the Bolsheviks the day before yesterday, for the Mensheviks yesterday, and who *almost* united them at the world-famous unity congress) – when such individuals receive a *manifesto* from members of our Party in which they carry on propaganda against an uprising. We must agitate also *in favour* of an uprising. Let the anonymous individuals come right out into the light of day, and let them bear the punishment they deserve for their shameful vacillations, even if it be only the ridicule of all class-conscious workers. I have at my disposal only one hour before I send the present letter to

Petrograd, and I therefore can say only a word or two about one of the "methods" of the sad heroes of the brainless *Novaya Zhizn* trend. Mr V. Bazarov attempts to polemicise against Comrade Ryazanov, who has said – and who is a thousand times correct in saying – that "all those who create in the masses a mood of despair and indifference are preparing an uprising".

The sad hero of a sad cause "rejoins" as follows:

"Have despair and indifference ever conquered?"

O contemptible fools from *Novaya Zhizn*! Do they know such examples of uprising in history, in which the masses of the oppressed classes were victorious in a desperate battle without having been reduced to despair by long sufferings and by an extreme sharpening of all sorts of crises, in which those masses had not been seized by indifference towards various lackey-like pre-parliaments, towards idle playing at revolution, towards the Lieber-dans' reduction of the Soviets from organs of power and uprising to empty talking shops?

Or have the contemptible little fools from *Novaya Zhizn* perhaps discovered among the masses an indifference – to the question of bread, to the prolongation of the war, to and for the peasants?

12

Meeting of the Petrograd Soviet of Workers' and Soldiers' Deputies

October 25 (November 7), 1917[1]

1
Report on the Tasks of the Soviet Power Newspaper Report

Comrades, the workers' and peasants' revolution, about the necessity of which the Bolsheviks have always spoken, has been accomplished.

What is the significance of this workers' and peasants' revolution? Its significance is, first of all, that we shall have a Soviet government, our own organ of power, in which the bourgeoisie will have no share whatsoever. The oppressed masses will themselves create a power. The old state apparatus will be shattered to its foundations, and a new administrative apparatus set up in the form of the Soviet organisations.

From now on, a new phase in the history of Russia begins, and this, the third Russian revolution, should in the end lead to the victory of socialism.

One of our urgent tasks is to put an immediate end to the war. It is clear to everybody that in order to end this war, which is closely bound up with the present capitalist system, capital itself must be fought.

We shall be helped in this by the world working-class movement, which is already beginning to develop in Italy, Britain and Germany.

The proposal we make to international democracy for a just and immediate peace will everywhere awaken an ardent response among the international proletarian masses. All the secret treaties[2] must be immediately published in order to strengthen the confidence of the proletariat.

---

[1] The meeting opened at 2.35 p.m. on October 25 (November 7), and heard a report of the Revolutionary Military Committee on the overthrow of the Provisional Government and the triumph of the revolution. Lenin gave a report on the tasks facing Soviet power. The resolution motioned by Lenin (see below) was adopted by an overwhelming majority.

[2] The reference is to secret diplomatic documents, such as the secret treaties concluded by the tsarist and later by the bourgeois Provisional Government of Russia with the

Within Russia a huge section of the peasantry have said that they have played long enough with the capitalists, and will now march with the workers. A single decree putting an end to landed proprietorship will win us the confidence of the peasants. The peasants will understand that the salvation of the peasantry lies only in an alliance with the workers. We shall institute genuine workers' control over production.

We have now learned to make a concerted effort. The revolution that has just been accomplished is evidence of this. We possess the strength of mass organisation, which will overcome everything and lead the proletariat to the world revolution.

We must now set about building a proletarian socialist state in Russia.

Long live the world socialist revolution! [*Stormy applause.*]

2
Resolution

The Petrograd Soviet of Workers' and Soldiers' Deputies hails the victorious revolution of the proletariat and the garrison of Petrograd. The Soviet particularly emphasises the solidarity, organisation, discipline and complete unanimity displayed by the masses in this unusually bloodless and unusually successful uprising.

It is the unshakeable conviction of the Soviet that the workers' and peasants' government which will be created by the revolution, as a Soviet government, and which will ensure the urban proletariat the support of the whole mass of the poor peasantry, will firmly advance towards socialism, the only means of saving the country from the untold miseries and horrors of war.

The new workers' and peasants' government will immediately propose a just and democratic peace to all belligerent nations.

It will immediately abolish landed proprietorship and hand over the land to the peasants. It will institute workers' control over the production and

---

governments of Britain, France, Germany, Japan and other imperialist powers. From November 10 (23), 1917, these documents were published in *Pravda* and *Izvestia*, and in December were put out in a series entitled *Collection of Secret Documents from the Archives of the Former Ministry of Foreign Affairs*. Seven volumes were published from December 1917 to February 1918. By publishing the secret treaties, the Soviet Government's revolutionary propaganda struck a great blow for a general democratic peace, without annexations and indemnities, and exposed the imperialist nature of the First World War.

distribution of goods and establish national control over the banks, at the same time transforming them into a single state enterprise.

The Petrograd Soviet of Workers' and Soldiers' Deputies calls on all workers and all peasants to support the workers' and peasants' revolution devotedly and with all their energy. The Soviet expresses the conviction that the urban workers, in alliance with the poor peasants, will display strict, comradely discipline and establish the strictest revolutionary order, which is essential for the victory of socialism.

The Soviet is convinced that the proletariat of the West European countries will help us to achieve a complete and lasting victory for the cause of socialism.

Afterword

Afterword: Lenin's Choice

Slavoj Žižek

In academic politics today, the idea of dealing with Lenin immediately gives rise to two qualifications: yes, why not, we live in a liberal democracy, there is freedom of thought . . . provided that we treat Lenin in an "objective, critical and scientific way", not in an attitude of nostalgic idolatry, and, furthermore, from a perspective firmly rooted in the democratic political order, within the horizon of human rights – that is the lesson learned painfully through the experience of twentieth-century totalitarianism.

What are we to say to this? The problem lies in the further implicit qualifications which can easily be discerned by a "concrete analysis of the concrete situation", as Lenin himself would have put it.[1] "Fidelity to the democratic consensus" means acceptance of the present liberal-parliamentary consensus, which precludes any serious questioning of the way this liberal-democratic order is complicit in the phenomena it officially condemns, and, of course, any serious attempt to imagine a *different* sociopolitical order. In short, it means: say and write whatever you like – on condition that you do not actually question or disturb the prevailing political consensus. Everything is allowed, solicited even, as a critical topic: the prospect of a global ecological catastrophe; violations of human rights; sexism, homophobia, anti-feminism; growing violence not only in faraway countries, but also in our own megalopolises; the gap between the First and the Third World, between rich and poor; the shattering impact of the digitalization of our daily lives . . . today, there is nothing easier than to get international, state or corporate funds for a multidisciplinary research project on how to fight new forms of ethnic, religious or sexist violence. The problem is that all this occurs against the background of a fundamental *Denkverbot*: a prohibition on thinking.

Today's liberal-democratic hegemony is sustained by a kind of unwritten *Denkverbot* similar to the infamous *Berufsverbot* (prohibition on employing individuals with radical Left leanings in the state organs) in Germany in the late 1960s – the moment we show a minimal sign of engaging in political projects which aim seriously to challenge the existing order, the answer is immediately: "Benevolent as it is, this will inevitably end in a new Gulag!" The ideological function of constant references to the Holocaust, the Gulag, and more recent Third World catastrophes is thus to serve as the support of this *Denkverbot* by constantly reminding us how *things could have been much worse*: "Just look around and see for yourself what will happen if we follow your radical notions!" What we encounter here is the ultimate example of what Anna Dinerstein and Mike Neary have called the project of *disutopia*: "not just the temporary absence of Utopia, but the political celebration of the end of social dreams".[2] And the demand for "scientific objectivity" amounts to just another version of the same *Denkverbot*: the moment we seriously question the existing liberal consensus, we are accused of abandoning scientific objectivity for outdated ideological positions. This is the "Leninist" point on which one cannot and should not concede: *today, actual freedom of thought means freedom to question the prevailing liberal-democratic "post-ideological" consensus – or it means nothing.*

The Right to Truth

The perspective of the critique of ideology compels us to invert Wittgenstein's "What one cannot speak about, thereof one should be silent" into "What one should not speak about, thereof one cannot remain silent". If you want to speak about a social system, you cannot remain silent about its repressed excess. The point is not to tell the whole Truth but, precisely, to append to the (official) Whole the uneasy supplement which denounces its falsity. As Max Horkheimer put it back in the 1930s: "If you don't want to talk about capitalism, then you should keep silent about Fascism." Fascism is the inherent "symptom" (the return of the repressed) of capitalism, the key to its "truth", not just an external contingent deviation of its "normal" logic. And the same goes for today's situation: those who do not want to subject liberal democracy and the flaws of its multiculturalist tolerance to critical analysis, should keep quiet about the new Rightist violence and intolerance.

If we are to leave the opposition between liberal-democratic universalism and ethnic/religious fundamentalism behind, the first step is to acknowledge the existence of *liberal fundamentalism*: the perverse game of making a big fuss when the rights of a serial killer or a suspected war criminal are violated, while ignoring massive violations of "ordinary" people's rights.

More precisely, the politically correct stance betrays its perverse economy through its oscillation between the two extremes: either fascination with the victimized other (helpless children, raped women . . .), or a focus on the problematic other who, although criminal, and so on, also deserves protection of his human rights, because "today it's him, tomorrow it'll be us" (an excellent example is Noam Chomsky's defence of a French book advocating the revisionist stance on the Holocaust). On a different level, a similar instance of the perversity of Political Correctness occurs in Denmark, where people speak ironically of the "white woman's burden", her ethico political duty to have sex with immigrant workers from Third World countries – this being the final necessary step in ending their exclusion.

Today, in the era of what Habermas designated as *die neue Unübersichtlichkeit* (the new opacity),[3] our everyday experience is more mystifying than ever: modernization generates new obscurantisms; the reduction of freedom is presented to us as the dawn of new freedoms. The perception that we live in a society of free choices, in which we have to choose even our most "natural" features (ethnic or sexual identity), is the form of appearance of its very opposite: of the *absence* of true choices.[4] The recent trend for "alternate reality" films, which present existing reality as one of a multitude of possible outcomes, is symptomatic of a society in which choices no longer really matter, are trivialized. The lesson of the time-warp narratives is even bleaker, since it points towards a total closure: the very attempt to avoid the predestined course of things not only leads us back to it, but actually constitutes it – from Oedipus onwards, we want to avoid A, and it is through our very detour that A realizes itself.

In these circumstances, we should be especially careful *not to confuse the ruling ideology with ideology which seems to dominate*. More then ever, we should bear in mind Walter Benjamin's reminder that it is not enough to ask how a certain theory (or art) positions itself with regard to social struggles – we should also ask how it actually functions in these very struggles. In sex, the true hegemonic attitude is not patriarchal repression, but free promiscuity; in art, provocations in the style of the notorious "Sensation" exhibitions *are* the norm, the example of art fully integrated into the establishment. Ayn Rand brought this logic to its conclusion, supplementing it with a kind of Hegelian twist, that is, reasserting the official ideology itself as its own greatest transgression, as in the title of one of her late non-fiction books: "Capitalism, This Unknown Ideal", or in "top managers, America's last endangered species".

Indeed, since the "normal" functioning of capitalism involves some kind of disavowal of the basic principle of its functioning (today's model capitalist is someone who, after ruthlessly generating profit, then generously shares parts of it, giving large donations to churches, victims of ethnic or sexual abuse, etc., posing as a humanitarian), the ultimate act of transgression is to assert this principle directly, depriving it of its humanitarian mask. I am therefore tempted to reverse Marx's Thesis 11: the first task today is precisely *not* to succumb to the temptation to act, to intervene directly and change things (which then inevitably ends in a cul-de-sac of debilitating impossibility: "What can we do against global capital?"), but to question the hegemonic ideological co-ordinates. In short, our historical moment is still that of Adorno:

> To the question "What should we do?" I can most often truly answer only with "I don't know." I can only try to analyse rigorously what there is. Here people reproach me: When you practise criticism, you are also obliged to say how one should make it better. To my mind, this is incontrovertibly a bourgeois prejudice. Many times in history it so happened that the very works which pursued purely theoretical goals transformed consciousness, and thereby also social reality.[5]

If, today, we follow a direct call to act, this act will not be performed in an empty space – it will be an act within the hegemonic ideological co-ordinates: those who "really want to do something to help people" get involved in (undoubtedly honourable) exploits like *Médecins sans frontières*, Greenpeace, feminist and anti-racist campaigns, which are all not only tolerated but even supported by the media, even if they seemingly encroach on economic territory (for example, denouncing and boycotting companies which do not respect ecological conditions, or use child labour) – they are tolerated and supported as long as they do not get too close to a certain limit.[6]

This kind of activity provides the perfect example of interpassivity:[7] of doing things not in order to achieve something, but to prevent something from really happening, really changing. All this frenetic humanitarian, Politically Correct, etc., activity fits the formula of "Let's go on changing something all the time so that, globally, things will remain the same!". If standard Cultural Studies criticize capitalism, they do so in the coded way that exemplifies Hollywood liberal paranoia: the enemy is "the system", the hidden "organization", the anti-democratic "conspiracy", not simply capitalism and state apparatuses. The problem with this critical stance is not only that it replaces concrete social analysis with a struggle against abstract paranoiac fantasies, but that – in a typical paranoiac gesture – it unnecessarily *redoubles* social reality, as if there were a secret Organization *behind* the "visible" capitalist and state organs. What we should accept is that there is no need for a secret "organization-within-an-organization": the "conspiracy" is already in the "visible" organization as such, in the capitalist system, in the way the political space and state apparatuses work.[8]

Let us take one of the hottest topics in today's "radical" American academia: postcolonial studies. The problem of postcolonialism is undoubtedly crucial; however, postcolonial studies tend to translate it into the multiculturalist problematic of the colonized minorities' "right to narrate" their victimizing experience, of the power mechanisms which repress "otherness", so that, at the end of the day, we learn that the root of postcolonial exploitation is our intolerance towards the Other, and, furthermore, that this intolerance itself is rooted in our intolerance towards the "Stranger in Ourselves", in our inability to confront what we have repressed in and of ourselves – the politico-economic struggle is thus imperceptibly transformed into a pseudo-psychoanalytic drama of the subject unable to confront its inner traumas. . . . (Why pseudo-psychoanalytic? Because the true lesson of psychoanalysis is not that the external events which fascinate and/or disturb us are just projections of our inner repressed impulses. The unbearable fact of life is that there really are disturbing events out there: there *are* other human beings who experience intense sexual enjoyment while we are half-impotent; there *are* people submitted to terrifying torture. . . . Again, the ultimate truth of psychoanalysis is not that of discovering our true Self, but that of the traumatic encounter with an unbearable Real.) The true corruption of American academia is not primarily financial, it is not only that universities are able to buy many European critical intellectuals (myself included – up to a point), but conceptual: notions of "European" critical theory are imperceptibly translated into the benign universe of Cultural Studies chic. At a certain point, this chic becomes indistinguishable from the famous Citibank commercial in which scenes of East Asian, European, Black and American children playing is accompanied by the voice-over: "People who were once divided by a continent . . . are now united by an economy" – at this concluding highpoint, of course, the children are replaced by the Citibank logo.[9]

The great majority of today's "radical" academics silently count on the long-term stability of the American capitalist model, with a secure tenured position as their ultimate professional goal (a surprising number of them even play the stock market). If there is one thing they are genuinely afraid of, it is a radical shattering of the (relatively) safe life-environment of the "symbolic classes" in developed Western societies. Their excessive Politically Correct zeal when they are dealing with sexism, racism, Third World sweatshops, and so on, is thus ultimately a defence against their own innermost identification, a kind of compulsive ritual whose hidden logic is: "Let's talk as much as possible about the necessity of a radical change, to make sure that nothing will really change!" The journal *October* is typical of this: when you ask one of the editors what the title refers to, they half-confidentially indicate that it is, of course, *that* October – in this way, you can indulge in jargonistic analyses of modern art, with the secret assurance that you are somehow retaining a link with the radical revolutionary past. . . . With regard to this radical chic, our first gesture towards Third Way ideologists and practitioners should be one of praise: at least they play their game straight, and are honest in their acceptance of the global capitalist co-ordinates – unlike pseudo-radical academic Leftists who adopt an attitude of utter disdain towards the Third Way, while their own radicalism ultimately amounts to an empty gesture which obliges no one to do anything definite.

There is, of course, a strict distinction to be made here between authentic social engagement on behalf of exploited minorities (for example, organizing illegally employed chicano field workers in California) and the multiculturalist/postcolonial "plantations of no-risk, no-fault, knock-off rebellion"[10] which prosper in "radical" American academia. If, however, in contrast to "corporate multiculturalism", we define "critical multiculturalism" as a strategy of pointing out that "there are common forces of oppression, common strategies of exclusion, stereotyping, and stigmatizing of oppressed groups, and thus common enemies and targets of attack,"[11] I do not see the appropriateness of the continuing use of the term "multiculturalism", since the accent shifts here to the *common* struggle. In its normal accepted meaning, multiculturalism perfectly fits the logic of the global market.

Recently, the Hindus in India organized widespread demonstrations against McDonald's, after it became known that, before freezing its potato chips, McDonald's fried them in oil of animal (beef) fat origin; once the company had conceded the point, guaranteeing that all potato chips sold in India would be fried only in vegetable oil, the satisfied Hindus happily returned to munching the chips. Far from undermining globalization, this protest against McDonald's, and the company's quick answer, embody the Hindus' perfect integration into the diversified global order. The point is not only that the global market thrives on the diversification of demand, but that, on a purely formal level, the Hindus' defence of their tradition is already inscribed in the logic of modernity, that it is already a "reflected" gesture: the Hindus have *chosen* (to remain faithful to) their tradition, thereby transforming this tradition into one of the many options available to them.

A closer analysis should take into account the gap between the literal and the metaphorical dimension of the Hindu protest against McDonald's chips: it is clear that this protest functioned as a metaphorical stand-in for global discontent with Western cultural imperialism. We can thus imagine two further versions (not taking into account the third one: what if McDonald's were to lie, continuing to use beef fat, and the Hindus were to believe the company? Is it not true that in this case, everybody would have been satisfied?):

- What if, having obtained assurances that McDonald's had truly stopped using beef fat, the Hindus somehow felt frustrated? By complying with their literal demand, McDonald's prevented them from articulating their more fundamental protest against Western cultural imperialism?
- What if, after McDonald's had truly stopped using beef fat, the Hindu press had continued to spread the lie that this fat was still being used, and this lie had triggered a popular revolt against cultural imperialism with some really emancipatory results? Is it not true that in this case, a blatant lie would have served as the means of articulating a more global truth? (Consider also the analogous case of the trial of an African-American murderer: even if he really did commit the crime, the sentence is somehow "wrong", since it serves to sustain racist attitudes towards African-Americans.)

Mcdonald's "respect" for the Hindus is thus unremittingly *patronizing*, like our normal attitude towards small children: although we do not take them seriously, we "respect" their innocuous habits in order not to shatter their illusory world. When a visitor reaches a local village, with its local customs, is there anything more racist than his clumsy attempts to demonstrate how he "understands" these customs, and is able to follow them? Does not such behaviour reveal the same patronizing attitude as the one displayed by adults who adapt themselves to their small children by imitating their gestures and their way of speaking? Are not local inhabitants legitimately offended when the foreign intruder mimics their speech? The patronizing falsity of the visitor does not reside merely in the fact that he is only pretending to be "one of us" – the point is, rather, that we establish a real contact with the locals only when they disclose to us the distance they themselves maintain towards the letter of their own customs.[12] There is a well-known anecdote about Prince Peter Petrovič Njegos, an early-nineteenth-century Montenegrin ruler famous both for his battles against the Turks and for his epic poetry: when an English visitor to his court, profoundly touched by a local ritual, expressed his willingness to partake in it, Njegos cruelly rebuffed him: "Why should you make a fool of yourself too? Isn't it bad enough for us to play these silly games?" . . .

Furthermore, what about practices like burning wives after their husband's death, which is part of the same Hindu tradition as sacred cows? Should we (tolerant Western multiculturalists) also respect these practices? Here, the tolerant multiculturalist is compelled to resort to a thoroughly *Eurocentrist* distinction, a distinction that is totally foreign to Hinduism: the Other is tolerated with regard to customs which hurt no one – the moment we come up against some (for us) traumatic dimension, the tolerance is over. In short, tolerance is tolerance of the Other in so far as this Other is not an "intolerant fundamentalist" – which simply means: in so far as it is not the real Other. Tolerance is "zero tolerance" for the real Other, the Other in the substantial weight of its *jouissance*. We can see how this liberal tolerance reproduces the elementary "postmodern" operation of having access to the object deprived of its substance: we can enjoy coffee without caffeine, beer without alcohol, sex without direct bodily contact, right up to Virtual Reality, that is, reality itself deprived of its inert material substance – along the same lines, we even get the ethnic Other deprived of the substance of its Otherness. . . .

In other words, the problem with the liberal multiculturalist is that he or she is unable to maintain a true indifference towards the Other's *jouissance* – this *jouissance* bothers them, which is why their entire strategy is to keep it at a proper distance. This indifference towards the Other's *jouissance*, the thorough absence of envy, is the key component of what Lacan calls the subjective position of a "saint". Like the authentic "fundamentalists" (say, the Amish) who are indifferent, not bothered by the secret enjoyment of Others, true believers in a (universal) Cause, like Saint Paul, are pointedly indifferent to local customs and mores which simply *do not matter*. In contrast, the multiculturalist liberal is a Rortyan "ironist", always keeping his or her distance, always displacing belief on to Others – Others believe for them, in their place. And although they may appear ("for themselves") to reproach the believing Other for the particular content of his or her belief, what actually ("in itself") bothers them is *the form of belief as such*. Intolerance is intolerance towards the Real of a belief. These people in fact behave like the proverbial husband who concedes in principle that his wife may have a lover, only not *that* guy – that is to say, every particular lover is unacceptable: the tolerant liberal concedes the right to believe in principle, while rejecting every determinate belief as "fundamentalist".[13] The ultimate joke of multiculturalist tolerance is, of course, the way class distinction is inscribed into it: adding (ideological) insult to (politico-economic) injury, upper-class Politically Correct individuals use it to berate the lower classes for their redneck "fundamentalism".

One of the most refined forms of racist (or sexist) oppression is to deny the other the right to define their identity – we do it for them; we tell them who and what they really are. This practice is expanded with Politically Correct multiculturalism: when members of an old ethnic group, for example, make clear their desire to taste the pleasures of the "consumerist society", patronizing multiculturalists try to convince them that they are victims of Western capitalist ideology, and that they should resist it. This patronizing attitude can go right up to direct interference in naming itself: at a TV round-table discussion in Minnesota a couple of years ago, the enlightened white liberals tried to convince their partners to refer to themselves as "Native Americans", although they insisted that they unequivocally preferred the old term "Indians".

This brings us to the more radical question: is respect for the other's belief (say, belief in the sacredness of cows) really the ultimate ethical horizon? Is this not the ultimate horizon of postmodern ethics, in which, since reference to any form of universal truth is disqualified as a form of cultural violence, all that ultimately matters is respect for the other's fantasy? Or, to put it in an even more pointed way: OK, you can claim that lying to the Hindus about the beef fat is ethically problematic – does this mean, however, that you are not allowed to argue publicly that their belief (in the sacredness of cows) is already in itself a lie, a false belief? The fact that "ethical committees" are sprouting up everywhere today points in the same direction: how did ethics, all of a sudden, became an affair of bureaucratic (administrative), state-nominated committees invested with the authority to determine what course of action can still count as ethically acceptable? The "risk society" theorists' answer (we need committees because we are confronting new situations in which it is no longer possible to apply old norms, that is, ethical committees are the sign of "reflected" ethics) is clearly inadequate: these committees are the symptom of a deeper malaise (and, at the same time, an inadequate answer to it).

The ultimate problem with the "right to narrate" is that it uses a unique particular experience as a political argument: "Only a gay black woman can experience and tell what it means to be a gay black woman", and so on. Such recourse to a particular experience which cannot be universalized is always, and by definition, a conservative political gesture: ultimately, everyone can evoke his or her unique experience in order to justify their reprehensible acts.[14] Is it not possible for a Nazi executioner to claim that his victims did not really understand the inner vision which motivated him?

Along these same lines, Veit Harlan, *the* Nazi film director, spoke despairingly in the 1950s about the fact that Jews in the USA did not show any comprehension of his defence for making *The Jew Süss*, claiming that no American Jew could really understand his situation in Nazi Germany – far from exonerating him, this obscene (factual) truth is the ultimate lie. Furthermore, the fact that the greatest plea for tolerance in the history of cinema was made in a defence against "intolerant" attacks on an advocate for the Ku Klux Klan tells a lot about the extent to which – to use today's terms – the signifier "tolerance" is very much a "floating" one. For D. W. Griffith, *Intolerance* was not a way to exculpate himself for the aggressive racist message of *The Birth of a Nation*: quite the contrary, he was smarting at what he considered "intolerance" on the part of groups which attempted to have *The Birth of a Nation* banned because of its anti-Black thrust. In short, when Griffith complains about "intolerance", he is much closer to today's fundamentalists decrying the "Politically Correct" defence of the universal rights of women as "intolerant" towards their specific way of life than to today's multiculturalist assertion of differences.

Consequently, Lenin's legacy, to be reinvented today, is the politics of truth. Both liberal-political democracy and "totalitarianism" foreclose a politics of truth. Democracy, of course, is the reign of sophists: there are only opinions; any reference by a political agent to some ultimate truth is denounced as "totalitarian". What "totalitarianism" regimes impose, however, is also a mere semblance of truth: an arbitrary Teaching whose function is simply to legitimize the pragmatic decisions of the Rulers.[15] We live in the "postmodern" era, in which truth-claims as such are dismissed as an expression of hidden power mechanisms – as reborn pseudo-Nietzscheans like to emphasize, truth is a lie which is most efficient in asserting our will to power. The very question "Is it true?", apropos of some statement, is supplanted by the question "Under what power conditions can this statement be uttered?".

What we get instead of the universal truth is the multitude of perspectives, or – as it is fashionable to put it today – of "narratives"; as a result, the two philosophers of today's global capitalism are the two great Left-liberal "progressives", Richard Rorty and Peter Singer – both are honest in their radical stance. Rorty defines the basic co-ordinates: the fundamental dimension of a human being is the ability to suffer, to experience pain and humiliation – therefore, since humans are symbolic animals, the fundamental right is the right to narrate one's experience of suffering and humiliation.[16] Singer then provides the Darwinian background: "speciesism" (privileging the human species) is no different from racism: our perception of a difference between humans and (other) animals is no less illogical and unethical than our former perception of an ethical difference between, say, men and women, or Blacks and Whites.[17]

The problem with Singer is not only the rather obvious fact that while we, ecologically conscious humans, are protecting endangered animal species, our ultimate goal with regard to oppressed and exploited human groups is not just to "protect" them but, above all, to empower them to take care of themselves and lead a free and autonomous life. What gets lost in this Darwinist narrativism is simply the dimension of truth, *not* "objective truth" as the notion of reality from a point of view which somehow floats above the multitude of particular narratives. Without a reference to this universal dimension of truth, we ultimately all remain the "apes of a cold God"(as Marx put it in his 1841 poem[18]), even in Singer's progressive version of social Darwinism. Lenin's premiss – which today, in our era of postmodern relativism, is more pertinent than ever – is that universal truth and partisanship, the gesture of taking sides, are not only not mutually exclusive, but condition each other: the *universal* truth of a concrete situation can be articulated only from a thoroughly *partisan* position; truth is, by definition, one-sided.

This, of course, goes against the prevailing doxa of compromise, of finding a middle path among the multitude of conflicting interests. If we do not specify the criteria of the different, alternative, narrativization, then this endeavour runs the risk of endorsing, in the Politically Correct mood, ridiculous "narratives" like the ones about the supremacy of some aboriginal holistic wisdom, of dismissing science as just another narrative on a par with premodern superstitions. The Leninist answer to the postmodern multiculturalist "right to narrate" should thus be an unashamed assertion of the *right to truth*. When, in the débâcle of 1914, almost all the European Social-Democratic parties succumbed to war fervour and voted for military credits, Lenin's complete rejection of the "patriotic line", in its very isolation from the prevailing mood, stood for the singular emergence of the truth of the entire situation. Against the cliché according to which politics tears people apart, introducing disunity into the social body, we should claim that *the only real universality is the political one*: the universal link binding together all those who experience a fundamental solidarity, all those who became aware that their struggles are part of the very struggle which cuts across the entire social edifice.[19] To put it in Badiou's terms: universality (of the truth-procedure) can assert itself only in the guise of such a cut, of a radical division, at the very heart of the social body. How did De Gaulle emerge as the symbol of unified France? Through his "crazy" insistence in

1940, after the French defeat, that the war was not over, that the fight must go on – an insistence whose effects were deeply divisive.

In a closer analysis, we should show how the cultural relativism of the "right-to-narrate" orientation contains its own apparent opposite, a fixation on the Real of some trauma which resists its narrativization – this properly dialectical tension sustains today's academic "Holocaust industry". The postmodern logic of "everything is a discursive construction, there are no direct firm facts" was never used to deflate the Holocaust: Holocaust revisionists prefer to argue in the terms of empirical analysis. Their claims range from the "fact" that there is no written document in which Hitler ordered the Holocaust to the weird mathematics of: "Taking into account the number of gas ovens in Auschwitz, it was not possible to burn so many corpses . . .". In contrast to the revisionists, it is precisely the postmodern discursive constructionists (like Lyotard) who tend to elevate the Holocaust into the supreme ineffable metaphysical Evil – for them the Holocaust is the untouchable-sacred Real, the negative of contingent language games.[20] The problem with those who perceive every comparison between the Holocaust and other concentration camps and mass political crimes as an inadmissible relativization of the Holocaust is that they miss the point and reveal their own doubts: yes, the Holocaust *was* unique, but the only way to establish this uniqueness is to compare it with other similar phenomena, and thus demonstrate the limit of this comparison. If, instead of risking this comparison, you prohibit it, you get caught in the Wittgensteinian paradox of prohibiting speech about that about which we cannot speak: if we stick to the prohibition of the comparison, the gnawing suspicion emerges that if we were to be allowed to compare the Holocaust with other similar crimes, it would be deprived of its uniqueness. . . .

Materialism Revisited

Lenin's truth is ultimately that of *materialism*, and in fact, in the present climate of New Age obscurantism, it may appear attractive to reassert the lesson of Lenin's *Materialism and Empiriocriticism*: in today's popular reading of quantum physics, as in Lenin's time, the *doxa* is that science itself finally overcame materialism – matter is supposed to "disappear", to dissolve in the immaterial waves of energy fields.[21] It is also true (as Lucio Colletti emphasized) that Lenin's distinction between the philosophical and the scientific notion of matter eliminates the very notion of "dialectics in/of nature": the philosophical notion of matter as reality existing independently of mind precludes any intervention by philosophy into science. However . . . the "however" concerns the fact that, in *Materialism and Empiriocriticism*, there is no place for dialectics, for Hegel. What are Lenin's basic thesis? A refusal to reduce knowledge to phenomenalist or pragmatic instrumentalism (i.e. the assertion that, through scientific knowledge, we come to know the way things exist independently of our minds – the infamous "theory of reflection"), coupled with an insistence on the precarious nature of our knowledge (which is always limited, relative, and "reflects" external reality only in the infinite process of approximation). Does this not sound familiar? Is it not, in the Anglo-Saxon tradition of analytical philosophy, the basic position of Karl Popper, the archetypal anti-Hegelian? In his short article "Lenin and Popper",[22] Colletti recalls how, in a private letter written in 1970, first published in *Die Zeit*, Popper wrote: "Lenin's book on empiriocriticism is, in my opinion, truly excellent."[23]

This hard materialist core of *Empiriocriticism* persists in the *Philosophical Note-Books* (1915), despite Lenin's rediscovery of Hegel – why? In his *Note-Books*, Lenin is struggling with the same problem as Adorno in his "negative dialectics": how to combine Hegel's legacy of the critique of every immediacy, of the subjective mediation of all given objectivity, with the minimum of materialism that Adorno calls the "predominance of the objective"; this is why Lenin still clings to the "theory of reflection" according to which human thought mirrors objective reality):

> Here there are *actually*, objectively, *three* members: (1) nature; (2) human cognition = the human *brain* (as the highest product of this same nature); and (3) the form of reflection of nature in human cognition, and this form consists precisely of concepts, laws, categories, etc. Man cannot comprehend = reflect = mirror nature *as a whole*, in its completeness, its "immediate totality", he can only *eternally* come closer to this, creating abstractions, concepts, laws, a scientific picture of the world, etc., etc.[24]

Both Adorno and Lenin, however, take the wrong path here: the way to assert materialism is not by clinging to the minimum of objective reality *outside* the thought's subjective mediation, but by insisting on the absolute *inherence* of the external obstacle which prevents thought from attaining full identity with itself. The moment we concede this point, and externalize the obstacle, we regress to the pseudo-problematic of the thought asymptotically approaching the ever-elusive "objective reality", never able to grasp it in its infinite complexity.[25]

The problem with Lenin's "theory of reflection" lies in its implicit idealism: its very compulsive insistence on the independent existence of material reality outside consciousness is to be read as a symptomatic displacement, destined to conceal the key fact that *consciousness itself* is implicitly posited as external to the reality it "reflects". The very metaphor of reflection infinitely approaching the way things really are, the objective truth, betrays this idealism: what this metaphor leaves out of consideration is the fact that the partiality (distortion) of "subjective reflection" occurs precisely because the subject is included in the process it reflects – only a consciousness observing the universe from the outside would see the whole of reality "the way it really is", that is, a totally adequate "neutral" knowledge of reality would imply our ex-sistence, our external status with regard to it, just as a mirror can reflect an object perfectly only if it is external to it (so much for Lenin's theory of cognition as "mirroring" objective reality).[26] The point is not that there is independent reality out there, outside myself; the point is that I myself am "out there", part of that reality.[27] So the question is not whether there is a reality outside and independent of consciousness, but whether consciousness itself is outside and independent of reality: so, instead of Lenin's (implicitly idealist) notion of objective reality as existing "out there", separated from consciousness by layers of illusions and distortions, and cognitively approachable only through infinite approximation, we should assert that "objective" know-ledge of reality is impossible precisely because we (consciousness) are always-already part of it, in the midst of it – the thing that separates us from objective knowledge of reality is our very ontological inclusion in it.

This, of course, in no way entails that the tracing of the difference between idealism and materialism is not more crucial than ever today; but we should be careful to proceed in a truly Leninist way, discerning – through the "concrete analysis of concrete circumstances" – where this line of separation runs.[28] The line of separation between idealism and material-ism runs even within the field of religion, where the singular point of the emergence of materialism is signalled by Christ's words on the cross: "Father, why hast thou forsaken me?" – in this moment of total abandon-ment, the subject experiences and fully assumes the *nonexistence of the big Other*. More generally, the line of division is the one between the "idealist" Socratic–Gnostic tradition which claims that the truth is within us, just waiting to be (re)discovered through an inner journey, and the Judaeo-Christian "materialist" notion that truth can emerge only from an *external* traumatic encounter which shatters the subject's balance. "Truth" requires a struggle in which we have to fight our "spontaneous" tendency.

To put the same argument in a different way: the correct materialist position (which draws the radical Hegelian ontological consequence from Kant's antinomies) is that *there is no universe as a Whole*: as a Whole, the universe (the world) is Nothing – everything that exists is *within* this Nothing:

> The universe did not arise out of nothing: the universe arose inside nothing. Everything is nothing, seen from the inside. *The world without is really nothing seen from within.* We are inside nothing.
>
> Seen from without, there is zilch, nothing. Seen from within, there is everything we know. The whole universe.[29]

The line that separates materialism from idealism is very delicate here. On the one hand, there is the temptation to read this in the subjectivist mode (the universe "out there" emerges only through being perceived by the Mind); on the other, there is the obverse radical conclusion that consciousness is thoroughly included in the observed objects. This is where we again encounter the limitation of Lenin's "theory of reflection": only a consciousness observing the universe from the outside would see the whole of reality the way it really is. The very notion of the "whole universe" thus presupposes the position of an external observer, which is impossible to occupy. To put it in Gilles Deleuze's terms, what this means is *absolute* perspectivism: the distorting partial perspective is inscribed into the very material existence of things.

This is what "there is no world" means: there is no "true objective reality", since reality as such emerges from a distorted perspective, from a disturbance of the equilibrium of the primordial Void–Nothingness. This is the homology between Hegel and Nagarjuna's Buddhist thought: Nagarjuna also asserts that the Void as the ultimate reality does not assert the overall denial of beings, but just the fact that every positive entity is thoroughly relational, that it emerges in the void of the absent others which condition it – we arrive at the Void if we try to conceive of the world as a Whole.[30] You could also put it in the terms of Heideggerian epochality: "absolute perspectivism" means that our "world" is always disclosed to us within some finite horizon which arises against the background of an impenetrable self-concealment of Being. Every ontological disclosure is by definition partial, distorted, an "errance" of Being, and this limitation is its positive condition of possibility.

If there is a fundamental lesson common to Hegel and Lacan, it is the exact opposite of the common wisdom that one should discard non-essential appearances and go to the essentials: appearances matter; appearances are essential. We cannot simply oppose the way the thing is "in itself" and the

way it appears from our constrained, partial perspective: this appearance
has more weight than the thing in itself, because it designates the way the
thing in question is inscribed into the network of its relations with others.
In Marxism, "commodity fetishism" provides the co-ordinates of the way
commodities appear to subjects, *and this appearance determines their
objective social status*; in psychoanalysis, "fantasy" provides the frame
within which objects appear to the desiring subject, *and this frame constitutes the co-ordinates of what the subject experiences as "reality"*.

In the properly Hegelian relationship between the Finite and the Infinite,
we should not begin with the Finite and then proceed to ask how we can go
on to the Infinite – the moment we do this, the moment we start with (and
thus acknowledge) the Finite, we already miss the true Infinite, which is not
something beyond the Finite, but nothing but the lack-of-being of the Finite
itself, its negative self-cancellation. That's the crucial point, in which Alain
Badiou goes wrong when he insists on a strict frontier between the Political
and the Social (the domain of State, of history) – he concedes too much:
namely, that *society exists*. Against this concession, we should endorse the
thesis, articulated by Laclau and Mouffe,[31] that "society doesn't exist" –
that society is not a positive field, since the gap of the Political is inscribed
into its very foundations (Marx's name for the political which traverses the
entire social body is "class struggle"). Badiou concedes too much when he
accepts that there is the order of Being, and then goes on to how an Event
is possible. Just as society doesn't exist, we should formulate the basic
materialist thesis that "the world doesn't exist" (or, in Badiou's terms, that
there is no order of Being). The same goes for the relationship between
Necessity and Freedom: we should not first assert the causal network of
Necessity, and then ask how a break in it is possible, how Freedom can
emerge. Here we can also clearly locate Kant's ambiguity, his oscillation
between materialism and idealism – not in the normal sense (transcendental
constitution is idealist subjectivism; things-in-themselves are a remainder of
materialism), but in the guise of the oscillation between asserting, in a purely
immanent way, the nonexistence of the World as a Whole, and between the
idea of another noumenal domain of freedom behind phenomena.

From Aristotle and Aquinas, idealism asserts the existence of ontic objects
within the world, then posits God as its external Limit/Exception which
guarantees its ontological consistency. As a result, the formula of materialism is not to deny the Beyond, to claim that there is only the world of actual
finite "real" objects, but to claim that this very "real" object does not have
full ontological consistency – that from Outside, conceived of as a Whole,
it is nothing. Again, the formula of true atheism is not "God doesn't exist",

but "The world doesn't exist". The existence of the world implies its founding exception, which is God. Here, we should insist on the strict Hegelian determination of existence as the appearance of a hidden Essence: the World doesn't exist means that no hidden Ground-Essence appears in/ through it. (In the same way, for Freud in his *Moses and Monotheism*, the true formula of anti-anti-Semitism is "*The* Jew (Moses) doesn't exist . . .".) Here, the Lenin of *Materialism and Empiriocriticism*, with his inistence on the existence of objects there outside Consciousness, is secretly idealist: this fully constituted world can emerge only through immaterial Consciousness as its Exception.

What, however, if we were to connect the idea of truth as emerging from an external encounter with Lenin's (in)famous notion, from *What Is to Be Done?*, of how the working class cannot achieve its adequate class-consciousness "spontaneously", through its own "organic" development – of how this truth has to be introduced into it from outside (by Party intellectuals)? In quoting Kautsky at this point, Lenin makes a significant change in his paraphrase: while Kautsky speaks of how non-working-class intellectuals, who are outside the class struggle, should introduce science (providing objective knowledge of history) to the working class, Lenin speaks of consciousness which should be introduced by intellectuals who are outside the economic struggle, not outside the class struggle! Here is the passage from Kautsky which Lenin quotes approvingly –

> socialism and class struggle arise side by side and not one out of the other; each arises under different conditions. . . . The vehicle of science is not the proletariat, but the *bourgeois intelligentsia*. . . . Thus, socialist consciousness is something introduced into the proletarian class struggle from without and not something that arose within it spontaneously.[32]

– and here is Lenin's paraphrase of it:

> *all* worship of the spontaneity of the working-class movement, all belittling of the role of "the conscious element", of the role of Social-Democracy, *means, quite independently of whether he who belittles that role desires it or not, a strengthening of the influence of bourgeois ideology upon workers.* . . . the *only* choice is – either bourgeois or socialist ideology. There is no middle course . . . the *spontaneous* development of the working-class movement leads to its subordination to bourgeois ideology . . . for the spontaneous working-class movement is trade-unionism.[33]

It may sound the same, but it is not: for Kautsky, there is no room for politics proper, just the combination of the social (the working class and its struggle, from which intellectuals are implicitly excluded) and the pure neutral, classless, asubjective knowledge of these intellectuals. For Lenin, on the contrary, "intellectuals" themselves are caught in the conflict of ideologies (i.e. the ideological class struggle), which is inevitable. (It was Marx who made this point – from his youth, when he dreamt of the unity of German Idealist philosophy and the French revolutionary masses, to his insistence, in later years, that the leadership of the International should under no circumstances be left to the English workers: although they were the most numerous and best organized, they – in contrast to German workers – lacked theoretical stringency.) So when Lenin mentions the knowledge that intellectuals should deliver to the proletariat, it all depends on the exact status of this knowledge.

Lacan distinguishes four main modalities of knowledge: the servant's "know-how", practical knowledge of the artisan, farmer, and so on; the "disinterested" *theoria* (Plato in *Menon*: the philosopher confronting a slave) as the Master's reappropriation/transformation of knowledge which, however, is not yet modern scientific knowledge, since it still relies on the initiatory relationship between Master and his apprentice/pupil – as Plato emphasizes, this knowledge presupposes the transferential relationship of love; modern scientific knowledge, which is impersonal, not grounded in the figure of a Master, but existing in impersonal manuals and technical equipment, in principle accessible to all (here the subject is foreclosed, as Lacan put it); and bureaucratic knowledge, which is the process of registration, of "writing down", filing, cataloguing all that (should) exist(s).

Two interrelated paradoxes should be emphasized here, that of scientific knowledge and that of bureaucratic knowledge. When scientists tried to reconstruct the "software" for such a common activity as walking, they were amazed to learn how many complicated equations our brain has to solve effortlessly – as an engineer put it: "The upright two-footed locomotion of the human being seems almost a recipe for disaster in itself, and demands a remarkable control to make it practicable."[34] A leg has to change its point of support all at once, and the weight has to be unloaded to do so. The motors controlling a leg have to alternate between keeping the foot on the ground while it bears and propels the load, and taking the load off to make the leg free to move. All the while they have to keep the body's centre of gravity within the polygon defined by the feet, so that the body doesn't topple over. When we walk, we repeatedly tip over, and break our fall in the nick of time.[35] This complexity of instant spontaneous calculations, the knowledge the body has to possess in order to be able to walk, is what Lacan called "knowledge in the real" – and, of course, what we should not forget here is the basic hermeneutic point: it is only when we are already within the computational scientific horizon, when we observe a walking body from the engineering standpoint, trying to explicate the equations which allow this body to walk, that we are compelled to posit this kind of "knowledge in the real"; within a more "naive" approach, we simply refer to some innate or learned "dispositions". In short, this "knowledge in the real" emerges once we adopt the attitude of the external data-processing observer, and endeavour to translate the engaged living bodily agent's pre-reflexive know-how into the activity regulated by following explicit rules.

As for bureaucratic knowledge, its pervasiveness gives birth to a certain gap best exemplified by the French "certificat d'existence" or by strange stories, reported from time to time, on how (usually in Italy) some unfortunate individual, when he asks a certain favour from a state apparatus, is informed that, according to the registers, he is officially dead or nonexistent, and that, in order to be able to claim, he must first produce official documents which confirm his existence – is this not the bureaucratic version of "in-between the two deaths"?[36] A French businesswoman was recently summoned to the Préfecture because – as the official letter of invitation claimed – she had lost her *carte vitale* (the French health smart card). In fact, she had not lost it; so when, after waiting for over two hours, she got to the front of the queue and produced her card as proof that she had not lost it, the bureaucrat who was dealing with her said: "But the computer says you've lost it, so the one you have now is no longer valid – you'll have to hand it in to be destroyed, and then ask for a new one!" If there was ever such a thing as an ethics of bureaucracy, this is an example of it.

The interrelationship between these two modes of knowledge lies in the fact that they are the obverse of each other: "knowledge in the real" stands for the immediacy of a knowledge directly inscribed into the Real of the body itself, bypassing symbolic mediation; while bureaucratic knowledge brings home the absurd discord between the Symbolic and the Real.

To these four forms of knowledge we should, of course, add the paradoxical status of (supposed) knowledge in psychoanalysis: the analyst is supposed to know the secret of the analysand's desire. And undoubtedly, the infamous "knowledge" to be introduced to the working class from the outside by the Leninist Party is of the same nature as the (supposed) knowledge in psychoanalysis. The key question thus concerns the exact status of this externality: is it simply the externality of an impartial "objective" scientist who, after studying history and establishing that, in the long run, the working class has a great future ahead, decides to join the winning side? So when Lenin says: "The Marxian theory is omnipotent because it is true,"[37] everything depends on how we understand "truth" here: is it neutral "objective knowledge", or the truth of an engaged subject?[38] (One of the consequences of this notion of universal partisan truth concerns the stance we should adopt towards the populist New Right: we should quite "dogmatically" exclude them, rejecting any dialogue, not accepting their "normalization", their transformation into a "normal" political subject-partner. In short, we should fully accept the paradox: yes, it is we, the Leftists, who should reject any dialogue, and it is the Rightists who (in the present hegemony of liberal democracy, at least) simply want to be accepted as "normal partners in a dialogue" . . .).

The key to the status of this supposed knowledge in psychoanalysis is the paradoxical knowledge about the Other's knowledge. Take the final reversal in Edith Wharton's *The Age of Innocence*, in which the husband, who for years harboured an illicit passionate love for Countess Olenska, learns that his young wife *knew* about his secret passion all the time. Perhaps this could also offer a way of redeeming the unfortunate film *Bridges of Madison County*: if, at the end, the dying Francesca were to learn that her allegedly naive, down-to-earth husband knew all the time about her brief passionate affair with the *National Geographic* photographer, and how much this meant to her, but kept silent about it in order not to hurt her. That is the enigma of knowledge: how is it possible that the whole psychic economy of a situation radically changes not when the hero directly learns something (some long-repressed secret), but when he *find out that the other* (whom he mistakenly regarded as ignorant) *also knew it all the time*, and simply pretended not to know, to keep up appearances. Is there anything more humiliating than the situation of a husband who, after a long secret love affair, learns all of a sudden that his wife knew about it all the time, but kept silent about it out of politeness or, even worse, out of love for him?

Apropos of *Hamlet*, Lacan claims that the presupposition that the Other doesn't know maintains the bar that separates the Unconscious from the Conscious[39] – how? In *The Age of Innocence*, the hero lives under the illusion that his big desire is to be with the object of his passion: what he does not know (what he represses in his unconscious), and what he is forced to face when he learns that the Other (his wife) also knows, is the fact that he does *not* really want to abandon his family and live with his beloved – the true object of his desire was this entire situation, in which he was able to enjoy his passion only in secret. It is not the object of passion that is unconscious, it is the way I actually relate to it, the conditions under which I was attached to this object. So it is precisely when I think that, deep inside myself, I know (about my passion, about which the Other doesn't know), that I am duped about the lineaments of this passion. When a married man has a secret affair, and is convinced that he no longer loves his wife, how often it happens that when, for some reason (divorce; the wife's death), he is finally in a position to realize his desire, he breaks down. Or, even more simply, when he learns that his wife knows about the affair, and she offers to let him go, he is unable to do it. . . .

The outstanding documentary *The Thin Blue Line* quotes a memorable statement by an anonymous public prosecutor: "An average prosecutor can get a guilty person convicted; it takes a really good prosecutor to get an innocent person convicted." The logic of this paradox is the same as that of the motto of the Nazi henchmen formulated by Himmler: "It is easy to do a noble thing for your country, even to give your life for it; true heroism, however, consists in doing the necessary dirty job for it: to kill and torture for your country, to take the burden of evil on you!" That is the secret seductive lure of cynicism: living in truth and goodness is boring; the only authentic challenge is that of Evil, that is, the only space for extraordinary achievements is to be found in transgressive idiosyncrasies. In short, as Fernando Pessoa put it: "If you possess a truth, keep it to youself!"

Why should we not, then, in contrast to this stance, take the risk of shamelessly and courageously endorsing the boring classic criticism according to which Marxism is a "secularized religion", with Lenin as the Messiah, and so on? Yes, taking the proletarian standpoint is exactly like making a leap of faith and becoming fully engaged its Cause; yes, the "truth" of Marxism is perceptible only to those who accomplish this leap, not to neutral observers. What the externality means here is that this truth is none the less universal, not just the "point of view" of a particular historical subject: "external" intellectuals are needed because the working class cannot immediately perceive its own place within the social totality, which enables it to accomplish its "mission" – this insight has to be mediated through an external element.

And why not link these two externalities (that of the traumatic experience of the Divine Real, and that of the Party) to the third one, that of the analyst in the psychoanalytic cure? In all three cases, we are dealing with the same impossibility which bears witness to a materialist obstacle: it is not possible for the believer to "discover God in himself", through self-immersion, by spontaneously realizing his or her own Self – God must intervene from outside, disturbing our balance; it is not possible for the working class to actualize its historical mission spontaneously – the Party must intervene from the outside, shaking it out of its self-indulgent spontaneity; it is not possible for the patient/analyst to analyse himself – in contrast to Gnostic self-immersion, in psychoanalysis there is no self-analysis proper; analysis is possible only if a foreign kernel gives body to the object-cause of the subject's desire. Why, then, this impossibility? Precisely because not one of the three subjects (believer, proletarian, analyst) is a self-centred agent of self-mediation – all are decentred agents struggling with a foreign kernel.

In what is for some the most problematic song in *The Measure Taken*, a celebration of the Party, Brecht proposes something that is much more unique and precise than it may appear. That is to say, it seems that Brecht is simply elevating the Party into the incarnation of Absolute Knowledge, a historical agent which has complete and perfect insight into the historical situation – a subject supposed to know if ever there was one: "You have two eyes, but the Party has thousand eyes!" A close reading of this poem, however, makes it clear that something very different is going on: in reprimanding the young Communist, the Chorus says that the Party does *not* know all, that the young Communist may be right in his disagreement with the predominant Party line:

> Show us the way which we should take, and we
> shall follow it like you, but
> do not take the right way without us.
> Without us, this way is
> the falsest one.
> Do not separate yourself from us.[40]

This means that the authority of the Party is not that of determinate positive knowledge, but that of the form of knowledge, of a new type of knowledge linked to a collective political subject. The only crucial point on which the Chorus insists is that if the young comrade thinks that he is right, he should fight for his position *within* the collective form of the Party, not outside it – to put it in a somewhat pathetic way: if the young comrade is right, then the Party needs him even more than its other members. What the Party demands is that we agree to ground our "I" in the "we" of the Party's collective identity: fight with us, fight for us, fight for your truth against the Party line – *just don't do it alone*, outside the Party. Exactly as in Lacan's formula of the discourse of the analyst, what is important about the Party's knowledge is not its content, but the fact that it occupies the place of Truth.

God, Analyst, Party – the three forms of the "subject supposed to know", of the transferential object; this is why, in all three cases, we hear the claim "God/the Analyst/the Party is always right"; and, as it was clear to

Kierkegaard, the truth of this statement is always its negative – *man* is always wrong. This external element does not stand for objective knowledge, that is, its externality is strictly internal: the need for the Party stems from the fact that the working class is never "fully itself". So the ultimate meaning of Lenin's insistence on this externality is that "adequate" class-consciousness does not emerge "spontaneously", that it does not correspond to a "spontaneous tendency" of the working class; on the contrary, what is "spontaneous" is the *misperception* of one's social position, so that "adequate" class-consciousness has to be fought out through hard work. Here, again, the situation is homologous to the one in psychoanalysis: as Lacan emphasizes again and again, there is no primordial *Wissenstrieb* (drive-to-knowledge): the spontaneous human attitude is that of *je n'en veux rien savoir* – I don't want to know anything about it; and, far from realizing our innermost tendency, the psychoanalytic treatment has to proceed "against the grain".[41]

We can make the same point in terms of the opposition between *interpretation* and *formalization*:[42] the external agent (Party, God, Analyst) is not the one who "understands us better than we do ourselves", who can provide the true interpretation of what our acts and statements mean; rather, it stands for the *form* of our activity. What, then, is this Form? Let us take Ernst Nolte's "revisionist" argument concerning the relationship between Nazism and (Soviet) Communism: reprehensible as it was, Nazism not only appeared after Communism; it was also, with regard to its content, an excessive *reaction* to the Communist threat. Furthermore, all the horrors committed by Nazism merely copy the horrors already committed by Soviet Communism: secret police, concentration camps, genocidal terror. . . . Is this the Form we are talking about? Is the idea that Communism and Nazism share the same totalitarian Form, and that the difference between them concerns only the empirical agents which fill in the same structural places ("Jews" instead of "class enemy", etc.)? The usual liberal reaction to Nolte is a moralistic outcry: Nolte relativizes Nazism, reducing it to a secondary echo of the Communist Evil – how, however, can you even compare Communism, that thwarted attempt at liberation, with the radical Evil of Nazism?

In contrast to this dismissal, we should fully concede Nolte's central point: yes, Nazism was in fact a reaction to the Communist threat; it merely replaced the class struggle with the struggle between Aryans and Jews – the problem lies, however, in this "merely", which is by no means as innocent as it appears. We are dealing here with displacement [*Verschiebung*] in the Freudian sense of the term: Nazism displaces class struggle on to racial struggle, and thereby obfuscates its true site. What changes in the passage from Communism to Nazism is the Form, and it is in this change of Form that the Nazi ideological mystification resides: the political struggle is naturalized into the racial conflict, the (class) antagonism inherent to the social edifice is reduced to the invasion of a foreign (Jewish) body which disturbs the harmony of the Aryan community. So while we should fully admit that Nazism can be understood only as a reaction to the threat of (Soviet) Communism, as a displaced repetition of the Communist ideological universe, we should locate the Form which determines the concrete functioning of Nazism not in the abstract notion of "totalitarianism" which encompasses both Communism and Nazism as its two particular cases, but in the very displacement to which Nazism submits the Communist co-ordinates. This notion of Form is a properly dialectical one: Form is not the neutral frame of particular contents, but the very principle of concretion, that is, the "strange attractor" which distorts, biases, confers a specific colour on every element of the totality.

In other words, formalization is strictly correlative to focusing on the Real of an antagonism. In the Marxist perspective, "class struggle" is not the last horizon of meaning, the last signified of all social phenomena, but the formal generative matrix of the different ideological horizons of understanding. That is to say: we should not confuse this properly dialectical notion of Form with the liberal-multiculturalist notion of Form as the neutral framework of the multitude of "narratives" – not only literature, but also politics, religion, science, are all different narratives, stories we are telling ourselves about ourselves, and the ultimate goal of ethics is to guarantee the neutral space in which this multitude of narratives can coexist peacefully – in which everyone, from ethnic to sexual minorities, will have the right and opportunity to tell their story. Or, as Fernando Pessoa formulated it succinctly: "the Whole, the true and the genuine one, is an illness of our thoughts". The properly dialectical notion of Form signals precisely the *impossibility* of this liberal notion of Form: Form has nothing to do with "formalism", with the idea of a neutral Form, independent of its contingent particular content; it stands, rather, for the traumatic kernel of the Real, for the antagonism which "colours" the entire field in question. In this precise sense, class struggle is the Form of the Social: every social phenomenon is overdetermined by it, so that it is not possible to remain neutral towards it.

In this precise sense, both Marx and Freud were the two great formalizers. In his analysis of commodity fetishism, Marx asserts that the mystery of the commodity-form resides in this form itself, not in the content hidden beneath it, thereby echoing Freud's remark (in his masterpiece with the misleading title *The Interpretation of Dreams*) that the specificity of the dream resides in its form as such, not in the content encoded in this form.[43] For this precise reason, Marx's deployment of the commodity-form in Chapter 1 of *Capital* is not a "narrative", a *Vorstellung*, but a *Darstellung*, the deployment of the inner structure of the universe of merchandise – the narrative, on the contrary, is the story of "primitive accumulation", the myth capitalism proposes about its own origins. Along the same lines, Hegel's *Phenomenology of Spirit* – contrary to Richard Rorty's reading – does not suggest a grand narrative of the birth and deployment of subjectivity, but the *form* of subjectivity; as Hegel himself emphasizes in the Foreword, it focuses on the "formal aspect [*das Formelle*]". This is how we should also approach the absence of grand all-encompassing narratives today – this is Fredric Jameson's subtle description of the deadlock of the dialogue between the Western New Left and the Eastern European dissidents, of the absence of any common language between them:

> To put it briefly, the East wishes to talk in terms of power and oppression; the West in terms of culture and commodification. There are really no common denominators in this initial struggle for discursive rules, and what we end up with is the inevitable comedy of each side muttering irrelevant replies in its own favorite language.[44]

At the same time, Jameson insists that Marxism still provides the universal meta-language that enables us to situate and relate all other partial narrativizations/interpretations – is he simply inconsistent? Are there two Jamesons: one postmodern, the theorist of the irreducible multiplicity of narratives; the other the more traditional partisan of Marxist universal hermeneutics? The only way to save Jameson from this predicament is to insist that here Marxism is not the all-encompassing interpretative horizon, but the matrix which enables us to account for (to generate) the multiplicity of narratives and/or interpretations. It is also here that we should introduce the key dialectical distinction between the founding figure of a movement and the later figure who formalized this movement: Lenin did not just adequately translate Marxist theory into political practice – rather, he "formalized" Marx by defining the Party as the political form of its historical intervention – just as Saint Paul "formalized" Christ, and Lacan "formalized" Freud.[45]

The Inner Greatness of Stalinism

When, after Lenin's death, Marxism split into official Soviet Marxism and so-called Western Marxism, they both misread this externality of the Party as designating the position of neutral objective knowledge – in the steps of Kautsky, Soviet Marxism simply adopted this position, while Western Marxists rejected it as the theoretical legitimization of "totalitarian" Party rule. Those few libertarian Marxists who wanted to redeem Lenin – partially, at least – tended to oppose the "bad" Jacobin–elitist Lenin of *What Is to Be Done?*, relying on the Party as the professional intellectual elite which enlightens the working class from outside, to the "good" Lenin of *State and Revolution*, who envisioned the prospect of abolishing the State, of the broad masses directly taking the administration of public affairs into their own hands. This opposition, however, has its limits: the key premiss of *State and Revolution* is that you cannot fully "democratize" the State; that the State "as such", in its very notion, is a dictatorship of one class over another; the logical conclusion from this premiss is that, *in so far as we still dwell within the domain of the State*, we are legitimately entitled to exercise full violent terror, since, within this domain, every democracy is a fake. So, since the State is an instrument of oppression, it is not worth trying to improve its apparatuses, the protection of the legal order, elections, laws guaranteeing personal freedom . . . – all this becomes irrelevant.[46] The element of truth in this criticism is that you cannot separate the unique constellation which enabled the revolutionary takeover in October 1917 from its later "Stalinist" turn: the very constellation that made the revolution possible (peasants' dissatisfaction, a well-organized revolutionary elite, etc.) led to the "Stalinist" turn in its aftermath – that is the real Leninist *tragedy*. Rosa Luxemburg's famous alternative "socialism or barbarism" ended up as the ultimate infinite judgement, asserting the speculative identity of the two opposed terms: "Really Existing Socialism" *was* barbarism.[47]

In the diaries of Georgi Dimitroff, recently published in German,[48] we get a unique glimpse into how Stalin was fully aware of what brought him to power, giving an unexpected twist to his well-known slogan "People (cadres) are our greatest wealth". When, at a dinner in November 1937, Dimitroff praises the "great luck" of the international workers – that they had such a genius as their leader, Stalin – Stalin answers: "*I do not agree with him.* He even expressed himself in a non-Marxist way. . . . *Decisive* are the middle cadres" (7 November 1937). He puts it even more clearly a paragraph earlier:

> Why did we win over Trotsky and others? It is well known that, after Lenin, Trotsky was the most popular in our land. . . . But we had the support of the middle cadres, and they explained our grasp of the situation to the masses . . . Trotsky did not pay any attention to these cadres.

Here, Stalin spells out the secret of his rise to power: as a rather anonymous General Secretary, he nominated tens of thousands of cadres who owed their rise to him. . . . This is why Stalin did not yet want Lenin dead in the early 1922, rejecting his demand to be given poison to end his life after his debilitating stroke: if Lenin were to die in early 1922, the question of succession would not yet be resolved in Stalin's favour, since Stalin, as General Secretary, had not yet penetrated the Party apparatus sufficiently with his own appointees – he needed another year or two, so that when Lenin actually died, he would be able to count on the support of thousands of mid-level cadres, nominated by him, to win over the great old figures of the Bolshevik "aristocracy".

We should therefore stop the ridiculous game of opposing the Stalinist terror to the "authentic" Leninist legacy betrayed by Stalinism: "Leninism" is a thoroughly *Stalinist* notion. The gesture of back-projecting the emancipatory-utopian potential of Stalinism, into a preceding time, thus indicates our minds' inability to endure the "absolute contradiction", the unbearable tension, intrinsic to the Stalinist project itself.[49] It is therefore crucial to distinguish "Leninism" (as the authentic core of Stalinism) from the actual political practice and ideology of Lenin's period: the actual greatness of Lenin is not the same as the Stalinist authentic myth of Leninism. So what about the obvious counterargument that exactly the same goes for every ideology – including Nazism, which also, perceived from within, displays an "inner greatness" which seduced even such an outstanding philosopher as Heidegger? The answer should be simply a resounding *no*: the point is precisely that Nazism does *not* contain any authentic "inner greatness".

If we want to see Stalinist art at its purest, one name is sufficient: Brecht. Badiou was right to claim that "Brecht was a Stalinist, if, as one should, one understands Stalinism as the fusion of the politics and the philosophy of dialectical materialism under the jurisdiction of the latter. Or, let us say, Brecht practised a Stalinized Platonism."[50] This is what Brecht's "non-Aristotelian" theatre ultimately amounts to: a *Platonist* theatre in which the aesthetic charm is strictly controlled, in order to transmit the philosophico-political Truth which is *external* to it. Brechtian extraneation means that "aesthetic semblance has to distantiate itself from itself, so that, in this gap, the external objectivity of the True is *displayed*".[51] So when Badiou says that "extraneation is a protocol of philosophical surveillance",[52] we should shamelessly confer on this term all its secret-police connotations. So let us stop our ridiculous games of opposing some kind of "dissident" Brecht to Stalinist Communism: Brecht is the ultimate "Stalinist" artist; he was great not in spite of his Stalinism, but because of it. Do we really need proof?

Towards the end of the 1930s, Brecht shocked the guests at a New York party by claiming, about the accused in the Moscow show trials: "The more innocent they are, the more they deserve to be shot."[53] This statement is to be taken quite seriously, not just as perverse cockiness: its underlying premiss is that in a concrete historical struggle, the attitude of "innocence" ("I don't want to dirty my hands by getting involved in the struggle, I just want to lead a modest and honest life") embodies the ultimate guilt. In our world, *doing nothing is not empty, it already has a meaning* – it means saying "yes" to existing relations of domination. This is why, apropos of the Moscow trials, Brecht – while admitting that the methods of the prosecution were not very gentle – asked himself: is it possible to imagine how an honest and sincere Communist who entertained doubts about Stalin's policy of rapid industrialization ended up seeking help from foreign secret services and engaging in terrorist plots against the Stalinist leadership? His answer was "yes", and he proposed a detailed reconstruction of their reasoning.

No wonder, then, that when, on his way from his home to his theatre in July 1953, Brecht passed a column of Soviet tanks rolling towards the *Stalinallee* to crush the workers' rebellion, he waved at them, and wrote in his diary later that day that at that moment, he (never a Party member) was tempted for the first time in his life to join the Communist Party[54] – is this not an outstanding case of what Alain Badiou has called *la passion du réel* which defines the twentieth century? It was not that Brecht tolerated the cruelty of the struggle in the hope that it would bring a prosperous future: the harshness of the violence as such was perceived and endorsed as a sign of authenticity. For Brecht, the Soviet military intervention against the East Berlin workers was aimed not at the workers, but at "organized Fascist elements" which exploited the workers' dissatisfaction; for this reason, he claimed that the Soviet intervention actually prevented a new world war.[55]

Even on a personal level, Brecht "had a real liking for Stalin",[56] and he developed a line of argumentation justifying the revolutionary necessity of the dictatorship of a single individual;[57] his reaction to the "de-Stalinization" at the Twentieth Congress of the Soviet Communist Party in 1956 was: "Without a knowledge of dialectics, passages like the one from Stalin as the motor [of progress] to Stalin as its brake cannot be understood."[58] In short, instead of renouncing Stalin, Brecht played the pseudo-dialectical game of "what was progressive before, in the 1930s and 1940s, has now (in the 1950s) turned into an obstacle".... I am almost tempted to read the moment of Brecht's death (autumn 1956, just after the Twentieth Congress and before the Hungarian uprising) as timely: the merciful release of death freed him from having to confront the full pain of "de-Stalinization".

If we want to see Brecht at his best, we should focus on the great German Stalinist musical triad: Brecht (words), Hanns Eisler (music), Ernst Busch (performance).[59] If we need to convince ourselves of the authentic greatness of the Stalinist project, it is enough to listen to one of the supreme recordings of the twentieth century: Hanns Eisler's *Historic Recordings*, with (most of the) words by Brecht and (most of the) songs performed by Busch. In what is arguably their supreme achievent, the song "To Sing in the Prison [Im Gefängnis zu singen]" from *Die Mutter* (*The Mother*), the gap between the symbolic breakdown of the opponent and its actual defeat is directly alluded to, when the imprisoned worker Pawel addresses those in power:

> You have law-books and rulings
> You have prisons and fortresses . . .
> You have prison-guards and judges
> Who are well paid and ready to do anything.
> What for? . . .
> Just before you disappear – and that will happen soon –
> You will notice that all this was of no use to you.
>
> You have newspapers and printing-houses
> In order to fight against us and keep us quiet . . .
> You have priests and professors
> Who are well paid and ready to do anything.
> What for?
> Do you really have to be so afraid of truth?
>
> You have tanks and guns
> Tommy guns and hand-grenades . . .
> You have policemen and soldiers
> Who are well paid and ready to do anything.
> What for?
> Do you really have such mighty enemies? . . .
> Someday – and that will come soon –
> You will see that all this is of no use to you.[60]

The actual defeat of the enemy is thus preceded by symbolic breakdown, a sudden insight into how the struggle is meaningless, and all the arms and tools at its disposal *serve no purpose*. That is the ultimate premiss of the democratic struggle: for a priori structural reasons, and not only owing to some contingent miscalculation, the enemy misperceives the co-ordinates of the global situation, and assembles the wrong kind of forces in the wrong place. Two recent examples: what did the Shah's repressive apparatus amount to in 1979, when it was confronted by Khomeini's popular movement? It just collapsed. And of what use was the overblown network of *Stasi* agents and informers to the East German Communist *nomenklatura* in 1989, when it was confronted by the growing mass protests? Big oppressive regimes are never defeated in a head-on confrontation – at a certain point, when the "old mole" accomplishes its underground work of inner ideological disintegration, they just collapse.

Apart from the sublime masterpiece "In Praise of Communism" ("the Simplest, which is the most difficult to accomplish"), the third key song in *The Mother* is "The Song of the Patch and the Gown", which begins with an ironic depiction of humanitarians aware of the urgent need to help the poor:

> When our gown is tattered
> you always come running and say: this can no longer go on.
> Things must be remedied, and with all means!
> And, full of zeal, you run to the masters
> While we wait, freezing.
> And you come back, and triumphantly
> Show us what you gained for us:
> A small patch.
> OK, this is the patch.
> But where is
> The whole gown?[61]

This acerbic rhetorical question is repeated apropos of bread ("OK, this is a piece of bread, but where is the [whole] loaf?"[62]), and the song ends in a sweeping explosion of demands (". . . we need the whole factory, and the coal and the ore and the power in the state") – the properly revolutionary moment at which the *quid pro quo* of exchanges with those in power breaks down, and the revolutionaries brutally assert that they want *everything*, not just some "fair" part of it.

Here Brecht is at the very opposite end of the spectrum from Georg Lukács: precisely in so far as Lukács, the "soft" European humanist, played the role of "closet dissident", waging "guerrilla warfare" against Stalinism, and even joining the Imre Nagy government in 1956, thus endangering his very physical existence, he was the *ultimate Stalinist*. In contrast to Lukács, Brecht was unbearable to the Stalinist cultural establishment because of his very "over-orthodoxy" – there is no place for *The Measure Taken* in the Stalinist cultural universe.[63] If the young Lukács of *History and Class*

Consciousness was the philosopher of Lenin's historical moment, after the 1930s he turned into the ideal Stalinist philosopher who, for that very reason, in contrast to Brecht, missed the true greatness of Stalinism.

Lenin as a Listener of Schubert

Anti-Communist critics who insist on the continuity between Lenin and Stalinism like to dwell on Lenin's alleged insensitivity to the universal human dimension: not only did he perceive all social events through the narrow lens of the class struggle, of "us against them"; he was also, as a person, insensitive to the human suffering of real individuals. In order to answer this criticism, let us recall some details of the daily life of Lenin and the Bolsheviks in 1917 and the following years, which, in their very triviality, reveal their distance from the Stalinist *nomenklatura*.

When, on the evening of 24 October 1917, Lenin left his flat for the Smolny Institute to co-ordinate the revolutionary takeover, he took a tram and asked the conductress if there was any fighting going on in the town centre that day. In the years after the October Revolution, Lenin mostly drove around in a car with only his faithful driver and bodyguard, Gil; a couple of times they were shot at, stopped by the police and arrested (the policemen did not recognize Lenin); once, after visiting a school in the suburbs, they were even robbed of the car and their guns by bandits posing as police, then compelled to walk to the nearest police station. When Lenin was shot on 30 August 1918, this occurred while he was talking to a couple of women complaining in front of a factory he had just visited; the bleeding Lenin was driven by Gil to the Kremlin, in which no doctors were present; so his wife, Nadezhda Krupskaya, suggested that someone should run out to the nearest grocer's shop for a lemon. . . . The standard meal in the Kremlin *kantina* in 1918 was buckwheat porridge and thin vegetable soup. So much for the privileges of the *nomenklatura*!

Lenin's slanderers like to evoke his famous paranoiac reaction at listening to Beethoven's *appassionata* (he first started to cry, then claimed that a revolutionary cannot afford to let himself give way to such sentiments, because they make him too weak, wanting to pat his enemies on the head instead of fighting them mercilessly) as proof of his cold self-control and cruelty. Even on its own terms, however, is this really an argument *against* Lenin? Does it not, rather, bear witness to an extreme sensitivity to music that needs to be kept in check if he is to continue the political struggle? Who among today's cynical politicians still displays even a trace of such sensitivity? Is not Lenin in this case the very opposite of the high-ranking Nazis who, without any difficulty, combined such sensitivity with extreme cruelty in taking political decisions (it is reasonable to recall Heydrich, the Holocaust architect, who, after a hard day's work, always found time to listen to Beethoven's string quartets with his comrades) – is it not proof of Lenin's humanity that in contrast to this supreme barbarism, which lies in the very unproblematic unity of high culture and political barbarism, he was still extremely sensitive to the irreducible *antagonism* between art and power struggle?

Furthermore, I am tempted to develop a Leninist theory of this high-cultural barbarism. Hans Hotter's outstanding 1942 recording of Schubert's *Winterreise* seems to call for an intentionally anachronistic reading: it is easy to imagine German officers and soldiers listening to this recording in the Stalingrad trenches in the cold winter of 1942–43. Does not the topic of *Winterreise* evoke a unique consonance with the historical moment? Was not the whole Stalingrad campaign a gigantic *Winterreise*, where every German soldier could say of himself the very first lines of the cycle: "I came here a stranger, / As a stranger I depart"? Do the next lines not express their basic experience: "Now the world is so gloomy, / The road shrouded in snow. / I cannot choose the time / To begin my journey, / Must find my own way / In this darkness."

Here we have the endless meaningless march: "It burns under both my feet, / Even though I walk on ice and snow; / I don't want to catch my breath / Until I can no longer see the spires." The dream of returning home in the spring: "I dreamed of many-coloured flowers, / The way they bloom in May; / I dreamed of green meadows, / Of merry bird calls." The nervous waiting for the post: "From the high road a posthorn sounds. / Why do you leap so high, my heart?" The shock of the morning artillery attack: "The cloud tatters flutter / Around in weary strife. / And fiery red flames / Dart around among them." Utterly exhausted, the soldiers are refused even the solace of death: "I'm tired enough to drop, have taken mortal hurt. / Oh, merciless inn, you turn me away? / Well, onward then, still further, my loyal walking staff!"

What can one do in such a desperate situation but go on with heroic persistence, closing one's ears to the complaint of the heart, assuming the heavy burden of fate in a world deserted by God?

> If the snow flies in my face,
> I shake it off again.
> When my heart speaks in my breast,

> I sing loudly and gaily.
> I don't hear what it says to me,
> I have no ears to listen;
> I don't feel when it laments,
> Complaining is for fools.
> Happy through the world along
> Facing wind and weather!
> If there's no God upon the earth,
> Then we ourselves are Gods!

The obvious counterargument is that all this is merely a superficial parallel: even if there is an echo of the atmosphere and emotions, they are in each case embedded in an entirely different context: in Schubert, the narrator wanders around in winter because his beloved has abandoned him; while the German soldiers were on the way to Stalingrad because of Hitler's military plans. It is precisely in this displacement, however, that the elementary ideological operation consists: the way for a German soldier to be able to endure his situation was to avoid the reference to concrete social circumstances which would become visible through reflection (what the hell were they doing in Russia? what destruction did they bring to this country? what about killing the Jews?), and, instead, to indulge in a Romantic bemoaning of his miserable fate, as if the wider historical catastrophe simply materializes the trauma of a rejected lover. Is this not the supreme proof of emotional abstraction, of Hegel's idea that emotions are abstract, an escape from the concrete sociopolitical network accessible only to thinking?

And here I am tempted to take a further Leninist step: in our reading of the *Winterreise*, we did not just link Schubert to a contingent later historical catastrophe, we did not just try to imagine how this song cycle resonated with the embattled German soldiers in Stalingrad. What if the link to this catastrophe enables us to read what was wrong with the Schubertian Romantic position itself? What if the position of the Romantic tragic hero, narcissistically focused on his own suffering and despair, elevating them to a source of perverted pleasure, is already in itself a fake one, an ideological screen masking the true trauma of the wider historical reality? We should thus accomplish the properly Hegelian gesture of *projecting the split between the authentic original and its later reading coloured by contingent circumstances back into the authentic original itself*: what looks at first like a secondary distortion, a reading twisted by contingent external circumstances, tells us something about what the authentic original itself not only represses, leaves out, but *had the function of repressing*.

That is the Leninist answer to the famous passage from the Introduction to the *Grundrisse* manuscript, in which Marx points out how "the difficulty lies not in understanding that the Greek arts and epic are bound up with certain forms of social development. The difficulty is that they still afford us artistic pleasure and that in a certain respect they count as a norm and as an unattainable model."[64] This universal appeal is rooted in its very ideological function of enabling us to abstract from our concrete ideologico-political constellation by taking refuge in the "universal" (emotional) content. So, far from signalling some kind of trans-ideological human heritage, the universal attraction of Homer relies on the universalizing gesture of ideology.

Does this mean that every pathetic universal reference to humanity is, by definition, ideological? What about Lenin's appeals against patriotic fervour during World War I? Were they not an exemplary case of practising what Badiou[65] calls the universal function of "humanity", which has nothing whatsoever to do with so-called "humanism"? This "humanity" is neither a notional abstraction nor the pathetic imaginary assertion of all-encompassing brotherhood, but a universal function which actualizes itself in unique ecstatic experiences, like those of the soldiers from opposing trenches starting to fraternize.

In Jaroslav Hašek's legendary comic novel *The Good Soldier Schweik*, the adventures of an ordinary Czech soldier who undermines those in command by simply following orders too literally, Schweik finds himself at the front-line trenches in Galicia, where the Austrian army is confronting the Russians. When the Austrian soldiers start to shoot, the desperate Schweik runs into the no-man's-land in front of their trenches, waving desperately and shouting: "Don't shoot! There are men on the other side!" This is what Lenin was aiming at in his call to the tired peasants and other working masses in summer 1917 to stop fighting, dismissed as part of a ruthless strategy to win popular support, and thus gain power, even if it meant the military defeat of his own country (remember the standard argument that when, in spring 1917, Lenin was allowed by the German state to travel on a sealed train through Germany on his way from Switzerland to Sweden, Finland and then Russia, he was *de facto* functioning as a German agent). The barrier which broke down here is best exemplified by the eerie event which took place on the evening of 7 November 1942, when, in his special train rolling through Thuringia, Hitler was discussing the day's major news with several aides in the dining car; since Allied air raids had damaged the tracks, the train frequently slowed down:

> While dinner was served on exquisite china, the train stopped once more at a siding. A few feet away, a hospital train marked time, and from their tiered cots, wounded soldiers peered into the blazing light of the dining room where Hitler was immersed in conversation. Suddenly he looked up at the awed faces staring in at him. In great anger he ordered the curtains drawn, plunging his wounded warriors back into the darkness of their own bleak world.[66]

The miracle of this scene is redoubled: the people on each side experienced what they saw through the window as a fantasmatic apparition: for Hitler, it was a nightmarish view of the results of his military adventure; for the soldiers, it was an unexpected encounter with the Leader himself. The true miracle here would have been if a hand had stretched through the window – say, Hitler reaching out to a wounded soldier. But of course it was precisely such an encounter, such an intrusion into his reality, that Hitler dreaded; so instead of stretching out his hand, he – in panic – ordered the curtains drawn. . . . How, then, can we penetrate this barrier, and reach out to the Real Other?

There is a long literary tradition of elevating the face-to-face encounter with an enemy soldier as *the* authentic war experience (see the writings of Ernst Jünger, who celebrated such encounters in his memoirs of the trench attacks in World War I): soldiers often fantasize about killing the enemy soldier in a face-to-face confrontation, looking him in the eyes before stabbing him. Far from preventing further fight, this kind of mystical communion of blood serves precisely as its fake "spiritual" legitimization. One step further from such obscurantist ideology is accomplished by sublime moments of solidarity like the one which took place in the battle for Stalingrad: on 31 December 1942, New Year's Eve, Russian actors and musicians visited the besieged city to entertain the troops. The violinist Mikhail Goldstein went to the trenches to perform a one-man concert for the soldiers:

> The melodies he created drifted out through loudspeakers to the German trenches and the shooting suddenly ceased. In the eerie quiet, the music flowed from Goldstein's dipping bow.
>
> When he finished, a hushed silence hung over the Russian soldiers. From another loudspeaker, in German territory, a voice broke the spell. In halting Russian it pleaded: "Play some more Bach. We won't shoot."
>
> Goldstein picked up his violin and started a lively Bach *gavotte*.[67]

The problem with this violin performance is, of course, that it in fact functioned as just one brief sublime moment of suspension: immediately afterwards, the shooting went on. Thus this performance not only did not prevent the shooting, it even sustained it, providing the shared background of the two engaged parties. I am tempted to risk the hypothesis that it did not prevent the shooting precisely because it was all too noble and "deep": something much more superficial is needed to do the job. A much more effective experience of universal humanity – that is, of the meaninglessness of the conflict we are engaged in – can take the form of a simple exchange of gazes which says everything.

During an anti-apartheid demonstration in the old South Africa, while a troop of white policemen were dispersing and pursuing black demonstrators, a policeman was running after a black lady, a rubber truncheon in his hand. Unexpectedly, the lady lost one of her shoes; automatically obeying his "good manners", the policeman picked up the shoe and gave it to her; at this moment they exchanged glances, and both became aware of the inanity of their situation – after such a gesture of politeness, after handing her the lost shoe and waiting for her to put it back on, it was simply impossible for the policeman to continue to run after the lady, and to hit her with the truncheon; so, after politely nodding to her, he turned round and walked away. . . . The moral of this story is *not* that the policeman suddenly discovered his innate goodness – we are *not* dealing here with a case of natural goodness prevailing over racist ideological training; on the contrary, in all probability the policeman's psychological stance was that of any other racist. What triumphed here was simply his "superficial" training in politeness.

When the policeman stretched out his hand in order to pass the lady her shoe, his gesture was more than a moment of physical contact. The white policeman and the black lady literally lived in two different socio-symbolic universes with no possibility of direct communication: for each of them, the barrier which separated the two universes was suspended for a brief moment, and it was as if a hand from another, spectral, universe reached into their ordinary reality. In order to transform this magic moment of the suspension of symbolic barriers into a more substantial achievement, however, something more is needed – like, for example, the sharing of obscene jokes.

In ex-Yugoslavia, jokes circulated about each ethnic group, which was stigmatized through a certain feature – the Montenegrins were supposed to be extremely lazy; the Bosnians were stupid; the Macedonians were thieves; the Slovenes were mean. . . . Significantly, these jokes waned with the rise of ethnic tensions in the late 1980s: none of them was heard in 1990, when the hostilities erupted. Far from being simply racist, these jokes, especially those in which members of different nationalities meet – the "A Slovene, a Serb and an Albanian went shopping, and . . ." type – were one of the key forms of the actual existence of the official "brotherhood and unity" of

Tito's Yugoslavia. In this case, the shared obscene jokes functioned not as a means of excluding the others who were not "in", but as the means of their *inclusion*, of establishing a minimal symbolic pact. Indians (Native Americans) smoke the proverbial pipe of peace, while we, from the more primitive Balkans, have to exchange obscenities. To establish actual solidarity, the shared experience of high culture is not enough – we have to exchange with the Other the embarrassing idiosyncrasy of obscene enjoyment.

During my military service, I became very friendly with an Albanian soldier. It is a well known fact that Albanians are very sensitive to sexual insults which refer to their closest family members (mother, sister); I was in fact accepted by my Albanian friend when we left the superficial game of politeness and respect behind, and greeted each other with formalized insults. The first move was made by the Albanian: one morning, instead of the usual "Hello!", he greeted me with "I'll screw your mother!"; I knew that this was an offer to which I had to respond appropriately, so I snapped back: "Go ahead, you're welcome – after I've finished with your sister!" This exchange soon lost its openly obscene or ironic character, and became formalized: after only a couple of weeks, the two of us no longer bothered with the whole sentence; in the morning, when we saw each other, he just nodded and said "Mother!", to which I simply responded "Sister!"

This example reveals the dangers of such a strategy: the obscene solidarity all too often emerges at the expense of a third party – in this case, it involves male-bonding solidarity at the expense of women. (Can we imagine the reverse version: a young woman greeting her friend with "I'll screw your husband!", to which the friend responds: "Go ahead – after I've finished with your father!"?) Perhaps this is why the relationship between Jacqueline and Hilary du Pré strikes us as so "scandalous": the fact that, with her sister's approval, Jacqueline had an affair with her brother-in-law is so unbearable because it involves the reversal of the classic Lévi-Straussian logic of women as objects of exchange between men – in this case, it was the *man* who served as the object of exchange between women.

There is another problem here, that of power and authority: the example of my obscene ritual with the Albanian soldier works only because there was a presupposed equality between me and the Albanian – we were both common soldiers. Had I been an officer, it would have been much too risky – practically unthinkable – for the Albanian to make his first move. If, however, the Albanian had also been an officer, the situation would have been even more obscene: his gesture would have been an offer of false obscene solidarity masking the underlying power relations – a paradigmatic case of the "postmodern" exercise of power. The traditional figure of authority (boss, father) insists on being treated with proper respect, following the formal rules of authority; the exchange of obscenities and mocking remarks has to take place behind his back. Today's boss or father, on the contrary, insists that we should treat him as a friend; he addresses us with intrusive familiarity, bombarding us with sexual innuendos, inviting us to share a drink or a vulgar joke – all this is intended to establish the link of male bonding, while the relationship of authority (our subordination to him) not only remains intact, but is even treated as a kind of secret which should be respected and not talked about. For the subordinated, such a constellation is much more claustrophobic than traditional authority: today, we are deprived even of the private space of irony and mockery, since the master is on both levels: an authority as well as a friend.

This conundrum, however, is not as intractable as it may appear: in every concrete situation, we "spontaneously" always know which applies – that is, if the exchange of obscenities is "authentic" or a fake intimacy masking a relationship of subordination. The true problem is a more radical one: is a direct contact in the Real, without the underlying symbolic frame, feasible at all? The contact with the Real Other is inherently fragile – every such contact is extremely precarious and fragile; the authentic reaching out to the Other can revert at any moment to a violent intrusion into the Other's intimate space. . . . The way out of this predicament seems to be provided by the logic of social interaction best expressed in Henry James's masterpieces: in this universe, where *tact* reigns supreme, where an open explosion of one's emotions is considered the utmost vulgarity, everything is said, the most painful decisions are made, the most delicate messages are transmitted – however, it all takes place in the guise of a formal conversation. Even when I blackmail my partner, I do it with a polite smile, offering him or her tea and cakes. . . . Is it, then, that while a brutal direct approach misses the Other's kernel, a tactful dance can reach it? In *Minima Moralia*, Adorno pointed out the utter ambiguity of tact clearly discernible in James's work: respectful consideration for the other's sensitiveness, care not to violate his or her intimacy, can easily become brutal insensitivity to the other's pain.[68]

There is an old anecdote about two competing shopkeepers on the same street. When the first puts up a sign saying "My grocery is the best on this street!", the other answers by putting up a sign saying "My grocery is the best in the entire neighbourhood!" – and then it goes on and on: "Mine is the best in the whole town . . . in the whole country . . . on earth . . . in the whole universe . . .", until finally, the winner is the one who simply returns to the original sign: "My grocery is the best on this street!" And does not the same go for the gradual replacement of (sexually, racially . . .) aggressive

idioms with more "correct" ones, like the chain of substitutions *Nigger –
negro – black – African-American*; or *crippled – disabled – bodily challenged?* This replacement potentially proliferates and enhances the very
(racist) effect it tries to banish, adding insult to injury. As long as "crippled"
contains an indelible mark of aggressivity, this mark will not only be more
or less automatically transferred on to any of its "correct" metaphorical
substitutes; this substitution will even open up further possibilities of spicing
up the basic aggressivity with supplementary irony or patronizing politeness
(recall all the ironic uses of "challenged" generated by the PC use of this
term). We should therefore claim that the only way effectively to abolish
the hatred effect is, paradoxically, to create the circumstances in which we
can *return to the first link in the chain*, and use it in a non-aggressive way.
The strategy of returning to the first link, of course, is risky; however, the
moment it is fully accepted by the group targeted by it, it can definitely
work. When radical feminists call each other "bitch", it is wrong to dismiss
this strategy as a mere ironic identification with the male aggressor; rather,
the point is that it functions as an autonomous act of neutralizing the
aggressive sting.[69]

Did Lenin Love His Neighbour?

Atom Egoyan's film *Exotica* tackles the fragile status of the frontier that
separates public from private space. When we share a common space with
outsiders – say, when a delivery man or a repair man enters our apartment
– we politely ignore each other, refraining from probing into the other's
privacy (what do they desire, what are their secret dreams?); *Exotica*,
however, constantly violates this frontier, suddenly establishing a more
intimate contact between two people brought together by some official duty.
The Lacanian big Other is, among other things, one of the names for this
Wall which enables us to maintain the proper distance, guaranteeing that
the other's proximity will not overwhelm us – when we talk with a clerk,
we "do not get personal". (The paradox is that this very Wall is not just
negative: at the same time, it generates fantasies about what lurks behind it,
about what the other really desires.[70]) Our late capitalist daily life involves
an unprecedented disavowal of the other's experience:

> In order to pass a homeless person crouched in a doorway and *keep walking*,
> in order to *enjoy* dinner when children are hungry, in order to *rest* at night
> when suffering is incessant – atomized daily function demands that we

systematically foreclose our affections for and connections with others (in the words of dominant culture, our economy is comprised of individuals who respect each other's individuality). Behind the caricature of the bleeding-heart liberal is the truth of politics: how you feel is how you act.[71]

Here we are dealing not with individual psychology, but with capitalist subjectivity as a form of abstraction inscribed in and determined by the very nexus of "objective" social relations:

> Indifference towards specific labours corresponds to a form of society in which individuals can with ease transfer from one labour to another, and where the specific kind is a matter of chance for them, hence of indifference. Not only the category, labour, but labour in reality has here become the means of creating wealth in general, and has ceased to be organically linked with particular individuals in any specific form. Such a state of affairs is at its most developed in the most modern form of existence of bourgeois society, in the United States. Here, then, for the first time, the point of departure of modern economics, namely the abstraction of the category "labour", "labour as such", labour pure and simple, becomes true in practice.[72]

So, just as Marx described how, within the market economy, abstraction is inscribed into individual experience itself (a worker directly experiences his particular profession as a contingent actualization of his abstract capacity to work, not as an organic component of his personality; an "alienated" lover experiences his sexual partner as a contingent fill-in that satisfied his need for sexual and/or emotional gratification; etc.), abstraction is also inscribed into the way we relate to others at the most immediate level: we *ignore* them in the fundamental sense of the word, reducing them to bearers of abstract social functions. And the point here, of course, is that "systems of power necessitate specific emotional configurations":[73] the fundamental "coldness" of the late capitalist subject is supplanted/concealed by the phantom of a rich private emotional life which serves as a fantasy-screen protecting us from the shattering experience of the Real of other people's suffering. Today, the old joke about a rich man telling his servant "Throw out this destitute beggar – I'm so sensitive that I can't stand seeing people suffer!" is more appropriate than ever. The necessary price of this abstraction is that the very sphere of privacy gets "reified", turned into a domain of calculated satisfactions: is there anything more depressingly anti-erotic than the proverbial appeal of a yuppie to his partner: "Let's spend some quality time together!"? No wonder, then, that the obverse of this distance are brutal and humiliating intrusions into the other's intimate space: from confessionary talk-shows to cam-websites where we can observe other people defecating from the bottom of the toilet bowl.

It is a well-known fact that people find it much easier to confide their innermost dreams and fears to total strangers than to those who are close to them: phenomena like cyberspace chat-rooms and psychoanalytic treatment obviously rely on this paradox. The fact that we are telling it to a stranger totally outside our circle of acquaintances guarantees that our confession will not further stir up the *imbroglio* of passions in which we are enmeshed – not being one of our neighbouring others, the stranger is, in a way, the *big Other itself*, the neutral receptacle for our secrets. Today's "shared solipsism", however, moves on a different level: it is not only that we use strangers to confide the secrets of the loves and hatreds which structure our relationships with people whom we know and are close to; it is as if we are able to engage in these relationships themselves only against the background of a guaranteed distance. Things which, until now, had the status of an exception (like the proverbial passionate night of sex with a total stranger, in the knowledge that the next morning each of us will go his or her own way, never to meet again) are gradually imposing themselves as the new norm. (Among recent films, it is Patrice Chéreau's *Intimacy* which explores this issue most convincingly: on the morning after a wild night of sex with a stranger, when we find ourselves face to face with him or her, sharing an embarrassed proximity, is it possible to establish intimate personal contact?)

This disappearance of the frontier between public and private means that precise details of intimate life are becoming part of the public persona, accessible to everyone in books or on websites, not the obscene secret about which we whisper in private – to put it in a slightly nostalgic conservative way, the scandal lies in the very fact that there is no scandal any more. It began with models and movie stars: the (fake) video clip of Claudia Schiffer in passionate fellatio on two penises simultaneously is publicized everywhere; if we look on the Internet for data about Mimi MacPherson (the younger sister of the better-known Australian model Elle MacPherson), we find sites about her outstanding ecological activity (running a whale-observation company), interviews with her as a businesswoman, sites of "decent" photos of her, *plus* the stolen video of her masturbating and then copulating with her lover. And what about Catherine Millet's latest book,[74] in which this world-renowned art critic describes in a cold dispassionate style, without shame or guilt – and, as a result, also without any enthusiastic feeling of transgression – the details of her exuberant sexual life, up to her regular participation in big orgies, in which she was penetrated by or played with dozens of anonymous penises in a single session?

There are no a priori boundaries here – we can well imagine that, in the near future, some politician will (discreetly, at first) allow a hard-core video of his or her sexual shenanigans to circulate in public, to convince the voters of his or her force of attraction or potency. Almost a hundred years ago, Virginia Woolf wrote that, around 1912, human nature changed; perhaps this is a much more appropriate way of describing the radical shift in the status of subjectivity signalled by today's disappearance of the divide between public and private, discernible in phenomena like "Big Brother" reality soaps.[75]

So, in the conditions of late capitalism, our affective life is irrevocably split: on the one hand there is the sphere of "privacy", of intimate islands of emotional sincerity and intense engagements which, precisely, serve as obstacles which blind us to wider forms of suffering; on the other there is the (metaphorical and literal) screen through which we perceive this wider suffering, bombarded daily with TV reports on ethnic cleansing, rapes, tortures, natural catastrophes, with which we deeply sympathize and which sometimes move us to engage in humanitarian activities. Even when this engagement is quasi-"personalized" (like the photo and letter from a child in Africa whom we support through regular financial contributions), ultimately, the payment here retains its fundamental subjective function isolated by psychoanalysis: we give money in order to keep the suffering others at a proper distance which allows us to indulge in emotional sympathy without endangering our safe isolation from their reality. This split of the victims is the truth of the discourse of victimization: me (the harassed one) versus others (in the Third World or the homeless in our cities) with whom I sympathize at a distance. In contrast to this ideologico-emotional baggage, the authentic work of Love does not lie in helping the other by, as it were, throwing him scraps of our wealth across a safe barrier: it is, rather, the work of dismantling this barrier, of directly reaching out to the foreclosed suffering Other.

Such authentic work of Love should be opposed to feel-good anti-racism in the style of *Guess Who's Coming to Dinner?*, in which the black fiancé of the white upper-middle-class girl is educated, rich, and so on – his only fault is the colour of his skin: it is easy for the girl's parents to overcome the barrier and love such a "neighbor"; what, however, about the proverbial African-American from Spike Lee's *Do the Right Thing*, who annoys the Whites when he walks around with the boombox turned up loud? It is *this* excessive and intrusive *jouissance* that we should learn to tolerate – is he not the ideal subject of "cultural harassment"?[76] And is not the obsession with "sexual harassment" also a form of intolerance – or "zero tolerance", to use the popular Orwellian term of the law enforcers – for the other's enjoyment? This enjoyment is by definition excessive – every attempt to define its "proper measure" fails, since sexual seduction and proposal are in themselves intrusive, disturbing. Is the ultimate theme of the struggle against "harassment" not, therefore, the idea of each individual's right to be *left alone by his or her neighbours*, protected from their intrusive *jouissance*?

Why does Hamburg have three long-distance railway stations: the main station *Hamburg-Hauptbahnhof*, *Hamburg Dammtor*, and *Hamburg-Altona*, all on the same line? The distinction between the first two, the apparently "irrational" fact that, a short walk from the main station, there is another one, *Dammtor* station, is easy to explain: the ruling class wanted a station where its members could board the train unperturbed by the lower-class crowd. More enigmatic is the third station, *Altona*. It is not clear where this term comes from: while according to some sources it *refers* to the fact that this Danish settlement was perceived as standing "*all to nah*" ("all too near") to Hamburg itself, the more probable explanation is "*all ten au*", "by the brook". The fact, however, is that since the early sixteenth century, the citizens of Hamburg have been complaining continually about this small, originally Danish, settlement northwest of the city centre. As for the "all too near" theory, we should repeat the old Italian proverb: *se non è vero, è ben' trovato* – even if it's not true [on the factual level], it rings true! This is how a symptom is organized for Freud: as a hysterical accusation which, on the factual level, is clearly not true, but none the less "rings true" in so far as an unconscious desire resonates in it. And, in the same way, the symbolic function of the third station, *Altona* – to keep the intruders who are always "all too near" at a proper distance – also serves to displace/mystify the basic social antagonism (class struggle) into the fake antagonism between "us" (our nation, in which all classes are united in the same social body) and "them" (the foreign intruders).

The connection between these two oppositions provides the minimal co-ordinates of what Ernesto Laclau has conceptualized as the struggle for *hegemony*. The key feature of the concept of hegemony is the contingent connection between intrasocial differences (elements within the social space) and the limit that separates Society itself from non-Society (chaos, utter decadence, dissolution of all social links) – the limit between the Social and its exteriority, the non-Social, can articulate itself only in the guise of a difference (by mapping itself on to a difference) between elements of social space. The struggle within the social body (between *Hauptbahnhof* and *Dammtor*, the oppressed and the ruling class) is always, by a structural necessity, mirrored in the struggle between the social body "as such" ("all of us, workers and rulers") and those who are outside ("them", the foreigners who are "all too near", in *Altona*).[77] That is to say: class struggle is ultimately the struggle for the meaning of society "as such", the struggle for which of the two classes will impose itself as the stand-in for society "as such", thereby degrading its other into the stand-in for the non-Social (the destruction of, the threat to, society).

To simplify: Does the masses' struggle for emancipation pose a threat to civilization as such, since civilization can thrive only in a hierarchical social order? Or is it that the ruling class is a parasite threatening to drag society into self-destruction, so that the only alternative to socialism is barbarism? This, of course, in no way implies that the way we relate to "them" is secondary, and that we should simply shift the focus back to the antagonism which splits "our" society from within: the way we relate to "them", to the third element, is the key indicator of where we actually stand with regard to the inherent antagonism. Is not the basic operation of today's neo-Fascist populism precisely to combine working-class interpellation with racist interpellation ("cosmopolitan multinational companies as the true enemy of our honest workers")? This is why – to take the extreme example – for Jews in today's Israel, "Love thy neighbour!" means "Love the Palestinians!" *or it means nothing at all.*[78]

The courts in most Western societies know the measure of imposing an "order of restraint": when someone sues another person for harassing him or her (stalking, making unwarranted sexual advances, etc.), the harasser can be legally prohibited from knowingly approaching the victim within more than a hundred yards. Necessary as this measure is in view of the obvious reality of harassment, there is none the less something of the defence against the Real of the Other's desire in it: is it not obvious that there is something dreadfully *violent* about openly displaying one's passion for another human being to this being him- or herself? Passion, by definition, *hurts* its object; and even if its addressee gladly agrees to occupy this place, he or she can never do so without a moment of awe and surprise. Or – another variation on Hegel's dictum "Evil resides in the very gaze which perceives Evil all around" – intolerance towards the Other resides in the very gaze which perceives intolerant intruding Others all around.

We should be especially suspicious about an obsession with the sexual harassment of women when it is voiced by men: after barely scratching the "pro-feminist" PC surface, we soon encounter the good old male-chauvinist myth about how women are helpless creatures who should be protected not only from intruding men, but ultimately also from *themselves*. The problem is not that they will be unable to protect themselves, but that they might start to enjoy being sexually harassed – that the male intrusion will set free in them a self-destructive explosion of excessive sexual enjoyment. . . . In short, what we should focus on is *what kind of notion of subjectivity is implied in the obsession with different modes of harassment?* Is it not the "narcissistic" subjectivity for which everything others do (talk to me, look at me . . .) is potentially a threat, so that – as Sartre put it long ago – *l'enfer, c'est les autres?*

With regard to woman as an object of disturbance, the more she is covered, the more our (male) attention focuses on her, on what lies beneath the veil. The Taleban not only forced women to appear in public completely veiled, they also prohibited them from wearing shoes with too solid (metal or wooden) heels, and ordered them to walk in such a way that they would not make too loud a clicking noise, which might attract men's attention and thus distract them, disturbing their inner peace and dedication. This is the paradox of surplus-enjoyment at its purest: the more the object is veiled, the more intensely disturbing is the minimal trace of its remainder.

And is not this the case even with the growing prohibition on smoking? First, all offices were declared "smoke-free", then flights, then restaurants, then airports, then bars, then private clubs; then, on some university campuses, fifty yards around the entrances to the buildings; then – in a unique case of pedagogical censorship, reminding us of the famous Stalinist practice of retouching the photos of the *nomenklatura* – the US postal service removed the cigarette from stamps with photo-portraits of blues guitarist Robert Johnson, and of Jackson Pollock; now we have the recent attempts to impose a ban on lighting up on the pavement or in a park. Christopher Hitchens was right to point out not only that medical evidence for the threat of "passive smoking" is at best extremely shaky, but that these prohibitions themselves, intended "for our own good", are "fundamentally illogical, presaging a supervised world in which we'll live painlessly, safely – and tediously".[79]

Is not the target of such prohibitions again the Other's excessive, risky *jouissance*, embodied in the act of "irresponsibly" lighting a cigarette and inhaling deeply, with unabashed pleasure – in contrast to Clintonite yuppies who do it without inhaling (or have sex without actual penetration, or food without fat, or . . .)? On top of all this, the notion of the danger of "passive smoking" is clearly part of the post-AIDS fear not only of direct physical contact with others, but also of more ethereal forms of contact (the "invisible" exchange of fluids, bacteria, viruses . . .). What makes smoking such an ideal scapegoat is the fact that the proverbial "smoking gun" is easy to target here, providing a Politically Correct agent of conspiracy, the large tobacco companies, and thus disguising envy of the Other's enjoyment in the acceptable anti-corporate clout. The ultimate irony is not only that the tobacco companies' profits have not yet been affected by anti-smoking campaigns and legislation, but that even most of the billions of dollars the tobacco companies have agreed to pay will go to the medico-pharmaceutical industrial complex, which is the single strongest industrial complex in the USA, twice as strong as the infamous military–industrial complex.

What makes Fred Walton's film *When a Stranger Calls* so interesting is the unexpected twist after the first twenty minutes, which tell the standard story of the anonymous murderer harassing the babysitter alone in the house with two children with repeated phone calls: after he is apprehended (and we learn that he was in the house all the time, calling from another phone line, and that he has already killed the two children), we are thrown into *his* subjective perspective. This reversal of narrative perspective displays a clear class connotation: the first and last parts of the film take place in upper-middle-class surroundings (the crimes occur during babysitting, when the mother and father are out partying; the murderer's question "Did you check on the children?" is in fact addressed at the parents). Not only does the pathological harasser/murderer belong to the lower classes; he is also portrayed as the ultimate disturbing neighbour, whose offers of friendship and desperate pleas for communication are all brutally rejected (he is beaten up in a desolate low-class bar, ignored by people who walk past him on the street). This rejection also gives a clue to the motivation of his attacks: at the end of the film's second part (in which his narrative perspective predominates), we see him, hidden among dustbins, repeating his mantra: "Nobody sees me! Nobody hears me! I don't exist!" It is from this position of *subjective nonexistence* that he performs the act, and commits his horrible crimes.

There is an extraordinary scene towards the beginning of Kieslowski's *Decalogue 8*: in the middle of a university ethics class, an anonymous haggard-looking young man (a homeless drunkard?) enters the large class-room and looks around perplexed. All the participants are embarrassed and annoyed, not knowing what to do; finally, a formally dressed black man (a student from an African country?) says in English: "Get out!", and the intruder leaves the room.[80] The irony of this scene is double: first, the participants, who are intensely discussing love of one's neighbour, blatantly not only ignore, but even throw out, the actual neighbour in distress; second, the person who breaks the impasse by ordering the distressed neighbour to leave is a black student – the exemplary object of racial intolerance in Real Socialist countries, in which African students were despised by local students, who perceived them as financially and politically privileged but intellectually inept foreigners who posed a sexual threat by seducing white girls.

In the magnificent Chapter IIC ("*You* Shall Love Your Neighbor") of *Works of Love*, Kierkegaard develops the claim that the ideal neighbour whom we should love is a dead one – the only good neighbour is a dead neighbour. His line of reasoning is surprisingly simple and consistent: in contrast to poets and lovers, whose object of love is distinguished by its preference, by its particular outstanding qualities, "to love your neighbor means equality": "Forsake all distinctions so that you can love your neighbor."[81] It is only in death, however, that all distinctions disappear: "Death erases all distinctions, but preference is always related to distinctions."[82] A further consequence of this reasoning is the crucial distinction between two perfections: the perfection of the object of love, and the perfection of love itself. The lover's, poet's or friend's love contains a perfection that belongs to its object and is, for this very reason, imperfect as love; in contrast to this love:

> precisely because one's neighbor has none of the excellences which the beloved, a friend, a cultured person, an admired one, and a rare and extraordinary one have in high degree – for that very reason love to one's neighbor has all the perfections. . . . Erotic love is determined by the object; friendship is determined by the object; only love to one's neighbor is determined by love. Since one's neighbor is every man, unconditionally every man, all distinctions are indeed removed from the object. Therefore genuine love is recognizable by this, that its object is without any of the more definite qualifications of difference, which means that this love is recognizable only by love. Is not this the highest perfection?[83]

To put it in Kant's terms: here Kierkegaard is trying to articulate the contours of a non-pathological love, a love which would be independent of its (contingent) object, a love which (to paraphrase again Kant's definition of moral duty) is motivated not by its determinate object, but by the mere *form* of love – I love for the sake of love itself, not for the sake of what distinguishes its object. The implication of this stance is bizarre, if not outright morbid: perfect love is *thoroughly indifferent to the beloved object*.

No wonder Kierkegaard was so obsessed with the figure of Don Juan: do not Kierkegaard's Christian love for the neighbour and Don Juan's serial seductions share this crucial indifference to the object? For Don Juan, too, the quality of the seduced object did not matter: the ultimate point of Leporello's long list of conquests, which categorizes them according to their

characteristics (age, nationality, physical features), is that these characteristics are irrelevant – the only thing that matters is the pure numerical fact
of adding a new name to the list. In this precise sense, is not Don Juan a
properly *Christian* seducer, since his conquests were "pure", non-pathological in the Kantian sense, done for the sake of it, not because of any
particular and contingent properties of their objects? The poet's preferred
love object is also a dead person (paradigmatically the beloved woman): he
needs her to be dead in order to articulate his mourning in his poetry (or,
as in courtly love poetry, a living woman is elevated to the status of a
monstrous Thing). In contrast to the poet's fixation on the singular dead
love object, the Christian, however, treats the still living neighbour as
already dead, erasing his or her distinctive qualities. The dead neighbour
means the neighbour deprived of the annoying excess of *jouissance* which
makes him or her unbearable. So it is clear where Kierkegaard cheats: in
trying to sell us, as the authentic difficult act of love, what is in fact an
escape from the effort of authentic love. Love for the dead neighbour is an
easy feast: it basks in its own perfection, indifferent to its object – what
about not only "tolerating" but loving the other *because of his or her very
imperfection*?

Is this love for the dead neighbour really just Kierkegaard's theological
idiosyncrasy? On a recent visit to San Francisco, while listening to a blues
CD in a friend's apartment, I uttered the unfortunate remark: "Judging by
the colour of her voice, the singer is definitely black. Strange, then, that she
has such a German-sounding name – Nina." Of course, I was immediately
admonished for Political Incorrectness: one should not associate someone's
ethnic identity with a physical feature or a name, because all this just bolsters
racial clichés and prejudices. To my ensuing query about how, then, one
should identify ethnic belonging, I got a clear and radical answer: in no way,
by means of no particular feature, because every such identification is
potentially oppressive in constraining a person to his or her particular
identity. . . . Is this not a perfect contemporary example of what Kierkegaard
had in mind? One should love one's neighbours (African-Americans, in this
case) only in so far as they are implicitly deprived of all their particular
characteristics – in short, in so far as they are treated as already dead. What
about loving them *for* the unique sharp-melancholic quality of their voices,
for the amazing libidinal combinations of their names (the leader of the anti-
racist movement in France two decades ago was named *Harlem Désir*!) –
that is to say, *for* the idiosyncrasy of their modes of *jouissance*?

Lacan's name for this "imperfection", for the obstacle which makes me
love someone, is *objet petit a*, the "pathological" tic which makes him or

her unique. In authentic love, I love the other not simply for being alive, but because of the very troubling excess of life in him or her. Even the common wisdom is somehow aware of this: as they say, there is something cold in perfect beauty; we admire it, but we fall in love with an *imperfect* beauty, because of this very imperfection. For Americans, at least, there is something all too cold in Claudia Schiffer's perfection: it is somehow easier to fall in love with Cindy Crawford because of her very small imperfection (the famous tiny mole near her lip – her *objet petit a*).[84] And I am tempted to add to the couple of Schiffer and Crawford the couple of the Federal Republic of Germany and the defunct German Democratic Republic: there still are people who love the GDR *inclusive of and for its very imperfections* – they love the memory of the bitter sulphur taste of the air due to the heavy industry pollution – but there is hardly anyone who loves the Federal Republic of Germany.[85]

This failure of Kierkegaard also explains the problems which emerge when we apply the Kierkegaardian triad of the Aesthetic, the Ethical and the Religious to the domain of sexual relations: which is the religious mode of the erotic, if its aesthetic mode is seduction and its ethical mode marriage? Is it at all meaningful to talk about a religious mode of erotics in the precise Kierkegaardian sense of the term? The point of Lacan is that this, precisely, is the role of *courtly love*: the Lady in courtly love suspends the ethical level of universal symbolic obligations, and bombards us with totally arbitrary ordeals in a way which is homologous to the religious suspension of the Ethical; these ordeals are on a par with God ordering Abraham to slaughter his son Isaac. And, contrary to the surface appearance, here that sacrifice reaches its apogee: it is only here that we finally confront the Other *qua* Thing that gives body to the excess of enjoyment over mere pleasure.

Just like Kierkegaard's love for the dead neighbour, this tragic vision of courtly love is not only false, but ultimately even unchristian. In Hitchcock's *Vertigo*, the low-class Judy – who, under the pressure exerted from and out of her love for Scottie, endeavours to look and act like the high-class fatal and ethereal Madeleine – turns out to *be* Madeleine: they are the same person, since the "true" Madeleine Scottie encountered was already a fake. This identity of Judy and Judy–Madeleine, however, reveals all the more clearly the absolute otherness of Madeleine with regard to Judy – a Madeleine who is nowhere, who is present only in the guise of the ethereal "aura" that envelops Judy–Madeleine.

In a strictly homologous gesture, Christianity asserts that there is nothing beyond appearance – nothing but the imperceptible X that changes Christ, an ordinary man, into God. In the *absolute* identity of man and God, the

Divine is the pure *Schein* of another dimension that shines through Christ, this miserable creature. It is only here that the iconoclasm is truly brought to its conclusion: what is in fact "beyond the image" is that X which makes the man Christ God. In this precise sense, Christianity reverses Jewish sublimation into a radical desublimation: not desublimation in the sense of a simple reduction of God to man, but desublimation in the sense of the descent of the sublime Beyond to the everyday level. Christ is a "ready-made God" (as Boris Groys put it); he is fully human, inherently indistinguishable from other humans in exactly the same way as Judy is indistinguishable from Madeleine in *Vertigo* – it is only an imperceptible "something", a pure appearance which can never be grounded in a substantial property, that makes him divine.

This is why Scottie's obsessive love for Madeleine is a fake: if his love were true, he should have accepted the full identity of (the common, vulgar) Judy and (the sublime) Madeleine.[86] It is in this identity of incongruous opposites, of the sublime and the ridiculous, that we find the comedy of love – or, as Fernando Pessoa puts it: "All love letters are / comical. / They would not be about love, if they were not / comical."

There is, nevertheless, an indifference which pertains to true love: not an indifference to its object, but an indifference to the positive qualities of the beloved object. This indifference of love is closely linked to that of the Lacanian "empty signifier": of course, this signifier is never really "empty" – a king, for example, is always identified with a series of personal idiosyncratic features which characterize him; however, we, his subjects, are aware at all times that these features are thoroughly indifferent and replaceable, that it is not these features which make him a king. The difference between the "empty" signifier and the "full" signifier lies not in the absence or presence of positive features of the object designated by it, but in the different *symbolic status* of these features: in the first case these features are a positive magnitude (the subject's qualities), while in the second they function as a negative magnitude, that is, their very "full presence" is a stand-in for – holds the place of – the "emptiness" of the signifier (of the symbolic mandate) "King". So "fullness" and "emptiness" are not directly opposed: the very "emptiness" of the empty signifier is sustained by a specific "negative" fullness. And the same goes for love: to say "I love you because . . . [you have a nice nose, attractive legs]" is a priori false. With love, it is the same as with religious belief: I do not love you because I find your positive features attractive but, on the contrary, I find your positive features attractive because I love you, and therefore observe you with a loving gaze. Consequently, all the "fullness" of the positive features which I adore in the beloved are a stand-in for the "emptiness" which I really love – even if they were obliterated, I would still love you.

How does all this relate to sex? The true miracle occurs when sex is "transubstantiated" into an act of love. There are four ways to disavow this impossible/real conjunction of love and sexual enjoyment:

1. the celebration of asexual "pure" love, as if sexual desire for the beloved demonstrates the love's inauthenticity;[87]
2. the opposite assertion of intense sex as "the only real thing", which reduces love to a mere imaginary lure;
3. the division of these two aspects, their allocation to two different people: one loves one's gentle wife (or the idealized inaccessible Lady), while one has sex with a "vulgar" mistress;
4. their false immediate merger, in which intense sex is supposed to demonstrate that one "truly loves" one's partner, as if, in order to prove that our love is a true one, every sexual act has to be the proverbial "fuck of the century".

All these four stances are wrong, an escape from assuming the impossible/real conjunction of love and sex; a true love is enough in itself, it makes sex irrelevant – but precisely because "fundamentally, it doesn't matter", we can fully enjoy it without any superego pressure. . . . And, paradoxically, this brings us back to Lenin: when, in 1916, Lenin's (at that point ex-)mistress Inessa Armand wrote to him that even a fleeting passion was more poetic and cleaner than kisses without love between man and woman, he replied:

> Kisses without love between vulgar spouses are *filthy*. I agree. These need to be contrasted . . . with what? . . . It would seem: kisses *with* love. But you contrast "a fleeting (why a fleeting) passion (why not love?)" – and it comes out logically as if kisses without love (fleeting) are contrasted to marital kisses without love. . . . This is odd.[88]

Lenin's reply is usually dismissed as proof of his petty-bourgeois sexual restraint, sustained by his bitter memory of the past affair; however, there is more to it: the insight that marital "kisses without love" and the extramarital "fleeting affair" are the two sides of the same coin – they both shrink from combining the Real of an unconditional passionate attachment with the form of symbolic proclamation. Lenin is profoundly right here, but not in the classic prudish sense of preferring "normal" marriage for love to illicit promiscuity. The underlying insight is that, against all appearances, love and sex are not only distinct, but ultimately *incompatible* – that they operate on completely different levels, like *agape* and *eros*: love is charitable, self-effacing, ashamed of itself; while sex is intense, self-assertive, possessive, inherently *violent* (or the opposite: possessive love versus generous indulging in sexual pleasures).[89] The true miracle, however, occurs when (exceptionally, not "as a rule"), these two series momentarily *coincide* – an achievement which is real/impossible in the precise Lacanian sense and, as such, marked by an inherent *rarity*.

Today, it is as if the nexus of three levels which characterized traditional sexuality (reproduction, sexual pleasure, love) is gradually dissolving: reproduction is left to biogenetic procedures which are making sexual intercourse redundant; sex itself is turned into recreational fun; while love is reduced to the domain of "emotional fulfilment".[90] In such a situation, it is all the more precious to be reminded of those rare miraculous moments in which two of these three dimensions can still overlap. I am almost tempted to paraphrase Brecht's "What is a bank robbery compared to the founding of a bank?" here: what is an extramarital affair compared to an affair which declares itself publicly in the form of marriage?

In a recent book against the "excesses" of May 1968 and, more generally, against the "sexual liberation" of the 1960s, *The Independent* reminded us what the radicals of '68 thought about child sex. A quarter of a century ago, Daniel Cohn-Bendit wrote about his experience in a kindergarten:

> My constant flirt with all the children soon took on erotic characteristics. I could really feel how from the age of five the small girls had already learned to make passes at me. . . . Several times a few children opened the flies of my trousers and started to stroke me. . . . When they insisted, I then stroked them.

Shulamith Firestone went even further, expressing her hopes that, in a world "without the incest taboo . . . relations with children would include as much genital sex as they were capable of – probably considerably more than we now believe".[91] Confronted with these statements, Cohn-Bendit played them down, claiming: "This did not really happen, I only wanted to provoke people. When one reads it today, it is unacceptable."[92] The question, however, still remains: how, at that time, was it possible to provoke people, presenting sexual games with pre-school children to them as something appealing, while today, the same "provocation" would immediately give rise to an outburst of moral disgust? After all, child sexual harassment is one of *the* notions of Evil today. Without directly taking sides in this debate, we should read it as a sign of the change in our mores from the utopian energies of the 1960s and early 1970s to stale contemporary Political Correctness, in which every authentic encounter with another human being is denounced as a victimizing experience. This, of course, does not imply that we should simply take the side of "sexual liberation": the problem is, rather, that "sexual liberation" in the style of Cohn-Bendit and hedonistic Politically Correct asceticism are intrinsically linked – the second attitude is the "truth", the consequent realization, of the first one: that is to say, unconstrained hedonism *has* to end up in some form of renewed asceticism.

In *Gasparone*, a silly German musical from 1937, the young Marika Roekk, reproached by her father for treating her rich and powerful fiancé unkindly, promptly answers: "I love him, so I have the right to treat him in any way I want!" There is some truth in this statement: far from obliging me to be "respectful" and "considerate" – all signals of cold distance – love, in a way, allows me to dispense with these formalities. Does this mean that love gives me a kind of *carte blanche*, justifying every brutality? No, and that is the miracle of love: *love sets its own standards*, so that, within a love-relationship, it is immediately clear when we are dealing with love and when we are not (as with Politically Incorrect terms, which can also be used as proof that I am a real friend of the person concerned).

From *passage à l'acte* to the Act Itself

This is also why authentic love for one's neighbour has nothing to do with compassion: one of the key lessons of psychoanalysis concerns the hypocrisy of compassion, that is, the secret pleasure [*Schadenfreude*] one gets from sympathizing with the other's difficult predicament. Nowhere is this clearer than in Lars von Trier's films. In his remarkable intervention at the Krzysztof Kieslowski conference at UCLA in April 2001, Fredric Jameson violently protested against the unexpected death by drowning of a young boy, the traumatic event around which Kieslowski's *Decalogue 1* turns: he emphatically claimed that Kieslowski should never be forgiven for killing the boy, that he should be held accountable for his death – just as, according to some late medieval legislation, if an author kills a popular fictional character in his narrative, we should be allowed to prosecute him for murder. . . . Brilliant as this idea is, it is probably misplaced: the author who should in fact *never* be forgiven for the way he treats his heroines in *Breaking the Waves* and *Dancer in the Dark* is Lars von Trier.

Dancer in the Dark is one of those painful films in which it is clear from the very beginning where the story will end: in total catastrophe. While we are watching, we secretly hope – believe, even – that something will happen which will prevent this unbearable ending, so that, paradoxically, the final shock is that there is no surprise: the horrible ending towards which the film has pointed all the time *does* materialize.

The story takes place in the USA in the 1960s: Selma (Björk), a Czech émigrée who works in a textile factory, is going blind because of an inherited disease; she works overtime to save money for the operation which would save her son from the same predicament. Her friendly neighbour, in whom she confides, steals the money from her; she kills him, is condemned to death and executed. . . . How can Selma live through such an ordeal? Her big passions are singing and musicals: after working hours, she participates in an amateur group practising for a performance of *The Sound of Music*, and the drab reality of her life is continuously suspended by the songs she imagines singing to herself. These songs, which grow organically out of the rhythmic sounds of her working environment (reminding us of the good old Marxist theories of the birth of music out of the collective work rhythm), become leaner and leaner, with diminishing orchestral accompaniment, until when she is on her way to her execution, we hear just her hesitant voice trying to linger with the melody. The ambiguity here is radical: does *Dancer* celebrate the magic power of music (and musicals) which allows us to survive horrifying reality, or does it condemn music as an escapist fantasy which makes us passively endure social reality?

So how is Selma able to sustain such a radical subjective stance? By adopting the fetishist position. What is a fetish? Patricia Highsmith's short story 'The Button' tells the story of a middle-aged New Yorker who lives a miserable life with his wife and their Down's Syndrome child; late one night, unable to stand his son's meaningless gibber any longer, he goes for a walk through the empty streets, where he bumps into a homeless drunken beggar. Although the beggar is in no way intrusive, the hero spills out all his anger and frustrations on him; after beating him senselessly to death, he tears a button off his dirty coat and runs home. From this evening on, he keeps the button in his pocket all the time, clinging to it as to a kind of superstitious prop – whatever misery befalls him, there will always be this button to remind him how – once, at least – he was really able to hit back. So he regains the ability to confront life with new hope, even to smile kindly at his handicapped son. . . . This is a fetish at its purest: the in-between element which enables the subject to endure miserable reality. And perhaps the true secret of *Dancer* is that it narrates a case of feminine fetishism, turning around the classic psychoanalytic doxa which opposes feminine hysteria and male (fetishist) perversion. Is it not that Selma is able to endure everything, even the most painful situations, because she has her fetish – singing – to which she clings all the time? Underlying all this is a question:

what *is* singing? Why do we sing? At the very beginning of *Eugene Onegin*, Pushkin presents a scene of women singing as they pick strawberries in a field – with the acerbic explanation that they are ordered to sing by their mistress, so that they cannot eat the strawberries as they pick them.

What, then, is the *social* dimension of such a fetishist stance? Let us take another film which deals with music and the working class, Mark Herman's *Brassed Off*, whose topic is the relationship between a "real" political struggle (the miners' struggle against the threatened pit closure legitimized in terms of technological progress) and the idealized symbolic expression of the miners' community, their playing in a brass band. At first, the two aspects seem to be opposed: to the miners caught in their struggle for economic survival, the "Only music matters!" attitude of their old band leader dying of lung cancer looks like the vain fetishized insistence of the empty symbolic form deprived of its social substance. Once the miners lose their political struggle, however, the "music matters" attitude, their insistence on going on playing and participating in a national competition, turns into a defiant symbolic gesture, a proper act of asserting fidelity to their political struggle – as one of them puts it, when there's no hope, there are only principles to follow. . . . In short, the symbolic act occurs when we arrive at this intersection or, rather, short circuit of the two levels, so that insistence on the empty form itself (we'll continue to play in our brass band, whatever happens . . .) becomes the sign of fidelity to the content (to the struggle against the closure, for the continuation of the miners' way of life).

This role of music achieved its highest expression in the legendary event at the Vorkuta Gulag camp Mine 29 in 1953. A few months after Stalin's death, strikes broke out in labour camps all across Siberia; the strikers' demands were modest and "reasonable": the release of the very old and the too young, a ban on random shooting by watch-tower guards, and so on. One by one, the camps succumbed to threats or false promises from Moscow, and only Mine 29 at Vorkuta held out, surrounded by two divisions of NKVD troops, with tanks. When the troops finally entered the main gate, they saw the prisoners standing behind it in a solid phalanx, their arms linked, singing. After a brief moment of hesitation, the heavy machine-guns opened up – the miners remained massed and erect, defiantly continuing to sing, the dead held up by the living. After about a minute, reality prevailed, and corpses started to litter the ground. However, this brief minute in which the strikers' defiance seemed to suspend the very laws of nature, transubstantiating their exhausted bodies into the appearance of an immortal singing collective Body, was an occurrence of the Sublime at its purest, the prolonged moment in which, in a way, time stood still.

What, then, if we risk putting *Dancer in the Dark* into this series, viewing Selma's singing not as an escapist gesture but as a gesture of heroic defiance? Furthermore, what if – before immersing ourselves in speculation about the relationship between voice and reality – we take note of the fact that in a society with universal healthcare, Selma's predicament (having to toil for her son's eye surgery while she is going blind herself) could not have emerged in the first place?

Furthermore, the film's supreme achievement is the avoidance of melo-dramatic effects where the events seem to call for them. The key scene is the exchange between Selma and the neighbour who stole her money out of despair that were his wife to discover that he was broke, she would leave him. So when Selma (in a calm and dignified way, without any pathetic reproaches) confronts him with his crime, the friendly neighbour answers her in a calm, rational way, admitting everything, and presenting her with a choice: if he were to lose the money, he would not be able to endure the fact that his wife has left him, so the only alternative for him would be suicide. So Selma has to make a choice: either she lets him keep her painfully earned money, or she kills him (he even gives her his gun), which she does. This scene is unique in its radical tension: the cruelty of what is going on (the victim confronting the criminal who has ruined her life) is expressed in the form of a sincerely open and compassionate exchange between two true friends, both victims of circumstance, so that when Selma kills the thief, the act is accomplished not with uncontrolled rage, but as a tender act of helping a friend, reminding us of the final scene of Brecht's *Die Massnahme*, when the three revolutionaries throw their young companion who has failed in his work to his death – political liquidation as an act of *pietà*.

All this brilliance, however, does not alter the fundamental fact that there is something terribly wrong with the film. *Dancer* is the final part of Von Trier's trilogy, which also includes *Breaking the Waves* and *The Idiots*. All three films focus on the same figure of feminine subjectivity: the fairytale figure of the girl walking alone in a forest, who endeavours to escape the sense of being exposed to the menacing darkness all around her by offering bits of what she has to the surrounding shadows. While they profess compassion with the excessively good heroine, the way these films depict her progressive suffering and inexorable self-destruction cannot but put us in the position of the sadistic observer secretly enjoying what he officially condemns: this sadistic pleasure is the obverse, the hidden truth, of compassion. And for this, Von Trier should never be forgiven. The only antidote to this murderous compassion is its apparent opposite: loving aggressivity.

In June 2001, Andrea Yates from Houston, Texas, drowned all five of her children (from Mary, aged six months, to Noah, aged seven) in a bathtub. At nine in the morning, after her husband had left for work, she filled the bathtub and began killing her children. When she picked Mary up and put her in the tub, Noah caught her in her act and tried to run away; she chased him and wrestled him into the tub. She did her job methodically, killing them one by one, holding them underwater (with, as we can imagine, their eyes staring back at her), then laying them out on the bed wrapped in sheets. Then she calmly called the police and her husband, informing them of her act, for which she assumed full responsibility – when a policeman asked her: "Do you realize what you have done?", she answered: "Yes, I do. I killed my children."

Her case revealed the misery of all the talk about "PPD" (postpartum depression). This obfuscates not only the subjective impasse this violent *passage à l'acte* was destined to resolve, but also the ideological co-ordinates of this Medeaesque act which, as the very names of the children (Mary, Luke, Paul, John, Noah – ironically, the last to be drowned . . .) reveal, took place in a devout Christian household. (In the case of Susan Smith, who drowned her two boys in a South Carolina lake in 1994, her religious faith played a crucial role: she thought that by killing the children she was sending them to heaven, and thus sparing them the misery of terrestrial life.)

The Yateses were an ideal Christian family: after their marriage, Rusty and Andrea decided that Andrea should give up her job (as a nurse in a cancer clinic), stay at home, and dedicate herself fully to the children. And she did so with utter dedication: in addition to feeding, bathing and disciplining the children, and teaching them readings and maths, she took care of her father, who suffered from Alzheimer's. So, far from being psychotic, her mindset was that of feminine obsessional neurosis: the object of her desire was the other's demand. She dedicated her life to serving others – she cared too much, she tried to be too good a mother, always thinking of other people, never of herself. Caught in this subservience to the other's demand, she was by definition unable to fulfil it: in accordance with the inexorable logic of the superego, the more she tried to comply with the demand to serve her neighbours, the more she felt inadequate, with attacks of depression and emotional detachment as the consequences of her predicament. After drowning her children, she told the police that she was a bad mother, and that her children were hopelessly damaged. This left her only two ways out: either to kill herself or to kill the children. First, in June 1999, after her father's death, unable to sustain the situation without him to care for, she tried to kill herself by overdosing; finally, she chose the other path.

At a press conference, her husband described his attitude towards Andrea:

My wife, I'm supportive of her. But . . . I know that the woman here is not
the woman who killed my children. . . . One side of me blames her because
. . . she did it. But the other side of me says, "Well, she didn't, because that
wasn't her; she wasn't in her right frame of mind."[93]

This, precisely, is an all-too-easy way out: we should assert here what Hegel
would have called the speculative identity of these two sides. How, then,
are we to read the bond between these two aspects of Andrea's psyche
(loving and self-effacing care; the outburst of murderous violence)? If
anything, there are too many explanations – a whole proliferation of them.
Feminists could claim that Andrea's act was a desperate wild rebellion
against the traditional mother-role; "risk society" theorists could interpret
it as the result of the inability of traditional family values to enable
individuals to cope with the dynamics of modern social life; conservatives
could focus on the unbearable stress modern life is putting on the family.

There is, in fact, something "premodern" in Andrea's refusal to follow
the path of today's narcissistic injunction: "Realize yourself" – she found
satisfaction in the old-fashioned self-obliterating attitude of serving others.
What made her burden unbearable was the fact that in contrast to premodern times, when the childcare was more collectivized (grandparents, brothers
and sisters and other relatives shared in it), the modern nuclear family tends
to confer this task on the mother alone. Abandoning her professional career
and dedicating herself to her offspring, she is subjected to the ideological
injunction to experience this predicament as supreme happiness: the pure
bliss of privacy and intimacy, as opposed to "alienated" professional work.
What about the obvious fact that between the ages of two and five, children
really *are* monsters, the closest a human being can come to "radical Evil":
creatures of insatiable demand, inflexible and stubborn, by definition never
satisfied? No wonder that in 1646, the General Court of Massachusetts Bay
enacted the "stubborn-child law" which allowed rebellious sons to be tried
and put to death. Kant knew that small children display a kind of "wild
freedom" that has no counterpart in the animal kingdom – a freedom in
which, perhaps, the noumenal dimension of the Real appears.

While all these readings are feasible, we should focus on the more
fundamental dimension underlying them: that of the violent *passage à l'acte*
as the only way to break out of an ideological deadlock. Here we are
dealing not with the simple tension between the impossible ideological
injunction and subjective resistance to it, but with the double-bind inherent
to this injunction itself: the injunction's "explicit" message is redoubled
(supplemented, sustained) by an implicit obscene message which says the

exact opposite. The "complete" message of the injunction is thus, in the case of the mother: be happy and find fulfilment in the very hell of your home, where your children bombard you with impossible demands, where all your hopes are thwarted! And is not a similar double-bind at work in the multicultural liberal injunction to be tolerant? Here again, the true message is: learn to love the disgusting Other whose display of excessive *jouissance* makes you sick! This injunction also contains an additional twist which explains why a liberal subject is ready to follow it: "Zero tolerance for any kind of harassment!", which means that you should tolerate the Other *in so far as he himself is tolerant*. Tolerance towards the Other thus passes imperceptibly into a destructive hatred of all ("fundamentalist") Others who do not fit our idea of tolerance – in short, against all *actual* Others. Or – to apply the same logic to the family haven: infinite dedication to one's children can turn into a destructive rage against real children who do not appreciate their mother's sacrifice.

It is against this double-bind that the (self-)destructive *passage à l'acte* explodes; and it is all too simple to oppose this *passage à l'acte* directly to the authentic political act. The first reaction to an ideological double-bind has to be a "blind" violent *passage à l'acte*, which can only later, in a subsequent move, be properly politicized. We simply *have to accept the risk* that a blind violent outburst will be followed by its proper politicization – there is no short cut here, and no guarantee of a successful outcome either. Horrible as it may sound, we should therefore *not* simply condemn acts like the one committed by Andrea: we should discern in them a hidden liberating potential. What is a *passage à l'acte* – this moment of "Speak, hands, for me!", as Casca puts it in Shakespeare's *Julius Caesar*?

Perhaps its ultimate cinematic expression is found in Paul Schrader's and Martin Scorsese's *Taxi Driver*, in Travis's (Robert de Niro) final outburst against the pimps who control the young girl he wants to save (Jodie Foster). The implicit suicidal dimension of this *passage à l'acte* is crucial: when Travis is preparing for his attack, he practises drawing the gun in front of the mirror; in what became the best-known scene in the film, he addresses his own image in the mirror with an aggressive-condescending "You talkin' to me?". In a textbook illustration of Lacan's notion of the "mirror stage", the aggressivity here is clearly aimed at oneself, at one's own mirror-image. This suicidal dimension re-emerges at the end of the slaughter scene when Travis, heavily wounded and leaning against the wall, mimics with the forefinger of his right hand a gun aimed at his bloodstained forehead and mockingly triggers it, as if to say: "The true aim of my outburst was myself." The paradox of Travis is that he perceives *himself* as part of the degenerate dirt of the city life he wants to eradicate, so that – as Brecht put it apropos of revolutionary violence in *The Measure Taken* – he wants to be the last piece of dirt after whose removal the room will be clean.[94]

In a real-life case of such a deadlock, in 1999 Private Barry Winchell from Fort Campbell US Army base beat to death a fellow soldier who harassed him all the time about his homosexuality. This event is usually quoted as proof of the failure of Bill Clinton's "Don't ask, don't tell" policy on gays in the army; what is perhaps more crucial is to perceive how this failure is linked to the tension between explicit symbolic rules and their supplement, the obscene unwritten rules that actually sustain a community. In his unit, Winchell was continually submitted to anti-gay gibes and taunts – not only by his fellow soldiers, but also by his immediate superior, Sergeant Kleifgen. Typically, when Kleifgen was asked why he did not intervene and order the platoon members to stop harassing Winchell, he replied: "Everybody was having fun" – in short, harassing Winchell functioned as the secret obscene male-bonding ritual that cemented the community. (In military jargon, "having fun" refers as a rule to cruel and humiliating ritualized procedures – take my own experience in the Yugoslav People's Army, where the supreme example of "having fun" was to pick out a soldier asleep in his bed, tie his testicles with a rope to one of his toes when his legs were not fully stretched, then put a piece of paper between his toes, and set it on fire; when the fire awakened the unfortunate soldier, his automatic reaction was, of course, to stretch out his leg repeatedly, trying to get rid of the burning piece of paper that was causing him pain – in military jargon, this was called "making him ride a bicycle", and the result could be heard hundreds of yards away. . . .)

Again, the "Don't ask, don't tell" policy put Winchell in an unbearable double-bind: he was afraid that if he complained to his superior officers about the harassment, he would break the second part of the policy rule ("don't tell") – that is to say, his complaint would involve the act of publicly declaring his gay sexual orientation, which would then eventually lead to his expulsion. In order to break up this double-bind deadlock, he resorted to a physical attack on his most persistent harasser, killing him with a baseball bat. So what should Winchell have done? In abstract terms, instead of acting out and beating the tormenting other to death, he should first have *beaten himself up*, that is, got rid of *his own* libidinal investment in the rituals of his humiliation, *his own* secret participation in them. More concretely, he should have devised a strategy for turning the system against itself by manipulating the split between its explicit rules and their obscene supplement – perhaps, say, he should have summoned up the courage to break the false spirit of group solidarity ("Whatever problems we have, we deal with them

among ourselves – a real man doesn't go outside and complain to others")
and simply *denounced his tormentors to the higher authorities for sexually
harassing him*; if his superiors had asked: "But *are* you gay?", he should
have accused *them* of breaking the "Don't ask, don't tell" rule.

A couple of years ago, a lesbian feminist claimed that today gays are the
privileged victims, so that the analysis of how gays are underprivileged
provides the key to understanding all other exclusions, repressions, violence,
and so on (religious, ethnic, class . . .). The problem with this theory is
precisely its implicit (or, in this case, even explicit) universal claim: it is
making exemplary victims of those who are *not* – of those who, much more
easily than religious or ethnic Others (not to mention the socially – "class"
– excluded), can be fully integrated into the public space, enjoying full
rights. Here, we should explore the ambiguity of the connection between
gay and class struggle. There is a long tradition of Leftist gay-bashing,
whose traces are discernible up to Adorno – I will mention only Maxim
Gorky's infamous remark from his essay "Proletarian Humanism" (*sic!* –
1934): "Exterminate [*sic!*] homosexuals, and Fascism will disappear."[95]

All this cannot be reduced to opportunistically flirting with the traditional
patriarchal sexual morality of the working classes, or with the Stalinist
reaction against the liberating aspects of the first years after the October
Revolution; we should remember that Gorky's provocative statement, as
well as Adorno's reservations about homosexuality ("Totality and homosexuality belong together" is one of the aphorisms in *Minima Moralia*[96]),
are all based on the same historical experience: that of the SA, the "revolutionary" paramilitary Nazi organization of street-fighting thugs, in which
homosexuality abounded right up to the top (Röhm). The first thing to note
here is that it was Hitler himself who purged the SA in order to make the
Nazi regime publicly acceptable by cleansing it of its obscene-violent excess,
and that he justified the slaughter of the SA leadership precisely by citing
their "sexual depravity".

In order to function as the support of a "totalitarian" community, homosexuality has to remain a publicly disavowed "dirty secret", shared by those
who are "in". Does this mean that when gays are persecuted, they deserve
only qualified support, a kind of "Yes, we know we should support you,
but none the less . . . (you are partly responsible for Nazi violence)"? All we
should insist on is that the political overdetermination of homosexuality is
by no means simple, that the homosexual libidinal economy can be co-opted
by different political orientations, and that it is *here* that we should avoid
the "essentialist" mistake of dismissing Rightist "militaristic" homosexuality
as a secondary distortion of "authentic" subversive homosexuality.[97]

The greatness of Pasolini's *Salò or The 120 Days of Sodom* (1975) is that it does not shirk this thoroughly ambivalent status of homosexuality. The only heroic anti-Fascist act of resistance in the film is committed by Ezio, one of the victims, who is denounced by his peers for breaking the prohibition imposed on them by their masters–libertines: every night, he makes love to the black maid at the villa. When the libertines and their guards burst into the room where the two are making love, pointing their guns, the naked Ezio springs to his feet and raises his fist in the Communist salute; this unexpected heroic act has a paralysing effect on the libertines – stunned, they take some time to shoot him down. Should we not read this pathetic scene against the background of the strange absence of actual sexual penetration in the film – a feature which indicates "a prohibition, or the libertines' exacting distaste for, sexual intercourse of any kind"?[98] This only apparently surprising fact is intrinsic to the very fundamental structure of perversion: in the perverse universe, in which "everything is permitted", this very universal permissiveness is based on the underlying fundamental prohibition of what is already in itself impossible – in short, the plethora of perversions supplants the impossibility of the sexual relationship.[99]

So when – in the long tradition which runs from medieval courtly love to the latest Hollywood film – love is elevated into an "impossibility", celebrated as something which cannot be fully actualized in real social life, we are dealing with a "decoy impossibility"[100] which masks the true impossibility, that of the *sexual relationship*: while, for Lacan, love as such emerges in order to supplement this second impossibility, it is as if today, in our sexually permissive society, the relation is turned around, with the impossibility displaced on to love – it is the proliferation of sexual relationships which covers up the impossibility of authentic love. Of course, against the spiritual temptation of taking this reversal at face value, we should insist that "love" here still refers to the impossibility of sexual relationship masked by the proliferating diversity of sexual relations.[101]

Do not these two features, read together, deliver the standard sexually conservative Leftist rejection of perversions – in short, a kind of elaborate illustration of Gorky's outrageous statement? Furthermore, what are the consequences of this implicit conclusion which seems to impose itself on Pasolini himself, who provocatively displayed his homosexuality in public? Is *Salò* to be read as a kind of masochistic self-indictment, a statement of disgust at oneself? The answer to this reading – according to which *Salò* makes public the obscene, sexually perverse underground of Fascism – is to cite the film's thorough ambiguity, which emerges the moment we include its position of enunciation: in order to formulate such a disgust – that is, to make a film like *Salò* – *you have to be gay*. In other words, it is only from a gay position that one can reveal the thorough ambiguity of the possible political connotations of homosexuality.

Welcome to the Desert of the Real!

The ultimate American paranoiac fantasy is that of an individual living in a small idyllic Californian city, a consumerist paradise, who suddenly starts to suspect that the world he lives in is a fake, a spectacle staged to convince him that he lives in a real world, while all the people around him are in fact actors and extras in a gigantic show. The most recent example of this is Peter Weir's *The Truman Show* (1998), with Jim Carrey playing a small-town clerk who gradually discovers that he is the hero of a permanent twenty-four-hour TV show: his home town is constructed on a gigantic studio set, with cameras following him everywhere. Among its predecessors, it is worth mentioning Phillip K. Dick's *Time out of Joint* (1959), in which the hero, leading a modest daily life in a small idyllic Californian city in the late 1950s, gradually discovers that the whole town is a fake staged to keep him satisfied. . . . The underlying experience of *Time out of Joint* and *The Truman Show* is that the late capitalist consumerist Californian paradise is, in its very hyperreality, in a way *unreal*, without substance, deprived of material *gravitas*.

The same "de-realization" of the horror went on after the World Trade Centre attack: while the number of victims, 6,000, is repeated all the time, it is surprising how little of the actual carnage we see – no dismembered bodies, no blood, no desperate faces of dying people . . . in clear contrast to the reporting of Third World catastrophes, where the whole point was to produce a scoop of some gruesome detail: Somalis dying of hunger, raped Bosnian women, men with their throats cut. These shots were always accompanied by the advance warning that "some of the images you will see are extremely graphic, and may hurt children" – a warning which we *never* heard in the reports on the WTC collapse. Is this not yet another proof of how, even in this tragic moment, the distance which separates Us from Them, from their reality, is maintained: the real horror happens *there*, not *here*?[102]

So it is not only that Hollywood stages a semblance of real life deprived of the weight and substance of materiality – in late capitalist consumerist society, *"real social life" itself somehow acquires the features of a staged fake*, with our neighbours behaving in "real" life like stage actors and extras. . . . The ultimate truth of the capitalist utilitarian de-spiritualized universe is the de-materialization of "real life" itself, its reversal into a spectral show. Christopher Isherwood, among others, gave expression to this unreal quality of American daily life, exemplified in the motel room: "American motels are unreal! . . . they are deliberately designed to be unreal. . . . The Europeans hate us because we've retired to live inside our advertisements, like hermits going into caves to contemplate." Peter Sloterdijk's notion of the "sphere" is literally realized here, as the gigantic metal sphere that envelopes and isolates the entire city.

Years ago, a series of science-fiction films like *Zardoz* or *Logan's Run* forecast today's postmodern predicament by extending this fantasy to the community itself: the isolated group living an aseptic life in a secluded area longs for the experience of the real world of material decay. Is not the endlessly repeated shot of the plane approaching and hitting the second WTC tower the real-life version of the famous scene from Hitchcock's *The Birds*, superbly analysed by Raymond Bellour, in which Melanie approaches the Bodega Bay pier after crossing the bay in a small boat? When, as she approaches the wharf, she waves to her (future) lover, a single bird (first perceived as a barely distinguishable dark blot) unexpectedly enters the frame from above right, and hits her on the head.[103] Was not the plane which hit the WTC tower literally the ultimate Hitchcockian blot, the anamorphic stain which de-naturalized the famous idyllic New York skyline?

The Wachowski brothers' hit *Matrix* (1999) brought this logic to its climax: the material reality we all experience and see around us is a virtual one, generated and co-ordinated by a gigantic mega-computer to which we are all connected; when the hero (played by Keanu Reeves) awakens into "real reality", he sees a desolate landscape littered with burnt ruins – what remains of Chicago after a global war. The resistance leader Morpheus utters the ironic greeting: "Welcome to the desert of the real." Did not something of a similar order take place in New York on 11 September? Its citizens were introduced to the "desert of the real" – to us, corrupted by Hollywood, the skyline and the shots we saw of the collapsing towers could not fail to remind us of the most breathtaking scenes in the big catastrophe productions. For the great majority of the public, the WTC explosions were events on the TV screen, and when we watched the oft-repeated shot of frightened people running towards the camera ahead of the giant cloud of dust from the collapsing tower, was not the framing of the shot itself reminiscent of the spectacular shots in the catastrophe movies, a special effect which outdid all others, since, as Jeremy Bentham knew, reality is the best appearance of itself?

When we hear how the attacks were a totally unexpected shock, how the unimaginable Impossible happened, we should remember the other defining catastrophe from the beginning of the twentieth century, that of the *Titanic*: this, also, was a shock, but the space for it had already been prepared in ideological fantasizing, since the *Titanic* was the symbol of the might of nineteenth-century industrial civilization. Does not the same hold for these attacks? Not only were the media bombarding us all the time with talk about the terrorist threat; this threat was also obviously libidinally invested – just recall the series of movies from *Escape from New York* to *Independence Day*. That is the rationale behind the often-mentioned association of the attacks with Hollywood disaster movies: the unthinkable which happened was the object of fantasy, so that, in a way, *America got what it had fantasized about* – and that was the greatest surprise. The ultimate twist in this link between Hollywood and the "war against terror" occurred when the Pentagon decided to solicit help from Hollywood: at the beginning of October, the press reported that a group of Hollywood scenarists and directors, specialists in catastrophe movies, was established at the instigation of the Pentagon, with the aim of imagining possible scenarios of terrorist attacks and how to fight them.

We should therefore invert the standard reading according to which the WTC explosions were the intrusion of the Real which shattered our illusory Sphere: quite to the contrary, it was prior to the WTC collapse that we lived in our own world, perceiving Third World horrors as something which were not actually part of our social reality, as things which existed (for us) as spectral apparitions on the (TV) screen – and what happened on 11 September was that *this fantasmatic screen apparition entered our reality*. It is not that reality entered our image: the image entered and shattered our reality (that is, the symbolic co-ordinates which determine what we experience as reality). The fact that, after 11 September, the opening of many "blockbuster" movies with scenes which bear a resemblance to the WTC collapse (high buildings on fire or under attack, terrorist action . . .) was postponed (or the films were even shelved), should therefore be read as *the "repression" of the fantasmatic background* responsible for the impact of the WTC collapse. Of course, the point is not to play a pseudo-postmodern game of reducing the WTC collapse to just another media spectacle, reading it as a catastrophe version of snuff porno movies; the question we should have asked ourselves when we stared at our TV screens on 11 September is simply: *Where have we already seen the same thing over and over again?*

This means that the dialectic of semblance and Real cannot be reduced to the rather elementary fact that the virtualization of our daily lives, the experience that we are living more and more in an artificially constructed universe, gives rise to the irresistible urge to return to the Real, to regain firm ground in some kind of real reality. *The real which returns has the status of a(nother) semblance*: precisely because it is real – that is, because of its traumatic/excessive nature – we are unable to integrate it into (what we experience as) our reality, and are therefore compelled to experience it as a nightmarish apparition. This is what the compelling image of the collapse of the WTC was: an image, a semblance, an effect, which, at the same time, delivered the thing itself. This effect of the Real is not the same as what, way back in the 1960s, Roland Barthes called *l'effet du réel*; it is, rather, its exact opposite, *l'effet de l'irréel*. That is to say: in contrast to the Barthesian *effet du réel*, in which the text makes us accept its fictional product as real, here, the Real itself, in order to be sustained, has to be perceived as a nightmarish unreal spectre. Usually we say that we should not mistake fiction for reality – consider the postmodern doxa according to which reality is a discursive product, a symbolic fiction which we misperceive as a substantial autonomous entity. The lesson of psychoanalysis here is the opposite one: we should not mistake reality for fiction; we should be able to discern, in what we experience as fiction, the hard kernel of the Real which we are able to sustain only if we fictionalize it. In short, we should discern which part of reality is "transfunctionalized" through fantasy, so that although it is part of reality, it is perceived in a fictional mode. Much more difficult than denouncing-unmasking (what looks like) reality as fiction is recognizing the part of fiction in "real" reality.

It is precisely now, when we are dealing with the raw Real of a catastrophe, that we should bear in mind the ideological and fantasmatic co-ordinates which determine its perception. If there is any symbolism in the collapse of the WTC towers, it is not so much the old-fashioned notion of the "centre of financial capitalism" but, rather, the notion that the two WTC towers stood for the centre of *virtual* capitalism, of financial speculation disconnected from the sphere of material production. The shattering impact of the attacks can be accounted for only against the background of the borderline which, today, separates the digitalized First World from the Third World "desert of the Real". It is the awareness that we live in an insulated artificial universe which generates the notion that some ominous agent is threatening us all the time with total destruction. In this paranoiac perspective, the terrorists are turned into an irrational abstract agency – abstract in the Hegelian sense of subtracted from the concrete socio-ideological network which gave birth to it. Every explanation which evokes social circumstances is dismissed as a covert justification of terror, and every particular entity is evoked only in a negative way: the terrorists are betraying the true spirit of Islam; they do not express the interests and hopes of the poor Arab masses.

Whenever we encounter such a purely evil Outside, we should summon up the courage to endorse the Hegelian lesson: in this pure Outside, we should recognize the distilled version of our own essence. For the last five centuries, the (relative) prosperity and peace of the "civilized" West has been bought at the price of ruthless violence and destruction of the "barbarian" Outside: a long story, from the conquest of America to the slaughter in the Congo. Cruel and indifferent as it may sound, we should also, now more than ever, bear in mind that the actual effect of these attacks is much more symbolic than real: in Africa, more people die of AIDS *every single day* than all the victims of the WTC collapse, and their deaths could easily have been avoided at relatively small financial cost. The USA simply got a taste of what goes on around the world on a daily basis – from Sarajevo to Grozny, from Rwanda and the Congo to Sierra Leone. If we add to the situation in New York rapist gangs and a dozen or so snipers blindly targeting people as they walk along the streets, we get an idea of what Sarajevo was like a decade ago.

When, in the days after 11 September 2001, our gaze was transfixed by the images of the plane hitting one of the WTC towers, we were all forced to experience the "compulsion to repeat" and *jouissance* beyond the pleasure principle: we wanted to see it again and again; the same shots were repeated *ad nauseam*; and the uncanny satisfaction we got from it was *jouissance* at its purest. It was when we watched the two WTC towers collapsing on the TV screen that it became possible for us to experience the falsity of "reality TV shows": even if these shows are "for real", people still *act* in them – they simply *play themselves*. The standard disclaimer in a novel ("Characters in this text are a fiction; any resemblance to real characters is purely accidental") holds also for the participants in reality soaps: what we see there are fictional characters, even if they play themselves for real.

Of course, the "return to the Real" in the WTC attacks can be given different twists: we have already heard some conservatives claiming that what made us so vulnerable was our very openness – with the inevitable conclusion lurking in the background that if we are to protect our "way of life", we will have to sacrifice some of our freedoms which were "misused" by the enemies of freedom. This logic should be rejected out of hand: is it not a fact that our "open" First World countries are the most controlled countries in the entire history of humanity? In the United Kingdom, all public spaces, from buses to shopping malls, are constantly videotaped, not to mention the almost total control of all forms of digital communication.

Along the same lines, Rightist commentators like George Will also immediately proclaimed the end of the American "holiday from history" – the impact of reality shattering the isolated tower of the liberal tolerant attitude and the Cultural Studies focus on textuality. Now, we are forced to strike back, to deal with real enemies in the real world. . . . Whom, however, do we strike at? Whatever the response, it will never hit the *right* target, bringing us full satisfaction. The ridicule of America attacking Afghanistan cannot fail to strike us: if the greatest power in the world destroys one of the world's poorest countries, in which peasants barely survive on barren hills, will this not be the ultimate case of impotent acting out? In many ways Afghanistan is an ideal target: a country that is already reduced to rubble, with no infrastructure, repeatedly destroyed by war for the last two decades . . . we cannot avoid the surmise that the choice of Afghanistan will also be determined by economic considerations: is it not best procedure to act out one's anger at a country for which no one cares, and where there is nothing to destroy? Unfortunately, the choice of Afghanistan recalls the anecdote about the madman who searches for a lost key beneath a streetlamp; asked why there, when he lost the key in a dark corner somewhere, he answers: "But it's easier to search under strong light!" Is it not the ultimate irony that the whole of Kabul already looks like downtown Manhattan?

To succumb to the urge to act and retaliate means precisely to *avoid* confronting the true dimensions of what occurred on 11 September – it means an act whose true aim is to lull us into the secure conviction that nothing has really changed. The true long-term threats are further acts of mass terror in comparison with which the memory of the WTC collapse will pale – acts that are less spectacular, but much more horrifying. What about bacteriological warfare, what about the use of lethal gas, what about the prospect of DNA terrorism (developing poisons which will affect only people who share a determinate genome)? In this new warfare, the agents claim their acts less and less publicly: not only are "terrorists" themselves no longer eager to claim responsibility for their acts (even the notorious Al Qaida did not explicitly appropriate the 11 September attacks, not to mention the mystery about the origins of the anthrax letters); "anti-terrorist" state measures themselves are draped in a shroud of secrecy; all this constitutes an ideal breeding ground for conspiracy theories and generalized social paranoia. And is not the obverse of this paranoiac omnipresence of the invisible war its desubstantialization? So, again, just as we drink beer without alcohol or coffee without caffeine, we are now getting war deprived of its substance – a virtual war fought behind computer screens, a war experienced by its participants as a video game, a war with no casualties (on our side, at least).

With the spread of the anthrax panic in October 2001, the West got the first taste of this new "invisible" warfare in which – an aspect we should always bear in mind – we, ordinary citizens, are, with regard to information about what is going on, totally at the mercy of the authorities: we see and hear nothing; all we know comes from the official media. A superpower bombing a desolate desert country and, at the same time, hostage to invisible bacteria – *this*, not the WTC explosions, is the first image of twenty-first-century warfare. Instead of a quick acting-out, we should confront these difficult questions: what will "war" mean in the twenty-first century? Who will "they" be, if they are, clearly, neither states nor criminal gangs? Here I cannot resist the temptation to recall the Freudian opposition of the public Law and its obscene superego double: along the same lines, are not "international terrorist organizations" the obscene double of the big multi-national corporations – the ultimate rhizomatic machine, omnipresent, yet with no clear territorial base? Are they not the form in which nationalist and/or religious "fundamentalism" accommodated itself to global capitalism? Do they not embody the ultimate contradiction, with their particular/exclusive content and their global dynamic functioning?

For this reason, the fashionable notion of the "clash of civilizations" must be thoroughly rejected: what we are witnessing today, rather, are clashes *within* each civilization. A brief look at the comparative history of Islam and Christianity tells us that the "human rights record" of Islam (to use an anachronistic term) is much better than that of Christianity: in past centuries, Islam was significantly more tolerant towards other religions than Christianity. It is also time to remember that it was through the Arabs that, in the Middle Ages, we in Western Europe regained access to our Ancient Greek legacy. While I do not in any way excuse today's horrific acts, these facts none the less clearly demonstrate that we are dealing not with a feature inscribed into Islam "as such", but with the outcome of modern sociopolitical conditions.

If we look more closely, what is this "clash of civilizations" really about? Are not all real-life "clashes" clearly related to global capitalism? The Muslim "fundamentalist" target is not only global capitalism's corrosive impact on social life, but *also* the corrupt "traditionalist" regimes in Saudi Arabia, Kuwait, and so on. The most horrifying slaughters (those in Rwanda, Congo, and Sierra Leone) not only took place – and are taking place – within the same "civilization", but are also clearly related to the interplay of global economic interests. Even in the few cases which would vaguely fit the definition of the "clash of civilisations" (Bosnia and Kosovo, southern Sudan, etc.), the shadow of other interests is easily discernible. A suitable dose of "economic reductionism" would therefore be appropriate here: instead of the endless analyses of how Islamic "fundamentalism" is intolerant towards our liberal societies, and other "clash-of-civilization" topics, we should refocus our attention on the economic background of the conflict – the clash of economic interests, and of the geopolitical interests of the United States itself (how to retain privileged links both with Israel and with conservative Arab regimes like those of Saudi Arabia and Kuwait).

Beneath the opposition of "liberal" and "fundamentalist" societies, "McWorld versus jihad", there is the embarrassing third term: countries like Saudi Arabia and Kuwait, deeply conservative monarchies but economically American allies, fully integrated into Western capitalism. Here, the USA has a very precise and simple interest: in order for it to be able to count on these countries for their oil reserves, *they have to remain non-democratic* (the underlying notion is, of course, that a democratic awakening could give expression to anti-American attitudes). This is an old story whose infamous first chapter after World War II was the CIA-orchestrated *coup d'état* against the democratically elected Prime Minister, Mossadeq, in Iran in 1953 – there was no "fundamentalism" there, not even a "Soviet threat", just a plain democratic awakening, with the idea that the country should take control of its oil resources and break up the monopoly of the Western oil companies.

The lengths to which the USA is ready to go in order to maintain this pact were made clear in the Gulf War in 1991, when the Jewish American soldiers stationed in Saudi Arabia had to be transported by helicopter to the aircraft carriers in the Gulf so that they could pray, since non-Muslim rituals are prohibited on Saudi soil – a fact which should undoubtedly be taken together with another fact, very rarely mentioned in the Western press: Tariq Aziz, the Iraqi Foreign Minister and one of the key figures of the Saddam regime, is not a Muslim but a Christian. This "perverted" position of truly "fundamentalist" conservative Arab regimes is the key to the (often comical) conundrums of American politics in the Middle East: they stand for the point at which the USA is forced explicitly to acknowledge the primacy of economy over democracy – that is, the secondary and manipulative character of legitimizing international interventions by talking about the protection of democracy and human rights.

On the subject of this "clash of civilizations", let us recall the letter from a seven-year-old American girl whose father is a pilot fighting over Afghanistan: she wrote that although she loves her father deeply, she is ready to let him die, to sacrifice him for her country. When President Bush quoted these lines, they were perceived as a "normal" outburst of American patriotism; let us conduct a simple mental experiment, and imagine an Arab Muslim girl pathetically reciting into the camera the same words about her father fighting for the Taleban – we do not have to give much thought to what our reaction would have been: morbid Muslim fundamentalism which does not stop even at cruel manipulation and exploitation of children.

Every feature attributed to the Other is already present in the very heart of the USA. Murderous fanaticism? Today in the USA there are more than two million populist Rightist "fundamentalists" who also practise a terror of their own, legitimized by (their understanding of) Christianity. Since America is, in a way, "harbouring" them, should the US Army have punished the USA itself after the Oklahoma bombing? And what about the way Jerry Falwell and Pat Robertson reacted to the events of 11 September, perceiving them as a sign that God removed His protection from the USA because of the sinful lives of the Americans, putting the blame on hedonist materialism, liberalism and rampant sexuality, and claiming that America got what it deserved? The fact that this very condemnation of "liberal" America, which matched the condemnation from the Muslim Other, came from the very heart of *l'Amérique profonde* should give us food for thought. On 19 October, George W. Bush himself had to concede that the most probable perpetrators of the anthrax attacks are not Muslim terrorists but America's own extreme Right Christian fundamentalists – again, does not the fact that the acts first attributed to an external enemy may turn out to be acts begotten in the very heart of *l'Amérique profonde* provide an unexpected confirmation of the thesis that this clash is a clash within each civilization?

In the aftermath of 11 September, Americans *en masse*, including liberals, rediscovered the innocence of their American pride, displaying flags and singing together in public – as if, after decades of ethico-political doubts about the American role in the world, the vicious destruction of the WTC towers de-culpabilized them, giving them the right to assert their identity in all its innocence. . . . Against this reclaimed innocence, we should emphasize more than ever that there is nothing "innocent" in this rediscovery of American innocence, in getting rid of the sense of historical guilt or irony which prevented many Americans from fully claiming their nationality. What this gesture amounted to was "objectively" assuming the burden of all that being "American" stood for in the past – an exemplary case of ideological interpellation, of fully assuming one's symbolic mandate, which enters the stage after the perplexity caused by some historical trauma.

In the traumatic aftermath of 11 September, when the old security seemed momentarily to be shattered, what could be more "natural" than to take refuge in the innocence of a firm ideological identification?[104] However, it is precisely such moments of transparent innocence, of "back to basics", when the gesture of identification seems "natural", that are, from the standpoint of the critique of ideology, the most obscure – even, in a certain way, *obscurity itself*; to quote Fernando Pessoa's superb formulation: "When I speak frankly, I don't know with what frankness I speak." Let us recall another such innocently transparent moment, the endlessly reproduced video-shot, from Beijing's Avenue of Eternal Peace at the height of the "troubles" in 1989, of a tiny young man with a can who stands alone in front of an approaching gigantic tank, and courageously tries to prevent its advance, so that when the tank tries to circumvent him by turning right or left, the man also moves aside, again standing in its path:

> The representation is so powerful that it demolishes all other understandings. This streetscene, this time and this event, have come to constitute the compass point for virtually all Western journeys into the interior of the contemporary political and cultural life of China.[105]

And, again, this very moment of transparent clarity (things are presented in their starkest form: a single man against the brute force of the State) is, to our Western gaze, sustained by a cobweb of ideological implications, embodying a series of oppositions: individual versus state, peaceful resistance versus state violence, man versus machine, the inner force of a tiny individual versus the impotence of the powerful machine. . . . These implications, against the background of which the shot exerts its full direct impact, these "mediations" which sustain that impact, are not present for a Chinese observer, since the above-mentioned series of oppositions is part of the European ideological legacy. The same ideological background also overdetermines, say, our perception of the horrifying images of tiny individuals jumping from the burning WTC towers to certain death.

Among the ideological reappropriations of 11 September, there are already calls for rethinking some of the basic ingredients of the modern notion of human dignity and freedom. Take Jonathan Alter's article in *Newsweek* of 5 November 2001, "Time to Think about Torture", with the ominous subtitle "It's a new world, and survival may well require old techniques that seemed out of the question". After flirting with the Israeli idea of legitimizing physical and psychological torture in cases of extreme urgency (so-called ticking-clock cases, when we know that a terrorist prisoner possesses information which may save hundreds of lives), and neutral statements like "Some torture clearly works", Alter concludes:

We can't legalize torture; it's contrary to American values. But even as we continue to speak out against human-rights abuses around the world, we need to keep an open mind about certain measures to fight terrorism, like court-sanctioned psychological interrogation. And we'll have to think about transferring some suspects to our less squeamish allies, even if that's hypocritical. Nobody said this was going to be pretty.

The obscenity of such statements is blatant. First, why use the WTC attack as justification? Are there not much more terrible atrocities going on all the time around the world? Second, what is *new* about this idea? Has not the CIA been teaching Latin American and Third World American military allies the practice of torture for decades? Hypocrisy has prevailed for years. Even Alan Dershowitz's liberal argument, cited by Alter, is suspicious: "I'm not in favour of torture, but if you're going to have it, it should damn well have court approval." The underlying logic – since we are doing it in any case, better legalize it, and thus present excesses! – is extremely dangerous: it gives legitimacy to torture, and thus opens up the space for *more* illicit torture. When, along the same lines, Dershowitz argues that torturing in the ticking-clock situation is not against the prisoner's rights as an accused person (the information obtained will not be used in trial against him, and the torture is done not as punishment, but only to prevent the mass killing to come), the underlying premiss is even more disturbing: so one should be allowed to torture people not as part of a deserved punishment, but simply because they know something? Why, then, not also legalize the torture of prisoners of war who may possess information which may save hundreds of our soldiers' lives?

In short, such debates, such calls to keep an open mind, are nothing less than the ultimate sign that the terrorists are winning the ideological war. Essays like Alter's, which do not advocate torture outright, but just introduce it as a legitimate topic of debate, are even more dangerous than an explicit endorsement of torture: while – at this moment, at least – an explicit endorsement would be too shocking, and therefore rejected, the mere introduction of torture as a legitimate topic allows us to entertain the idea while retaining a pure conscience (of course I'm against torture, but whom does it hurt if we merely discuss it?). Such legitimization of torture as a topic of debate changes the background of ideological presuppositions and options much more radically than its outright advocacy: it changes the entire field, while, without this change, outright advocacy remains an idiosyncratic view. The problem here is that of the fundamental ethical presuppositions: of course we can legitimize torture for the sake of short-term profit (saving hundreds of lives), but what about the long-term consequences for our symbolic universe? Where do we stop? Why not torture persistent criminals, a parent who has kidnapped his child from a divorced spouse? The idea that once we let the genie out of the bottle, torture can be kept at a reasonable level, is the worst legalistic illusion. Any consistent ethical stance *must* completely reject such pragmatic-utilitarian reasoning. Moreover, I am again tempted to conduct a simple mental experiment: let us imagine an *Arab* newspaper making a case for the torture of American prisoners, and the explosion of comments about fundamentalist barbarism and disrespect for human rights that would provoke.

So what about the phrase which reverberates everywhere: "Nothing will be the same after 11 September"? Significantly, this phrase is never further elaborated – it is just an empty gesture of saying something "deep" without really knowing what we want to say. So our first reaction to it should be: Really? Is it not, rather, that the only thing that actually changed was that America was forced to realize the kind of world it was part of? On the other hand, such changes in perception are never without consequences, since the way we perceive our situation determines the way we act in it. Remember the collapse of a political regime – for example, the collapse of the Communist regimes in Eastern Europe in 1990: at a certain moment, people became aware all of a sudden that the game was over, that the Communists had lost. The break was purely symbolic, nothing changed "in reality" – none the less, from this moment on, the final collapse of the regime was simply a matter of time.

What if something of the same order *did* occur on 11 September? We should bear in mind that Hollywood is the nerve centre of the American ideology which exerts a worldwide hegemonic role: what draws millions of Third World people to the USA – even those whose "official" ideology is opposed to everything America stands for – is not merely the prospect of material wealth, but also the "American Dream", the chance to participate in it. Hollywood is literally a "dream factory": its main function is to fabricate hegemonic ideological dreams, to provide individuals with co-ordinates for their private fantasies. So when the Hollywood machinery is perturbed, as in the post-11 September era, when the executives are desperately trying to guess and/or establish the new rules (no catastrophe movies; will single-hero movies like the James Bond series survive? Will there be a turn towards family melodramas or a turn towards direct patriotism?), this fact does bear witness to the deep ideological impact of the events of 11 September.

Perhaps the ultimate victim of the WTC attacks will be a certain figure of the big Other, the American Sphere. During Nikita Khrushchev's secret speech to the Twentieth Congress of the Soviet Party, denouncing Stalin's crimes, a dozen or so delegates had a nervous breakdown, and had to be carried out and given medical treatment; one of them, Boleslaw Bierut, the hardline General Secretary of the Polish Communist Party, even died of a heart attack some days later. (The model Stalinist writer Alexander Fadeyev shot himself a few days later.) The point is not that they were "honest Communists" – most of them were brutal manipulators without any subjective illusions about the nature of the Soviet regime. What broke down was their "objective" illusion, the figure of the "big Other" against the background of which they could exert their ruthless drive for power: the Other on to which they transposed their belief, the Other which, as it were, believed on their behalf, their subject-supposed-to-believe, disintegrated. And did not something homologous happen in the aftermath of 11 September? Was not 11 September 2001 the "Twentieth Congress" of the American Dream?

That day is already being appropriated for ideological causes: from the claims in all the main media that anti-globalization is now finished, to the notion that the shock of the WTC attacks revealed the substanceless character of postmodern Cultural Studies, their lack of contact with "real life". While the second notion is (partially) right for the wrong reasons, the first one is downright wrong. What is true is that the relatively trifling character of standard Cultural Studies critical topics was thereby revealed: what is the use of a Politically Incorrect expression with possible racist undertones, compared with the tortured death of thousands? The dilemma of Cultural Studies is this: will they stick to the same topics, directly admitting that their fight against oppression is a fight *within* First World capitalism's universe – which means that, in the Western First World's wider conflict with the external threat to it, one should reassert one's fidelity to the basic American liberal-democratic framework; or will they risk a step towards radicalizing their critical stance: will they problematize this framework itself? As for the end of anti-globalization, the dark hints from the first days after 11 September that the attacks could also have been the work of anti-globalization terrorists is, of course, nothing but a crude manipulation: the only way to conceive of what happened on 11 September is to locate it in the context of the antagonisms of global capitalism. We should always bear in mind apropos of Afghanistan that until the 1970s – that is, until the country became directly involved in the superpower struggle – it was one of the most tolerant Muslim societies, with a long secular tradition: Kabul was known as a city with a vibrant cultural and political life. The paradox, therefore, is that far from expressing some deep traditionalist tendency, the rise of the Taleban, an apparent regression into ultra-fundamentalism, was the result of the country being caught up in the whirlpool of international politics – it was not only a defensive reaction to this, it emerged directly through the support of foreign powers (Pakistan, Saudi Arabia, the USA itself).

Another victim of 11 September among some liberals seems to be the notion of the purity of moral intention: it is as if any claim to purity is suspected of breeding some kind of terrorism. We should remember Hegel's thesis on how the actual outcome of our act discloses our true intention: I am not allowed to defend myself by claiming: "But that wasn't what I wanted!", because I do not really know what I wanted. It is in the actual consequences of my act that the truth of my intention becomes visible: however unpleasant the outcome of my act, this is what I really wanted. . . . Attractive as this combination of Hegel and psychoanalysis may sound, we should bear in mind when confronted with it that Hegel's thesis is meaningful only within the idealist identity of the Actual and the Rational, of the Subject and Substance: we can trust that reality will reveal to us the true meaning of our acts only if we presuppose the pre-established harmony between our psychic structure and that of objective social reality – there is "Reason in History", as Hegel put it. And is not Freud's fundamental insight, repeatedly reasserted by Lacan, that we, human subjects, are not "at home in this world", that the reality in which we live is fundamentally foreign, hostile to our innermost intentions and drives?

This Hegelian position goes hand in hand with the mistrust of any form of moral purity, with its dismissal as the false position of the "Beautiful Soul" – and, in fact, it seems that today's ethico-religious "fundamentalisms" provide the most forceful argument against moral fanaticism. The worst thing to do when we are confronted with the onslaught of dedicated "fundamentalists", however, is to suspect ethical purity as such – to reactivate the old conservative wisdom according to which we should mistrust *les purs et les durs*: low-level minor corruption; a tolerance for human weaknesses enables the smooth functioning of the social machine, while rigid moral fanaticism necessarily reverts to utter corruption in which everything, every human consideration, is sacrificed for the Cause.

What is wrong with this suspicion is that it conflates two different forms of purity: "authentic" ethical purity and the false superego purity of turning oneself into the instrument of the Other's enjoyment. "Wise" tolerance for minor everyday corruption and fanaticist superego rigour are opposites within the same horizon, they are two sides of the same coin – or, to put it in Hegelese, there is an underlying identity of these opposites. That is to say, within this domain, corruption is the ultimate horizon, and the only choice is the one between tolerance of minor corruption and a direct intolerant onslaught against corruption, which coincides with the highest corruption. What Lacan, on the contrary, called the "act" is precisely an intervention which breaks out of this vicious cycle of minor corruption and rigour as the supreme corruption. So there is an infinite gap between religious fanaticist "fundamentalism" and authentic revolutionary intervention, although they both seem to share an "uncompromising" radical character; this gap does not concern only the sociopolitical dimension, but also the immanent structure of the act: the "fundamentalist" act is done for the big Other; in it, the subject instrumentalizes himself for the Other; while an authentic act authorizes itself only in itself – that is to say, it is not "covered" by the big Other; on the contrary, it intervenes at the very point of inconsistency of the big Other. This difference is the difference between Kant and Sade: Sade is not simply the truth of Kant; the Sadeian perverse position emerges, rather, when the radical Kantian ethical stance is compromised.

The supreme example here is, yet again, that of Antigone. From the standpoint of the Hegelian position mentioned above, Antigone is to be unambiguously condemned: the actual consequences of her act were catastrophic; she was an ethical rigourist if ever there was one, in contrast to her sister Ismene's tolerance and compromising attitude – is this what we want? The opposite of the rationality of the Real, or its closed circuit of Fate which gives us back our true message, is the act itself which intervenes in the very rational order of the Real, changing-restructuring its co-ordinates – an act is not irrational; rather, it creates its own (new) rationality. This is what Antigone accomplishes; this is the true consequence of her act. And this cannot be planned in advance – we have to take a risk, a step into the open, with no big Other to return our true message to us.

We do not yet know all the consequences this event will have for the economy, ideology, politics, warfare, but one thing is certain: the USA – which, hitherto, perceived itself as an island exempt from this kind of violence, witnessing this kind of thing only from the safe distance of the TV screen – is now directly involved. So the alternative is: will the Americans decide to fortify their "sphere" further, or will they risk stepping out of it? Either America will persist in – even strengthen – the deeply *immoral* attitude of "Why should this happen to us? Things like this just don't happen *here*!", leading to more aggressivity towards the threatening Outside – in short: to a paranoid acting-out. Or America will finally risk stepping through the fantasmatic screen separating it from the Outside World, accepting its arrival in the Real world, making the long-overdue move from "A thing like this shouldn't happen *here*!" to "A thing like this shouldn't happen *anywhere*!". That is the true lesson of the attacks: the only way to ensure that it will not happen *here* again is to prevent it happening *anywhere else*. In short, America should learn humbly to accept its own vulnerability as part of this world, enacting the punishment of those responsible as a sad duty, not as an exhilarating retaliation.

The WTC attacks again confronted us with the necessity of resisting the temptation of a double blackmail. If one simply, only and unconditionally condemns it, one cannot but appear to endorse the blatantly ideological position of American innocence under attack by Third World Evil; if one draws attention to the deeper sociopolitical causes of Arab extremism, one cannot but appear to blame the victim, which ultimately got what it deserved. . . . The only appropriate solution here is to reject this very opposition, and to adopt both positions simultaneously; this can be done only if one resorts to the dialectical category of *totality*: there is no choice between these two positions; both are biased and false. Far from offering a case apropos of which one can adopt a clear ethical stance, we encounter here *the limit of moral reasoning*: from the moral standpoint, the victims are innocent, the act was an abominable crime; however, *this very innocence is not innocent* – to adopt such an "innocent" position in today's global capitalist universe is in itself a false abstraction.

The same goes for the more ideological clash of interpretations: one could claim that the attack on the WTC was an attack on what is worth fighting for in democratic freedoms – the decadent Western way of life condemned by Muslim and other fundamentalists is the universe of women's rights and multiculturalist tolerance;[106] one could also claim, however, that it was an attack on the very centre and symbol of global financial capitalism. This, of course, in no way entails the compromise notion of shared guilt (the terrorists are to blame, but the Americans are also partly to blame . . .) – the point is, rather, that the two sides are not really opposed, that they belong to the same field. The fact that global capitalism is a totality means that it is the dialectical unity of itself and of its other – of the forces which resist it on "fundamentalist" ideological grounds.

As a result, of the two main stories which emerged after 11 September, *both were worse*, as Stalin would have put it. The American patriotic narrative – the innocence under siege, the surge of patriotic pride – is, of course, simplistic; however, is the Leftist narrative (with its *Schadenfreude*: the USA got what it deserved, what it had been doing to others for decades) really any better? The prevailing reaction of European – but also American – Leftists was nothing less than scandalous: every imaginable stupidity was said and written, up to the "feminist" point that the WTC towers were two phallic symbols waiting to be destroyed ("castrated"). Was there not something petty and miserable in the mathematics reminding us of Holocaust revisionism (what are 6,000 dead against millions in Rwanda, Congo, etc.)? And what about the fact that the CIA (co-)created the Taleban and Bin Laden, financing and helping them to fight the Soviets in Afghanistan? Why was this fact quoted as an argument *against* attacking them? Would it not be much more logical to claim that it is precisely their duty to rid us of the monster they created?

The moment we think in the terms of "Yes, the WTC collapse was a tragedy, but we should not be in full solidarity with the victims, since this would mean supporting US imperialism", the ethical catastrophe has already arrived: the only appropriate stance is an unconditional solidarity with *all* victims. The ethical stance proper is replaced here with the moralizing mathematics of guilt and horror, which misses the key point: the terrifying death of each individual is absolute and incomparable. In short, let us conduct a simple mental experiment: if you detect in yourself any reluctance to empathize fully with the victims of the WTC collapse, if you feel the urge to qualify your empathy with "Yes, but what about the millions who suffer in Africa . . .", you are not demonstrating your Third World sympathies, merely the *mauvaise foi* which bears witness to your implicit patronizing racist attitude towards Third World victims. (More precisely, the problem with such comparative statements is that they are both necessary and inadmissible: one *has* to make them, one *has* to make the point that much worse horrors take place all over the world on a daily basis – but one has to do so without getting involved in the obscene mathematics of guilt.)

No wonder this anti-Americanism was most discernible in "big" European nations, especially France and Germany: it is part of their resistance to globalization. We often hear the complaint that the recent trend towards globalization threatens the sovereignty of nation-states; here, however, we should qualify this statement: which states are most exposed to this threat? It is not the small states, but the second-rank (ex-)world powers, countries like the United Kingdom, Germany and France: what they fear is that once they are fully immersed in the newly emerging global empire, they will be reduced to the same level as, say, Austria, Belgium, or even Luxembourg. The refusal of "Americanization" in France, shared by many Leftists and Rightist nationalists, is thus ultimately the refusal to accept the fact that

France itself is losing its hegemonic role in Europe. The results of this refusal are often comical – at a recent philosophical colloquium, a French Leftist philosopher complained how, apart from him, there are now practically no French philosophers in France: Derrida is sold to American deconstructionism; academia is overwhelmed by Anglo-Saxon cognitivism.

Another simple mental experiment is called for here: let us imagine someone from Serbia claiming that he is the only remaining truly Serb philosopher – he would immediately be denounced and ridiculed as a nationalist. The levelling of weight between larger and smaller nation-states should therefore be counted among the beneficial effects of globalization: beneath the contemptuous deriding of the new Eastern European post-Communist states, it is easy to discern the contours of the wounded narcissism of the European "great nations". Here, a good dose of Lenin's sensitivity towards small nations (consider his insistence that, in the relationship between large and small nations, we should always allow for a greater degree of "small" nationalism) would be helpful.

Interestingly, the same matrix was reproduced within ex-Yugoslavia – not only by the Serbs themselves, but even by the majority of the Western powers, Serbia was self-evidently perceived as the only ethnic group with enough substance to form its own state. Throughout the 1990s, even radical democratic critics of Milošević who rejected Serb nationalism acted on the presupposition that, among the ex-Yugoslav republics, only Serbia had democratic potential: once it had overthrown Milošević, Serbia alone could turn into a thriving democratic state, while other ex-Yugoslav nations were too "provincial" to sustain their own democratic State. Is this not the echo of Friedrich Engels's famous scathing remarks about how the small Balkan nations are politically reactionary, since their very existence is a reaction, a survival of the past?

America's "holiday from history" was a fake: America's peace was bought at the price of catastrophes elsewhere. These days, the prevailing point of view is that of an innocent gaze confronting unspeakable Evil which struck from the Outside – and again, apropos of this gaze, we should summon up our strength and apply to it Hegel's well-known dictum that Evil resides (also) in the innocent gaze itself which perceives Evil all around. So there is an element of truth even in the most constricted Moral Majority vision of a depraved America dedicated to mindless pleasures, in the conservative horror at this netherworld of sexploitation and pathological violence: what they do not perceive is merely the Hegelian speculative identity between this netherworld and their own position of fake purity – the fact that so many fundamentalist preachers turn out to be sexual perverts in private is more than a contingent empirical fact. The infamous Jimmy Swaggart's claim that the fact that he visited prostitutes only gave additional strength to his preaching (he knew from intimate struggle what he was preaching against), although undoubtedly hypocritical on the immediate subjective level, is none the less *objectively true*.

And does not the same go for the statement by the Taleban leader Mullah Mohammad Omar who, on 25 September 2001, appealed to Americans to use their own judgement in responding to the devastating attacks on the World Trade Centre and the Pentagon rather than blindly following their government's policy to attack his country? "You accept everything your government says, whether it is true or false. . . . Don't you have your own thinking? . . . So it will be better for you to use your sense and understanding." Are not these statements, taken in an abstract decontextualized sense, absolutely appropriate? To this first great irony of the situation (irony in the precise Mozartian sense of the term: although you may be subjectively hypocritical, your statements are more true than you think), we should add a second: the fact that the first codename for the US operation against terrorists was "Infinite Justice" (later changed in response to a protest by Islamic clerics that only God can exercise infinite justice).

Taken seriously, this name is profoundly ambiguous: either it means that the Americans have the right ruthlessly to destroy not only all terrorists but also all those who gave them material, moral, ideological, etc., support (and this process will be, by definition, endless in the precise sense of Hegelian "bad infinity" – such work will never be really accomplished; some other terrorist threat will always be there . . .); or it means that the justice exercised must be truly infinite in the strict Hegelian sense – that, in relating to others, it has to relate to itself: in short, that it has to pose the question of how we who are exercising justice are involved in what we are fighting against. When, on 22 September 2001, Jacques Derrida received the Theodor Adorno award, he referred in his speech to the WTC attacks: "My unconditional compassion for the victims of 11 September does not prevent me from saying it aloud: with regard to this crime, I do not believe that anyone is politically guiltless." This self-relating, this inclusion of oneself in the picture, is the only true "infinite justice".

The worst thing to do apropos of the events of 11 September is to elevate them to a point of Absolute Evil, a vacuum which cannot be explained and/ or dialecticized. To posit them in a series with the Shoah is a blasphemy: the Shoah was carried out methodically by a vast network of state apparatchiks and their executors who, in contrast to the destroyers of the WTC towers, lacked the suicidal acceptance of their own death – as Hannah

Arendt has shown, they were anonymous bureaucrats doing their job, and an enormous gap separated what they did from their individual self-experience. This "banality of Evil" is missing in the case of the terrorist attacks: the terrorists fully assumed the horror of their acts; this horror was part of the fatal attraction which drew them towards committing them. Or, to put it in a slightly different way: the Nazis did their job of "solving the Jewish question" as an obscene secret hidden from the public gaze, while the terrorists blatantly displayed the spectacle of their act. The second difference is that the Shoah was a part of *European* history, it was an event which did not directly concern the relationship between Muslims and Jews: remember Sarajevo, which had by far the largest Jewish community in ex-Yugoslavia and, moreoever, was the most cosmopolitan Yugoslav city, a thriving centre of cinema and rock music – why? Precisely because it was the Muslim-dominated city, where the Jewish and Christian presence was tolerated, in contrast to the Christian-dominated large cities from which Jews and Muslims were purged long ago.

Why should the New York catastrophe be in any way privileged over, say, the mass slaughter of Hutus by Tutsis in Rwanda in 1994? Or the mass bombing and gas-poisoning of Kurds in the north of Iraq in the early 1990s? Or the Indonesian forces' mass killings in East Timor? Or . . . the list of countries where mass suffering was and is incomparably greater than the suffering in New York, but which do not have the good fortune to be in the limelight in order to be elevated by the media into the sublime victim of Absolute Evil, is long, and that is the point: if we insist on the use of this term, these are all "Absolute Evils". So should we extend the prohibition or explaining, and claim that none of these evils could and should be "dialect-icized"? And are we not obliged to go even a step further: what about "individual" horrible crimes, from those of the sadist mass murderer Jeffrey Dahmer to those of Andrea Yates, who drowned her five children in cold blood? Is there not something real/impossible/inexplicable about every one of these acts? Is it not that – as Schelling put it more than two hundred years ago – in each of them we confront the ultimate abyss of free will, the imponderable fact of "I did it because I did it!" which resists any explanation in psychological, social, ideological, etc., terms?

We should therefore reject Lacan's famous reading of the Holocaust (the Nazi extermination of the Jews) as, precisely, a holocaust in the old Jewish meaning of the term: a sacrifice to the obscure gods, intended to satisfy their terrible demand for *jouissance*; the annihilated Jews, rather, belong to the series of what the ancient Romans called *Homo sacer* – those who, although human, were excluded from the human community, which is why one could kill them with impunity; for that very reason, one could not sacrifice them (because they were not a worthy sacrificial offering). Have the events of 11 September something to do with the obscure God who demands human sacrifices? Yes, the spectacular explosion of the WTC towers was not simply a symbolic act (in the sense of an act whose aim is to "deliver a message"): it was primarily an explosion of lethal *jouissance*, a perverse act of making oneself an instrument of the big Other's *jouissance*. Yes, the culture of the attackers is a morbid culture of death, the attitude which finds the climactic fulfilment of one's own life in violent death. Yes, the ultimate aim of the attacks was not some hidden or obvious ideological agenda, but – precisely in the Hegelian sense of the term – to (re)introduce the dimension of absolute negativity into our daily lives: to shatter the insulated daily course of the lives of us, true Nietzschean Last Men. Sacrilegious as it may appear, the WTC attacks do share something with Antigone's act: they both undermine the "servicing of the goods", the reign of the pleasure–reality principle. The "dialectical" thing to do here, however, is not to include these acts in some grander narrative of the Progress of Reason or Humanity, which somehow, even if it does not redeem them, at least makes them part of an all-encompassing larger consistent narrative, "sublates" them in a "higher" stage of development (the naive notion of Hegelianism), but to make us question our own innocence, to discuss and assess our own (fantasmatic libidinal) investment and engagement in them.

So, rather than remain stuck in debilitating awe in the face of Absolute Evil, an awe which prohibits us from thinking about what is going on, we should remember that there are two fundamental ways of reacting to such traumatic events, which cause unbearable anxiety: the way of the superego and the way of the act. The way of the superego is precisely that of the sacrifice to the obscure gods of which Lacan speaks: the reassertion of the barbaric violence of the savage obscene law in order to fill in the gap of the failing symbolic law. And the act? One of the heroes of the Shoah for me is a famous Jewish ballerina who, as a gesture of special humiliation, was asked by the camp officers to perform a dance for them. Instead of refusing, she did it, and while she held their attention, she quickly grabbed the machine-gun from one of the distracted guards and, before being shot down herself, succeeded in killing more than a dozen officers . . . was not her act comparable to that of the passengers on the flight which crashed down in Pennsylvania who, knowing that they would die, forced their way into the cockpit and crashed the plane, saving hundreds of other lives?

*

Redemptive Violence

The thing to do, therefore, is not aggressively to protect the safety of our Sphere, but to shake ourselves out of the fantasy of the Sphere – how? David Fincher's *Fight Club* (1999), an extraordinary achievement for Hollywood, tackles this deadlock head-on. The film's insomniac hero (superbly played by Edward Norton) follows his doctor's advice and, in order to discover what true suffering is, joins a support group for victims of testicular cancer.[107] He soon discovers, however, how such practice of love for one's neighbour relies on a false subjective position (of voyeurist compassion), and soon gets involved in a much more radical exercise. On a flight, he meets Tyler (Brad Pitt), a charismatic young man who shows him the futility of a life filled with failure and empty consumer culture, and offers him a solution: why don't they fight, beating each other to pulp? Gradually, a whole movement develops out of this idea: secret after-hours boxing matches are held in the basements of bars all over the country. The movement quickly gets politicized, organizing terrorist attacks against big corporations . . . In the middle of the film there is an almost unbearably painful scene, reminiscent of the most bizarre David Lynch moments, which serves as a kind of clue to the surprising final twist: in order to blackmail his boss into paying him for not working, the narrator throws himself around the man's office, beating himself bloody before security staff arrive; in front of his embarrassed boss, the narrator thus enacts on himself the boss's aggressivity towards him. Afterwards, the narrator muses in a voice-over: "For some reason, I thought of my first fight – with Tyler." This first fight between the narrator and Tyler, which takes place in a parking lot outside a bar, is watched by five young men who laugh and exchange glances in wondrous amusement:

> Because the fight is being watched by people who do not know the partici-
> pants, we are led to believe that what we are seeing is what they are seeing:
> that is, a fight between two men. It isn't until the end that we are shown that
> they were watching the narrator throw himself around the parking lot, beating
> himself up.[108]

Towards the end of the film, we thus learn that the narrator did not know that he had been leading a second life until the evidence became so overwhelming that he could no longer deny the fact; Tyler has no existence outside the narrator's mind; when other characters interact with him, they are really interacting with the narrator, who has taken on the Tyler persona. However, it is obviously not sufficient to read the scene of Norton beating himself in front of his boss as an indication of Tyler's nonexistence – the unbearably painful and embarrassing effect of the scene bears witness to the fact that it discloses (stages) a certain disavowed fantasmatic truth. In the novel on which *Fight Club* is based, this scene is written as an exchange between what is really going on (Norton is beating himself up in front of his boss) and Norton's fantasy (the boss is beating up Tyler):

> At the projectionist union office, Tyler had laughed after the union president punched him. The one punch knocked Tyler out of his chair, and Tyler sat against the wall, laughing.
> "Go ahead, you can't kill me," Tyler was laughing. "You stupid fuck. Beat the crap out of me, but you can't kill me."
>   . . .
> "I am trash," Tyler said. "I am trash and shit and crazy to you and this whole fucking world."
>   . . .
> His honor shot the wingtip into Tyler's kidneys after Tyler curled into a ball, but Tyler was still laughing.
> "Get it out," Tyler said. "Trust me. You'll feel a lot better. You'll feel great."
>   . . .
> I am standing at the head of the manager's desk when I say, what?
> You don't like the idea of *this*?
> And without flinching, still looking at the manager, I roundhouse the fist at the centrifugal force end of my arm and slam fresh blood out of the cracked scabs in my nose.
>   . . .
> Blood gets on the carpet and I reach up and grip monster handprints of blood on the edge of the hotel manager's desk and say, please, help me, but I start to giggle.
>   . . .
> You have so much, and I have nothing. And I start to climb my blood up the pinstriped legs of the manager of the Pressman Hotel who is leaning back, hard, with his hands on the windowsill behind him and even his thin lips retreating from his teeth.
>   . . .
> There's a struggle as the manager screams and tries to get his hands away from me and my blood and my crushed nose, the filth sticking to the blood on both of us, and right then at our most excellent moment, the security guards decide to walk in.[109]

What does this self-beating stand for? On a first approach, it is clear that its fundamental function is to reach out and re-establish the connection with the real Other – to suspend the fundamental abstraction and coldness of capitalist subjectivity, best exemplified by the figure of the lone monadic individual who, alone in front of the PC screen, communicates with the entire world. In contrast to the humanitarian compassion which enables us to retain our distance towards the other, the very violence of the fight signals the abolition of this distance. Although this strategy is risky and ambiguous (it can easily regress into a proto-Fascist macho logic of violent male bonding), this risk has to be taken – there is no other direct way out of the closure of capitalist subjectivity.

The first lesson of *Fight Club* is thus that we cannot go *directly* from capitalist to revolutionary subjectivity: the abstraction, the foreclosure of others, the blindness to the other's suffering and pain, has first to be broken in a gesture of taking the risk and reaching directly out to the suffering other – a gesture which, since it shatters the very kernel of our identity, cannot fail to appear extremely violent. However, there is another dimension at work in *self*-beating: the subject's scatological (excremental) identification, which is equivalent to adopting the position of the proletarian who has nothing to lose. The pure subject emerges only through this experience of radical self-degradation, when I allow/provoke the other to beat the crap out of me, emptying me of all substantial content, of all symbolic support which could confer a modicum of dignity on me. So when Norton beats himself up in front of his boss, his message to the boss is: "I know you want to beat me, but you see, your desire to beat me is also my desire, so if you were to beat me, you would be fulfilling the role of the servant of my perverse masochistic desire. But you're too much of a coward to act out your desire, so I'll do it for you – here it is, you've got what you really wanted. Why are you so embarrassed? Aren't you ready to accept it?"[110] The gap between fantasy and reality is crucial here: the boss, of course, would never actually have beaten Norton up, he was merely fantasizing about doing it, and the painful effect of Norton's self-beating hinges on the very fact that he stages the content of the secret fantasy his boss would never be able to actualize.

Paradoxically, such a staging is the first act of liberation: by means of it, the servant's masochistic libidinal attachment to his master is brought to light, and the servant thus acquires a minimal *distance* towards it. Even on a purely formal level, the fact of beating oneself up reveals the simple fact that *the master is superfluous*. "Who needs you to terrorize me? I can do it myself!" So it is only through first beating up (hitting) *oneself* that one becomes free: the true goal of this beating is to beat out that in me which attaches me to the master. When, towards the end, Norton shoots at himself (surviving the shot, in fact killing only "Tyler in himself", his double), he thereby also liberates himself from the dual mirror-relationship of beating: in this culmination of self-aggression, its logic cancels itself; Norton will no longer have to beat himself – now he will be able to beat the true enemy (the system).[111] And, incidentally, the same strategy is occasionally used in political demonstrations: when a crowd is stopped by the police, who are ready to beat them, the way to bring about a shocking reversal of the situation is for the individuals in the crowd to start beating each other.

In his essay on Sacher-Masoch,[112] Gilles Deleuze elaborated this aspect in detail: far from bringing any satisfaction to the sadist witness, the masochist's self-torture frustrates him, depriving him of his power over the masochist. Sadism involves a relationship of domination, while masochism is the necessary first step towards liberation. When we are subjected to a power mechanism, this subjection is always and by definition sustained by some libidinal investment: the subjection itself generates a surplus-enjoyment of its own. This subjection is embodied in a network of "material" bodily practices, and for this reason we cannot get rid of our subjection through a merely intellectual reflection – our liberation has to be *staged* in some kind of bodily performance; furthermore, this performance *has* to be of an apparently "masochistic" nature, it *has* to stage the painful process of hitting back at oneself.[113] And did not Sylvia Plath adopt the same strategy in her famous poem "Daddy"?

> What she does in the poem is, with a weird detachment, to turn the violence against herself so as to show that she can equal her oppressors with her self-inflicted oppression. And this is the strategy of the concentration camps. When suffering is there whatever you do, by inflicting it upon yourself you achieve your identity, you set yourself free.[114]

This also resolves the problem of Plath's reference to the Holocaust: some of her critics say that her implicit equation of her oppression by her father to what the Nazis did to the Jews is an inadmissible exaggeration: what matters is not the (obviously incomparable) magnitude of the crime, but the fact that Plath felt compelled to adopt the concentration camp strategy of turning violence against herself as her only means of psychic liberation. For this reason, it is also far too simplistic to dismiss her thoroughly ambivalent hysterical attitude towards her father (her horror at his oppressive presence and, simultaneously, her obvious libidinal fascination with him – "Every woman adores a Fascist, the boot in the face . . ."): this hysterical knot[115] of libidinal investment in one's own victimization can never be undone.[116] That is to say, you cannot oppose the "redemptive" awareness of being oppressed to the "pathological" enjoyment the hysterical subject derives from this very oppression, interpreting their conjunction as the result of the "liberation from patriarchal domination as an unfinished project" (to paraphrase Habermas), that is, as the index of a split between the "good" feminist awareness of subjection and the persistent patriarchal libidinal economy which chains the hysteric to patriarchy, making her subordination into a *servitude volontaire*. If this were the case, then the solution would be simple: we should enact what, apropos of Proudhon, Marx characterized as the exemplary petty-bourgeois procedure – that of distinguishing in every phenomenon a "good" and a "bad" aspect, and then affirming the good and getting rid of the bad: in our case, struggling to keep the "good" aspect (awareness of oppression) and discard the "bad" one (finding pleasure in oppression). This "untying of the knot" does not work because *the only true awareness of our subjection is the awareness of the obscene excessive pleasure (surplus-enjoyment) we derive from it*; this is why the first gesture of liberation is not to get rid of this excessive pleasure, but actively to assume it – exactly what the hero of *Fight Club* does. In his *Autobiography*, Bertrand Russell reports how he tried to help T.S. Eliot and his wife Vivien in their marital troubles, "until I discovered that their troubles were what they enjoyed"[117] – in short, until he discovered that they enjoyed their symptom.

What, then, is a symptom? In his new book *The Shadow of the Sun*,[118] Ryszard Kapuscinski reports on the consequences of an enormous hole which had opened in the main street of Onitsha in Nigeria, holding up traffic for miles: the hole had become an institution. An entire new focus of urban life started to blossom around it: one crowd of boys unloading the next truck in line, another dragging the vehicle into the flooded pit and then heaving it out; rows of women around the edge, selling hot food, others hawking homemade lemonade and beer; boys selling cigarettes and chewing gum. "There arose, suddenly and spontaneously, thanks solely to that unfortunate hole, a dynamic, humming, bustling neighborhood."[119] Fresh-painted "Hotel" signs showed where local shops had been converted into refuges for drivers forced to spend nights waiting for their turn to get through; people with nothing to do stood around, turning the hole into a place for meetings and conversations – in short, a ridiculous contingent and meaningless obstacle triggered a swarm of social activity; people started to *enjoy their symptom*. The superficial solution, of course, would have been: why not simply *fill in the hole*, enabling the traffic to run through smoothly again? The mechanism here is in fact that of a hysterical symptom: when a hysterical subject encounters a similar contingent obstacle, he or she turns it into a focus of activity, rather than simply abolishing or bypassing it. And is it not the same in our societies with, say, ferries bringing passengers and cargo across a bay or a river? The embarcation points are, as a rule, places with a thriving social life which disappears once a bridge is constructed.

The same point could also be made in the terms of Heidegger's opposition between "substitutive-dominating solicitude" and "anticipatory-liberating solicitude": while it is fully concerned with what the other needs, substitutive solicitude ignores the "care" which the other should take upon himself in this activity of procuring something; anticipatory solicitude, in contrast, helps the other clearly to understand his "care", so that he can go freely towards it.[120] Does not this distinction apply perfectly to liberal humanitarians? Is not their solicitude "substitutive", in the sense that they want to help others (the poor, deprived, victims), instead of enabling them to help themselves (perhaps, even, in order to *prevent* them from helping themselves)? And is not this also what is wrong with the Politically Correct discourse of victimization – it continues to address the establishment with the voice of the victim who demands compensation, help from the Other? This is what is ultimately at stake in revolutionary violence: the transformation of the oppressed victim into an active agent, captured by Marx's famous statement that the emancipation of the proletariat can only be the act of the proletariat itself.

In an outstanding reading of Walter Benjamin's "Theses on the Philosophy of History",[121] Eric Santner elaborates Benjamin's notion that a present revolutionary intervention repeats/redeems past failed attempts: the "symptoms" – past traces which are retroactively redeemed through the "miracle" of the revolutionary intervention – are "not so much forgotten deeds, but rather forgotten *failures* to act, failures to *suspend* the force of social bond inhibiting acts of solidarity with society's 'others' ":

symptoms register not only past failed revolutionary attempts but, more modestly, past *failures to respond* to calls for action or even for empathy on behalf of those whose suffering in some sense belongs to the form of life of which one is a part. They hold the place of something that is *there*, that *insists* in our life, though it has never achieved full ontological consistency. Symptoms are thus in some sense the virtual archives of *voids* – or, perhaps, better, defenses against voids – that persist in historical experience.

Santner specifies how these symptoms can also take the form of perturbations of "normal" social life, like participation in the obscene rituals of the reigning ideology. Was not the infamous *Kristallnacht* in 1938 – that half-organized half-spontaneous outburst of violent attacks on Jewish homes, synagogues, businesses, and people themselves – a Bakhtinian "carnival" if ever there was one? We should read *Kristallnacht* precisely as a "symptom": the furious rage of such an outburst of violence makes it a symptom – the defence-formation covering the void of the failure to intervene effectively in the social crisis.

In other words, the very rage of the anti-Semitic pogroms is proof, *a contrario*, of the possibility of the authentic proletarian revolution: its excessive energy can be read only as a reaction to the ("unconscious") awareness of the missed revolutionary opportunity.[122] And is not the ultimate cause of *Ostalgie* (nostalgia for the Communist past) among many intellectuals (and even "ordinary people") in the defunct German Democratic Republic also a longing not so much for the Communist past, for what really went on under Communism, but, rather, for what *might have happened* there, for the missed opportunity of another Germany? Are not the post-Communist outbursts of neo-Nazi violence also a negative proof of the presence of these emancipatory chances, a symptomatic outburst of rage displaying an awareness of missed opportunities? We should not be afraid to draw a parallel with individual psychic life: just as an awareness of a missed "private" opportunity (say, the opportunity of engaging in a fulfilling love-relationship) often leaves its traces in the form of "irrational" anxieties, headaches, and fits of rage, the void of the missed revolutionary chance can explode in "irrational" fits of destructive rage.

According to Alain Badiou, the state of a situation whose function is to represent the multitude (for example, the State with regard to society) always involves an excess with regard to the situation it represents: the State apparatus is never a transparent representation of society; it relies on its own logic, which retroactively intervenes in and exerts violent pressure on what it represents.[123] At this point, we should add to his argument: not only is there an excess of State with regard to the multitude it represents; *the State is, at the same time, excessive with regard to itself* – that is to say, it generates its own excess which, although necessary for its functioning, has to remain unrecognized.

Apocalypse Now Redux (2000; Francis Ford Coppola's newly edited longer version of *Apocalypse Now*) stages, in the clearest possible way, the co-ordinates of this structural excess of State power. Is it not significant that in the figure of Kurtz, the Freudian "primordial father" – the obscene father-enjoyment beyond the reach of symbolic Law, the total Master who dares to confront the Real of terrifying enjoyment face to face – is presented not as a residue of some barbaric past, but as the necessary outcome of modern Western power itself? Kurtz was the perfect soldier – as such, through his overidentification with the military power system, he turned into the excess which the system has to eliminate.[124]

Badiou is right, however, in his emphasis on how the vicious cycle of superego violence has to be broken – this, precisely, is what does *not* happen in the film. The ultimate horizon of *Apocalypse Now* is the insight into how Power generates its own excess, which it must annihilate in an operation which has to imitate what it fights (Willard's mission to kill Kurtz does not appear in the official record – "It never happened", as the general who briefs Willard points out). We thereby enter the domain of secret operations, of what the Power does without ever admitting it. And does not the same go for today's figures presented by the official media as the embodiments of radical Evil? Is this not the truth behind the fact that Bin Laden and the Taleban emerged as part of the CIA-supported anti-Soviet guerrilla war in Afghanistan, and the fact that Noriega in Panama was an ex-CIA agent?[125] In all these cases, is not the USA fighting its own excess? And was not the same true of Fascism? The liberal West had to join forces with Communism to destroy its own excessive outgrowth. (Along the same lines, I am tempted to suggest what a truly subversive version of *Apocalypse Now* would have been like: to repeat the formula of the anti-Fascist coalition, and have Willard propose to the Vietcong a pact to destroy Kurtz.) What remains outside the horizon of *Apocalypse Now* is the perspective of a collective political act breaking out of this vicious cycle of the System which generates its superego excess, and is then compelled to annihilate it: a revolutionary violence which no longer relies on the superego obscenity. This "impossible" act is what takes place in every authentic revolutionary process.

So, back to *Fight Club*: is not the very idea of the "fight club", the evening encounters between men who play the game of beating each other up, the very model of such a false transgression/excitation, of the impotent *passage à l'acte* which bears witness to the failure actually to intervene in the social body? Does not *Fight Club* stage an exemplary case of the *inherent transgression*: far from effectively undermining the capitalist system, it enacts the obscene underside of the "normal" capitalist subject? And does not the same go for the politicized violence – the attack on bank headquarters – which concludes the film? Is not *Fight Club the* film about the emergence of American terrorism? Is not the final scene – the modern glass buildings exploding as a result of terrorist attacks – strangely reminiscent of the WTC collapse? This aspect was developed in detail by Diken and Laustsen, in their outstanding "Enjoy your fight!", the most pertinent analysis of *Fight Club*:[126]

The normalized and law abiding subject is haunted by a spectral double, by a subject that materializes the will to transgress the law in perverse enjoyment. . . . Thus *Fight Club* is hardly an "anti-institutional" response to contemporary capitalism, just as creativity, perversion or transgression are not necessarily emancipatory today. . . . Rather than a political act, *Fight Club* thus seems to be a trancelike subjective experience, a kind of pseudo-Bakhtinian carnivalesque activity in which the rhythm of everyday life is only temporarily suspended. . . . The problem with *Fight Club* is that it falls into the trap of presenting its problématique, violence, from a cynical distance. *Fight Club* is of course extremely reflexive and ironic. It can even be said that it is an irony on fascism.

The ultimate ground of this irony is that, in accordance with late capitalist global commodification, *Fight Club* offers as an "experiential commodity" the very attempt to explode the universe of commodities: instead of concrete political practice, we get an aestheticist explosion of violence. Furthermore, following Deleuze, Diken and Laustsen discern in *Fight Club* two dangers which invalidate its subversive thrust: first, there is the tendency to go to the extreme of the spectacle of ecstatic (self-)destruction – revolutionary politics is obliterated in a depoliticized aestheticist orgy of annihilation; second, the revolutionary explosion "deterritorializes, massifies, but only in order to stop deterritorialization, to invent new territorializations": "in spite of a deterritorializing start, *Fight Club* ends up transforming into a fascist organization with a new name: Project Mayhem. Violence is now turned outwards, which culminates in a plan for 'organized' terror to undermine the foundations of the consumerist society." These two dangers are complementary, since "the regression to the undifferentiated or complete disorganization is as dangerous as transcendence and organization".

Is the solution really the "just measure" between the two extremes: neither the new Organization nor the regression to undifferentiated violence? What we should problematize here is, rather, the very opposition between de- and re-territorialization – that is to say, Deleuze's idea of the irreducible tension between the "good" schizophrenic-molecular collectivity and the "bad" paranoiac-molar one: molar/rigid versus molecular/supple; rhizomatic *flows*, with their molecular segmentarity (based on mutations, de-territorialization, connections, and accelerations), versus *classes* or *solids*, with their rigid segmentarity (binary organization, resonance, overcoding).[127] This opposition (a variation on Sartre's old thesis, from his *Critique of Dialectical Reason*, about the reversal of the praxis of authentic group dialectics into the "practico-inert" logic of the alienated institution – Deleuze himself often directly refers to Sartre) is a false ("abstract") universalization, in so far as it offers no space to articulate the key distinction between the two different logics of the very connection between micro- and macro-, local and global: the "paranoiac" State which "re-territorializes" the schizophrenic explosion of the molecular multitude is not the only imaginable frame of the global collective social organization; the Leninist *revolutionary party* gives body to (or, rather, announces) a totally different logic of collectivity. (Beneath this opposition is, of course, Deleuze's profoundly anti-Leninist distrust of any form of firm global Organization. What is interesting here, however, is that Alain Badiou himself, who draws attention to this anti-Leninist thrust of Deleuze, seems to rely on the same opposition in his "anti-Statist" assertion of the utopian goal of pure *presence* of the multitude, without any state of *re-presentation* which totalizes this multitude, and thus generates a remainder for which there is no place within the totality – significantly, Badiou also refers here to Sartre.[128]) What disappears in this perspective is simply the fundamental Marxist insight that the molar State has to "totalize" the molecular multi-tude *because a radical "antagonism" is already at work within this multitude.*

As Deleuze saw very clearly, we cannot provide in advance an unambig-uous criterion which will allow us to distinguish "false" violent outburst from the "miracle" of the authentic revolutionary breakthrough. The ambi-guity is irreducible here, since the "miracle" can occur only through the repetition of previous failures. And this is also why violence is a necessary ingredient of a revolutionary political act. That is to say: what is the criterion of a political act proper? Success as such clearly does not count, even if we define it in the dialectical terms of Merleau-Ponty: as the wager that the future will retroactively redeem our present horrible acts (this is how Merleau-Ponty, in *Humanism and Terror*, provided one of the more intelligent justifications of the Stalinist terror: retroactively, it will become justified if its final outcome is true freedom);[129] neither does reference to some abstract-universal ethical norm. The only criterion is the absolutely inherent one: that of the enacted utopia.

In a genuine revolutionary breakthrough, the utopian future is neither simply fully realized, present, nor simply evoked as a distant promise which justifies present violence – it is rather as if, in a unique suspension of temporality, in the short circuit between the present and the future, we are – as if by Grace – briefly allowed to act *as if* the utopian future is (not yet fully here, but) already at hand, there to be seized. Revolution is experienced not as a present hardship we have to endure for the sake of the happiness and freedom of future generations, but as the present hardship over which this future happiness and freedom already cast their shadow – in it, we are already free even as we fight for freedom; we are already happy even as we fight for happiness, no matter how difficult the circumstances. Revolution is not a Merleau-Pontyan wager, an act suspended in the *futur antérieur*, to be legitimized or de-legitimized by the long-term outcome of present acts; it is, as it were, *its own ontological proof*, an immediate index of its own truth.

Let us recall the staged performance of "Storming the Winter Palace" in Petrograd on the third anniversary of the October Revolution, 7 November 1920. Tens of thousands of workers, soldiers, students and artists worked round the clock, living on kasha (tasteless wheat porridge), tea and frozen apples, and preparing the performance in the very place where the event "really happened" three years earlier; their work was co-ordinated by army officers, as well as by avant-garde artists, musicians and directors, from Malevich to Meyerhold. Although this was acting, not "reality", the soldiers and sailors were playing themselves – many of them had not only actually participated in the events of 1917, but were also simultaneously involved in the real battles of the Civil War that were raging in the vicinity of Petrograd, a city under siege and suffering from severe food shortages. A contemporary commented on the performance: "The future historian will record how, throughout one of the bloodiest and most brutal revolutions, all of Russia was acting";[130] and the formalist theoretician Viktor Shklovski noted that "some kind of elemental process is taking place where the living fabric of life is being transformed into the theatrical".[131] We can all remember the infamous self-celebratory First of May parades that were one of the supreme signs of recognition of Stalinist regimes – if we need proof of how Leninism functioned in an entirely different way, are not such performances the supreme proof that the October Revolution was definitely *not* a simple *coup d'état* by a small group of Bolsheviks, but an event which unleashed a tremendous emancipatory potential?

The archetypal Eisensteinian cinematic scene that depicts the exuberant orgy of revolutionary destructive violence (what Eisenstein himself called "a veritable bacchanalia of destruction") belongs to the same series: when, in *October*, the victorious revolutionaries penetrate the wine cellars of the Winter Palace, they indulge in an ecstatic orgy of smashing thousands of bottles of expensive wine; in *Bohzin Meadow*, after the village Pioneers discover the body of the young Pavlik, brutally murdered by his own father, they force their way into the local church and desecrate it, robbing it of its relics, squabbling over an icon, sacrilegiously trying on vestments, laughing heretically at the statuary. . . .[132] In this suspension of goal-orientated instrumental activity, we in fact get a kind of Bataillean "unrestrained expenditure" – the pious desire to deprive the revolution of this excess is simply the desire to have a revolution without revolution. It is against this background that we should approach the delicate issue of revolutionary violence which is an authentic act of liberation, not just a blind *passage à l'acte*.[133]

And did we not get exactly the same scene in the Great Cultural Revolution in China, with thousands of Red Guardists ecstatically destroying old historical monuments, smashing old vases, defacing old paintings, chipping at old walls?[134] In spite of (or, rather, *because of*) all its horrors, the Great Cultural Revolution undoubtedly contained elements of such an enacted utopia. At the very end, before such activity was blocked by Mao himself (since he had already achieved his goal of re-establishing his full power and getting rid of the top *nomenklatura* competition), there was the "Shanghai Commune": one million workers who simply took the official slogans seriously, demanding the abolition of the State and even of the Party itself, and the direct communal organization of society. It is significant that it was at this very point that Mao ordered the restoration of order. The (often noted) parallel between Mao and Lacan is fully justified here: the dissolution of the École Freudienne de Paris in 1979 was Lacan's "Great Cultural Revolution", mobilizing his young followers (who, incidentally, were mostly ex-Maoists from 1968!) in order to get rid of the inner circle of his "mandarins". In both cases, the paradox is that of a leader who triggers an uncontrolled upheaval, while trying to exert full personal power – the paradoxical overlapping of extreme dictatorship and extreme emancipation of the masses.

It is with regard to political terror that we can locate the gap which separates Lenin's era from Stalinism:[135] in Lenin's time, terror was openly admitted (Trotsky sometimes even boasted, in an almost cocky way, about the non-democratic nature of the Bolshevik regime and the terror it used), while in Stalin's time the symbolic status of the terror changed completely: terror turned into the publicly non-acknowledged obscene shadowy supplement of the public official discourse. It is significant that the climax of terror (1936–37) came after 1935, when the new constitution was accepted – this constitution was supposed to end the state of emergency, and proclaim that things had gone back to normal: the suspension of the civil rights of whole strata of the population (kulaks, ex-capitalists) was revoked, the franchise was now universal, and so on. The key idea of this constitution was that now, after the stabilization of the Socialist order and the annihilation of the enemy classes, the Soviet Union was no longer a class society:

the subject of the State was no longer the working class (workers and peasants), but the people. This does not mean, however, that the Stalinist constitution was a mere hypocrisy concealing the social reality – the possibility of terror is inscribed into its very core: since the class war is now officially over, and the Soviet Union is conceived of as the classless country of the People, those who (are still presumed to) oppose the regime are no longer mere class enemies in a conflict that tears the social body apart, but enemies of the People, vermin, worthless scum which must be excluded from humanity itself.

This repression of the regime's own excess was strictly correlative to the invention of the psychological individual which took place in the Soviet Union in the late 1920s and early 1930s. Russian avant-garde art of the early 1920s (Futurism, Constructivism) not only zealously endorsed industrialization, it even endeavoured to reinvent a new industrial man – no longer the old man of sentimental passions and roots in tradition, but the new man who gladly accepts his role as a bolt or screw in the gigantic co-ordinated industrial Machine. As such, it was subversive in its very "ultra-orthodoxy", in its overidentification with the core of the official ideology: the image of man or woman that we get in Eisenstein, Meyerhold, Constructivist paintings, and so on, emphasizes the beauty of his or her mechanical movements, his or her thorough de-psychologization. What was perceived in the West as the ultimate nightmare of liberal individualism, as the ideological counterpoint to "Taylorization", to the Fordist assembly line, was hailed in Russia as the *utopian* prospect of liberation: consider how Meyerhold violently advocated the "behaviourist" approach to acting – no longer emphatic familiarization with the person the actor is playing, but ruthless bodily training to achieve cold physical discipline, the actor's ability to perform a series of mechanized movements.[136] What the Russian avant-garde artists were doing here was simply drawing the consequences of Lenin's own celebration of "Taylorization" as the new scientific way to organize production.

Does this vision (and practice) of mechanized production really harbour an emancipatory potential? The first thing to do here is to ask an elementary question: What is a factory? Leslie Kaplan's essay-poem *L'excès-usine*,[137] with its description of the "hell" of factory life, reveals the dimension overlooked in standard Marxist depictions of the workers' "alienation". Kaplan opposes the self-enclosed universe of the factory to the open environment of the previous work process: the factory space is a timeless space in which fiction and reality ultimately coincide – that is to say, the very reality of this space functions as a fantasmatic space cut off from its environs. What is lacking in this space is the full "background noise" which provides a life-world context for human individuals: in a factory, as Kaplan puts it, instead of the rich tapestry of the background environment, there is only whiteness – in short, it is as if, when we go into a factory, we enter an artificial universe deprived of the substantial wealth of the texture of real life. In this space, (historical-narrative) memory itself is threatened: workers are cut off from their ancestral roots, and this also affects their own utopian potential: reduced to robots endlessly repeating the same mechanical gestures, they lose the very capacity to dream, to devise projects of alternative reality. What they experience is no longer nostalgia for a determinate past (say, of their previous more "organic" farmers' lives), but, as Kaplan puts it perspicaciously, an "absolute nostalgia" for an empty Otherness whose sole positive content is, again, factory life itself – say, the empty corridors of a factory.

However, is this loss of historical memory, of the capacity to dream, really just a negative experience? What if this disintegration of our embeddedness in the concrete life-world is (a necessary step towards) the emergence of free subjectivity? What if, in order to emerge as a subject, I have first to lose all the wealth of my objective being, so that, at this level of objective being, I am nothing but a corporeal machine? *This* is what was unbearable to and in the official Stalinist ideology, so that Stalinist "socialist realism" *was* actually an attempt to reassert "Socialism with a human face", to reinscribe the process of industrialization into the constraints of the traditional psychological individual: in Socialist Realist texts, paintings and films, individuals are no longer depicted as parts of the global Machine, but as warm passionate people.

Against Pure Politics

This reference to liberating violence also allows us to distinguish Lenin's notion of universal humanity from the recent tendency to introduce moralistic-legalistic reasoning into political struggles. When "apolitical" human rights are evoked as the rationale for a political – even a military – intervention, our first, naive reaction cannot fail to be that of spontaneous rejoicing: isn't it comforting to see NATO forces intervene not for any specific economic or strategic reasons, but simply because a country is cruelly violating the basic human rights of an ethnic group? Is this not the only hope in our globalized era – to see some internationally acknowledged force as a guarantee that all countries will respect a certain minimum of ethical (and, ideally, also health, social, ecological) standards? What can we have against a respected international tribunal in The Hague prosecuting criminal politicians?

Of course, the no less spontaneous reaction of a Leftist radical is that of contemptuous distrust: first, the neutrality of the reference to human rights is obviously a fiction – in the present constellation, this reference to human rights serves the global New Order dominated by the USA. The question to be asked apropos of every particular intervention on behalf of human rights is thus always: On what criteria did this selection rely? Why Albanians in Serbia and not also Palestinians in Israel, Kurds in Turkey, and so on? Why is Cuba boycotted, while a much harsher North Korean regime gets free help to develop "safe" atomic energy capacities? Here, of course, we enter the shady world of international capital and its strategic interests. Furthermore, this purely humanitarian-ethical legitimization of an intervention thoroughly de-politicizes it, changing it into an intervention into humanitarian catastrophe, grounded in purely moral reasons, not an intervention into a well-defined political struggle. In this way, the reality of a political struggle is transformed into a moral struggle between Good and Evil – in short, the moralization of politics runs the risk of imperceptibly turning into the politicization of morals, in which the political opponent is transformed into the personification of moral Evil.

But is this standard Leftist answer good enough? What it amounts to is a rehashing of the old Marxist denunciation of a false ideological universality: "Universal human rights in fact privilege individuals in highly developed First World countries. . . ." The problem with this rehashing is that it misses the unique chance of turning human rights themselves into a terrain of hegemonic struggle, rather than surrendering them to the enemy. Let us recall the fate of the reference to human rights in the late eighteenth century: of course, at the beginning, they were "in fact" the rights of white male property-owners, silently excluding the lower classes, women, other races, and so forth. Their very universal form, however, set in motion an unstoppable process of expansion: first women said "Why not us too?", then Blacks (in Haiti) said the same, then the workers. . . .

And it is well worth following the same strategy today. There will always be a bitter taste to the tragicomedy of Milošević's arrest at the end of March 2001, and to his extradition to The Hague in June: in both cases, the act was executed in order to comply with the deadline set by the USA if it was to grant Yugoslavia generous financial aid. This bitter taste does not result only from a suspicion that the world powers singled out Milošević and elevated him into a personification of Evil; it also attests to the new

Yugoslav government's reluctance to admit Yugoslav responsibility for the war in the 1990s, its intention to cling to the myth of Yugoslavs as victims of Western aggression. Much more important – and the first step in the right direction – was the unexpected arrest of Augusto Pinochet two years earlier. Whatever its ultimate outcome, the immediate ideological repercussions were immense: when Pinochet arrived in London, he was perceived in Chile as an all-powerful untouchable *éminence grise*; after his arrest, the psychological barrier was broken, he was just a frail old criminal inventing humiliating excuses to avoid arrest. The limitation of the Pinochet case, however, is that he comes from a small marginal country.

What, then, comes after Pinochet and Milošević? The true achievement would have been to go for the jugular – to pursue this logic to the very end: to arrest someone who "really matters". And here Henry Kissinger is arguably the ideal candidate:[138] the accusation that he is a war criminal is an old and well-substantiated one (remember the famous BBC talk at which the moderator asked him directly: "How does it feel to be a war criminal?" – Kissinger, of course, immediately stormed out of the studio). Furthermore, he is no longer politically active, so the USA cannot claim that his arrest would in any way impede the functioning of its state apparatuses. This, then, would have been an authentic political *act*: if, when Kissinger was on a world tour promoting a new book, some (preferably West European) country arrested him just as they arrested Pinochet. This gesture would put the international human rights machinery to the test, forcing its functionaries to clarify their stance and make a choice: either the US Empire would force his release, thus exposing the big fake of human rights, or. . . .

Sometimes, the most cunning politics is that of utter naivety – or, to paraphrase Gandhi's ingenious quip apropos of British civilization: "Universal Human Rights? A good idea – maybe we should test it out!" Is not the May 2001 decision of the US Senate (orchestrated by Jesse Helms) to reject any jurisdiction of The Hague and other international tribunals over American citizens – a decision which took European Community governments by surprise – already a clear sign of the open and brutal exclusivism of US human rights policies? The only way to give some actual content to the "anti-terrorist alliance" which is emerging after the 11 September attacks is to confer the ultimate competence on some kind of international court – which means that this court will also have to have the right to prosecute US citizens. No wonder that after I finished reading Christopher Hitchens's *The Trial of Henry Kissinger*, I had a kind of inverted Martin Luther King egalitarian dream: I saw, in the row of prisoners sitting on the benches of the Hague tribunal, Milošević alongside Kissinger; I imagined these two hardened unscrupulous cynics sitting together at a table during breaks in the trial, sipping whisky and sharing their cheap wisdom. This, then, should be the message to those in power who referred to human rights in their arrest of Noriega, in their bombing of Iraq, in their economic blockade of Cuba, in the pursuing of the Yugoslav war criminals by the Hague tribunal: *arrest Kissinger or shut up!*

I am tempted to go even further here – what about the catastrophic short-sighted madness of President Bush's decision, at the end of March 2001, to renege on his electoral promise to implement the Kyoto treaty on global warming, which sets limits for carbon dioxide emissions? Some of his critics were fully justified in claiming that this action amounted to the Americans' betrayal of their responsibility as global citizens: what right has the USA now to condemn Brazil for destroying the rainforest, or China for building a dam on the Yellow River? The total cynicism of this decision lies in its justification: presumably, only in this way can we prevent a hike in electricity and oil prices, which would hit poor people hardest. This stance of "first economy, then ecology" forgets that it was the very "de-regulation" of the electricity supply in California which caused the power crisis.

It is here that liberal-capitalist globalization should be counteracted with a truly democratic globalization: why not start a big global campaign for a kind of international ecological court, aiming (in the long term, at least) to achieve some kind of legal status with executive authority, setting clear criteria for what constitutes an ecological crime, and with the power to impose at least some kind of measures against the people and institutions responsible? Why not mobilize the full force of the legalistic-moralistic discourse, treating (in this case) Bush not merely as a political adversary, but as a criminal who should be publicly treated as such, and boycotted?[139]

Perhaps, on a more general level, I should take the risk of applying to the logic of political subversion Lacan's opposition of masculine (universality and its constitutive exception) and feminine (no exception to the set, which renders the set non-all) formulas of sexuation.[140] The normal oppositional logic remains on the masculine side: it either assumes the position of a simple exception/externality with regard to the system (clinging to some element – pure love, some version of non-alienated human essence, the correct class position, scientific insight – which is supposed to guarantee that one is outside the system, able to attack it without being contaminated by it), or asserts the absolute closure of the system (late capitalism contains, in an unprecedented way, its own excess, so that all attempts to break out, to transgress its domain, are inherent transgressions taken into account by the system in advance).

The way to break out of this impasse is to reformulate the problem in terms of the feminine side of the formulas of sexuation: there is nothing which is simply external to the system, which is not part of it; at the same time, the system is non-all, it is never able to totalize itself, fully to contain the excesses it generates. This means that the system's excesses are thoroughly and irredeemably ambivalent (or "undecidable", to use a more fashionable term): the very element which was engendered by the system in order to guarantee its closure can turn into a threat – even the most trivial Hollywood melodramas can be "transfunctionalized" into the bearers of explosive utopian potential. Nowhere is this more obvious than in the case of religion: it can function as the "opium of the people", as the imaginary supplement which makes us endure unbearable reality, *or* it can turn against the very conditions which gave birth to it, as was the case with different sects and heresies.[141]

The two formulas of sexuation could be condensed into the triad Universal/Particular/Singular, by introducing a split into universality itself – in Hegelese: between "abstract" and "concrete" universality, or, in Lacanese: between (not only "All S are P", but) "S *as such is* P", and "there is no S which is not P". First, we have the opposition between universality and its exception – for example: "Man (as such) is a rational being", supplemented by "Some men are not fully rational" (and – the racist implication – therefore not fully human). Or, the more directly politicized version: "A citizen of the USA is, by definition, free", supplemented by "Some of them do not deserve (are not ready and fit for) full freedom." The crucial insight here is the one into the structural necessity of this exception: as Hegel put it, the *differentia specifica* is at the same time the difference between genus and its species. "Man as such is free" *means* that "Some people are not free." Or, with regard to the logic of explicit symbolic norms and their obscene supplement: "the Law is neutral and equal for all" *means* that there is a set of obscene unwritten rules which privilege some and exclude others, and these obscene rules are the condition for the law to function effectively and regulate social relations. In Kantian terms, the obscene unwritten rules which posit exceptions to the norm (i.e. the way we are not only permitted, but even obliged, to violate the norm) are a kind of transcendental schema which mediates between the symbolic norm and "real life".

The "feminine" counterpoint to this logic of universality and its constitutive exception is: "There is no man who is not a rational being (or, more precisely, there is nothing in/of man which is outside rationality)" and, for that very reason, "Not-all of man is rational." The logic here is not that of the exception to the universality, but of some abject, some singularity, which directly gives body to the falsity of "its" universality. This is the logic of the singular symptomal element, like the proletariat for Marx: it does not function only as an exception to its universality; rather, it directly belies, undermines, this universality – the very existence of the proletariat means that the whole of the capitalist system is "irrational". (Perhaps this is also how we should read Hegel's "Everything rational is actual and everything actual is rational" from his Foreword to the *Philosophy of Right*: "There is nothing actual which is not rational.") This is how proper dialectical "concrete universality" works: "there is nothing which is not political" (or, in traditional terms, "there is nothing which is not affected by class struggle"), which, precisely, does not mean that "politics is everything", but, rather, that the political class struggle is that "pathological" diagonal feature which affects every element of the social edifice, submitting it to a kind of anamorphic distortion.

In Iceland, some thirty miles northeast of Reykjavik, you can see *das Ding* in one of its historical configurations, under the name of "Althing", the site of the annual caucus of (almost) all inhabitants during which they debated common issues and established new laws. So what do you actually see there? A high cliff (from which the "law-speaker" proclaimed new laws by shouting) separated by a rift valley from the plain to the east (where the crowd gathered). This, then, is the first surprise: the Icelanders chose as their gathering place the site of a geological rupture (the divide between the North American and the Eurasian continental plates, which are physically tearing apart – this is why there are so many earthquakes in Iceland), as if they intended to indicate how politics is, in its very notion, the field of intractable antagonistic struggle. Interestingly enough, the Althing functioned from 930 until 1798, roughly the period of the French Revolution, when the last assembly was held – again, as if to indicate how modern parliamentary democracy is incompatible with the active engagement of all citizens, and thus belying the assertion that the Althing was the first democratic parliament in the history of humanity. This Thing is not simply the mute presence of the Real – it *speaks*, imposing its decrees and judgements. When the assembled population had reached a conclusion, the speakers on top of the cliff informed them by shouting what the Thing had concluded.

That is the difference between the Althing and the modern democratic parliament or national assembly: in the Althing, the Thing coincides with the big Other (the symbolic order); while in modern democracy, the Thing (enjoyment) is evacuated from the Other, the Other is the neutral order of laws, blind to the particularity of enjoyment. If, none the less, we concede that the Althing was an exemplary site of political antagonism, then, perhaps, a guide to Iceland culture provides the reason in a quite open and brutal way: "The essence of Icelandic conversation is insult." Is not insulting the adversary (attempting to undermine his symbolic status) inscribed into the very heart of the political process? Is this insulting not the fundamental *modus operandi* of political debate?

From this point, we should return to the thesis that one of the basic features of democracy is the transformation of (political) enemy into adversary, of unconditional antagonism into agonistic competition: an adversary is not a mortal threat to power, since the place of it is originally empty, a place for whose (temporal) occupation different agents can legitimately compete.[142] Whenever we hear that we need to suspend the logic of exclusion or excommunication in the field of politics, however, we should always bear in mind that such an agonistic thriving multitude of adversaries, not enemies, has by definition to rely on some (explicit or implicit) symbolic *pact* which defines the rules of this agonistic competition. For this simple reason, wide as this field of agonistic competition can be, the translation of antagonism into agonism, of enemy into adversary, can never be complete – there will always be some "indivisible remainder" of those who do not recognize this pact. And are not the terms in which we have to define this exclusion necessarily ethico-legalistic?

This means that the key political struggle is not so much the agonistic competition, within the field of the admissible, of political subjects who acknowledge each other as legitimate adversaries, but, rather, the struggle for the delimitation of this field, for the definition of the line which will separate the legitimate adversary from the illegitimate enemy.

Classic liberal democracy, for example, involves the excommunication of the extreme (Fascist) Right and (terrorist or Communist) Left: there is no pact with them; coalitions are out of the question. Why should the Leftist strategy not be to impose an even more radical exclusion: does not the struggle between Right and Left often revolve around the inclusion of the far Right, with the Right accepting its inclusion and the Left insisting on its exclusion (Haider in Austria, the neo-Fascist *Alleanza nazionale* in Italy, etc.)? Why not, instead of condemning out of hand the introduction of moralistic and legalistic categories into the political struggle proper, *extend* their application, censuring the extreme Right as ethically Evil, as morally inacceptable, as a pariah to be shunned? In short, why not openly *endorse* the politicization of ethics, in the sense of abolishing the distance between the two, of changing the legal and moral terrain into another battlefield of political hegemony, of resorting to direct ethico/legal arguments and measures to discredit the enemy?[143] The goal of radical Leftist politics should therefore be the very opposite of unprincipled tolerant pluralism: to create the public space in which some (racist, etc.) statements and practices are inadmissible, that is, simply *not possible* – those who utter or practise them exclude themselves from the communal space. This is why, every time a radical Rightist stance (from Holocaust revisionism to anti-feminism) becomes "acceptable" in public debates, the Left suffers a defeat.

Do we thereby in fact court some kind of dangerous "extremism", which is also one of the standard criticisms of Lenin? Lenin's critique of "Leftism as the Infantile Disorder of Communism" has been more than pertinent over recent decades, when the Left has often succumbed to the terrorist temptation. Political "extremism" or "excessive radicalism" should always be read as a phenomenon of ideologico-political *displacement*: as an index of its opposite, of a limitation, of a refusal actually to "go right to the end".

What was the Jacobins' recourse to radical "terror" if not a kind of hysterical acting-out bearing witness to their inability to disturb the very fundamentals of economic order (private property, etc.)? And does not the same go even for the so-called "excesses" of Political Correctness? Don't they, also, reveal a retreat from disturbing the real (economic, etc.) causes of racism and sexism? Perhaps, then, the time has come to raise as a problem the classic topos, shared by practically all "postmodern" Leftists, according to which political "totalitarianism" somehow results from the predominance of material production and technology over the intersubjective communication and/or symbolic practice, as if the root of political terror resides in the fact that the "principle" of instrumental reason, of the technological exploitation of nature, is extended also to society, so that people are treated as raw material to be transformed into New Men. What if the exact *opposite* were the case? What if political "terror" indicates precisely that the sphere of (material) production is *denied* in its autonomy and *subordinated* to political logic? Is it not that all political "terror", from the Jacobins to the Maoist Cultural Revolution, presupposes the foreclosure of production proper, its reduction to the terrain of political conflict?

Take Badiou's exalted defence of Terror in the French Revolution, in which he quotes the justification of the guillotine for Lavoisier: "*La république n'a pas besoin de savants.* [The Republic has no need for scientists.]" Badiou's thesis is that the truth of this statement emerges if we cut it short, depriving it of its caveat: "*La république n'a pas de besoins.* [The Republic has no needs.]" The Republic gives body to the purely political logic of equality and freedom, which should follow its path with no consideration for the "servicing of goods" destined to satisfy the needs of individuals.[144]

In the revolutionary process proper, freedom becomes an end in itself, caught in its own paroxysm – this suspension of the importance of the sphere of the economy, of (material) production, brings Badiou close to Hannah Arendt, for whom, as for Badiou, freedom is opposed to the domain of the provision of goods and services, the maintenance of households and the exercise of administration, which do not belong to politics proper: the only place for freedom is the communal political space.

In this precise sense, Badiou's (and Sylvain Lazarus's[145]) plea for the reappraisal of Lenin is more ambiguous than it may appear: what it actually amounts to is nothing less than an abandonment of Marx's key insight into how the political struggle is a spectacle which, in order to be deciphered, has to be referred to the sphere of economics ("if Marxism had any analytical value for *political* theory, was it not in the insistence that the problem of freedom was contained in the social relations implicitly declared 'unpolitical' – that is, naturalized – in liberal discourse"[146]). No wonder the Lenin Badiou and Lazarus prefer is the Lenin of *What Is to Be Done?*, the Lenin who (in his thesis that socialist-revolutionary consciousness has to be brought to the working class from outside) breaks with Marx's alleged "economism" and asserts the autonomy of the Political, not the Lenin of *The State and Revolution*, fascinated by modern centralized industry, imagining (depoliticized) ways of reorganizing the economy and the state apparatus.

This "pure politics" of Badiou, Rancière and Balibar, more Jacobin than Marxist, shares with its great opponent, Anglo-Saxon Cultural Studies and their focus on struggles for recognition, the degradation of the sphere of the economy. That is to say: what all the new French (or French-orientated) theories of the Political, from Balibar through Rancière and Badiou to Laclau and Mouffe, aim at is – to put it in traditional philosophical terms – the reduction of the sphere of the economy (of material production) to an "ontic" sphere deprived of "ontological" dignity. Within this horizon, there is simply no room for the Marxian "critique of political economy": the structure of the universe of commodities and capital in Marx's *Capital* is not just that of a limited empirical sphere, but a kind of socio-transcendental a priori, the matrix which generates the totality of social and political relations.

The relationship between economy and politics is ultimately that of the well-known visual paradox of "two faces or a vase": you see either two faces or a vase, never both – you have to make a choice.[147] In the same way, you either focus on the political, and the domain of the economy is reduced to the empirical "servicing of goods", or you focus on the economy, and politics is reduced to a theatre of appearances, to a passing phenomenon which will disappear with the arrival of the developed Communist (or technocratic) society in which, as Engels put it, the "administration of people" will vanish in the "administration of things".[148]

The "political" critique of Marxism (the claim that if you reduce politics to a "formal" expression of some underlying "objective" socioeconomic process, you lose the openness and contingency constitutive of the political field proper) should therefore be supplemented by its obverse: the field of economy is, *in its very form*, irreducible to politics – this level of the form of the economy (of the economy as the determining form of the social) is what French "political post-Marxists" miss when they reduce the economy to one of several positive social spheres. In Badiou, the root of this notion of pure "politics", radically autonomous with regard to history, society, economy, State, even Party, is his opposition between Being and Event – this is where Badiou remains "idealist". From the materialist standpoint, an Event emerges "out of nowhere" within a specific constellation of Being – the space of an Event is the minimal "empty" distance between two beings, the "other" dimension which shines through this gap.[149]

So, Lenin the ultimate political strategist should in no way be separated from Lenin the "technocrat" dreaming about the scientific reorganization of production. The greatness of Lenin is that although he lacked the proper conceptual apparatus to think these two levels together, he was aware of the *urgency* of doing so – an impossible yet necessary task.[150] What we are dealing with here is another version of the Lacanian "il n'y a pas de rapport . . .": if, for Lacan, there is no sexual relationship, then, for Marxism proper, there is *no relationship between economy and politics*, no "meta-language" that enables us to grasp the two levels from the same neutral standpoint, although – or, rather, because – these two levels are inextricably intertwined. The "political" class struggle takes place in the midst of the economy (recall that the very last paragraph of *Capital* Volume III, where the text stops abruptly, tackles the class struggle), while, at the same time, the domain of the economy serves as the key that enables us to decode political struggles. No wonder the structure of this impossible relationship is that of a Moebius strip: first, we have to progress from the political spectacle to its economic infrastructure; then, in a second step, we have to confront the irreducible dimension of the political struggle at the very heart of the economy.

Here, Lenin's stance against economism as well as against pure politics is crucial today, apropos of the split attitude towards the economy in (what remains of) radical circles: on the one hand, the above-mentioned pure

"politicists" who abandon the economy as the site of struggle and intervention; on the other, the economists, fascinated by the functioning of today's
global economy, who preclude any possibility of a political intervention
proper. Today, more than ever, we should go back to Lenin: yes, the
economy is the key domain; the battle will be decided there, we have to
break the spell of global capitalism – but the intervention should be truly
political, not economic. Today, when everyone is "anti-capitalist", right up
to the Hollywood "socio-critical" conspiracy movies (from *Enemy of the
State* to *The Insider*) in which the villains are the big corporations, with
their ruthless pursuit of profit, the signifier "anti-capitalism" has lost its
subversive sting. What we should be discussing, rather, is the self-evident
opposite of this "anti-capitalism": the trust that the democratic substance
of honest Americans can break up the conspiracy. *This* is the hard kernel of
today's global capitalist universe, its true Master-Signifier: democracy.

The limit of democracy is the State: in the democratic electoral process,
the social body is symbolically dissolved, reduced to a pure numerical
multitude. The electoral body is precisely not a body, a structured whole,
but a formless abstract multitude, a multitude without a State (in both
Badiouian senses of this term: the State as the re-presented unity of the
multitude, and the State with its apparatuses). The point is thus not that
democracy is intrinsic to the State, sustained by its apparatuses, but that it
structurally *ignores* this dependency. When Badiou says that the State is
always in excess with regard to the multitude it represents, this means that
it is precisely this excess which is structurally overlooked by democracy: the
democratic illusion is that the democratic process can control this excess of
the State.

That is why the anti-globalization movement is not enough: at some
point, we will have to tackle the problem of the self-evident reference to
"freedom and democracy". That is the ultimate Leninist lesson for today:
paradoxically, it is only in this way, by problematizing democracy – by
making it clear that liberal democracy a priori, in its very notion (as Hegel
would have put it), cannot survive without capitalist private property – that
we can become truly anti-capitalist. Did not the disintegration of Communism in 1990 provide the ultimate confirmation of the most "vulgar"
Marxist thesis that the actual economic base of political democracy is
the private ownership of the means of production, that is, capitalism, with
its class distinctions? The big urge after the introduction of political
democracy was "privatization", the frantic effort to find – at any price, in
whatever way – new owners, who can be descendants of former owners
whose property was nationalized when the Communists took power, ex-

Communists, apparatchiks, Mafiosi . . . anybody, as long as we get a "base" of democracy.[151] The ultimate tragic irony is that all this is taking place *too late* – at exactly the moment when, in First World "post-industrial" societies, private ownership has started to lose its central regulative role.

The battle to be fought is therefore twofold: first, yes, anti-capitalism. However, anti-capitalism without tackling the problem of capitalism's *political* form (liberal parliamentary democracy) is not sufficient, no matter how "radical" it is. Perhaps *the* lure today is the belief that we can undermine capitalism without actually problematizing the liberal-democratic legacy which – as some Leftists claim – although engendered by capitalism, acquired autonomy and can serve to criticize capitalism. This lure is strictly correlative to its apparent opposite: to the pseudo-Deleuzian love–hate fascinating/fascinated poetic depiction of Capital as a rhizomatic monster/vampire which de-territorializes and swallows up everything – indomitable, dynamic, always rising from the dead, each crisis making it stronger, Dionysos–Phoenix reborn. . . . It is in this poetic (anti-)capitalist reference to Marx that Marx is *really* dead: appropriated and deprived of his political sting.

Marx was fascinated by the revolutionary "de-territorializing" impact of capitalism which, in its inexorable dynamic, undermines all stable traditional forms of human interaction – everything solid melts into air, up to the corpses of the Jews who disappeared into the smoke of the Auschwitz gas ovens. . . . He criticized capitalism because its "de-territorialization" was not thorough enough, because it generated new "re-territorializations" – the ultimate obstacle to capitalism is capitalism itself, that is to say, capitalism unleashes a dynamic it is no longer able to contain. Far from being outdated, this claim seems to gain relevance with today's growing deadlocks of globalization, in which the inherently antagonistic nature of capitalism belies its worldwide triumph. The problem, however, is: is it still possible to imagine Communism (or another form of post-capitalist society) as a formation which liberates the de-territorializing dynamic of capitalism, freeing it of its intrinsic constraints?

Marx's fundamental vision was that a new, higher social order (Communism) is possible – an order that would not only maintain but even raise to a higher degree, and fully release in reality, the potential of the self-increasing spiral of productivity which, in capitalism, on account of its inherent obstacle/contradiction, is thwarted again and again by socially destructive economic crises. What Marx overlooked is that – to put it in classic Derridean terms – this inherent obstacle/antagonism as the "condition of impossibility" of the full deployment of productive forces is simultaneously its "condition of possibility": if we abolish the obstacle, the intrinsic contradiction of capitalism, we do not get the fully unbridled drive to productivity finally delivered of its impediment, we lose precisely this productivity that seemed to be generated and simultaneously thwarted by capitalism – if we take away the obstacle, the very potential thwarted by this obstacle dissipates . . . that would be a possible Lacanian critique of Marx, focusing on the ambiguous overlap between surplus-value and surplus-enjoyment.[152]

While this constant self-propelling revolutionizing still holds for high Stalinism, with its total productive mobilization, "stagnant" late Real Socialism legitimized itself (between the lines, at least) as a society in which we can live peacefully, avoiding capitalist competitive stress. This was the last line of defence when, from the late 1960s onwards, after the fall of Khruschchev (the last enthusiast who prophesied during a visit to the USA, that "your grandchildren will be Communists"), it became clear that Real Socialism was losing its competitive edge in the war with capitalism. So stagnant late Real Socialism *was* already, in a way, "socialism with a human face": silently abandoning great historical tasks, it provided the security of everyday life going on in benevolent boredom. Today's *Ostalgie* for defunct Socialism mostly consists in such a conservative nostalgia for that self-satisfied, restricted way of life; even nostalgic anti-capitalist artists from Peter Handke to Joseph Beuys celebrate this aspect of Socialism: the absence of stressful mobilization and frantic commodification. Erich Mielke himself, the chief of the GDR secret police, admitted in simple terms the Communist regime's inability to cope with the capitalist logic of self-propelling excess: "Socialism is so good; so people demand more and more. That's the way things are."[153] Of course, this unexpected shift tells us something about the deficiency of the original Marxist project itself: it reveals the limitation of its goal of unbridled productive mobilization.

How was it that Wim Wenders's *Buena Vista Social Club* (1999), a rediscovery and celebration of pre-revolutionary Cuban music, of the tradition obliterated for many years by the fascinating image of the Revolution, was none the less perceived as a gesture of opening towards today's – "Castro's" – Cuba? Would it not be much more logical to see in this film the nostalgic-reactionary gesture *par excellence*, that of discovering and resuscitating traces of a long-forgotten pre-revolutionary past (musicians in their seventies and eighties, the old dilapidated streets of Havana, as if time has stood still for decades)? It is precisely at this level, however, that we should locate the paradoxical achievement of the film: it depicts the very nostalgia for the pre-revolutionary nightclub musical past as part of the post-revolutionary Cuban present (this is clear in the very first scene, where the old musician comments on old photos of Fidel and Che). This is what made this "apolitical" film a model *political* intervention: by demonstrating how the "pre-revolutionary" musical past was incorporated into post-revolutionary Cuba, it undermines the standard perception of Cuban reality. The price for this, of course, is that the image of Cuba we get is an image of a country where time is at a standstill: nothing happens, no industrial activity; there are old cars, empty railway tracks; people just walk around – and, occasionally, they sing and play music. Wenders's Cuba is therefore the Latin American version of the nostalgic image of Eastern Europe: a space outside history, outside the dynamic of today's second modernization. The paradox (and, perhaps, the final message of the film) is that this was the ultimate function of the Revolution: not to accelerate social development but, on the contrary, to carve out a space in which time stands still.

For They Know Not What They Believe

Capitalism is not just one historical epoch among others – in a way, the once fashionable (and today forgotten) Francis Fukuyama was right: global capitalism *is* "the end of history". Christopher Nolan's outstanding neo-*noir* thriller *Memento* (2000) is, among other things, a perfect metaphor for where we stand today with regard to historical memory. As always, *memento* ultimately refers to *mori* – the film is the story (told in flashback, from the final killing of the alleged murderer to the original crime) of a young man whose wife was raped and killed in his presence, and who, as a consequence of this trauma, suffers from an uncanny mental disorder: while he can remember past events prior to the murder, he can keep in his mind what has happened since the trauma only for a couple of minutes, so the only way for him to organize his recent experience is through external material inscriptions (all the time he takes Polaroid photos, writes notes on scraps of paper, or even has the crucial data tattooed on to his body). With the help of these meagre resources, he desperately tries to trace the murderer and avenge his wife's death; the ending is ambiguous: either there was a crime, but he himself was the murderer; or there was no crime at all, and he simply needs this traumatic point of reference to justify and co-ordinate his recent activities.

Is this not, in a way, the predicament of every one of us today? Are we all not split between the remembrance of the old historical past and the post-historical present which we are unable to insert into the same grand narrative with the past, so that the present is experienced as a confused succession of fragments which rapidly evaporate from our memory? In short, the problem of our post-historical era is not that we cannot remember the past, our history proper (there are more than enough narratives of that), but that we cannot remember the present itself – that we cannot historicize-narrate it properly, that is, acquire a proper cognitive mapping with regard to it: either we refer to some elusive trauma (like the Holocaust) whose unbearable truth is that we ourselves are (co-)responsible for it, or we construct such traumas in order to make sense of our present.

In what precise sense, then, is capitalism "post-historical"? A certain excess which was, as it were, kept in check in previous history, perceived as a local perversion, a limited deviation, is elevated in capitalism to the very principle of social life, in the speculative movement of money begetting more money, of a system which can survive only by constantly revolution-izing its own conditions – that is to say, in which *the thing can survive only as its own excess*, constantly exceeding its own "normal" constraints.

Let us take the case of consumption: before modernity, we were dealing with a direct opposition between moderate consumption and its excess (gluttony, etc.); with capitalism, the excess (the consumption of "useless things") becomes the rule, that is, the elementary form of buying is the act of buying things we "don't really need". There is an ecological limit to growth, of course: it is clear, for example, that the prospect of rapid development in China, with millions of new cars, would – in the present world constellation – provoke a global ecological catastrophe. However, we should not underestimate capitalism's ability to colonize domains which seem to resist it – to turn catastrophes caused by its own development into incentives to further development. If it is one of capitalism's highest achievements to turn every human catastrophe (from illness to war) into a source of lucrative investment, why should it not also do this with ecology? The notion that a serious ecological catastrophe will awaken us from capitalism and turn us into devoted no-growth, no-profit producers fatefully underestimates capitalism's capacity to turn catastrophes into blessings in disguise.[154] This is why we should remain faithful to Marx's fundamental insight: unbridled capitalist expansion encounters its limit not in an external factor – the available ecological resources, for example – but in itself: the limit of capitalism is absolutely intrinsic to it – or, as Marx himself put it, the limit of capitalism is capital itself.[155]

And perhaps it is only today, under the global capitalism in its "post-industrial" digitalized form, that – to put it in Hegelian terms – really existing capitalism is reaching the level of its notion: perhaps we should reiterate Marx's old anti-evolutionist dictum (incidentally, taken verbatim from Hegel) that the anatomy of man provides the key to the anatomy of a monkey – that in order to deploy the inherent notional structure of a social formation, you must start with its most developed form. Marx located the elementary capitalist antagonism in the opposition between use- and exchange-value: in capitalism, the potentials of this opposition are fully realized, the domain of exchange-value acquires autonomy, is transformed into the spectre of self-propelling speculative capital which uses the productive capacities and needs of actual people only as its dispensable temporal embodiment. Marx derived the very notion of economic crisis from this gap: a crisis occurs when reality catches up with the illusory self-generating mirage of money begetting more money – this speculative madness cannot go on indefinitely; it has to explode in ever stronger crises. The ultimate root of the crisis, for Marx, is the gap between use-value and exchange-value: the logic of exchange-value follows its own path, its own mad dance, irrespective of the real needs of real people.

It may appear that this analysis is more relevant than ever today, when the tension between the virtual universe and the real is reaching almost tangibly unbearable proportions: on the one hand, we have crazy solipsistic speculations about futures, mergers, and so on, following their own inherent logic; on the other, reality is catching up in the form of ecological catastrophes, poverty, the collapse of social life in the Third World, mad cow disease. This is why cyber-capitalists can appear to be the paradigmatic capitalists today; this is why Bill Gates can dream of cyberspace as providing the frame for what he calls "frictionless capitalism".

What we have here is an ideological short circuit between the two versions of the gap between reality and virtuality: the gap between real production and the virtual/spectral domain of Capital, and the gap between experiential reality and the Virtual Reality of cyberspace. The true horror of the slogan "frictionless capitalism" is that although actual "frictions" continue, they become invisible, repressed into the netherworld outside our "postmodern" post-industrial universe; this is why the "frictionless" universe of digitalized communication, technological gadgets, and so on, is always haunted by the notion that there is a global catastrophe just around the corner, threatening to explode at any moment.

It actually seems that the cyberspace gap between my fascinating screen persona and the miserable flesh which is "me" offscreen translates into immediate experience the gap between the Real of the speculative circulation of capital and the drab reality of the impoverished masses. On today's market, we find a whole series of products deprived of their malignant property: coffee without caffeine, cream without fat, beer without alcohol. . . . Virtual Reality simply *generalizes* this procedure of offering a product deprived of its substance: it provides *reality itself* deprived of its substance, of the hard resistant kernel of the Real – just as decaffeinated coffee smells and tastes like the real coffee without being real coffee, Virtual Reality is experienced as reality without being so.[156] In the case of Virtual Reality, the difference does not concern only quantity: coffee without caffeine is still part of reality, whereas Virtual Reality suspends the very notion of reality . . .[157] Is a recourse to "reality" which will sooner or later catch up with the virtual game, however, really the only way to conduct a genuine critique of capitalism? What if the problem of capitalism is not this solipsistic mad dance, but precisely the opposite: that it continues to disavow its distance from "reality", that it presents itself as serving the real needs of real people? The originality of Marx is that he played both cards simultaneously: the origin of capitalist crises is the gap between use- and exchange-value, *and* capitalism constrains the free deployment of productivity.

The problem with the deconstructionist or Deleuzian poetry of capital is that it totally suspends Marx's intention to provide an actual economic analysis of existing capitalism, not a critical philosophy of commodity fetishism and reification. Let us take Derrida's *Specters of Marx*:[158] does it not contain a tension between Derrida's "official" anti-capitalist claim (his call for a "New International" against global capitalism) and his analysis of the irreducible spectrality which has to supplement the gap of every positive ontological edifice, as the proto-transcendental a priori which opens up the space for the spectrality of capital? Does this not compel Derrida to conclude that, ultimately, Marx's critique of capitalism and his revolutionary project of a Communist society constituted an attempt to reduce (or, rather, contain) the dimension of spectrality and *différance* within the positive ontological frame of unalienated humanity in which the collective "general intellect"[159] regulates its reproduction as a totally (self-)transparent process? In short, is not Derrida's conclusion that *capital is différance*: a movement which never reaches completion (the full circle of its circulation); which always *postpones* the final settling of accounts?

Capitalism expands by repeatedly "borrowing from the future", by referring to some indefinite future moment of "full reimbursement" which is forever deferred, like the constant rescheduling of the debts of Second and Third World countries by the IMF, with the fictional notion (which is operative, although no one believes in it) that, at some future moment, these debts will be repaid. It was John Maynard Keynes who, in his criticism of the idea that, in the long term, reality has to catch up with capital's speculative movement, added acerbically that in the long term we are all dead: actual economic life, however, is precisely the endless postponement of this full settling of accounts. So, when Kojin Karatani, in his otherwise admirable Derridean reading of Marx's *Capital*, claims that capitalism is already its own deconstruction, that it is no longer a stable self-centred system disrupted by excesses and interferences, but a system which, precisely, maintains itself through incessant self-revolutionizing; a system whose instability is its very strength; one which is, in a way, in excess with regard to itself (this, incidentally, is ultimately just a deconstructionist rephrasing of Marx's formulations from the *Communist Manifesto*), he ultimately arrives at a purely formal definition of capitalism as a self-referential system sustained by its very structural imbalance:

> The self-referential formal system is dynamic because of incessant internal slippage (self-differentiation). It cannot maintain a definitive meta-level or center that systematizes a system. Rather, like the "multiplicity of subjects" that Nietzsche once proposed, it is multicentered.... In short, the self-referential formal system is always disequilibriated and excessive.[160]

How, then, is radical anti-capitalism possible within these co-ordinates? Is the notion of the anti-capitalist struggle as the struggle between two spectralities, the "bad" spectrality of capital and the "good" spectrality of the messianic promise of justice and democracy-to-come, strong enough? Are we not – in so far as we remain within this frame – compelled to apply the deconstructive logic of supplement to this opposition itself, and to claim that the "good" spectrality of the messianic promise is always-already contaminated by the "bad" spectrality of capital? The standard deconstructionist notion of how capitalism is an order which generates/contains its own excess, so that it *is* already its own *différance*, lacking any fixed centre to be subverted, thus confuses what Marx so convincingly – and, I am tempted to add, seductively – describes as the intrinsic "theological whimsies" of capital with his theory of the class struggle, and of how capitalism has inexorably to produce an excess it will no longer be able to contain.

Let us take a closer look at Marx's classic description of the passage from money to capital, with its explicit allusions to the Hegelian and Christian background. First, there is the simple act of market exchange, in which I sell in order to buy – I sell the product I own or made in order to buy another one which is of some use to me: "The simple circulation of commodities – selling in order to buy – is a means of carrying out a purpose unconnected with circulation, namely, the appropriation of use-values, the satisfaction of wants."[161] What happens with the emergence of capital is not just the simple reversal of C–M–C (Commodity–Money–Commodity) into M–C–M – that is, investing money into some commodity in order to sell it again, and thus get back (more) money; the key effect of this reversal is the *externalization* of circulation: "The circulation of money as capital is, on the contrary, an end in itself, for the expansion of value takes place only within this constantly renewed movement. The circulation of capital has therefore no limits."[162] Crucial here is the difference between the capitalist and the traditional miser, hoarding his treasure in a secret hideout, and the capitalist who augments his treasure by throwing it into circulation:

> The restless never-ending process of profit-making alone is what he aims at. This boundless greed after riches, this passionate chase after exchange-value, is common to the capitalist and the miser; but while the miser is merely a capitalist gone mad, the capitalist is a rational miser. The never-ending augmentation of exchange-value, which the miser strives after, by seeking to save his money from circulation, is attained by the more acute capitalist, by constantly throwing it afresh into circulation.[163]

None the less, this madness of the miser is not something which simply disappears with the rise of "normal" capitalism, or its pathological deviation. It is, rather, *inherent* to it: the miser has his moment of triumph in the economic *crisis*. In a crisis, it is not – as you would expect – money which loses its value, and we have to resort to the "real" value of commodities; commodities themselves (the embodiment of "real [use-]value") become useless, because there is no one to buy them. In a crisis:

> money suddenly and immediately changes from its merely nominal shape, money of account, into hard cash. Profane commodities can no longer replace it. The use-value of commodities becomes value-less, and their value vanishes in the face of their own form of value. The bourgeois, drunk with prosperity and arrogantly certain of himself, has just declared that money is a purely imaginary creation. "Commodities alone are money," he said. But now the opposite cry resounds over the markets of the world: only money is a commodity. . . . In a crisis, the antithesis between commodities and their value-form, money, is raised to the level of an absolute contradiction.[164]

It is crucial how, in this elevation of money to the status of the only true commodity ("The capitalist knows that all commodities, however scurvy they may look, or however badly they may smell, are in faith and in truth money, inwardly circumcised Jews"[165]), Marx resorts to the precise Pauline definition of Christians as "inwardly circumcised Jews": Christians do not need real external circumcision (that is, the abandonment of ordinary commodities with use-values, dealing only with money), since they know that each of these ordinary commodities is already "inwardly circumcised", that its true substance is money. It is even more crucial that Marx describes the passage from money to capital in the precise Hegelian terms of the passage from substance to subject:

> In truth, however, value is here [in capital] the active factor in a process, in which, while constantly assuming the form in turn of money and commodities, it at the same time changes in magnitude, differentiates itself by throwing off surplus-value from itself; the original value, in other words, expands sponta-neously. For the movement, in the course of which it adds surplus-value, is its own movement, its expansion, therefore, is automatic expansion. Because it is value, it has acquired the occult quality of being able to add value to itself. It brings forth living offspring, or, at the least, lays golden eggs. . . .
>
> In simple circulation, C–M–C, the value of commodities attained at the most a form independent of their use-values, i.e., the form of money; but the same value now in the circulation M–C–M, or the circulation of capital, suddenly presents itself as an independent substance, endowed with a motion of its own, passing through a life-process of its own, in which money and commodities are mere forms which it assumes and casts off in turn. Nay, more: instead of simply representing the relations of commodities, it enters now, so to say, into private relations with itself. It differentiates itself as original value from itself as surplus-value; as the father differentiates himself from himself *qua* the son, yet both are one and of one age: for only by the surplus-value of 10 pounds does the 100 pounds originally advanced become capital, and so on as this takes place, so soon as the son, and by the son, the father is begotten, so soon does their difference vanish, and they again become one, 110 pounds.[166]

In short, capital is money which is no longer a mere substance of wealth, its universal embodiment, but value which, through its circulation, generates more value, value which mediates-posits itself, retroactively positing its own presuppositions. First, money appears as a mere means of the exchange of commodities: instead of endless bartering, we first exchange our product for the universal equivalent of all commodities, which can then be exchanged for any commodity we may need. Then, once the circulation of capital is set in motion, the relationship is inverted, the means turns into an end in itself – the very passage through the "material" domain of use-values (the production of commodities which satisfy individuals' particular needs) is posited as a moment of what is substantially the self-movement of capital itself – from this moment on, the true aim is no longer the satisfaction of individuals' needs, but simply more money, the endless repeating of the circulation as such. . . . This arcane circular movement of self-positing is then equated with the central Christian tenet of the identity of God the Father and His son, of the immaculate conception by means of which the single Father directly (without a female spouse) begets his only son, and thus forms what is arguably the ultimate single-parent family.

Is capital, then, the true Subject/Substance? Yes and no: for Marx, this self-engendering circular movement is – to put it in Freudian terms – precisely the capitalist "unconscious fantasy" which parasitizes upon the proletariat as "pure substanceless subjectivity"; for this reason, capital's speculative self-generating dance has a limit, and it brings about the conditions of its own collapse. This insight allows us to solve the key interpretative problem of the quote above: how are we to read its first three words: "*In truth, however*"?

First, of course, they imply that this truth has to be asserted against some false appearance or experience: the everyday experience that the ultimate goal of capital's circulation is still the satisfaction of human needs, that capital is simply a means of bringing about this satisfaction in a more efficient way. This "truth", however, is *not* the reality of capitalism: in reality, capital does not engender itself, but exploits the worker's surplus-value. So there is a necessary third level to be added to the simple opposition of subjective experience (of capital as a simple means of efficiently satisfying people's needs) and objective social reality (of exploitation): the "objective deception", the disavowed "unconscious" fantasy (of the mysterious self-generating circular movement of capital), which is the truth (albeit not the reality) of the capitalist process. To quote Lacan again, truth has the structure of a fiction: the only way to formulate the truth of capital is to describe this fiction of its "immaculate" self-generating movement. And this insight also allows us to locate the weakness of the above-mentioned "deconstructionist" appropriation of Marx's analysis of capitalism: although it emphasizes the endless process of deferral which characterizes this movement, as well as its fundamental inconclusiveness, its self-blockage, the "deconstructionist" retelling still describes the *fantasy* of capital – it describes what individuals believe, although they don't know it.[167]

All this means that the urgent task of economic analysis today is, again, to repeat Marx's "critique of political economy", without succumbing to the temptation of the multitude of ideologies in "post-industrial" societies. The key change concerns the status of private property: the ultimate element of power and control is no longer the last link in the chain of investments, the firm or individual who "really owns" the means of production. The ideal capitalist today functions in a wholly different way: investing borrowed money, "really owning" nothing, even in debt, but none the less controlling things. A corporation is owned by another corporation, which is again borrowing money from banks, which may ultimately manipulate money owned by ordinary people like ourselves. With Bill Gates, the "private property of the means of production" becomes meaningless, at least in the normal meaning of the term.[168]

The paradox of this virtualization of capitalism is ultimately the same as that of the electron in elementary particle physics. The mass of each element in our reality is composed of its mass at rest plus the surplus provided by the acceleration of its movement; an electron's mass at rest, however, is zero; its mass consists only of the surplus generated by the acceleration of its movement, as if we are dealing with a nothing which acquires some deceptive substance only by magically spinning itself into an excess of itself. Does not today's virtual capitalist function in a similar way – his "net value" is zero, he directly operates just with the surplus, borrowing from the future?[169]

"Cultural Capitalism"

This virtual capitalism, brought to its logical conclusion, confronts us with the Master-Signifier at its purest. Just imagine a totally "outsourced" company – let us imagine, say, that Nike "outsources" not only its material production (to Indonesian or Central American contractors), the distribution of its products, and its marketing strategy and advertising campaigns, but also the design itself, to some selected top designer agency, and, moreover, borrows money from a bank. Nike would therefore be "nothing in itself" – nothing but the pure brand name "Nike", the "empty" Master-Signifier which connotes the cultural experience pertaining to a certain "lifestyle". This is where the polemics against the fetishized role of the logo in our daily lives goes wrong: it overlooks how the efficiency of different logos is parasitical upon a certain gap (between the Master-Signifier and the chain of "normal" signifiers) which pertains to language as such – there is no such thing as a language whose terms directly designate reality, bypassing "lifestyle" connotations.

Two new labels have recently established themselves in the fruit juice (and also ice-cream) market: "forest fruit" and "multivitamin". Both are associated with a clearly identified flavour, but the point is that the connection between the label and what it designates is ultimately contingent: the label cannot be directly grounded in its designated content. A different combination of forest fruits would produce a different flavour, and it would be possible to generate the same flavour artificially (the same, of course, goes for "multivitamin" juice), so that we can easily imagine a child who, on being given authentic home-made forest fruit juice, complains to his mother: "That's not what I want! I want the *real* forest fruit juice!" It is all too easy to dismiss this as an example of the way fixed designations function within commodity fetishism: what such examples reveal is a gap which pertains to language "as such": there is always a gap between what a word actually means (in this case, the flavour recognized as "multivitamin") and what its meaning would be were it to function literally (any juice enriched with a multitude of vitamins). The autonomous "symbolic efficiency" is so strong that it can sometimes generate effects which are almost uncannily mysterious; I clearly remember how I reacted when, for the first time, I tasted "*zuppa inglese* [sherry trifle – literally 'English soup']" Italian ice cream: although I had no idea whatsoever what this "English soup" tastes (or should taste) like, the effect of recognition was instant and spontaneous – I immediately "knew" that what I was licking tasted like *zuppa inglese*. . . .

Jeremy Rifkin has called this new stage of commodification "cultural capitalism".[170] In "cultural capitalism", the relationship between an object and its symbol-image is turned around: the image does not represent the product; rather, the product represents the image.[171] We buy a product – an organic apple, for example – because it represents the image of a healthy lifestyle. This reversal is brought to its extreme when a secondary association becomes the ultimate point of reference, as in the case of Mozart's Piano Concerto No. 20: since the 1960s, when the second movement was used for the soundtrack of the popular Swedish sentimental love story *Elvira Madigan*, even "serious" recordings of it usually add the film's title: Mozart, Piano Concerto No. 20 ("Elvira Madigan"), so that when we buy and listen to the CD, the experience we buy is that of an insipid Romantic melodrama. . . . Along the same lines, the main reason why so many people still continue to go to "real" shops is not so much that you can "see and feel" the product itself, but that you can "enjoy browsing itself as a recreational activity".[172]

As the example of buying an organic apple indicates, the very ecological protest against the ruthless capitalist exploitation of natural resources is already caught in the commodification of experiences: although ecology perceives itself as a protest against the digitalization/virtualization of our daily lives, and advocates a return to the direct experience of sensual material reality, in all its unpredictable fragility and substance, ecology itself is branded as a new lifestyle – what we are really buying when we buy "organic food", and so on, is already a certain cultural experience, the experience of a "healthy ecological lifestyle". The same goes for every return to "reality": a recent TV advertisement shown on all the main US channels features a group of ordinary people at a barbecue with country music and dancing, with the accompanying message: "Beef. Real food for real people." The irony is that the beef offered here as the symbol of a certain lifestyle (that of "real" grass-roots working-class Americans) is much more chemically and genetically manipulated than the "organic" food consumed by "artificial" yuppies.

Ultimately, Nation itself is turning into an experiential commodity: we buy things which enable us to experience ourselves as participating in a Nationhood. . . . And I am tempted to risk even a step further, following Benedict Anderson's thesis on nations as "imagined communities":[173] what if nations were "artificial" formations from the very outset? Is not the rise of modern nations (as opposed to premodern "organic" communities) co-dependent with the rise of capitalism, that is, of commodity production? Is not "nation" the undead spectre of a Community which starts to haunt us after the market economy has killed the "living" organic communities? Nation is an "imagined community" not only in the sense that its material base is the mass media, not the direct mutual acquaintance of its members; it is "imagined" also in a more radical sense of an "imaginary supplement" to the social reality of disintegration and irresolvable antagonisms. Nation thus functioned from the very beginning as a fetish: the point is not to believe in the National Cause, but to use this belief as a prop which enables us to engage in our egotistic pursuits ("we are really doing it for our nation").

The ultimate example of not only commodity fetishism, but, in a much more literal way, fetishism itself commodified, is today's Japan, where you can buy from vending machines, alongside cans of Coke and prepacked food, panties guaranteed to have been worn by young girls. What we are witnessing today, the defining feature of "postmodern" capitalism, is the direct commodification of our experience itself: what we are buying on the market are less and less products (material objects) which we want to own, and more and more life-experiences – experiences of sex, eating, communicating, cultural consumption, participating in a lifestyle. Material objects are increasingly there simply to serve as props for this experience, which is increasingly offered for free to seduce us into buying the true "experiential commodity",[174] like the free cellular phones we get if we sign a one-year contract:

As cultural production comes to dominate the economy, goods increasingly take on the qualities of props. They become mere platforms or settings around which elaborate cultural meanings are acted out. They lose their material importance and take on symbolic importance. They become less objects and more tools to help facilitate the performance of lived experiences.[175]

This is the trend – from "Buy this DVD player, and get five DVDs for free!" to "Commit yourself to buying DVDs from us regularly (or, even better, buy access to a cable which allows you free access to digitalized movies), and we'll give you a DVD player for free!" – or, to quote Mark Slouka's succinct observation: "As more of the hours of our days are spent in synthetic environments . . . life itself is turned into a commodity. Someone makes it for us; we buy it from them. We become the consumers of our own lives."[176] Here the logic of market exchange is brought to a kind of Hegelian self-relating identity: we no longer buy objects, we ultimately buy (the time of) our own life. Michel Foucault's notion of turning one's Self itself into a work of art thus finds unexpected confirmation: I buy my bodily fitness by visiting fitness clubs; I buy my spiritual enlightenment by enrolling in transcendental meditation courses; I buy my public persona by going to restaurants frequented by people with whom I want to be associated.

Although this shift may appear to be a break with the capitalist market economy, we could argue that it brings its logic to its consequent climax. The industrial market economy involves the temporal gap between the purchasing of a commodity and its consumption: from the seller's point of view, the affair is over the moment he sells his commodity – what happens afterwards (what the purchaser does with it, the direct consumption of the commodity) does not concern him; in the commodification of experience, this gap is closed, *the consumption itself is the commodity bought.* The possibility of closing this gap, however, is inscribed into the very nominalistic logic of the modern society and its community. That is to say: since the purchaser buys a commodity for its use-value, and since this use-value can be broken down into its various components (when I buy a Land Rover, I do so in order to drive myself and other people around, *and* to signal my participation in a certain lifestyle associated with the Land Rover), there is a logical next step towards commodifying and selling these components directly (hiring a car instead of buying it, etc.). At the end of all this, therefore, is the solipsistic fact of subjective experience: since the subjective experience of individual consumption is the ultimate goal of the entire production process, it is logical to bypass the object, and to commodify and sell this experience directly. And perhaps, instead of interpreting this commodification of experiences as the result of a shift in the prevailing mode of subjectivity (from the classical bourgeois subject focused on possessing objects, to the "postmodern" Protean subject focused on the wealth of his experiences), we should, rather, conceive of this Protean subject itself as the effect of the commodification of experiences.[177]

This, of course, compels us to reformulate completely the classic Marxist topic of "reification" and "commodity fetishism", in so far as this topic still relies on the notion of the fetish as a concrete object whose stable presence obfuscates its social mediation. Paradoxically, fetishism reaches its acme precisely when the fetish itself is "de-materialized", turned into a fluid "immaterial" virtual entity; money fetishism will culminate with the passage to its electronic form, when the last traces of its materiality will disappear – electronic money is the third form, after "real" money which directly embodies its value (gold, silver) and paper money which, although it is a "mere sign" with no intrinsic value, still clings to its material existence. And it is only at this stage, when money becomes a purely virtual point of reference, that it finally assumes the form of an indestructible spectral presence: I owe you a thousand dollars, and no matter how many material notes I burn, I will still owe you a thousand dollars – the debt is inscribed somewhere in virtual digital space. . . . Does not the same go for warfare? Far from heralding twenty-first-century warfare, the WTC twin towers explosion and collapse in September 2001 were, rather, the last spectacular cry of twentieth-century warfare. What awaits us is something much more uncanny: the spectre of an "immaterial" war where the attack is invisible – viruses, poisons which can be anywhere and nowhere. On the level of visible material reality, nothing happens, no big explosion, yet the known universe starts to collapse; life disintegrates. . . . We are entering a new era of paranoiac warfare, in which our biggest task will be to identify the enemy and his weapons. It is only with this thorough "de-materialization", when Marx's famous thesis from *The Communist Manifesto* according to which, in capitalism, "all that is solid melts into air'[178] acquires a much more literal meaning than the one Marx had in mind, when not only is our material social reality dominated by the spectral/speculative movement of Capital, but this reality itself is progressively "spectralized" (the "Protean Self" instead of the old self-identical Subject, the elusive fluidity of its experiences instead of the stability of the owned objects); in short: when the usual relationship between solid material objects and fluid ideas is turned around (objects are progressively dissolved in fluid experiences, while the only stable things are virtual symbolic obligations) – it is only at this point that what Derrida called the spectral aspect of capitalism[179] is fully actualized.

Convincing as it may sound, however, Rifkin's vision has its limitations:

he passes all too rapidly from an "industrial" to a "post-industrial" order, in which (so we are repeatedly told) market and ownership no longer play the key role. What about the obvious all-pervasive fact that *the market is still here*? First, "cultural capitalism"'s focus on marketing experiences, not objects, has to rely on a complex material infrastructure (food, machinery, etc.); second, experiences themselves still have to be sold, and thus marketed – there are people who *own* them (in the guise of copyrights on brand names, etc.). So, instead of claiming that market and ownership no longer play the key role, we should, rather, argue that the character of ownership is changing: what matters is less and less the ownership of material objects, and more and more the ownership of "immaterial" formulas of experiences (copyrights, logos . . .).

The key insight is that *"cultural capitalism" is not a totality* – if we are to grasp it in its totality, we have to include both poles: the production of cultural experiences as well as "real" material production. What characterizes "late capitalism" is the split between the production of cultural experiences as such and its (partially invisible) material base, between the Spectacle (of theatrical experience) and its secret staging mechanisms; far from disappearing, material production is still here, transfunctionalized into the supporting mechanism for the stage production. In today's ideological perception, work itself (manual labour as opposed to the "symbolic" activity of cultural production), not sex, appears as the site of obscene indecency to be concealed from the public eye. The tradition which goes back to Wagner's *Rheingold* and Lang's *Metropolis*, the tradition in which the work goes on underground, in dark caves, culminates today in the "invisibility" of the millions of anonymous workers sweating in Third World factories, from Chinese Gulags to Indonesian or Brazilian assembly lines – the West can afford to babble about the "disappearing working class", even as its traces are easily discernible all around us: all we need to do is to look at the little label "Made in . . . (China, Indonesia, Bangladesh, Guatemala)" on mass products, from jeans to Walkmans.

What is crucial in this tradition is the equation of labour with *crime* – the idea that labour, hard work, is an indecent criminal activity to be hidden from the public eye. The only place in Hollywood cinema where we see the production process in all its intensity is when the hero of an action film penetrates the master-criminal's secret domain and finds a site of intense labour (distilling and packaging drugs, constructing a rocket that will destroy New York . . .). When, in a James Bond movie, the master-criminal, after capturing Bond, usually takes him on a tour of his illegal factory, is this not the closest Hollywood comes to the proud socialist-realist presentation of factory production? And the function of Bond's intervention, of course, is to explode this site of production in a fireball, allowing us to return to the daily semblance of our existence in a world where the working class is "disappearing".[180]

Today, the two superpowers, the USA and China, relate more and more as Capital and Labour. The USA is turning into a country of managerial planning, banking, services, and so on, while its "disappearing working class" (except for migrant Chicanos and others who work predominantly in the service economy) is reappearing in China, where the majority of US products, from toys to electronic hardware, are manufactured in ideal conditions for capitalist exploitation: no strikes, limited freedom of movement for the workforce, low wages. . . . Far from being simply antagonistic, the relationship between China and the USA is, at the same time, deeply symbiotic. The irony of history is that China fully deserves the title "workers' state": it is the state of the working class for American capital. Although Rifkin is aware that the cyber-commodification of experience of "cultural capitalism" affects only 20 per cent of humankind, he does not develop this *structural co-dependency* between this 20 per cent and the remaining 80 per cent.

How, then, are we to situate not only Third World manual labour sweatshops but *digital* sweatshops like the one in Bangalore, where tens of thousands of Indians programme software for Western corporations? Is it adequate to designate these Indians as the "intellectual proletariat"? Will they be the final revenge of the Third World? What are the consequences of the (for the conservative Germans, at least) unsettling fact that, after decades of importing hundreds of thousands of physical immigrant workers, Germany has now discovered that it needs at least tens of thousands of intellectual immigrant workers, mostly computer programmers? The disabling alternative of today's Marxism is what to do about the growing importance of "immaterial production" today (cyber-workers)? Do we insist that only those involved in "real" material production are the working class, or do we take the fateful step of accepting that these "symbolic workers" are the (true) proletarians of today? We should resist this step, because it obfuscates the division between immaterial and material production, the split in the working class between (as a rule, geographically separated) cyber-workers and material workers (programmers in the USA or India; sweatshops in China or Indonesia).

Perhaps it is the figure of the unemployed (jobless) person who stands for the pure proletarian today: the substantial determination of an unemployed person remains that of a worker, but he or she is prevented from either actualizing or renouncing it, so that he or she remains suspended in the potentiality of a worker who cannot work. Perhaps today we are, in a sense, "all jobless": jobs tend to be based more and more on short-term contracts, so that the jobless state is the rule, the zero-level, and the temporary job the exception. This, then, should also be the answer to advocates of "post-industrial society" whose message to workers is that their time is over, that their very existence is obsolete, and that all they can count on is purely humanitarian compassion: there is less and less room for workers in the universe of today's capital, and we should draw the only logical conclusion from this fact. If today's "post-industrial" society needs fewer and fewer workers to reproduce itself (20 per cent of the workforce, on some accounts), then *it is not workers who are in excess, but Capital itself.*

This limitation of Rifkin's vision also accounts for the weakness of his proposed solution to our crisis – you can almost touch the discrepancy between the outstanding first part of his book and the "regression" into postmodern New Age jargon in the second part. Rifkin's premiss is culture as the communal soil of human existence, which precedes the economy: if we are able to produce and exchange objects, we have to share a common space of cultural understanding, and every material production is ultimately parasitic upon this space. As a result, when the market threatens to colonize and swallow up culture, it unknowingly drains off its own resources; we should therefore find a new balance between market and culture by revitalizing civil society and community life, affirming their autonomy against market forces – we need not only access to commodities, but even more access to our shared cultural substance. . . . This pseudo-solution cannot fail to remind us of the pseudo-Oriental New Age talk about the need to establish the balance of opposite principles – in this case, of the market economy and its cultural foundation.

Rifkin is not alone – many other analysts have also pointed out how the current expansion of global causes a progressive disintegration of societal links: the old "organic" forms of civil society and political organization are increasingly replaced with forms of interaction organized on the market model; the ultimate consequence of this stance is the idea, proposed by some neoliberal ideologues, that the political logic of decision-making as such should be replaced with the economic one – the true voting in our societies goes on every day, when, by buying a product or service, we "vote" for it against its competitors; along the same lines, we should strive to treat the state apparatus as just another "service organization" a society chooses to buy among a choice of competitors. (Is not the logical consequence of this stance that the state flag itself, the symbol of national community, is turned into just another company logo?) It is becoming increasingly clear, however, that the market cannot play the role of pre-market forms of social life: a shopping mall cannot replace a political meeting proper; an opinion poll cannot serve as a substitute for genuine electoral engagement; paid courses on "spiritual growth" cannot replace real educational interaction.

Furthermore, does not the rise of so-called "gated communities" – residential quarters isolated from their environs, the upper-class equivalent of ghettos – show how the First World and the Third World can no longer be simply opposed as distinct political unities: they are developing more and more within each political unity (state, city)? So when, a decade ago, Francis Fukuyama launched his pseudo-Hegelian thesis on the "end of history", he was right, although not in the way he thought: in so far as the proper opposite of history is nature, the "end of history" means that the social process itself is more and more "naturalized", experienced as a new form of "fate", as a blind uncontrollable force. There are multiple reactions to and symptoms of this threat: desperate attempts to revive old forms of "organic" communal life, from conservative grass-roots organizations to more liberal attempts at the revival of civil society; calls for stronger state control and recourse to violent measures to maintain "law and order"; and so on. These reactions are doomed to failure precisely in so far as they are mere reactions: instead of challenging the market logic itself, they resign themselves to mere damage limitation.

A Cyberspace Lenin?

So where is Lenin in all this? According to the prevailing doxa, in the years after the October Revolution Lenin's loss of faith in the creative capacities of the masses led him to emphasize the role of science and the scientists, to rely on the authority of the expert: he hailed "the beginning of that very happy time when politics will recede into the background, . . . and engineers and agronomists will do most of the talking".[181] Technocratic post-politics? Lenin's ideas about how the road to socialism runs through the terrain of monopoly capitalism may sound dangerously naive today:

> Capitalism has created an accounting *apparatus* in the shape of the banks, syndicates, postal service, consumers' societies, and office employees' unions. *Without big banks socialism would be impossible*. . . . Our task is here merely to *lop off* what *capitalistically mutilates* this excellent apparatus, to make it

even bigger, even more democratic, even more comprehensive. . . . This will be country-wide *book-keeping*, country-wide *accounting* of the production and distribution of goods, this will be, so to speak, something in the nature of the *skeleton* of socialist society.[182]

Is this not the most radical expression of Marx's notion of the *general intellect* regulating all social life in a transparent way, of a post-political world in which the "administration of people" is supplanted by the "administration of things"? It is easy, of course, to play against this quote the tune of the "critique of instrumental reason" and "administered world [*verwaltete Welt*]": the "totalitarian" potential is inscribed in this very form of total social control. It is easy to observe sarcastically that in the Stalinist epoch, the apparatus of social administration did actually become "*even bigger*". Furthermore, is not this post-political vision the very opposite of the Maoist notion of the eternity of the class struggle ("everything is political")?

However, are things really so unambiguous? What if we replaced the (obviously dated) example of the central bank with the World Wide Web, today's perfect candidate for the General Intellect? Dorothy Sayers claimed that Aristotle's *Poetics* is in fact the theory of the detective novel *avant la lettre* – since poor Aristotle didn't yet know about the detective novel, he had to refer to the only examples at his disposal, the tragedies. . . .[183] Along the same lines, Lenin was in fact developing the theory of the role of the World Wide Web, but since the World Wide Web was unknown to him, he had to refer to the unfortunate central banks. Consequently, can we also say that "*without the World Wide Web socialism would be impossible. . . . Our task is here merely to lop off* what *capitalistically mutilates* this excellent apparatus, to make it *even bigger*, even more democratic, even more comprehensive"? In this context, I am tempted to revive the old, opprobrious and half-forgotten Marxian dialectics of the productive forces and the relations of production: it is already a cliché to claim that, ironically, it was this very dialectics which buried Really Existing Socialism: Socialism was unable to sustain the passage from industrial to post-industrial economy.

One of the tragicomic victims of the disintegration of Socialism in ex-Yugoslavia was an old Communist apparatchik interviewed by Ljubljana student radio in 1988. The Communists knew they were losing power, so they desperately tried to please everyone. When this old cadre was asked provocative questions about his sex life by the student reporters, he desperately tried to prove that he was in touch with the younger generation; since, however, the only language he had at his disposal was wooden bureaucratese, the result was an uncanny obscene mixture – statements like "Sexuality is an important component of my daily activity. Touching my wife between her thighs gives me great new incentives for my work of building socialism." And when we read East German official documents from the 1970s and early 1980s, formulating their project of turning the GDR into a kind of Silicon Valley of the Eastern European Socialist bloc, we cannot avoid the same impression of a tragicomic gap between form and content: while they were fully aware that digitalization was the way of the future, they approached it in terms of the old Socialist logic of industrial planning – their very words betrayed the fact that they did not understand what was really going on, the social consequences of digitalization.

However, does capitalism really provide the "natural" frame of relations of production for the digital universe? Is there not also, in the World Wide Web, an explosive potential for capitalism itself? Is not the lesson of the Microsoft monopoly precisely the Leninist one: instead of fighting this monopoly through the state apparatus (remember the court-ordered splitting-up of the Microsoft Corporation), would it not be more "logical" simply to *nationalize* it, making it freely accessible?[184] So today, I am thus tempted to paraphrase Lenin's well-known slogan "Socialism = electrification + the power of the soviets": "Socialism = free access to the Internet + *the power of the soviets*." (The second element is crucial, since it specifies the only social organization within which the Internet can realize its liberating potential; without it, we would have a new version of crude technological determinism.)

The key antagonism of the so-called new (digital) industries is thus how we can maintain the form of (private) property, the only form within which the logic of profit can prevail (consider the Napster problem: Napster was an organization offering software for the free circulation of copyright recordings of pop music). And do not the legal complications in biogenetics point in the same direction? The crucial element of the new international trade agreements is the "protection of intellectual property": in a merger, whenever a big First World company takes over a Third World company, the first thing they do is close down the research department. Phenomena emerge here which subject the notion of property to extraordinary dialectical paradoxes: in India, local communities suddenly discover that medical practices and materials they have been using for centuries are now owned by American companies, so they have to be bought from them; now that the biogenetic companies are patenting genes, we are all discovering that parts of ourselves, our genetic components, are already under copyright, owned by others.

The outcome of this crisis of private property and the means of production, however, is by no means guaranteed – this is where we should take into account the ultimate paradox of Stalinist society: against capitalism – which is a class society, albeit in principle egalitarian, without direct hierarchical divisions – "mature" Stalinism is a classless society articulated in precisely defined hierarchical groups (top *nomenklatura*, technical intelligence, the army . . .). This means that even for Stalinism, the classic Marxist notion of the class struggle is no longer adequate to describe its hierarchy and domination: in the Soviet Union from the late 1920s onwards, the key social division was defined not by property, but by direct access to power mechanisms and to the privileged material and cultural conditions of life (food, accommodation, healthcare, freedom of travel, education). And perhaps the ultimate irony of history will be that, just as Lenin's vision of "central bank Socialism" can be properly read only retrospectively, from today's World Wide Web, the Soviet Union provided the first model of a developed "post-property" society, of the true "late capitalism" in which the ruling class will be defined by direct access to the (informational, administrative) means of social power and control, and to other material and social privileges: the point will no longer be to own companies, but directly to run them, to have the right to use a private jet, to have access to the best healthcare, and so on – privileges which will be acquired not by owning property, but by other (educational, managerial, etc.) mechanisms.

This, then, is the approaching crisis which will hold out the perspective of a new emancipatory struggle, of the complete reinvention of the political: not the old Marxist choice between private property and its nationalization, but the choice between a hierarchical and an egalitarian post-property society. Here, the old Marxist thesis on how bourgeois freedom and equality are based on private property and market conditions takes an unexpected twist: what market relations enable are (at least) "formal" freedom and "legal" equality: since social hierarchy can be sustained through property, there is no need for its direct political assertion.

If, then, the role of property is diminishing, the danger is that its gradual disappearance will create the need for some new (racist or expert-rule) form of hierarchy, directly founded in individual qualities, and thus cancelling even the "formal" bourgeois equality and freedom. In short, in so far as the determining factor of social power will be inclusion in/exclusion from the privileged set (of access to knowledge, control, etc.), we can expect an increase in various modes of exclusion, up to downright racism. The first clear sign of this is the new alliance between politics (government) and natural sciences: in the newly emerging biopolitics, the government is instigating an "embryo industry", a control over our genetic legacy that is outside democratic control, justified by an offer no one can refuse: "Don't you want to be cured of cancer, diabetes, Alzheimer's . . .?" While politicians are making such "scientific" promises, however, scientists themselves remain deeply sceptical, often emphasizing the need for decisions to be reached through a wider social consensus.

The ultimate problem of genetic engineering lies not in its unpredictable consequences (what if we create monsters – for example, humans with no sense of moral responsibility?) but in the way biogenetic engineering fundamentally affects our notion of education: instead of educating a child to be a good musician, will it be possible to manipulate his or her genes so that he or she will be "spontaneously" inclined towards music? Instead of instilling in a child a sense of discipline, will it be possible to manipulate his or her genes so that he or she will "spontaneously" tend to obey orders?

One of the most nightmarish prospects opened up by the identification of the genome is that of a DNA warfare which will give new meaning to the notion of "ethnic cleansing": it is well known (although not widely reported) that secret army agencies all over the world are already using the latest biogenetic results to experiment with lethal chemical substances which, when disseminated, will affect only members of a certain ethnic group. The situation here is radically open – if two classes of people gradually emerge, the "naturally born" ones and the genetically manipulated ones, it is not even clear in advance which class will occupy the higher level in the social hierarchy: will the "naturals" consider the manipulated ones as mere tools, not truly free beings, or will the much more perfect manipulated ones consider "naturals" as belonging to a lower rung of evolution?

So the struggle ahead has no guaranteed outcome – it will confront us with an unprecedented need to act, since it will concern not only a new mode of production, but a radical rupture in what it means to be a human being.[185] Today, we can already discern the signs of a kind of general unease – recall the series of protests usually listed under the name "Seattle". The ten-year honeymoon of triumphant global capitalism is over; the long-overdue "seven-year itch" is here – witness the panicky reactions of the mass media, which, from *Time* magazine to CNN, started all of a sudden to warn us about the Marxists manipulating the crowd of "honest" protesters. The problem now is the strictly Leninist one: how do we actualize the media's accusations? How do we invent the organizational structure which will confer on this unrest the form of the universal political demand? Otherwise, the momentum will be lost, and all that will remain will be marginal disturbances, perhaps organized like a new Greenpeace, with a certain efficiency, but also strictly limited goals, marketing strategy, and so on. In short, without the form of the Party, the movement remains caught in the vicious cycle of "resistance", one of the big catchwords of "postmodern" politics, which likes to oppose "good" resistance to power to a "bad" revolutionary takeover of power – the last thing we want is the domestication of anti-globalization into just another "site of resistance" against capitalism.

As a result, the key "Leninist" lesson today is: politics without the organizational form of the Party is politics without politics, so the answer to those who want just the (quite adequately named) "New Social Movements" is the same as the Jacobins' answer to the Girondin compromisers: "You want revolution without a revolution!" Today's dilemma is that there are two ways open for sociopolitical engagement: either play the game of the system, engage in the "long march through the institutions", or become active in new social movements, from feminism through ecology to anti-racism. And, again, the limit of these movements is that they are not political in the sense of the Universal Singular: they are "single-issue movements" which lack the dimension of universality – that is to say, they do not relate to the social totality.

Against Post-politics

In "A Contribution to the Critique of Hegel's Philosophy of Right", Marx deploys something like the logic of hegemony: at the climax of revolutionary enthusiasm, a "universal class" emerges, that is, some particular class imposes itself as universal, and thereby engenders global enthusiasm, since it stands for society as such against the *ancien régime*, antisocial crime as such (like the bourgeoisie in the French Revolution). What then follows is the disillusion so sarcastically described by Marx: the day after, the gap between the Universal and the Particular becomes visible again; capitalist vulgar profit emerges as the actuality of universal freedom, and so on.[186]

For Marx, of course, the only universal class whose singularity (exclusion from the society of property) guarantees its actual universality is the proletariat. This is what Ernesto Laclau rejects in his version of the logic of hegemony: for Laclau, the short circuit between the Universal and the Particular is *always* illusory, temporary, a kind of "transcendental paralogism".[187] However, is Marx's proletariat really the negative of positive full essential humanity, or "only" the gap of universality as such, irrecoverable in any positivity?[188] In Alain Badiou's terms, the proletariat is not another particular class, but a singularity of the social structure and, as such, the universal class, the non-class among the classes.

What is crucial here is the properly temporal-dialectical tension between the Universal and the Particular. When Marx says that in Germany, because of the compromised pettiness of the bourgeoisie, it is too late for partial bourgeois emancipation, and that for this reason, in Germany, the condition of every particular emancipation is *universal* emancipation, one way to read this is to see in it the assertion of the universal "normal" paradigm and its exception: in the "normal" case, partial (false) bourgeois emancipation will be followed by universal emancipation through the proletarian revolution; while in Germany, the "normal" order gets mixed up. There is, however, another, much more radical way to read it: the very German exception, the German bourgeoisie's inability to achieve partial emancipation, opens up the space for a possible *universal* emancipation.

The dimension of universality thus emerges (only) where the "normal" order that links the succession of particulars is disrupted. For this reason, there is no "normal" revolution; each revolutionary explosion is grounded in an exception, in a short circuit of "too late" and "too early". The French Revolution occurred because France was not able to follow the "normal" English path of capitalist development; the very "normal" English path resulted in the "unnatural" division of labour between the capitalists, who held socioeconomic power, and the aristocracy, which was left with political power. And, according to Marx, this was how Germany produced the ultimate revolution in thought (German Idealism as the philosophical counterpart of the French Revolution): precisely because it lacked a political revolution.

The structural necessity of this non-contemporaneity, of this discrepancy, is what gets lost in Habermas: the basic point of his notion of "modernity as an unfinished project" is that the project of modernity contained two facets: the development of "instrumental reason" (scientific-technological manipulation and domination of nature) and the emergence of intersubjective communication free of constraints; hitherto, only the first facet has been fully deployed, and our task is to bring the project of modernity to completion by actualizing the potential of the second facet. What, however, if this discrepancy is structural? What if we cannot simply supplement instrumental Reason with communicational Reason, since the primacy of instrumental Reason is constitutive of modern Reason as such? Habermas is fully consistent in applying the same logic to today's globalization – his thesis is that of "globalization as an unfinished project":

> The discrepancy between progressive economic integration and the political integration which lags behind can be overcome only through a politics which aims at constructing a higher-level capacity of political acting which would be able to keep pace with deregulated markets.[189]

In short, there is no need to fight capitalist globalization directly – we need only to supplement it with an adequate political globalization (a stronger central political body in Strasbourg; the imposition of pan-European social legislation, etc.). However, what if, again, modern capitalism, which generates economic globalization, cannot simply be supplemented by political globalization? What if such an extension of globalization to the political project forced us radically to redefine the contours of economic globalization itself?[190]

In short, Habermas's basic attitude is nothing less than *a disavowal of the twentieth-century* – he acts as if the twentieth century, in its specific dimension, *did not take place*: as if what happened in it were basically just contingent detours, so that the underlying conceptual narrative – that of enlightened democratic liberalism, with its indefinite progress – can be told without them.[191] Along the same lines, in order to characterize the demise of the Socialist regimes in 1990, Habermas coined the term "catch-up revolution":[192] the West (Western liberal democracy) has nothing to learn from the Eastern European Communist experience, since in 1990, these countries simply caught up with the social development of the Western liberal-democratic regimes. Habermas thereby writes off this experience as simply accidental, denying any fundamental structural relationship between Western democracy and the rise of "totalitarianism" – any notion that "totalitarianism" is a symptom of the inner tensions of the democratic project itself.

The same goes for Habermas's treatment of Fascism: against Adorno's and Horkheimer's notion of Fascist "barbarism" as the ineluctable outcome of the "dialectic of Enlightenment", the Fascist regimes are for him a contingent detour (delay, regression) which does not affect the basic logic of modernization and Enlightenment. The task is thus simply to abolish this detour, not to rethink the Enlightenment project itself. This victory over "totalitarianism", however, is a Pyrrhic one: what Habermas needs here is a Hitchcockian lesson (remember Hitchcock's claim that a film is only as interesting as its main evil character). Dismissing the "totalitarian" deadlock as a mere contingent detour leaves us with a comfortable, but ultimately *impotent*, position of someone who, unperturbed by the catastrophes around him, clings to the basic rationality of the universe.

The promise of the "Seattle" movement lies in the fact that it is the very opposite of its usual media designation (the "anti-globalization protest"): it is the first kernel of a new *global* movement, global with regard to its content (it aims at a global confrontation with today's capitalism) as well as its form (it is a global movement, a mobile international network ready to intervene anywhere from Seattle to Prague). It is more global than "global capitalism", since it brings into the game its victims – that is, those who are excluded from capitalist globalization, as well as those who are included in a way which reduces them to proletarian misery.[193] Perhaps I should take the risk here of applying Hegel's old distinction between "abstract" and "concrete" universality: capitalist globalization is "abstract", focused on the speculative movement of Capital; whereas the "Seattle" movement stands for "concrete universality", both for the totality of global capitalism *and* for its excluded dark side. The *reality* of capitalist globalization is best exemplified by the victory in June 2001 of the Russian nuclear lobby, which forced the parliament's decision that Russia would import nuclear waste from developed Western countries.

Here, Lenin's reproach to liberals is crucial: they merely exploit the working classes' discontent to strengthen their position *vis-à-vis* the conservatives, instead of identifying with it to the end.[194] Is this not also true of today's Left liberals? They like to evoke racism, ecology, workers' grievances, and so on, to score points over the conservatives – *without endangering the system*. Remember how, in Seattle, Bill Clinton himself deftly referred to the protesters on the streets outside, reminding the assembled leaders inside the guarded palaces that they should listen to the demonstrators' message (the message which, of course, Clinton interpreted, depriving it of its subversive sting, which he attributed to the dangerous extremists introducing chaos and violence into the majority of peaceful protesters). This Clintonesque stance later developed into an elaborate "carrot-and-stick" strategy of containment: on the one hand, paranoia (the notion that there is a dark Marxist plot lurking behind it); on the other hand, in Genoa, none other than Berlusconi provided food and shelter for the anti-globalization demonstrators – on condition that they "behaved properly", and did not disturb the official event. It is the same with all New Social Movements, up to the Zapatistas in Chiapas: establishment is always ready to "listen to their demands", depriving them of their proper political sting. The system is by definition ecumenical, open, tolerant, ready to "listen" to all – even if you insist on your demands, they are deprived of their universal political sting by the very form of negotiation. The true Third Way we have to look for is *this* third way between institutionalized parliamentary politics and the New Social Movements.

As a sign of this emerging uneasiness and need for a true Third Way, it is interesting to see how, in a recent interview, even a conservative liberal like John le Carré had to admit that, as a consequence of the "love affair between Thatcher and Reagan" in most of the developed Western countries, and especially in the United Kingdom, "the social infrastructure has practically stopped working"; this then leads him to make a direct plea for, at least, "re-nationalizing the railways and water".[195] We are in fact approaching a state in which (selective) private affluence is accompanied by a global (ecological, infrastructural) degradation which will soon start to affect us all: the quality of water is not a problem confined to the UK – a recent survey showed that the entire reservoir from which the Los Angeles area gets its water is already so polluted by man-made toxic chemicals that it will soon be impossible to make it drinkable even through the use of the most advanced filters. Le Carré expressed his fury at Blair for accepting the basic Thatcherite co-ordinates in very precise terms: "I thought last time, in 1997, that he was lying when he denied he was a socialist. The worst thing I can say about him is that he was telling the truth."[196] More precisely, even if, in 1997, Blair was "subjectively" lying, even if his secret agenda was to save whatever can be salvaged of the socialist agenda, he was "objectively" telling the truth: his (eventual) subjective socialist conviction was a self-deception, an illusion which enabled him to fulfil his "objective" role, that of completing the Thatcherite "revolution".

How, then, are we to respond to the eternal dilemma of the radical Left: should we strategically support centre-Left figures like Bill Clinton against the conservatives, or should we adopt the stance of "It doesn't matter, we shouldn't get involved in these fights – in a way, it's even better if the Right is directly in power, since, in this way, it will be easier for the people to see the truth of the situation"? The answer is a variation on Stalin's answer to the question: "Which deviation is worse, the Rightist or the Leftist one?": *they are both worse.* What we should do is adopt the stance of the proper dialectical paradox: in principle, of course, one should be indifferent to the struggle between the liberal and conservative poles of today's official politics – however, *one can only afford to be indifferent if the liberal option is in power.* Otherwise, the price may appear much too high – consider the catastrophic consequences of the German Communist Party's decision in the early 1930s not to focus on the struggle against the Nazis, with the justification that the Nazi dictatorship was the last desperate stage of capitalist domination, which would open the eyes of the working class, shattering their belief in "bourgeois" democratic institutions.

Along these lines, even Claude Lefort, whom no one can accuse of Communist sympathies, recently made a crucial point in his answer to François Furet: today's liberal consensus is the result of a hundred and fifty years of Leftist workers' struggle and pressure upon the State; it incorporated demands which were dismissed by liberals with horror a hundred years ago – even less.[197] If we need proof, we should simply look at the list of the demands at the end of the *Communist Manifesto*: apart from two or three of them (which, of course, are the crucial ones), all the others are today part of the consensus (at least the disintegrating Welfare State consensus): universal franchise; free education; universal healthcare and care for the elderly; a limitation on child labour. . . . In short, today's "bourgeois democracy" is the result not of liberalism's intrinsic development, but of the proletarian class struggle.

It is true that, today, it is the radical populist Right which usually breaks the (still) prevailing liberal-democratic consensus, gradually making acceptable hitherto excluded ideas (the partial justification of Fascism, the need to constrain abstract citizenship on grounds of ethnic identity, etc.). However, the hegemonic liberal democracy is using this fact to blackmail the Left radicals: "We shouldn't play with fire: against the new Rightist onslaught, we should insist more than ever on the democratic consensus – any criticism of it, wittingly or unwittingly, helps the New Right!" This is the key line of separation: we should reject this blackmail, taking the risk of disturbing the liberal consensus, even up to questioning the very notion of democracy.

The ultimate answer to the criticism that radical Left proposals are utopian should thus be that, today, the true utopia is the belief that the present liberal-democratic capitalist consensus can go on indefinitely, without radical change. We are therefore back with the old '68 slogan *"Soyons réalistes, demandons l'impossible!"*: in order to be a true "realist", we must consider breaking out of the constraints of what appears "possible" (or, as we usually put it, "feasible").

If there is a lesson to be learned from Silvio Berlusconi's electoral victory in May 2001, it is that the true utopians are the Third Way Leftists – why? The main temptation to be avoided apropos of Berlusconi's victory in Italy is to use it as a pretext for yet another exercise in the tradition of the conservative-Leftist *Kulturkritik* (from Adorno to Virilio), which bemoans the stupidity of the manipulated masses, and the eclipse of the autonomous individual capable of critical reflection. This, however, does not mean that the consequences of this victory are to be underestimated. Hegel said that all historical events have to happen twice: Napoleon had to lose twice, and so on. And it seems that Berlusconi also had to win the election twice for us to become aware of the full consequences of this event: the first time can be written off as a mere accidental curiosity, while the second demonstrates that we are dealing with a deeper necessity.

So what did Berlusconi achieve? His victory provides a depressing lesson about the role of morality in politics: the ultimate outcome of the great moral-political catharsis – the anti-corruption campaign of "clean hands" which, a decade ago, ruined Christian Democracy, and with it the ideological polarity of Christian Democrats and Communists which dominated postwar Italian politics – is Berlusconi in power. It is something like Rupert Murdoch winning a British election: a political movement run as a business-publicity enterprise. Berlusconi's *Forza Italia* is no longer a political party, but – as its name indicates – more like a sports fan club. If, in the good old Socialist countries, sport was directly politicized (remember the DDR's enormous investment in its top athletes), now, politics itself is turned into a sporting contest. And the parallel goes even further: if the Communist regimes nationalized industry, Berlusconi is, in a way, privatizing the state itself. For this reason, all the Leftists' and liberal democrats' worry about the danger of neo-Fascism lurking beneath Berlusconi's victory is misplaced and, in a way, much too optimistic: Fascism is still a determinate political project, while in the case of Berlusconi, there is ultimately *nothing* lurking beneath, no secret ideological project, just the sheer assurance that things will function, that he will do better. In short, Berlusconi is *post-politics at its purest*.[198] The ultimate sign of "post-politics" in all Western countries is the growth of a managerial approach to government: government is reconceived as a managerial function, deprived of its properly political dimension.

The true stake of today's political struggles is: which of the two former main parties, the conservatives or the "moderate Left", will succeed in presenting itself as truly embodying the post-ideological spirit, against the other party dismissed as "still caught in the old ideological machine"? If the 1980s belonged to the conservatives, the lesson of the 1990s seemed to be that, in our late capitalist societies, Third Way social democracy (or, even more relevantly, post-Communism in the ex-Socialist countries) actually functions as the representative of capital as such, in its totality, against its particular factions represented by the various "conservative" parties, which then, in order to present themselves as addressing the entire population, also try to satisfy the particular demands of the anti-capitalist strata (say, of domestic "patriotic" middle-class workers threatened by cheap immigrant labour – recall the CDU, which, against the Social Democratic proposal that Germany should import 50,000 Indian computer programmers, launched the infamous slogan "Kinder statt Inder! / Children rather than Indians!"). This economic constellation explains to a great extent how and why Third Way Social Democrats can simultaneously stand both for the interests of big capital and for the multiculturalist tolerance which aims at protecting the interests of ethnic minorities.

The Third Way dream of the Left was that the pact with the Devil might work out: OK, no revolution, we accept capitalism as the only game in town, but at least we will be able to save some of the achievements of the Welfare State, and build a society that is tolerant towards sexual, religious and ethnic minorities. If the trend announced by Berlusconi's victory persists, a much darker prospect is discernible on the horizon: a world in which the unlimited rule of capital is supplemented not by Left-liberal tolerance, but by a typical post-political mixture of pure publicity spectacle and Moral Majority concerns (remember that the Vatican gave Berlusconi its tacit support!). If there is a hidden ideological agenda to Berlusconi's "post-politics", it is – to put it bluntly – the disintegration of the fundamental post-World War II democratic pact. In recent years, there have already been numerous signs that the post-World War II anti-Fascist pact is slowly cracking: from "revisionist" historians to the New Right populists, so-called "taboos" are disappearing. . . . Paradoxically, those who undermine this pact refer to the very liberal universalized logic of victimization: sure, there were victims of Fascism, but what about other victims of the Postwar expulsions? What about the Germans evicted from their homes in Czechoslovakia? Do they not also have some right to (financial) compensation?

The immediate future belongs not to outright Rightist provocateurs like Jean-Marie le Pen or Pat Buchanan, but to people like Berlusconi and Haider: these advocates of global capital in the sheep's clothing of populist nationalism. The struggle between them and the Third Way Left is the struggle over who will be more effective in counteracting the excesses of global capitalism: Third Way multiculturalist tolerance or populist homophobia. Will this boring alternative be Europe's answer to globalization? Berlusconi is therefore post-politics at its worst: even *The Economist*, that staunch voice of anti-Left liberalism, was accused by Berlusconi of being part of a "Communist plot" when it asked some searching questions about how a convicted criminal can become Prime Minister! What this means is that, for Berlusconi, all opposition to his post-politics is rooted in a "Communist plot". And in a way, he is right: this *is* the only true opposition; all the others – liberals or Third Way Leftists – are basically playing the same game as he is, only with a different gloss. Is the Third Way

Left really able to offer a global alternative to Berlusconi's politics? And the hope is that Berlusconi will also be right about the second aspect of his paranoiac cognitive mapping: that his victory will give an impetus to the more radical Left.

Return versus Repetition

Where, then, are we today? The entire history of the Soviet Union can be comprehended as analogous to Freud's famous image of Rome, a city whose history is deposited in its present in the guise of different layers of archaeological remainders, each new level covering up the preceding one, like (another model) the seven layers of Troy; so that history, in its regress towards ever older epochs, proceeds like an archaeologist, discovering new layers by probing deeper and deeper into the ground. Was not the (official ideological) history of the Soviet Union the same accumulation of exclusions, of turning people into non-persons, of a retroactive rewriting of history?

Quite logically, "de-Stalinization" was indicated by the opposite process of "rehabilitation", of admitting "errors" in the past politics of the Party. The gradual "rehabilitation" of the demonized Bolshevik ex-leaders can thus serve as perhaps the most sensitive index of how far (and in what direction) the "de-Stalinization" of the Soviet Union was going. The first to be rehabilitated were the senior military leaders shot in 1937 (Tukhachevsky and others); the last to be rehabilitated, in the Gorbachev era, just before the collapse of the Communist regime, was Bukharin – this last rehabilitation, of course, was a clear sign of the turn towards capitalism: the Bukharin who was rehabilitated was the one who, in the 1920s, advocated a pact between workers and peasants (owners of their land), launching the famous slogan "Enrich yourselves!", and opposed forced collectivization. Significantly, however, one figure was *never* rehabilitated, excluded by the Communists as well as by the anti-Communist Russian nationalists: Trotsky, the "wandering Jew" of the Revolution, the true anti-Stalin, the arch-enemy, opposing "permanent revolution" to the idea of "building socialism in one country".

I am tempted here to risk a parallel with Freud's distinction between primordial (founding) and secondary repression in the Unconscious: Trotsky's exclusion amounted to something like the "primordial repression" of the Soviet State, to something which can never be readmitted through "rehabilitation", since the entire Order relied on this negative gesture of exclusion.[199] Trotsky is the one for whom there is no room either in pre-1990 Really Existing Socialism or in post-1990 Really Existing Capitalism, in which even those who are nostalgic for Communism do not know what to do with Trotsky's permanent revolution – perhaps the signifier "Trotsky" is the most appropriate designation of that which is worth redeeming in the Leninist legacy. Here we should look at "Hölderlin's Hyperion", a bizarre but crucial short essay by Georg Lukács written in 1935, in which Lukács praises Hegel's endorsement of the Napoleonic Thermidor against Hölderlin's intransigent fidelity to the heroic revolutionary utopia:

> Hegel comes to terms with the post-Thermidorian epoch and the close of the revolutionary period of bourgeois development, and he builds up his philosophy precisely on an understanding of this new turning-point in world history. Hölderlin makes no compromise with the post-Thermidorian reality; he remains faithful to the old revolutionary ideal of renovating "polis" democracy and is broken by a reality which has no place for his ideals, not even on the level of poetry and thought.[200]

Here Lukács is referring to Marx's notion that the heroic period of the French Revolution was the necessary enthusiastic breakthrough followed by the unheroic phase of market relations: the true social function of the Revolution was to establish the conditions for the prosaic reign of the bourgeois economy, and the true heroism lies not in blindly clinging to the early revolutionary enthusiasm, but in recognizing "the rose in the cross of the present", as Hegel liked to paraphrase Luther – that is, in abandoning the position of the Beautiful Soul, and fully accepting the present as the only possible domain of actual freedom. Thus it was this "compromise" with social reality which enabled Hegel to take his crucial philosophical step forward: that of overcoming the proto-Fascist notion of "organic" community in his *System der Sittlichkeit* manuscript, and engaging in a dialectical analysis of the antagonisms of bourgeois civil society. (That is the properly dialectical paradox of the proto-Fascist endeavour to return to a premodern "organic" community: far from being simply "reactionary", Fascist "feudal Socialism" is a kind of compromise solution, an *ersatz* attempt to build socialism within the constraints of capitalism itself.) It is obvious that Lukács's analysis is deeply allegorical: it was written a couple of months after Trotsky launched his thesis that Stalinism was the Thermidor of the October Revolution. Lukács's text should therefore be read as an answer to Trotsky. he accepts Trotsky's characterization of Stalin's regime as "Thermidorian", giving it a positive twist – instead of bemoaning the loss of utopian energy, we should, in a heroically resigned way, accept its consequences as the only actual space of social progress.

For Marx, of course, the sobering "morning after" which follows the revolutionary intoxication indicates the original limitation of the "bourgeois" revolutionary project, the falsity of its promise of universal freedom: the "truth" of universal human rights are the rights of commerce and private property. If we read Lukács's endorsement of the Stalinist Thermidor, it implies (argubly against his conscious intention) an utterly pessimistic anti-Marxist perspective: the proletarian revolution itself is also characterized by the gap between its illusory universal assertion of freedom and the ensuing awakening in the new relations of domination and exploitation, which means that the Communist project of realizing "actual freedom" failed.

What, then, are we to do in these circumstances? The problem with those few remaining orthodox "Leninists" who behave as if we can simply recycle the old Leninism, and continue to talk about the corrupted leaders' betrayal of the working masses' revolutionary impulses, is that it is not quite clear from which subjective position of enunciation they speak: they either engage themselves in passionate discussions about the past (demonstrating with admirable erudition how and where anti-Communist "Leninologists" falsify Lenin, etc.), in which case they avoid the question of *why (apart from a purely historical interest) this matters at all today*; or, the closer they get to contemporary politics, the closer they are to adopting a purely jargonistic pose which threatens no one.

When, in the last months of 2000, the Milošević regime in Serbia was finally toppled, many Marxists in the West raised the question: "What about the coal miners whose strike led to the disruption of the electricity supply, and thus, in effect, brought Milošević down? Was that not a genuine workers' movement, which was then manipulated by the politicians, who were nationalists or corrupted by the CIA?" The same symptomatic point emerges apropos of every new social upheaval (like the disintegration of Real Socialism ten years ago): in each of these cases, they identify some working-class movement which allegedly displayed a true revolutionary – or, at least, Socialist – potential, but was first exploited and then betrayed by pro-capitalist and/or nationalist forces. In this way, we can continue to dream that Revolution is round the corner: all we need is the authentic leadership which would be able to organize the workers' revolutionary potential. If we can believe its members, Solidarność was originally a workers' democratic-socialist movement, later "betrayed" by its leadership, which was corrupted by the Church and the CIA.

There is, of course, an element of truth in this approach: the ultimate irony of the disintegration of Communism was that the great revolts (the GDR in 1953; Hungary in 1956; Solidarity in Poland) were originally *workers'* uprisings which only later paved the way for the classic "anti-

Communist" movements – before succumbing to the "external" enemy, the regime got a message about its falsity from those whom these "workers' and peasants' states" evoked as their own social base. This very fact, however, also demonstrates how the workers' revolt lacked any substantial socialist commitment: in all cases, once the movement exploded, it was smoothly hegemonized by the standard "bourgeois" ideology (political freedom, private property, national sovereignty, etc.).

This mysterious working class whose revolutionary thrust is repeatedly thwarted by treacherous nationalist and/or liberal politicians is the *fetish* of some of the remaining Trotskyists, these actual Hölderlins of today's Marxism – the singular point of disavowal which enables them to sustain their overall interpretation of the state of things. Their fetishist fixation on the old Marxist–Leninist framework is the exact opposite of the fashionable talk about "new paradigms", about how we should leave behind old "zombie-concepts" like working class, and so on – the two complementary ways of avoiding the effort to think the New which is emerging today. The first thing to do here is to cancel this disavowal by fully admitting that this "authentic" working class simply *does not exist*.[201] And if we add to this position four further ones, we get a pretty clear picture of the sad predicament of today's Left: the acceptance of Cultural Wars (feminist, gay, anti-racist, etc., multiculturalist struggles) as the dominant terrain of emancipatory politics; the purely defensive stance of protecting the achievements of the Welfare State; the naive belief in cyber-communism (the idea that the new media are directly creating conditions for a new authentic community); and, finally, the Third Way, capitulation itself. Let us just hope that the present anti-globalization movement will introduce a new dimension by, finally, again conceiving of capitalism neither as a solution nor as one of the problems, but as *the* problem itself.

The reference to Lenin should serve as the signifier of the effort to break the vicious circle of these false options. The first thing to do is to learn to decode the way the basic political conflict continues to function as the secret point of reference of even seemingly "apolitical" antagonisms.

Let us take Krzysztof Kieslowski's *Decalogue*, a series conspicuous for its "apolitical" stance: the first thing that strikes the viewer who is aware of the historical circumstances in which *Decalogue* was shot is the total absence of any reference to politics: although the series was shot in the most turbulent period of post-World War II Polish history (the state of emergency imposed by General Jaruzelski's *coup d'état* in order to curb Solidarity), Kieslowski resisted the temptation to score easy points by spicing up the story with direct dissident thrills. A close analysis, however, demonstrates how this very avoidance of explicit politicization was, in its proper historical context, a political gesture *par excellence* – the gesture of rejecting not only the ruling Communist regime but also the "dissident" opposition, at least in its classic anti-Communist form. Furthermore, the political dimension is not simply absent, but *actively erased*: in so far as the conflict between science and religion in *Decalogue 1* is the encoded formulation of the *political* struggle between ("scientific" atheist) Communists and (religious) Solidarity dissidents,[202] the catastrophe in which science and religion suspend each other announces the depoliticization of the universe of the *Decalogue*, a limitation to the world of middle-class privacy, with its typical traumas (ethical choices, fidelity, abortion).

From here, I am tempted to return to Kieslowski's earlier *Blind Chance* – this is the film's storyline. Witek runs to catch a train. Three variations follow on how such a seemingly banal incident could influence the rest of his life. One: he catches the train, meets an honest Communist, and becomes a Party activist himself. Two: while running for the train, he knocks down a railway guard, is arrested, brought to trial and sentenced to unpaid labour in a park, where he meets someone from the opposition. He, in turn, becomes a militant dissident. Three: he simply misses the train, returns to his interrupted studies, marries a fellow student and leads a peaceful life as a doctor unwilling to get mixed up in politics. He is sent abroad to a symposium; the plane he is on explodes in midair. . . . In so far as there are reasons to claim that the only "true" story is the third one (the first two being just Witek's hallucinated alternatives when he is approaching death), the film indicates the escape into privacy after the deadlock of the struggle between Communists and dissidents – in short, *Blind Chance* provides the key to decode *Decalogue 1*.

However, is this triad really complete, are the options really exhausted, as the final catastrophe (the hero's death in the plane crash) seems to indicate, functioning as a kind of closure? What if there is a *fourth* option: repoliticization *beyond* the opposition Communism/dissidence, and its sublation in post-Communist post-political society?[203] This politicization is not simply external to the previous one; its base should, rather, be conceived as the intersection of the two apparently opposite poles of Communism and dissidence. Does not *Decalogue 10* point in this direction, with its society of philatelists, a kind of secret authentic community, thriving under Socialism because it is allowed contact with foreign countries?[204] Are not these philatelists, then, the model for other societies in which the communal spirit survives, from psychoanalytic associations to subversive half-illegal political organizations? There is yet another aspect to this: Fredric Jameson has pointed out how, today, the standard doxa against conspiracy theories (they are the political epistemology of the poor, projecting their perplexity into the fantasy of a secret enemy which pulls the strings, and the reference to whom thus explains all) is no longer sufficient. Today, a lot of ongoing phenomena have to be explained through some kind of conspiracy theory (acts of semi-clandestine government agencies; the strategies of large companies). And, in order to fight them, we are more and more in need of our own half-clandestine organizations. Perhaps Lenin's formula of the Party from his much-vilified *What Is to Be Done?* has acquired new relevance today.

John Berger recently made a salient point apropos of a French poster for the Internet investment brokers Selftrade: under the image of a hammer and sickle cast in solid gold and embedded with diamonds, the caption reads: "And what if everybody profited from the stock market?" The strategy of this poster is obvious: today, the stock market fulfils egalitarian Communist criteria: everybody can participate in it. Berger indulges in a simple mental experiment: "Imagine a communications campaign today using an image of a swastika cast in solid gold and embedded with diamonds! It would of course not work. Why? The Swastika addressed potential victors not the defeated. It invoked domination not justice."[205] The hammer and sickle, in contrast, invoked the hope that "history would eventually be on the side of those struggling for fraternal justice".[206] The irony is thus that, at the very moment when this hope is officially proclaimed dead by the hegemonic ideology of the "end of ideologies", a paradigmatically "post-industrial" enterprise (is there anything more "post-industrial" than dealing with stocks on the Internet?) has to mobilize this dormant hope in order to get its message through.[207] "Repeating Lenin" means giving new life to this hope, which still continues to haunt us.

As a result, *repeating* Lenin does not mean a *return* to Lenin – to repeat Lenin is to accept that "Lenin is dead", that his particular solution failed, even failed monstrously, but that there was a utopian spark in it worth saving.[208] Repeating Lenin means that we have to distinguish between what Lenin actually did and the field of possibilities he opened up, the tension in Lenin between what he actually did and another dimension: what was "in Lenin more than Lenin himself". To repeat Lenin is to repeat not what Lenin *did* but what he *failed to do*, his missed opportunities. Today, Lenin looks like a figure from a different time zone: it is not that his notions of the centralized Party, and so on, seem to pose a "totalitarian threat" – it is rather that they seem to belong to a different epoch to which we can no longer properly relate.

Instead of reading this fact as proof that Lenin is outdated, however, we should, perhaps, risk the opposite conjecture: what if this impenetrability of Lenin is a sign that there is something wrong with *our* epoch? What if the fact that we experience Lenin as irrelevant, "out of sync" with our postmodern times, imparts the much more unsettling message that our time itself is "out of sync", that a certain historical dimension is disappearing from it?[209] If, to some people, such an assertion appears dangerously close to Hegel's infamous quip when his deduction that there should be only eight planets circulating around the Sun was proved wrong by the discovery of the ninth planet (Pluto): "So much the worse for the facts!", then we should be ready fully to assume this paradox.

How did the ideology of Enlightenment evolve in eighteenth-century France? First there was the epoch of salons, in which philosophers tried to shock their benefactors, the generous Counts and Countesses, even Kings and Empresses (Holbach Frederick the Great, Diderot Catherine the Great) with their "radical" ideas on equality, the origin of power, the nature of man, and so on – all this remaining a kind of intellectual game. At this stage, the idea that someone could take these ideas literally, as the blueprint for a radical sociopolitical transformation, would probably have shocked the ideologues themselves, who were either part of the entourage of an enlightened nobleman or a lone pathetic figure like Rousseau – their reaction would have been that of Ivan Karamazov, disgusted upon learning that his bastard half-brother and servant have acted on his nihilistic ruminations, killing his father. This passage from intellectual game to an idea which actually "seizes the masses" is the moment of *truth* – in it, the intellectual gets his own message back in its inverted/true form. In France, we go from the gentle reflections of Rousseau to the Jacobin Terror; within the history of Marxism, it is only with Lenin that this passage occurs, that the games are *really* over. And it is up to us to repeat this same passage, and accomplish the fateful step from ludic "postmodern" radicalism to the domain in which the *games are over*.

There is an old joke about socialism as the synthesis of the highest achievements of the whole of human history to date: from prehistoric societies it took primitivism; from the Ancient world it took slavery; from medieval society brutal domination; from capitalism exploitation; and from socialism the name. . . .[210] Could not something similar be said about our attempt to repeat Lenin's gesture? From conservative cultural criticism it takes the idea that today's democracy is no longer the site where crucial decisions are made; from cyberspace ideologues the idea that the global digital network offers a new space for communal life, and so on; and from Lenin more or less just the name itself. . . . This very fact could, however, be turned in an argument *for* the "return to Lenin": the extent to which the signifier "Lenin" retains its subversive edge is easily demonstrated – when, for example, one makes the "Leninist" point that today's democracy is exhausted, that the key decisions are not taken there, one is directly accused of "totalitarianism"; when a similar point is made by sociologists, or even Václav Havel, they are praised for the depth of their insight. . . . *This* resistance is the answer to the question "Why Lenin?": it is the signifier "Lenin" which *formalizes* this content found elsewhere, transforming a series of common notions into a subversive theoretical formation.

Notes

1. There is also, of course, a false reference to "concrete circumstances" – recall Silvio Berlusconi who, in September 2001, after the widespread critical reaction against his remarks on the superiority of Western Christian civilization over Islam, countered that the scandal was cooked up by journalists who used his remarks out of context. It is significant that when people defend themselves in this way, they never give us a positive definition of *the context in which such remarks are acceptable* (the same happened to the British representative of Louis Farrakhan, who also claimed that Farrakhan's anti-Semitic remarks were "torn out of their proper context"; when he was given time to elaborate this "proper context" in a TV interview, he naturally refused to do so). To put it in Hegelian terms, such a direct and unspecified reference to "context" is *abstraction at its purest.*

2. Quoted from Peter McLaren, *Che Guevara, Paulo Freire, and the Pedagogy of Revolution,* Oxford: Rowan & Littlefield 2000, p. xxv.

3. See Jürgen Habermas, *Die Neue Unübersichtlichkeit,* Frankfurt: Suhrkamp Verlag 1985.

4. Here I draw on Anna Kornbluh, "The Family Man", unpublished manuscript (UCLA, March 2001).

5. Theodor W. Adorno, *Vermischte Schriften I,* Frankfurt: Suhrkamp Verlag 1997, p. 404.

6. Furthermore, the struggle against Eurocentric racism often generates a racism of its own. Shepard Krech's *The Ecological Indian: Myth and History* (New York: Norton 1999) demonstrates convincingly how the myth of Native Americans living in undisturbed balance with nature, instead of trying to dominate and transform it, is the ultimate racist myth, implicitly reducing Native Americans to beings who, like animals, left no traces on their land, while "aggressive" Western man cultivated it. This notion obliterates the key fact that the preservation and conservation of natural resources are decidedly Western concepts, foreign in fundamental ways to a Native American worldview.

7. For this notion, see Chapter 3 of Slavoj Žižek, *The Plague of Fantasies*, London and New York: Verso 1997.

8. Conspiracy theories are the obverse of the Enlightenment conviction that Reason (rational conscious intention) rules the world: if this is the case, then Reason's very (apparent) failure to establish its reign has to be accounted for in the terms of Reason – not simply as Reason's failure to master the complexity of real life, but as the result of some dark powers which are *rationally* plotting against the rule of Reason (from the idea that the masses are ignorant and act against their interests because reactionary forces of religion are manipulating them to the Stalinist notion that, behind the "difficulties" in the construction of socialism, there must be some counter-revolutionary plot). Does not all this confirm Adorno's and Horkheimer's thesis that modern anti-Semitism (the conspiracy theory *par excellence*) is grounded in the Enlightenment?

9. I owe this example to Anna Kornbluh (UCLA), whose unpublished paper "Multiculturalism and Multinational Corporate Capitalism" includes a justified critique of some of my formulations concerning multiculturalism in Chapter 4 of *The Ticklish Subject* (London and New York: Verso 1999).

10. McLaren, *Che Guevara*, p. x.

11. Douglas Kellner, *Media Culture*, London: Routledge 1995, p. 97.

12. Parallel to this attitude of "respect for the Other's specific customs", which in fact involves a humiliating condescension, is the false imposed subjectivization we often encounter in the pedagogical process: after explaining some point in an allegedly "objective", impartial way, the teacher turns to a pupil and asks him: "Now, in order to prove that you were able to follow my explanation, please put it *in your own words . . .*".

13. The "bourgeois" way out of this predicament is the displacement of tolerance on to the State: the State should be neutral, indifferent, so that we, individuals, can go on hating and struggling, while the State guarantees the neutral frame which prevents us from actually hurting others.

14. There is, of course, an element of partial truth in this position. I myself am mindful of how, every time I visit my Western friends, they explain to me in detail the real stakes of the post-Yugoslav war, everything I always wanted to know about Slovene nationalism and "egotism", and so on – an exemplary case of Leftist racism, if ever there was one. The way to fight it, however, is to provide a better concrete analysis, not to counter them with "Only someone from ex-Yugoslavia can really grasp what the war was about."

15. Alain Badiou, *D'un désastre obscur*, Paris: Éditions de l'Aube 1998, p. 50.

16. See Richard Rorty, *Contingency, Irony, Solidarity*, Cambridge: Cambridge University Press 1989.

Along similar lines, Habermas, Rorty's great opponent, elevates the rise of the "public sphere" of civil society, the space of free discussion that mediates between private lives and political/state apparatuses in the Enlightenment era. The problem is that this space of enlightened public debate was always redoubled by the fear of the irrational/passionate crowd which can, through contamination (what Spinoza called *imitatio affecti*), explode into murderous violence based on superstitions manipulated by priests or other ideologues. So the enlightened space of rational debate was always based on certain exclusions: on the exclusion of those who were not considered "rational" enough (the lower classes, women, children, savages, criminals . . .) – they needed the pressure of "irrational" authority to keep them in check; that is to say, for them, Voltaire's well-known saying "If God did not exist, it would be necessary to invent him" is valid.

17. See Peter Singer, *The Essential Singer: Writings on an Ethical Life*, New York: Ecco Press 2000.

18. Quoted in Robert Payne, *Marx*, New York: Simon & Schuster 1968, p. 61.

19. The liberal lack of solidarity and the ensuing social disintegration are best exemplified by the well-known story of two white men in the wilderness who suddenly see a hungry lion approaching them: while the first one panics, the second one calmly starts to put on his running shoes. The first one asks him: "But why are you doing that? Don't you know that a lion can run faster than any man?" The second one answers: "I don't intend to run faster than the lion – I just want to run faster than *you!*"

20. This also enables us to answer Dominick la Capra's criticism according to which the Lacanian notion of lack conflates two levels that should be kept apart: the purely formal "ontological" lack constitutive of the symbolic order as such, and the particular traumatic experiences (exemplarily: the Holocaust) which could also not have occurred – particular historical catastrophes like the Holocaust thus seem to be "legitimized" as directly grounded in the fundamental trauma that pertains to the human condition itself. (See Dominick la Capra, "Trauma, Absence, Loss", *Critical Inquiry*, vol. 25, no. 4, Summer 1999, pp. 696–727.)

This distinction between structural and contingent-historical trauma, convincing as it may appear, is doubly inadequate in its reliance on the Kantian distinction between the formal/structural a priori and the contingent/empirical a posteriori. First, *every* trauma, trauma "as such", in its very concept, is experienced as something contingent, as an unexpected meaningless disturbance – trauma is by definition not "structural", but something which disturbs the structural order. Second, the Holocaust was not simply a historical contingency but something which, in its unique combination of mythical sacrifice and technological instrumental efficiency, realized a certain destructive potential inscribed into the very logic of so-called Western civilization. We cannot adopt towards it the neutral position of a safe distance, from which we dismiss the Holocaust as an unfortunate accident: the Holocaust is, in a way, the "symptom" of our civilization, the singular point in which the universal repressed truth about it emerges. To put it in somewhat pathetic terms: any account of Western civilization which does not account for the Holocaust thereby invalidates itself.

21. For an Althusserian attempt to salvage Lenin's *Empiriocriticism*, see Dominique Lecourt, *Une crise et ses enjeux*, Paris: Maspero 1973.

22. First published in 1990 in the Italian weekly magazine *L'Espresso*, then reprinted in Colletti, *Fine della filosofia*, Roma: Ideazione 1996.

23. When, in a typical gesture of transferential pathos, Lenin repeats again and again how Marx and Engels always called their philosophy "dialectical materialism", it is easy for an anti-Leninist Marxologist to draw attention to the fact that Marx and Engels *never once* used this term (it was Georgi Plekhanov who introduced it). This situation put the Soviet editors of the collected works of Marx and Engels in a nice dilemma: in the Index, there *had* to be an entry "dialectical materialism", which they then filled in with references to the pages where Marx or Engels talks about dialectics, the materialist concept of history. . . . However, this is not the whole story: there is a truth-effect in this hallucinatory projection of a later concept back into Marx.

24. See V.I. Lenin, "Conspectus of Hegel's Book *The Science of Logic*", in *Collected*

Works, Moscow: Progress Publishers 1966, vol. 38, p. 179. I owe this parallel to Eustache Kouvélakis, Paris (private conversation).

25. For a more detailed critique of Adorno's "predominance of the objective", see Chapter 2 of Slavoj Žižek, *On Belief*, London: Routledge 2001.

26. In a passage in his *Note-Books*, Lenin is on the verge of this insight when he notes how the very "abstraction" of thought, its failure immediately to grasp the object in its infinite complexity, its distance from the object, its stepping-back from it, brings us closer to what the object actually is: in its very "one-sided" reduction of the object to some of its abstract properties in the concept, this apparent "limitation" of our knowledge (sustaining the dream of a total intuitive knowledge) is the very essence of knowledge:

> Thought proceeding from the concrete to the abstract – provided it is *correct* (NB: and Kant, like all philosophers, speaks of correct thought) – does not get away *from* the truth but comes closer to it. The abstraction of *matter*, of a *law* of nature, the abstraction of *value*, etc., in short *all* scientific (correct, serious, not absurd) abstractions reflect nature more deeply, truly and *completely*. From living perception to abstract thought, *and from this to practice*, – such is the dialectical path of cognition of *truth*, of cognition of objective reality." (Lenin, "Conspectus", p. 168)

He is on the verge – and then again regresses to the prevailing evolutionary notion of the infinite approaching reality.

27. To put it in brutal and direct terms: it is obvious that "Lenin did not really understand Marx" – if nothing else, the Hegelian complexity of Marx's "critique of political economy" was beyond his reach; the paradox, however, is that it is only because Lenin did not "understand Marx" that he was able to organize the October Revolution, the first properly Marxist revolution. This means that the split must have already been operative in Marx himself: if a certain ignorance of Marx's theory was a positive condition of bringing about a Marxist revolution, then Marx's revolutionary theory itself, although it perceived itself as the theoretical moment of a global revolutionary praxis, had to involve a gap with regard to revolutionary practice – had to misperceive the conditions of revolutionary intervention.

28. In general terms, the task of materialism is not just successfully to "reduce" the experience of Meaning to material movement; we should aim higher: to demonstrate how materialism can beat idealism at its own game by giving a better account of the experience of Meaning itself, in its uniqueness. Dialectical materialism here is strictly opposed to mechanical materialism, which is reductionist by definition: it does not acknowledge the radical heteronomy of the effect with regard to the cause, that is, it conceives of the sense-effect as a simple appearance, the appearance of an underlying "deeper" material Essence. Idealism, on the contrary, denies that the sense-effect is an effect of material processes, fetishizing it into a self-generated entity; the price it pays for this denial is the *substantialization* of the sense-effect: idealism covertly qualifies the sense-effect as a new Body (the immaterial body of Platonic Forms, for example). Paradoxical as it may sound, only dialectical materialism can think the effect of Sense, of the sense *qua* event, in its specific autonomy, without its reduction to some version of substantial being (this is why vulgar mechanical materialism constitutes the necessary complement to idealism).

29. Tor Norretranders, *The User Illusion*, Harmondsworth: Penguin 1999, p. 353.

30. What Buddhism seems unable to conceptualize is the status of subjectivity.

31. Ernesto Laclau and Chantal Mouffe, *Hegemony and Socialist Strategy*, London: Verso 1985.

32. Quoted from V.I. Lenin, *What Is to Be Done?*, New York: International Publishers 1999, p. 40.

33. Ibid., p. 40–41.

34. Quoted from Steven Pinker, *How the Mind Works*, Harmondsworth: Penguin 1999, p. 11.

35. Ibid., pp. 10–12.

36. Jacques-Alain Miller himself relates to Lacan as S_2 to S_1: he is Lacan's "bureaucrat", registering things, editing them, as in his first two great interventions, the essay "Suture" and the preparation of the detailed "Index raisonné" to the French edition of *Écrits*. His very presence exerted a retroactive influence on Lacan himself, forcing him to formulate his position in a much more concise way.

However, if Lacan was already the "formalizer" of Freud, is Miller again, in a kind of deconstructionist spurious infinity, the "formalizer" of Freud? Or, to take a step further: if Lacan is to Freud what Lenin is to Marx (as Lacan himself ironically hints in his *Seminar XX: Encore*), is Miller to both of them what *Stalin* is to Marx and Freud: the "bureaucratizer", introducing the reign of institutional terror (and, in effect, a lot of ex-Millerians *do* accuse Miller of "Stalinism", even going as far as demanding public confessions from people who betrayed him)? To this I am tempted to reply: why not? The only thing this homology teaches us is the difference between psychoanalytic and political organization: what, in politics, is self-destructive terror is of a totally different order in the psychoanalytic community – here, the Stalin figure is a "good" one.

37. V.I. Lenin, "Three Sources and Three Component Parts of Marxism", in *Collected Works*, Moscow: Progress Publishers 1966, vol. 19, p. 23.

38. It is here that Saint Paul can still show us the way: the endeavour of his "political theology" was precisely to ground a new collective (of believers) which avoided the debilitating choice between the "Roman" way (the multiculturalist tolerant empire of legal rights) and the "Jewish" way (ethnic fundamentalism). (See Jacob Taubes's outstanding *Die Politische Theologie des Paulus*, Munich: Wilhelm Fink Verlag 1993.) Is Saint Paul's dilemma not also ours: how to assert, against the narrow "fundamentalist" threat, a universalism of Truth which leaves behind the aseptic formalist universalism of liberal-democratic discourse?

39. See Jacques Lacan, *Le désir et son interprétation* (unpublished seminar 1958–59).

40. Bertolt Brecht, *Die Massnahme*, Frankfurt: Suhrkamp Verlag 1998, p. 67. It was Alain Badiou who drew my attention to this passage.

41. This attitude of *je n'en veux rien savoir* ("I don't want to know anything about it") is perhaps best exemplified by a classic scene from a spy or crime film: a dying criminal or spy gives the ordinary person who is accidentally there, in the wrong place at the wrong time, the forbidden piece of information (a spoken confession, a tape, a photo . . .). The innocent bystander is well aware that this knowledge is dangerous, contagious and potentially lethal, so he is horrified at the prospect of possessing it. There are situations in which the most terrible thing an enemy can do to us is to entrust us with a piece of such forbidden knowledge.

42. I owe this distinction to Alain Badiou (private conversation).

43. When, in "The Civil War in France", Marx praised the Paris Commune as the "finally discovered *form* in which the class struggle could be pursued to its end" (Karl

Marx, *Selected Writings*, ed. by David McLellan, Oxford: Oxford University Press 1977, p. 599), the term "form" should also be given all its Hegelian dialectical weight.

44. Quoted from Susan Buck-Morss, *Dreamworld and Catastrophe*, Cambridge, MA: MIT Press 2000, p. 237. On a different level, there are in Palestine today two opposed narratives (the Jewish one and the Palestinian one) with absolutely no common horizon, no "synthesis" in a broader meta-narrative; thus the solution cannot be found in any all-encompassing narrative.

45. This difference between interpretation and formalization is also crucial if we are to introduce some (theoretical) order into the recent debates on the Holocaust: although it is true that the Holocaust cannot be adequately interpreted or narrated in short, rendered meaningful; that all attempts to do this fail, and have to end in silence, *it can and should be "formalized"*, situated in its structural conditions of possibility.

46. One of the desperate strategies to try to redeem the utopian potential of the twentieth century is to claim that if the twentieth century was able to generate unprecedented Evils (Holocaust and Gulag), it thereby provided a negative proof that the same excess should also be possible in the opposite direction, that is, that radical Good is also feasible. . . . What, however, if this opposition is false? What if we are dealing here with a deeper identity: what if twentieth-century radical Evil was precisely the outcome of attempts directly to realize radical Good?

47. One possible counterargument here is that the category of the tragic is not appropriate to the analysis of Stalinism: the problem is not that the original Marxist vision got subverted by its unintended consequences; the problem is *this vision itself*. If Lenin's – and even Marx's – project of Communism were to be fully realized according to their true core, things would have been much worse than Stalinism – we would have a version of what Adorno and Horkheimer called "*die verwaltete Welt* (the administered society)", a totally self-transparent society run by the reified "general intellect", from which every last residue of human autonomy and freedom would have been obliterated. . . . The way to answer this criticism is to make a distinction between Marx's analysis of the capitalist dynamic and his positive vision of Communism, as well as between this vision and the actuality of the revolutionary turmoil: what if Marx's analysis of the capitalist dynamic is not dependent on his positive determinations of Communist societies? And what if his theoretical expectations themselves were shattered by the actual revolutionary experience? (It is clear that Marx himself was *surprised* by the new political form of the Paris Commune.)

48. Georgi Dimitroff, *Tagebücher 1933–1943*, Berlin: Aufbau Verlag 2000.

49. One of the few historians who is ready to confront this excruciating tension is Sheila Fitzpatrick, who pointed out that the year 1928 was a shattering turning-point, a true second revolution – not a kind of "Thermidor" but, rather, the consequent radicalization of the October Revolution. See *Stalinism: New Directions*, ed. Sheila Fitzpatrick, London: Routledge 2001.

50. Alain Badiou, *Petit manuel d'inesthétique*, Paris: Éditions du Seuil 1998, p. 16.

51. Ibid.

52. Ibid.

53. Quoted in Sydney Hook, *Out of Step*, New York: Dell 1987, p. 493.

54. See Carola Stern, *Männer lieben anders. Helene Weigel und Bertolt Brecht*, Reinbek bei Hamburg: Rowohlt 2001, p. 179.

55. Bertolt Brecht, *Gesammelte Werke*, vol. 20, Frankfurt: Suhrkamp Verlag 1967, p. 327.

56. *The Cambridge Companion to Brecht*, ed. Peter Thomson, Cambridge: Cambridge University Press 1994, p. 162.

57. See Bertolt Brecht, "Über die Diktaturen eizelner Menschen", in *Schriften*, vol. 2, Frankfurt: Suhrkamp Verlag 1973, pp. 300–301.

58. Brecht, *Gesammelte Werke*, vol. 20, p. 326.

59. Eisler occupies a privileged position among Brecht's three composers: Kurt Weill, Eisler and Paul Dessau. Each of them is identified with a specific stage of Brecht's work: Weill is the composer of his pre-Marxist carnivalesque-sarcastic rejection of the bourgeois universe, which culminates in *The Beggar's Opera*; Eisler is the composer of the most "Stalinist" Brecht, the Brecht of the "learning plays" and *The Mother*; Dessau is the composer of Brecht's "mature" epic theatre. Paradoxically, Eisler was also the most avant-garde of the three: right up to his death in 1961, he acknowledged his debt to Arnold Schoenberg (who also, right up to his death, recognized Eisler as one of his three true followers, together with Berg and Webern). There is something tragic in Eisler's utopia, to which he stuck to the bitter end: to overcome the split between his "serious" music (mostly chamber music and outstanding songs, some of them set to words by Hölderlin) and his "*Kampflieder* [struggle-songs]", and to compose a piece which would be at the same time dodecaphonic and popular (acceptable to the working masses).

60. Eisler's *Historic Recordings*, Berlin Classics, LC 6203; Bertolt Brecht, *Die Mutter*, Frankfurt: Suhrkamp 1980, pp. 47–8 (trans. Slavoj Žižek).

61. Ibid., pp. 21–2 (trans. Slavoj Žižek).

62. As usual, Brecht was borrowing here from an earlier Busch song, the "Ballad on Charity", composed by Eisler in 1930, with words by Kurt Tucholsky: the song's refrain is "Gut, das ist der Pfennig, und wo ist die Mark? [OK, this is a penny, but where is the mark?"].

63. In the German Democratic Republic, literature was classified into six categories:

1. the undisputed Socialist classics, that is, writers directly acknowledging themselves as Communists and endorsing the leading role of the Party;
2. "problematic" authors who, although committed Marxists, were not totally controlled by the Party, and were thus always under suspicion and tightly controlled (like Brecht);
3. authors who belonged to the "humanist heritage", that is, great names of the classic past and "progressive" contemporary authors, from Goethe and Schiller to Thomas Mann;
4. "tolerated" authors who were still published, albeit in limited editions;
5. authors who were not published, since they were rejected as bourgeois decadents and reactionaries (Kafka, Joyce, Nietzsche);
6. outright anti-Communist authors who were totally ignored, not even mentioned in literary histories and encyclopaedias.

One of the best indicators of the dynamics of "liberalization" was the passage of an author from one category to another: in the mid-1980s, for example, Kafka, Joyce and Freud went from (5) to (4), a selection of their works was published, albeit in limited editions; and Heinrich von Kleist went from (4) to (3), that is, he regained the status of belonging to the "great humanist heritage". The most interesting feature of this classification, however, is that it involves two levels, the explicit one and the implicit one: while (2) and (6) are necessary, they have to remain unacknowledged, excluded from the explicit set of categories, and, consequently, extremely close to each other.

Categories (2) and (6) did not exist for the public discourse: only the other four
categories were publicly used – that is to say, there were Communist classics, great
progressive humanists, tolerated authors and prohibited authors. Outright anti-Communist works (say, Arthur Koestler's *Darkness at Noon*) were not simply prohibited,
they were literally *unmentionable* – their prohibition itself was prohibited; one did not
talk about them. Things were even more delicate with category (2), a kind of strange
inversion of (6): while these authors were published and (to a certain extent) publicly
celebrated, there was a kind of strange unease about their work – however, public
articulation of this unease was strictly controlled, or even prohibited. The *nomenklatura*
simply did not know what to do with them. they were "ours", committed Communists,
but in such a way that they threatened to slip directly into category (6) – this was
Brecht's place. If, say, Brecht had crossed the threshold of tolerance, and become a
"dissident", he would have gone straight into (6), into the category of those who were
unmentionable – there would have been no other place for him.

    64. Karl Marx, *Grundrisse*, Harmondsworth: Penguin 1972, p. 112.

    65. See Alain Badiou, *Conditions*, Paris: Éditions du Seuil 1992.

    66. William Craig, *Enemy at the Gates*, Harmondsworth: Penguin 2000, p. 153. It is
deeply symptomatic how Jean-Jacques Annaud's film *Enemy at the Gates*, roughly based
on Craig's Stalingrad book, changes this scene (reported by Craig) of Hitler finding
himself face to face with the wounded soldiers: the film replaces Hitler with its only
truly interesting character, who is also, ironically, the one who is entirely invented: the
German sniper Major König, sent to kill the Russian ace sniper Vassily Zaitsev.

    What makes König (played superbly by Ed Harris) so fascinating is the combination
of cultural refinement (one could easily imagine *him* listening to *Winterreise*!), radical
Evil (in order to provoke Zaitsev into an uncontrollable outburst of rage, which will
expose him, he places in no-man's-land, between the front lines, the young boy who
acted as a kind of secret messenger between König and Zaitsev), and melancholic
resignation. As such, König is definitely the point of our (the spectators') libidinal
identification, against the Russian couple of Vassily and Tania, whose love dialogue
about who snores more like a pig is blatantly racist. His refined Evil is indicated by the
way he justifies his act to the boy ("I hate what I will have to do to you!"), and his deep
resignation by the way he accepts his death at the end: when he realizes that he is
exposed to Zaitsev, he simply takes off his cap and, with a melancholic smile, awaits the
shot.

    67. Craig, *Enemy at the Gates*, pp. 307–8.

    68. See Theodor W. Adorno, *Minima Moralia*, Frankfurt: Suhrkamp Verlag 1997,
pp. 38–41.

    69. In the late 1950s – when, as part of the process of de-Stalinization in the USSR,
hundreds of thousands of prisoners were released from the Gulag, and their sentences
proclaimed invalid – the ultimate counterargument of the intransigent Stalinists was that
one should not do this out of consideration for the investigators, prosecutors and judges
who passed the sentences in the first place – they believed that what they were doing
served the revolution, so what a shock it would be for them to have to accept that the
trial was a fake!

    70. This topic of *Exotica* is crucial for today's shift of the line of separation between
private and public. Recall the US Attorney General's decision, on 12 April 2001, that
the execution of Timothy McVeigh, the Oklahoma City bomber, would be broadcast on
a closed-circuit television link, enabling the survivors and the victims' relatives to watch

it. Does not this decision indicate the end of the modern logic of punishment, described by Foucault in *Discipline and Punish*, in which the act of capital punishment is no longer a public spectacle, but is to be performed behind the closed doors of a prison? With this legal decision, we are not simply returning to the premodern notion (and practice) of execution as a public spectacle: the fact that McVeigh's execution was broadcast only to the select few who were considered entitled to it (because they were affected by the crime) creates a space of shared, collective privacy.

71. Kornbluh, "The Family Man".

72. Marx, *Grundrisse*, p. 89. When Kierkegaard located the ultimate evil of modernity in the reign of the anonymous Public sustained by the press (daily newspapers), his violent criticism targeted the same abstraction:

> The abstraction of the press (for a newspaper, a journal, is no political concretion and only an individual in an abstract sense), combined with the passionlessness and reflectiveness of the age, gives birth to that abstraction's phantom, the public. (Søren Kierkegaard, *The Present Age*, New York: Harper & Row 1962, p. 64)

That is to say: here "abstraction" is, for Kierkegaard, also "real": it designates not a theoretical entity but actual life-experience itself, the way individuals relate to themselves when they "discuss problems" from the non-engaged position of an external observer – in this case, we "abstract" ourselves from our embeddedness in a concrete situation.

73. Kornbluh, "The Family Man".

74. Catherine Millet, *La vie sexuelle de Catherine M.*, Paris: Éditions du Seuil 2001.

75. Despite this radical rupture, however, today's digitalization designates the culminating point of the properly metaphysical tradition. Adorno said somewhere that every great philosophy is a variation on the ontological proof of God's existence: an attempt to pass directly from thought to being, first formulated by Parmenides in his assertion of the sameness of thinking and being. (Even Marx follows this line of thought: is not his idea of "class-consciousness" precisely that of a thought which directly intervenes into social being, as Georg Lukács showed vividly in *History and Class Consciousness?*) Consequently, is not cyberspace digital ideology – in its attempt to pass "from the bit to the It", to generate the very density of being from the digital formal-structural order – the last stage of this development?

76. The situation in Poland in the 1990s provides a unique example of such a love of one's neighbour: the unexpected friendship between General Jaruzelski and the former dissident Adam Michnik – two true neighbours, radical strangers to each other, coming from two different (ideological) universes, and none the less able to establish contact.

77. Here we should be attentive to the dialectical character of the notion of "as such". All of us probably remember the strange fact of how, when, with a sigh of relief, we suddenly become fully aware that our toothache has gone, this is a sign that it will soon come back. Similar occurrences abound: when, in the middle of the night, you wake up satisfied that you have no need to urinate, this means that very soon the urge will be there, and so on. The underlying logic is clear enough: the very explicit awareness of the absence of the unpleasant feeling is a reaction to the subconsciously perceived fact that the unpleasant feeling is already forming. Even on this level of the utmost trifling intimacy, Hegel's saying holds true: the owl of Minerva flies at dusk, that is, you become fully aware of something only when this thing is sliding away. . . .

78. While unconditionally rejecting the Israeli occupation of the West bank, we

should, of course, no less unconditionally oppose the anti-Semitic outbursts in Western Europe which justify themselves as the "exported *intifada*," that is, as gestures of solidarity with the oppressed Palestinians (from attacks on synagogues in Germany to hundreds of anti-Semitic incidents in France in autumn 2000). We should display no "understanding" here: there should be no room for the logic of "But you should understand that attacks on Jews in France are a reaction to the Israeli military brutality!", just as there is no room for the logic of "But you can understand the Israeli military reaction – who wouldn't be afraid, after the Holocaust and two thousand years of anti-Semitism!" Here, again, we should oppose the double blackmail: if one is pro-Palestinian, one is *eo ipso* anti-Semitic, and if one is against anti-Semitism, one must *eo ipso* be pro-Israel. The solution is not a compromise, a "just measure" between the two extremes – we should, rather, go right to the end in *both* directions – in the defence of Palestinian rights as well as in fighting anti-Semitism.

79. Christopher Hitchens, "We Know Best", *Vanity Fair*, May 2001, p. 34. And is not the same "totalitarian" vision often discernible in opposition to the death penalty? To put it in Foucauldian terms: is not the abolition of the death penalty part of a certain "biopolitics" which considers crime to be the result of social, psychological, ideological, etc., circumstances: the notion of the morally/legally responsible subject is an ideological fiction whose function is to cover up the network of power relations; individuals are not responsible for the crimes they commit, so they should not be punished?

Is not the obverse of this thesis, however, that those who control the circumstances control the people? Lenin's position – the unambiguous introduction of the class struggle as the line of separation with regard to the death penalty – is much more honest:

> It is right to argue against the death penalty only when it is applied by the exploiters against the mass of the working people with the purpose of maintaining exploitation. It is hardly likely that any revolutionary government whatever could do without applying the death penalty to the exploiters (i.e. the landowners and capitalists). (V.I. Lenin, "The Impending Catastrophe and How to Combat It", see above, p. 85.)

80. It was Ken Rinehard (UCLA) who drew my attention to this scene.

81. Søren Kierkegaard, *Works of Love*, New York: Harper 1994, p. 75.

82. Ibid., p. 74.

83. Ibid., pp. 77–8.

84. How, exactly, do we fall in love? During a class on German literature, a French friend of mine was recently beguiled by the way an older and embittered colleague recited, with great force, a poem by Celan; later, she approached him and was surprised to learn that his name was François (her mother's name being Françoise) – this uncanny coincidence functioned as the detail which pushed her into risking a full love-relationship.

Is this not an exemplary case of the distinction between Imaginary and Symbolic? First there is a simple imaginary fascination which, if it is to develop into full-blown love, has to be supported by a symbolic identification. Here there is a clear parallel with Freud's insight into the difference between the thought articulated in a dream and the dream's unconscious desire: an everyday thought is submitted to the dream-work (encoded in a dream) only if a "deeper" unconscious desire gets attached to it. In the same way, it was the totally imbecilic coincidence of names which channelled the maternal identification into a simple fascination. My friend felt deeply indebted towards her mother, as if her birth had ruined her mother's career and turned her into an embittered housewife; for this reason, in her love life she had a clear preference for older and not particularly attractive men who, instead of giving her sexual pleasure, needed her to help them – this was her elementary fantasy frame, and a man become a potential partner if he fulfilled these criteria. Her mother, not her father, was thus the Third through whom she desired, the object-cause of her desire, the symptom she was enjoying in entertaining a painful and frustrating relationship with her partner. This is why it would not be true to say that even without the coincidence of names, the elementary force of erotic attraction she felt for her colleague would have found another basis – on the contrary, without the fortuitous coincidence of names, there would have been no love, merely a passing attraction.

There is, of course, something deeply depressing about this insight. Is this all there is to it? Is there no "true" love? Is all we can do simply to learn to live with our symptoms, to accept the imbecilic contingency which rules our lives? Lacan's ultimate wager is that this is *not* the case: there is love beyond symptomatic identification, love which directly touches the other in the Real of his or her being.

85. To avoid misunderstanding, we should, of course, retain the full awareness of the totally unacceptable terrorist measures of the GDR authorities against the dissidents; simply consider the recently disclosed fact that when the leading dissidents were interrogated, they were seated close to a flimsy wall on the other side of which was a strong source of radiation. The idea, of course, was to cause cancer – and indeed, a large number of them died of it.

86. For a more detailed discussion of this paradox of love, see Chapter 2 of Žižek, *On Belief*.

87. That was Otto Weininger's failing – no wonder Hitler said: "Weininger was the only Jew who deserved to live."

88. Quoted from Robert Service, *Lenin*, London: Macmillan 2000, p. 232.

89. In Catherine Breillat's *Romance*, there is a fantasmatic scene which perfectly stages this radical split between love and sexuality: the heroine imagines herself lying naked on her belly on a small low table divided in the middle by a partition with a hole just big enough for her body. With the upper side of her body, she faces a nice tender guy with whom she exchanges gentle loving words and kisses, while her lower part is exposed to one or more sex-machine studs who penetrate her wildly and repeatedly.

90. For this idea of a nexus, I am indebted to Rüdiger Safranski, "Theorie über die Liebe oder Theorie aus Liebe?", intervention at the colloquium *Über die Liebe*, Schloss Elmau (Germany), 15 August 2001. And, incidentally, do we not encounter here yet again the triad RIS: the Real of biogenetic reproduction, the Imaginary of intense pleasure experiences, the Symbolic of intersubjective relations?

91. Both quotes from Maureen Freely, "Polymorphous Sexuality in the Sixties", *The Independent*, 29 January 2001, The Monday Review, p. 4.

92. Quoted from *Konkret*, vol. 3 (March 2001), p. 9.

93. Quoted from "Motherhood and Murder", *Newsweek*, 2 July 2001, p. 24.

94. Two decades after *Taxi Driver*, Andrew Davis's *The Fugitive* provided a less ambiguous version of the violent *passage à l'acte* serving as a lure, a vehicle of ideological displacement. Towards the end, the innocent persecuted doctor (Harrison Ford) confronts his colleague (Jerome Kraabe) at a large medical convention, accusing him of falsifying medical data on behalf of a large pharmaceutical company. At this precise point, when you would expect that the focus would shift to the company – corporate capital – as the true culprit, Kraabe interrupts his talk, invites Ford to step aside, and

then, outside the convention hall, they engage in a passionate violent fight, beating each other until their faces are red with blood. This scene is tell-tale in its openly ridiculous character, as if, in order to get out of the ideological mess of playing with anti-capitalism, one should make a move which directly reveals the cracks in the narrative. Another aspect here is the transformation of the bad guy (Kraabe) into a vicious, sneering, pathological character, as if psychological depravity (which accompanies the dazzling spectacle of the fight) should replace the anonymous non-psychological drive of capital: the much more appropriate gesture would have been to present the corrupt colleague as a psychologically sincere and privately honest doctor who, because of the financial difficulties of the hospital in which he works, was lured into swallowing the pharmaceutical company's bait.

95. Quoted from Siegfried Tornow, "Männliche Homosexualität und Politik in Sowjet-Russland", in *Homosexualität und Wissenschaft II*, Berlin: Verlag Rosa Winkel 1992, p. 281.

96. Adorno, *Minima Moralia*, p. 52.

97. One of the detrimental clinical consequences of the Cultural Studies Politically Correct stance is the (implicit, but thereby all the more effective) prohibition on articulating the structural discontent/unease which pertains to lesbian subjectivity: conceptualizing the clinical fact that most lesbian relationships are characterized by an uncanny coldness, emotional distance, impossibility of love, radical narcissism, as well as unease with one's own position, as if drawing the logical conclusion from this fact (and not just dismissing it as the effect of internalized patriarchal repression) would be equivalent to endorsing the classic patriarchal wisdom.

Along the same lines, the problem with the argument that homosexuals remain faithful to the primordial same-sex "passionate attachment" (in short: in a first mythical stage, we were all homosexuals, and heterosexuality emerges as the betrayal of this primordial object of desire) is that it can easily be turned into an argument *against* homosexuality: in so far as culture means the work of mediation, of displacement, it implicitly posits homosexuality as the "primitive" starting point which has to be left behind in the course of cultural development. For this reason, the apparently "conservative" notion of homosexuality as relying on (or resulting from) some kind of "unnatural" derailment seems much more promising, theoretically as well as politically: it asserts homosexuality as the stance of courageously daring to take unexplored paths.

98. Gary Indiana, *Salò or The 120 Days of Sodom*, London: BFI Publishing 2000, p. 71.

99. I am tempted to add: not only the wealth of perversions, but wealth *as such*, since amassing wealth for its own sake *is* perversion at its purest. Against the cliché "True, money's not everything, but it comes pretty close to it!", the authentic Freudian claim is, rather: "Sex isn't everything, but it comes pretty close to it!" – and money is precisely what fills in the gap, the distance, on account of which sex is never "everything". In this precise sense, money is an "anal (partial) object": a perverse supplement that is necessary to provide some kind of consistency to our sexuality.

100. I borrow this term from Kornbluh, "The Family Man".

101. Milan Kundera once said that, in true love, you always want to keep your beloved within view – you are afraid even to blink, fearing that in that brief moment, the magic will disappear and the beloved will turn into just another ugly person. . . . True love is precisely the opposite of this fear: I let my beloved breathe, since I trust that even when I cannot see him or her, the bond between us will remain firm.

102. Another case of ideological censorship: when firefighters' widows were interviewed on CNN, most of them gave the expected performance: tears, prayers . . . all except one who, without a tear, said that she did not pray for her husband, because she knew that prayer would not bring him back. Asked if she dreamed of revenge, she calmly said that this would be a true betrayal of her husband: had he survived, he would have insisted that the worst thing to do is to succumb to the urge to retaliate . . . there is no need to add that this fragment was shown only once, and then disappeared from the repetitions of the interviewers.

103. See Chapter 3 of Raymond Bellour, *The Analysis of Film*, Bloomington, IN: Indiana University Press 2000.

104. I draw here on my critical elaboration of Althusser's notion of interpellation in Chapter 3 of *The Metastases of Enjoyment*, London and New York: Verso 1995.

105. Michael Dutton, *Streetlife China*, Cambridge: Cambridge University Press 1998, p. 17.

106. Recall, along these lines, the Taleban Foreign Minister's answer to a question from Western journalists: why do women in Afghanistan not play a greater role (or, rather, *any* role) in public affairs: "How can you trust a person who, every month, bleeds for a couple of days!"

107. Among other superb moments, the screenplay of *Fight Club* contains what is arguably the best pro-choice line in the history of cinema (unfortunately, it was not included in the film itself): in the midst of the intense lovemaking with the hero, Helena Bonham-Carter gasps: "I love you. I want to have your abortion." *This*, not the proverbial "I want to have your child", is the ultimate expression of love: the gesture of *sacrificing* the offspring, and thus asserting the love-relationship as the absolute end in itself.

108. Ira Nayman, "The Man Who Wasn't There", *Creative Screenwriting*, vol. 8, no. 2 (March–April 2001), p. 58.

109. Chuck Palahniuk, *Fight Club*, New York: Henry Holt & Company 1996, pp. 114–17.

110. The only similar case is *Me, Myself and Irene*, in which Jim Carrey beats himself up – here, of course, in a comic (albeit painfully exaggerated) way, as one part of a split personality pounding the other part. There is, however, a scene in Don Siegel's *Dirty Harry* which somehow presages the self-beating in *Fight Club*: the serial killer, in order to denounce "Dirty Harry" (Inspector Callahan, played by Clint Eastwood) for police brutality, hires a thug to beat his face to a pulp – even when his face is soaked in blood, he continues to encourage him: "Hit me harder!"

111. For a more detailed account of the notion of act as "striking back at oneself", see Slavoj Žižek, *The Fragile Absolute*, London and New York: Verso 2000.

112. See Gilles Deleuze, *Masochism and Coldness*, New York: Zone Books 1993.

113. It is a clear indication of the constraints imposed by the Politically Correct perspective that almost all critical reactions to *Fight Club* remained blind to this emancipatory potential of violence: they saw in the film the reassertion of violent masculinity as a paranoid reaction to recent trends which undermine traditional masculinity; consequently, they either condemned the film as proto-Fascist, or commended it as a critique of this proto-Fascist attitude.

114. Quoted in Claire Brennan, *The Poetry of Sylvia Plath*, Cambridge: Icon Books 2000, p. 22.

115. I borrow this term from Elisabeth Bronfen's study of hysteria, *The Knotted Subject*, New York: Columbia University Press 2000.

116. We should note here that Plath also used the term "Holocaust" in order to describe her first night of love with Ted Hughes: "Arrived in Paris early Saturday evening exhausted from sleepless holocaust night with Ted in London" (*The Unabridged Journals of Sylvia Plath*, ed. Karen V. Kukil, New York: Anchor Books 2000, p. 552). "Holocaust" is thus, for her, not only an unimaginable (indescribable) horror, but also an unimaginable enjoyment – in short, the indescribable excess as such. Furthermore, most of the circumstantial evidence indicates that Sylvia and Ted, in the true spirit of courtly love, realized this intense sexual experience without having full sexual intercourse – after all, Sylvia was well versed in the art of achieving "practical satisfaction" while maintaining "technical virginity" (ibid., p. 147).

117. *The Autobiography of Bertrand Russell*, London: Routledge 2000, p. 295.

118. Ryszard Kapuscinski, *The Shadow of the Sun*, New York: Knopf 2001.

119. Ibid., p. 183.

120. See Martin Heidegger, *Sein und Zeit*, Tübingen: Max Niemeyer Verlag 1963 (10th edn), p. 121–2.

121. See Eric Santner, "Miracles Happen: Benjamin, Rosenzweig, and the Limits of the Enlightenment" (unpublished paper, 2001), which contains a (fully justified) constructive criticism of my own reading of "Theses" in *The Sublime Object of Ideology* (London: Verso 1989).

122. In so far as these past failures herald their revolutionary redemption to come, they "prognosticate" the future revolutionary miracle which will retroactively redeem them. Furthermore, in so far as Alain Badiou's name for the miracle is "Event" (see Alain Badiou, *L'être et l'événement*, Paris: Éditions du Seuil 1989), we can deploy from Benjamin's "Theses" a kind of critique *avant la lettre* of Badiou: an Event does not occur out of nowhere; not only does it take place within what Badiou calls a *site événementielle*, it is even "prognosticated" by a series of past failed Events.

123. A recurrent theme in Badiou, *L'être et l'événement*.

124. Two figures who anticipate Kurtz are crucial here: Kilburne, the eccentric commander of the helicopter squad (Robert Duvall), a clear precursor of Kurtz – Kurtz in so far as he is still acceptable to the military establishment (recall his numerous half-psychotic idiosyncrasies); and the leader of the isolated French community in Cambodia, a group clinging to their colonial past on an abandoned plantation.

125. Incidentally, why, after Noriega's arrest, did he not stand public trial? What could he have divulged about his CIA contacts?

126. Bülent Diken and Carsten Bagge Laustsen, "Enjoy your fight! – 'Fight Club' as a symptom of the Network Society" (unpublished manuscript).

127. For the most systematic exposition of these two levels, see Gilles Deleuze and Félix Guattari, *A Thousand Plateaus*, Minneapolis: University of Minnesota Press 1987. In psychoanalysis, one talks about paranoia, but very rarely about schizophrenia – is only *paranoia*, then, a strict psychoanalytic concept, while *schizophrenia* is not a concept, merely a name for descriptive features (and an entity within the medical, not the psychoanalytic, discourse)? I am none the less tempted to propose the following distinction: in both cases, the foreclosed symbolic (Law) returns in the Real; in paranoia, however, it returns "in the mind", in the guise of hallucinations and paranoiac delusions; while in schizophrenia, the foreclosed returns by directly inscribing itself in the bodily Real (as catatonic numbness, etc.). It is imperative to distinguish this schizophrenic

inscription of the foreclosed (say, symbolic castration) from the hysterical inscription in a conversion symptom: in schizophrenia, castration itself is inscribed, while the hysterical symptom is a compromise solution which gives body to the denial of castration. (For this point I am indebted to Élisabeth Doisneau, Brussels.)

128. See Badiou, *L'être et l'événement*.

129. See Maurice Merleau-Ponty, *Humanism and Terror: The Communist Problem*, Oxford: Polity Press 2000.

130. Quoted from Buck-Morss, *Dreamworld and Catastrophe*, p. 144.

131. Ibid.

132. The distinction between "high" and "late" modernism (elaborated by Fredric Jameson in his lectures on modernism (not yet published; delivered in February 2001 at the Kulturwissenschaftliches Institut in Essen) seems crucial here. The early "substantial" modernism was not yet modernism "for itself", an autonomous artistic style, but it was still conceived as a global project for the total overhaul of society itself; we go on to modernism "for itself" with the reappropriation of American Abstract Expressionism by the establishment, and its use for Cold War propaganda.

How can we forget the extent to which the international explosion of Abstract Expressionism in the early 1950s was orchestrated by the CIA as part of its Cold War strategy to undermine the cultural impact of Communism by launching in Europe an American art which was highly "nonconformist", yet totally unacceptable to the Communists? The very decision to elevate Jackson Pollock (and not, say, Mark Rothko) into the emblematic figure of Abstract Expressionism was made by the CIA for non-artistic reasons: in his physical appearance and lifestyle, Pollock perfectly fitted the ideological notion of the American individualist – aggressively male, spontaneous, a hard drinker. . . . So it was that in a little over a year, Pollock progressed from cheap Greenwich Village bars to the front page of *Life* magazine. (See the amusing report in Chapter 16 of Frances Stonor Saunders, *The Cultural Cold War*, New York: The New Press 1999.)

The key underlying opposition of "high" modernism was that between art and culture: "culture" was the keyword for the mediation between art and society, so the assertion of art's autonomy had to insist on the opposition between art and its degradation/vulgarization in (mass) culture. It is only at this moment, with the ascendancy of "late" modernism, that the concept of artistic modernism as such was posited. If, then, modernism involves a certain narrative (of the "progress" from realism to modernism), and if this narrative emerges only with post-World War II "late" modernism, could we not say that the "repressed" of this narrative is "high" modernism itself, its trans-aesthetic utopian excess of political energy, its endeavour to transform "real life" itself?

We can see how "late" modernism is a necessary mediator between "high" modernism and postmodernism: it is only within the "late" modernist universe that realism can be appropriated as a contingent style. Let us take the triad (in art theory) of realism, modernism, and postmodernism – when, exactly, do we pass from modernism to postmodernism? On the abstract conceptual level, there is only one precise answer: when *realism itself* (re)appears, is (re)appropriated, as a "modernist" procedure. This goes for all today's "realist" writers, up to the bestselling novels of John Irving: here realism is not practised as a substantial stance; it is rather that the realist *code* is practised as one among the available procedures – deprived of its substance, it is used as a pastiche. In other words, postmodernism appears when modernism reaches its point of closure –

when its constitutive tension with and opposition to the realist tradition is sublated/ internalized, since realism now no longer indicates a substantially different approach to reality itself, simply one of the contingent historical codes within the modernist horizon.

Today, of course, "late" modernism is paying the price for its original sin of elitism, in the guise of the newly discovered populism of Cultural Studies: take the (rare, but nevertheless paradigmatic) cases of Cultural Studies authors who, while dismissing "high culture" as elitist, argue that, when individuals do not react to them as the ideological text expects them to, but inscribe them into their own subversive context, soap operas and shopping malls can be reappropriated as "sites of resistance" against the hegemonic ideology. (There is no need to add that a true Marxist should vehemently oppose this reading: such "subverting" is simply the "inherent transgression" which, far from undermining the hegemonic ideology, in effect sustains it.)

133. On this point, the crucial figure of Soviet cinema is not Eisenstein but Alexander Medvedkin, appropriately called by Christ Marker "the last Bolshevik" (see Marker's outstanding documentary *The Last Bolshevik* [1993]). While he wholeheartedly supported official policies, including forced collectivization, Medvedkin made films which staged this support in a way which retained the initial ludic utopian-subversive revolutionary impulse; for example, in *Happiness* (1935), in order to combat religion, he shows a priest who imagines seeing a nun's breasts through her habit – an outrageous scene for a Soviet film in the 1930s. Thus Medvedkin enjoys the unique privilege of being an enthusiastically orthodox Communist film-maker whose films were *all* banned, or at least heavily censored.

134. Although it is also possible to argue that this violence *was* in fact an impotent *passage à l'acte*: an outburst which displayed an inability to break with the weight of the past symbolic tradition. In order to get rid of the past effectively, you do not need to smash monuments physically – changing them into part of the tourist industry is much more effective. Is this not what the Tibetans are painfully discovering today? The true destruction of their culture will occur not through the Chinese destroying their monuments, but through the proliferation of Buddhist theme parks in downtown Lhasa.

135. I am tempted to question the very term "Leninism": was it not invented under Stalin? And does the same not go for Marxism (as a teaching), which was basically a Leninist invention, so that Marxism is a Leninist notion and Leninism a Stalinist one?

136. See Chapters 2 and 3 of Buck-Morss's outstanding *Dreamworld and Catastrophe*.

137. See Leslie Kaplan, *L'excès-usine*, Paris: Hachette 1984.

138. See Christopher Hitchens, *The Trial of Henry Kissinger* (New York and London: Verso 2001), which makes a conclusive case against this miserable figure who exemplifies vulgar cynical opportunistic *Realpolitik* masquerading as "wisdom". After his retirement from active politics, whenever there was a backlash against some emancipatory struggle, he was there, raising his voice in support, even if the interests he was defending were those of the Communist *nomenklatura* on its deathbed: in 1981, after Jaruzelski's *coup d'état*, he voiced his "understanding" of Russian geopolitical interests; in 1991, on the first day of the abortive anti-Gorbachev coup by the old Soviet *nomenklatura*, he was there again, emphasizing the necessity for a strong, stable Russian state. Moreover, while still active – first as National Security Adviser and then as Secretary of State under Nixon and Ford – he was always there to bomb or otherwise destroy the poor and helpless, from Chile to Cambodia, and to make a "strategic" deal with the powerful, right up to Mao Ze Dong. The first association which comes to mind when one hears

his name is Margaret Thatcher's apt characterization of Giulio Andreotti, the Italian ex-Prime Minister involved with the Mafia: it is not only that he is immoral; after watching a TV interview with him, one cannot avoid the impression that he almost elevated immoral cynicism into a kind of perverted ethical attitude – he is immoral not for some egotistic reasons, but out of principle, as if there is something deep in his nature which explodes in revulsion whenever he scents the possibility that someone might act out of moral consideration.

139. What, then, is the underlying subjective position of those who carry out the energy policies of the Bush presidency? Are they not aware of the facts (that if the present trend goes on, catastrophe awaits all of us; that the USA is squandering an "unfairly" large *per capita* amount of the Earth's (limited) energy resources)? The only possible answer is: yes, they are very well aware of them, but they don't care. Their implicit reasoning goes something like this: we know that there will be a catastrophe in a decade or two, but instead of worrying about it, let us, rather, enjoy our privileges as long as we can – this cynical reasoning is the hidden truth of Bush's obscene rumblings about growing energy consumption as part of the sacred American way of life. Here, I am tempted to revive the old Stalinist designation of capitalist regimes as "decadent": is "decadence" not the most appropriate term for a political regime which knowingly abandons the perspective of its own long-term survival?

140. Again I rely here on Kornbluh, "The Family Man", where she also evokes the perfect example of Woody Allen's *Husbands and Wives*, a film which juxtaposes two strategies of coping with a marriage in crisis: the couple who embark on an open transgression of their marital vow (each of the partners gets a new lover) save their marriage; while the couple who persist in the form of marriage see their marriage irreparably destroyed. The message is clear: only a proper dose of the appropriate transgression (promiscuity) can save a marriage, while sticking to the form of marriage in a crisis is the most effective way to destroy it. (Although Allen's universe is Jewish, does he not here apply the proverbial Catholic lesson on how to save a marriage in crisis: a couple of visits to a prostitute may ease the tension, and thus reinforce the marital bond.) And do not these two strategies obey the logic of Lacan's formulas of sexuation? The first couple proceed in a "masculine" way: they risk the exception (promiscuity) to sustain the universal form (of marriage); while the second couple allow for no exception, and thus lose the very universal bond. (For an explanation of the "formulas of sexuation", see Chapter 2 of Slavoj Žižek, *Tarrying with the Negative*, Durham, NC: Duke University Press 1993.)

Consider the two versions of misunderstanding: a man says: "I can understand everything you said (or did), *except that* – how could you have done *that*?"; while a woman would, rather, say: "There's nothing of what you said (or did) that I don't understand; nevertheless, the whole of it, put together, doesn't make sense to me." Or, with regard to meaning: the "masculine" version is to posit a traumatic/meaningless excess which grounds and guarantees meaning – that is how monotheism operates: "There is One God, He just is what He is", that is, a meaningless traumatic Void. Far from undermining meaning, such an excess of the pure Divine Name (of the signifier without signified) guarantees it, in contrast to the "feminine" formula " There is nothing (no element) which is deprived of meaning" – and, for that very reason, meaning is non-all; it never builds a consistent Whole.

The basic paradox of the phallic function (it relies on its constitutive exception, so that without its exception it is no longer operative: the woman suspends the phallic function by the very fact that she is wholly, without remainder, included in it) can also be exemplified by the paradox of metaphysics: perhaps the very tendency to "overcome metaphysics" is metaphysical, so that the only true overcoming of metaphysics would be the gesture of fully accepting its closure (it was Foucault who emphasized that in so far as philosophy as such is Platonism, all philosophers define themselves as anti-Platonists).

Lacan has been criticized for the fact that these "formulas of sexuation" are inconsistent, since they combine intuitionist and constructionist approaches: the masculine universal proposition is "constructionist" (all X are submitted to the phallic function); while the feminine *pas-tout* is obviously "intuitionist", referring to the impossibility of representing the All of Woman in intuition. What, however, if this inconsistency is Lacan's point? What if the way we are sexualized in our capacity of "beings of language" relies precisely on the gap between the constructionist and intuitionist approach to a universal function – on the fact that while one can construct a universal proposition, one can never "fill it up" completely with specific examples; one can never reach it by proceeding from case to case, one by one?

141. This, however, in no way implies that a true subversion has to *appear* as such in a direct and obvious way; in Hollywood cinema of the 1940s, for example, the truly subversive works were not those which directly tackled the issues of class struggle. One of the few sites of true subversion was the Ernst Lubitsch tradition of comedies and its variation, Howard Hawks's screwball comedies. Recall the final scene of Hawks's *Gentlemen Prefer Blondes*, in which Marilyn Monroe explains why a woman should marry a man for his money: it is only in this case, when the woman's "pathological" bias in appreciating the man's qualities is suspended (since he has money, his financial status will not distort her perspective), that she can genuinely ponder the worth of her partner, appreciating him for what he is, and thus – perhaps – decide to fall in love with him.

142. This point was forcefully developed by Chantal Mouffe in *The Democratic Paradox*, London and New York: Verso 2000.

143. Recall Brecht's famous scandalous saying: "A Communist tells the truth when it is necessary, and he lies when it is necessary; he is kind when it is necessary, and he is brutal when it is necessary; he is honest when it is necessary, and he cheats when it is necessary. . . . Of all virtues, he has only one: that he fights for Communism." This *ethical suspension of morality* is specifically Christian-modern; as such, it is to be strictly opposed to the "pagan" one, in which morality concerns my relationship to others and ethics my "care of the Self" in the Foucauldian sense: what I make of myself.

144. See Alain Badiou, "L'Un se divise en Deux", intervention at the symposium *The Retrieval of Lenin*, Essen, 2–4 February 2001.

145. See Sylvain Lazarus, "La forme Parti", intervention at the symposium *The Retrieval of Lenin*.

146. Wendy Brown, *States of Injury*, Princeton, NJ: Princeton University Press 1995, p. 14.

147. See Fredric Jameson, "The Concept of Revisionism", intervention at the symposium *The Retrieval of Lenin*. I am even tempted to claim that this absence of a common language involves the logic of sexual difference as laid out by Lacan in his "formulas of sexuation": it is "masculine" politics versus the feminine "economy". And does the same not go for the Lacanian opposition between desire and drive? The two terms are absolutely incompatible; there is no common meta-language or code which would enable us to translate one into the other.

148. Is it not that the same "vase/two faces" paradox occurs in the case of the

Holocaust and the Gulag? Either we elevate the Holocaust into the ultimate crime, and the Stalinist terror is thereby half-redeemed, reduced to a minor role of an "ordinary" crime; or we focus on the Gulag as the ultimate result of the logic of modern revolutionary terror, and the Holocaust is thereby at best reduced to another instance of the same logic. Somehow, it does not seem possible to deploy a truly "neutral" theory of totalitarianism without giving a hidden preference either to the Holocaust or to the Gulag.

In the history of Communism in Slovenia, there was a traumatic moment in which the Nazi concentration camps and the Stalinist show trials and Gulag intersected: in 1949, there was in Ljubljana, the Slovene capital, a public trial usually referred to as the "Dachau trial": the accused were former Communists who were arrested by the Nazis and survived the Dachau camp. Most of them occupied important positions in the new nationalized industries after World War II, and they were made into scapegoats for the economic failures of the new regime: they were accused of collaborating with the Gestapo in Dachau, betraying their colleagues (the reason they survived), and, after the war, of continuing to work for Western secret services, sabotaging the construction of socialism; after they had been made to confess their guilt publicly, most of them were condemned to death and shot immediately, while some were imprisoned in "Goli Otok [the Naked Island]" on the Adriatic, a smaller Yugoslav version of the Gulag. Their despair was total: after surviving Dachau, they found no sympathetic "big Other" to tell about their ordeal; on the contrary, they were condemned for surviving (no doubt the prosecution also played on the so-called survivor's guilt). In this way, they found themselves in the horrifying void, deprived of any symbolic support, their entire life rendered totally meaningless. . . .

149. For a more detailed elaboration of this point, see Chapter 2 of Žižek, *On Belief*.

150. And the achievement of Lukács's *History and Class Consciousness* is that it is one of the few works which succeed in bringing these two dimensions together: on the one hand, the topic of commodity fetishism and reification; on the other, the topic of the Party and revolutionary strategy – that is why this book is profoundly *Leninist*.

151. See Badiou, *D'un désastre obscur*, p. 30.

152. For a further development of this point, see Chapter 3 of Žižek, *The Fragile Absolute*.

It is often said that the ultimate product of capitalism is piles of trash – useless computers, cars, TVs and VCRs . . .: places like the famous "resting place" of the hundreds of abandoned planes in the Mojave desert confront us with the obverse truth of the capitalist dynamic, its inert objectal remainder. And it is against this background that we should read the ecological dream-notion of total recycling (in which every remainder is used again) as the ultimate capitalist dream, even if it is expressed in terms of maintaining the natural balance of Planet Earth: the dream of the self-propelling circulation of capital, which would succeed in leaving no material leftover – proof of how capitalism can appropriate ideologies which seem to oppose it.

153. *Ich liebe euch doch alle! Befehle und Lageberichte des MfS Januar–November 1989*, ed. Armin Mitter and Stefan Wolle, Berlin: BasisDruck 1990, p. 120.

154. In fact, there are already predictions that the "next industrial revolution" will be focused on the natural environment as the main field of capitalist investment and innovation – see Paul Hawken, Amory Lovins and Hunter Lovins, *The Natural Capitalism: The Next Industrial Revolution*, London: Earthscan 1999.

155. This is precisely what Michael Hardt and Antonio Negri are trying to do in

their *Empire* (Cambridge, MA: Harvard University Press 2000), a book which sets its goal as rewriting *The Communist Manifesto* for the twenty-first century. Hardt and Negri describe globalization as an ambiguous "de-territorialization": victorious global capitalism permeates every pore of our social lives, the most intimate of spheres, and installs an ever-present dynamic which is no longer based on patriarchal or other hierarchic structures of domination; instead, it gives rise to an unstable, hybrid identity. On the other hand, this fundamental corrosion of all important social links lets the genie out of the bottle: it frees the potential centrifugal forces that the capitalist system is no longer fully able to control. It is precisely because of its global triumph that the capitalist system is more vulnerable than ever today – Marx's old formula is still valid: capitalism digs its own grave.

Hardt and Negri describe this process as the transition from the Nation-State to global Empire, a transnational entity comparable to Ancient Rome, in which hybrid scattered identities materialize. Hardt and Negri therefore deserve great praise for enlightening us about the contradictory nature of today's "turbocapitalism", and attempting to identify the revolutionary potentials of its dynamic. This heroic attempt sets itself against the standard view of those on the Left who are struggling to limit the destructive powers of globalization, and to rescue (what there is left to rescue of) the Welfare State. This standard Leftist view is imbued with a profoundly conservative mistrust of the dynamic of globalization and digitalization, which is quite contrary to the Marxist confidence in the powers of progress.

Nevertheless, we immediately get a sense of the limits of Hardt and Negri's attempt: the lack of concrete insight in their social-economic analysis is concealed in the Deleuzean jargon of multitude, de-territorialization, and so on – no wonder the three "practical" proposals with which this book ends appear anticlimactic. The authors propose to concentrate our political struggle around three global rights: the right to global citizenship; the right to a minimum income; and the reappropriation of the new means of production (i.e. access to and control of education, information, and communication). It is paradoxical that Hardt and Negri, the poets of mobility, variety, hybridization, and so on, formulate these three demands in the classic terminology of universal human rights: the problem with these demands is that they oscillate between formal emptiness and impossible radicalism.

Let us take the right to global citizenship: theoretically, this right, of course, should be approved; however, if this demand is to be taken more seriously than a celebratory formal declaration in the typical UN style, then it would mean the abolition of state borders – under present conditions, such a step would trigger an influx of cheap labour from India, China and Africa towards the USA and Western Europe, which would in turn result in a populist revolt against immigrants, a revolt of such violent proportions that people like Haider would look like models of multicultural tolerance. The same goes for the other two demands: for instance, a universal (worldwide) right to a minimum income – of course, why not? But how should we create the necessary socioeconomic and ideological conditions for such a shattering transformation? (Incidentally, the opposition of these two readings is deeply Kantian: if we read any of *Empire*'s three demands as a formal declaration, we conceive of it as a *regulatory* principle; while if we take it literally, and demand its direct actualization, we impose it as a *constitutive* principle.) This critique is not aimed only at minor empirical details: the main problem with *Empire* is that its fundamental analysis of how (if at all) the present global socioeconomic process will create the necessary space for such radical measures is inadequate. Hardt and Negri fail to repeat, in today's conditions, Marx's argument that the prospect of the proletarian revolution emerges out of the inherent antagonisms of the capitalist mode of production – and in this respect, *Empire* remains a pre-Marxist book.

156. I am tempted to include in this series the subject itself: is not the so-called postmodern "Protean subject" precisely a "subject (or, rather, subjectivity) without subject", deprived of the radical (self-relating) negativity which makes it a subject?

157. Along the same lines, the passage from symptom to what Lacan calls *le sinthome* runs through the symptom's *generalization*: a symptom is the exception which disturbs the "normal" run of things, bringing to light its repressed truth; while the *sinthome* emerges when we accept that *there are only exceptions* (disturbances, imbalances) – that the very "density" of reality indicates that "something went wrong", that the balance of the primordial Void was disturbed. The fact that "there is something rather than nothing" is a *pathological* phenomenon in the most radical sense of the term.

158. See Jacques Derrida, *Specters of Marx*, New York: Routledge 1993.

159. Marx, *Grundrisse*, p. 706.

160. Kojin Karatani, *Architecture as Metaphor*, Cambridge, MA: MIT Press 1995, p. 117.

161. Karl Marx, *Capital*, Volume I, New York: International Publishers 1867, p. 253.

162. Ibid., p. 254. It is with this shift to the universal form of circulation as an end in itself that we pass from premodern ethics, grounded in a reference to some substantial supreme Good, to paradigmatically modern Kantian ethics in which it is ultimately only the form of duty that matters, that is, in which duty is to be accomplished for the sake of duty. This means that Lacan's emphasis on how Kant's ethics is the ethics intrinsic to the Galilean–Newtonian universe of modern science has to be supplemented by an insight into how Kant's ethics is also the ethics intrinsic to the capitalist logic of circulation as an end in itself.

163. Ibid., pp. 254–5.

164. Ibid., pp. 236–7.

165. Ibid., p. 171.

166. Ibid., pp. 171–3.

167. This deconstructionist reading of Marx's critique of political economy should therefore be opposed to the great Marxist tradition of conceiving the global dimension of commodity fetishism: the class and commodity structure of capitalism is not just a phenomenon limited to the particular "domain" of economy, but the structuring principle that overdetermines the social totality, from politics to art and religion. *This* global dimension of capitalism is also suspended in today's multiculturalist progressive politics: its "anti-capitalism" is reduced to the level of how today's capitalism breeds sexist/racist oppression, and so on.

168. The main reference for this crisis of property (ownership) is, of course, Jeremy Rifkin's *The Age of Access*, New York: J.P. Tarcher 2001. However, for a more fundamental insight, avoiding Rifkin's flirting with the "new paradigm" topos, see Immanuel Wallerstein's *The End of the World as We Know It*, Minneapolis: University of Minnesota Press 2001.

169. Another figure of this inexplicable excess occurs in many cinema comedies in which the hero, stranded alone in a small town, is forced to take his expensive car to the local mechanic who, to the hero's horror, proceeds to take the whole car to pieces; when, a day or two later, the mechanic puts the car together again, to everyone's

surprise, it runs perfectly, although there is always a part or two left over, the remainders which the mechanic could not find a place for when he put the car back together. . . .

170. See Rifkin, *The Age of Access*. Along similar lines, Gerhard Schulze has proposed the concept of *Erlebnisgesellschaft*, the "society of [lived] experience", in which the prevailing norms are those of pleasure and the quality of life-experiences – see Gerhard Schulze, *Die Erlebnisgesellschaft. Kultursoziologie der Gegenwart*, Frankfurt and New York: Campus Verlag 1992.

171. Fuat Firat and Alladi Venkatesh, quoted from Rifkin, *The Age of Access*, p. 173.

172. Quoted from ibid., p. 35.

173. See Benedict Anderson, *Imagined Communities*, London: Verso 1991.

174. Rifkin, *The Age of Access*, p. 35.

175. Ibid., p. 173.

176. Quoted from ibid., p. 171.

177. For an attempt to assert the potentially liberating aspects of the rise of the "Protean subject", see Robert Lifton, *The Protean Self: Human Resilience in an Age of Fragmentation*, Chicago: University of Chicago Press 1999.

178. Karl Marx and Frederick Engels, *The Communist Manifesto*, Harmondsworth: Penguin 1985, p. 83.

179. See Derrida, *Specters of Marx*.

180. For a more detailed account of this tension, see Chapter 3 of Slavoj Žižek, *Did Somebody Say Totalitarianism?*, London and New York: Verso 2001.

181. Quoted from Neil Harding, *Leninism*, Durham, NC: Duke University Press 1996, p. 168.

182. Ibid., p. 146.

183. See Dorothy L. Sayers, "Aristotle on Detective Fiction", in *Unpopular Opinions*, New York: Harcourt, Brace and Company 1947, pp. 222–36.

184. In this context, the myth to be debunked is that of the diminishing role of the state. What we are witnessing today is a shift in its functions: while it is partially withdrawing from its welfare functions, the state is strengthening its apparatuses in other domains of social regulation. In order to start a business now, one has to rely on the state to guarantee not only law and order, but the entire infrastructure (access to water and energy, means of transportation, ecological criteria, international regulations, etc.), to an incomparably greater extent than a hundred years ago.

The recent electricity supply débâcle in California makes this point very forcefully: for a couple of weeks in January and February 2001, the privatization ("deregulation") of the electricity supply changed Southern California, one of the most highly developed "post-industrial" landscapes in the entire world, into a Third World country with regular blackouts. Of course, defenders of deregulation claimed that it was not thorough enough, thereby engaging in the old false syllogism of "My fiancée is never late for the appointment, because the moment she is late, she is no longer my fiancée": deregulation, by definition, works, so if it doesn't work, it wasn't really deregulation. . . . Does not the recent mad cow disease panic (which probably presages dozens of similar phenomena awaiting us in the near future) also indicate a need for strict state and global institutionalized control of agriculture?

185. It is this sense of urgency which is lacking in the otherwise admirable work of Immanuel Wallerstein, with its long-term systemic approach: today, can we really afford the comfortable position of an observer who predicts that a new world order will emerge over the next fifty years and last for around five hundred? Along the same lines, when,

in *Utopistics* (New York: New Press 1998), Wallerstein claims that the October Revolution and the ensuing Soviet state were just a subordinate event which, far from undermining the global capitalist system, fully fitted within its frame, does he not underestimate the extent to which the October Revolution and its aftermath were none the less conceived of as an attack on the global capitalist system?

Whatever we think about the horrors of the Soviet regime, is it not true that throughout the twentieth century, the "Communist bloc" was the *only* "enemy" which seriously challenged the capitalist hegemony, and thus provoked a panic reaction by the capitalist empire? Even if "Really Existing Socialism" in fact ended up as a component of the capitalist world system, this, rather, bears witness to the *failure* of the Socialist project, not to its intrinsic nature. Far from marking the collapse of ideology, the events of 1990 (the disintegration of Really Existing Socialism) represented one of the most massive assertions of ideology: the combination of inconsistent desires for freedom, material prosperity, and so on, which sustained the mass protest, was ideology at its purest.

What is obfuscated in Wallerstein's account is thus the properly dialectical tension between the Universal and the Particular: although, in principle, it is true that Really Existing Socialism proved to be just a species of capitalism, there is something fundamentally wrong with simply classifying capitalism and Socialism (and, perhaps, other exceptions to "classic" capitalism, like Fascism or the Third World populist-authoritarian "nationalist" socioeconomic orders) as species of the neutral universal genus "capitalism". The only true species of capitalism is capitalism itself, while other species, especially Socialism, were precisely failed attempts to break out of the capitalist frame – they are, as it were, species of capitalism by default. To put it in somewhat pathetic terms: the fact that Socialism ended up as a species of the universal capitalist order was paid for by the millions of dead, victims of the failed struggle to break out.

186. See Karl Marx, "A Contribution to the Critique of Hegel's Philosophy of Right", in *Early Writings*, New York: Vintage 1975, p. 244.

187. See Ernesto Laclau, "The Politics of Rhetoric", intervention at the conference *Culture and Materiality*, University of California, Davis, 23–25 April 1998. When today's postmodern political philosophers emphasize the paradox of democracy, how democracy is possible only against the background of its impossibility, do they not reproduce the paradoxes of Kantian practical reason discerned long ago by Hegel?

188. See Eustache Kouvélakis's commentary to *L'Introduction à la Critique de la Philosophie du Droit de Hegel*, Paris: Ellipses 2000.

189. Jürgen Habermas, "Warum braucht Europa eine Verfassung?", *Die Zeit*, 29 June 2001, Feuilleton, p. 7.

190. The hidden truth of Habermas's thesis emerges in his direct Eurocentrism: no wonder Habermas is full of praise for the European "way of life", no wonder he characterizes the project of political globalization (of constructing a transnational political entity) as the fulfilment of European civilization.

191. The last great figure of this liberalism was Ernst Cassirer, so it is not surprising that part of the recent disavowal of the twentieth century is the revival of Cassirer in Germany, nor that other philosophers – not only Habermas – have suggested that we should go back to the famous Cassirer–Heidegger debate in Davos in 1929 which, with Cassirer's "defeat" and Heidegger's brutal refusal to shake hands with his interlocutor at the end, marks the philosophical end of the nineteenth century: what if Heidegger did *not* win? What if this is simply our misperception?

192. See Jürgen Habermas, *Die nachholende Revolution*, Frankfurt: Suhrkamp Verlag 1990.

193. Indonesia provides an excellent illustration of this logic of globalization: after Suharto's rise to power in 1965, foreign investors started to invade the country in search of a cheap workforce; this workforce became dispensable once foreign companies had also bought tracts of fertile land, where they grow crops for export (rubber, pineapples) instead of food for local consumption. In this way, the local population finds itself doubly dependent on foreign countries: they work for foreign companies and they eat imported food.

The reality behind the "sweatshops" in Indonesia is thus more complex than it may seem: of course we should protest at the way the local workforce is treated by the multinationals; but it is no less true that if a local worker loses his or her job with a multinational, a much worse fate awaits him or her. This, again, in no way exonerates the multinational, since the very fact that the sacked worker, as it were, has nowhere to retreat to, that there is no local community where he or she can find refuge and work, is the result of the inclusion of Indonesia in global capitalism in recent decades.

194. I owe this point to Alan Shandro's intervention "Lenin and the Logic of Hegemony", at the symposium *The Retrieval of Lenin*.

195. John le Carré, "My vote? I would like to punish Blair", interview with David Hare, *The Daily Telegraph*, Thursday 17 May 2001, p. 23.

196. Ibid.

197. See Claude Lefort, *La complication*, Paris: Fayard 1999.

198. On this notion of post-politics, see Chapter 4 of Žižek, *The Ticklish Subject*.

199. It is fashionable to claim that the irony of Stalin's politics from 1928 onwards was that it *was* in fact a kind of "permanent revolution", a permanent state of emergency in which revolution repeatedly devoured its own children. This claim, however, is misleading: the Stalinist terror was the paradoxical result of the attempt to *stabilize* the Soviet Union into a state like any other, with firm boundaries and institutions – that is to say, terror was a gesture of panic, a defence reaction against the threat to State stability.

200. Georg Lukács, "Hölderlin's Hyperion", in *Goethe and His Age*, London: Allen & Unwin 1968, p. 137.

201. Their other fetish is their belief that things took a bad turn in the Soviet Union only because Lenin did not succeed in joining forces with Trotsky in his effort to depose Stalin. This fetish is discernible in Trotsky himself who, precisely because of his "structural dogmatism" (his sticking to the global "Marxist" schema of historical development), cannot do otherwise than understand Stalinism as the product of Stalin's own personality.

202. See Fredric Jameson's intervention at the symposium on Kieslowski (UCLA, April 2001).

203. This society retroactively reveals the limitation of both poles of the previous opposition, Communists and dissidents: in their very victory, the dissidents dug their own grave – is this not the lesson of the fact that, in post-Communist Poland, the ex-Communist government, acting in the interests of capital, closed down the Gdansk shipyards, cradle of the Solidarity movement?

204. See Jameson, intervention at Kieslowski symposium. This should make us attentive to other seemingly marginal but none the less key appearances of the political dimension in Kieslowski's work. Take the key scene of *The Double Life of Véronique*,

the meeting of the two Véroniques in the main square where a Solidarity political demonstration is taking place: this encounter is presented in a vertiginous circular shot which reminds us of the famous 360-degree shot from Hitchcock's *Vertigo*. The camera's circular movement thus indicates that we are on the verge of the vortex in which different realities combine, that this vortex is already exerting its influence: if we take one step further – that is to say, if the two Véroniques were actually to confront and recognize each other – reality would disintegrate, because such an encounter of a person with her own double, with *herself* in another time–space dimension, is precluded by the very fundamental structure of the universe. (We can easily imagine a Hollywood version of this impossible encounter along the lines of Disney's *The Parent Trap*, in which the same actress (Hayley Mills) plays the role of the two twin sisters: after getting acquainted, the two Véroniques would change places, the Polish one returning to France and the French one staying in Poland.) No wonder that this revolving movement takes place in the square where the police are trying to disperse demonstrators: the vortex which threatens to dissolve reality is echoed in the prospect of the political revolution which threatens to dissolve the existing sociopolitical order. And, interestingly, in the second – French – part of *Véronique*, this momentary appearance of political reality is echoed by another intrusion of the political: the terrorist bomb explosion outside Gare Saint-Lazare in Paris, where Véronique will meet the mysterious stranger who had been sending her coded messages: political demonstrations in the East; terrorist attacks in the West.

205. John Berger, "The Hammer and Sickle", *Janus* 5 (2000), p. 16.

206. Ibid., p. 17. The key difference between Nazism and Stalinism is, of course, that the Nazi regime did not actually intervene in the basic relations of production, while Stalinist forced collectivization did indicate a will radically to change these relations.

207. Or, to indulge in a similar mental experiment: in the last days of Really Existing Socialism, the protesting crowds often sang official songs, including national anthems, reminding the authorities of their unfulfilled promises. What better thing for an East German crowd to do in 1989 than simply to sing the GDR national anthem? Because its words ("Deutschland einig Vaterland [Germany, the united Fatherland]") were no longer appropriate to the emphasis on East Germany as a new Socialist nation, it was *forbidden* to sing it in public from the late 1950s to 1989: at official ceremonies, only the orchestral version was performed. (The GDR was thus the only country in which singing the national anthem constituted a criminal act!) Can one imagine the same thing under Nazism?

208. One should, perhaps, rehabilitate Marx's (implicit) distinction between the working class (an "objective" social category, a topic of sociological study) and the proletariat (a certain *subjective* position – the class "for itself", the embodiment of social negativity, to use an old and rather unfortunate expression). Instead of searching for the disappearing working class, we should, rather, ask: who occupies, who is able to subjectivize, its position as proletarian today?

209. On a more general methodological level, we should also invert the standard pseudo-Nietzschean view according to which the past we construct in our historiography is a symptom, an articulation of our present problems: what if, on the contrary, we ourselves – our present – are a symptom of the unresolved deadlocks of the past?

210. For a detailed Lacanian reading of this joke, see Chapter 2 of Žižek, *Tarrying with the Negative*.

Index